PRAISE FOR *MY POLITICAL JOURNEY*

"This invaluable memoir is a fascinating, generous-hearted, at times funny, skilfully written insider's view from the trenches of Jamaica's politics. It covers the struggle from colonialism to federation to Jamaican independence, and growing national self-realization. It's as much the story of a young country's possibilities as it is of the extraordinary life of one man, a son of rural Jamaica. A devoted regionalist and social democrat with unfailing faith in his people, P.J. Patterson's book reflects a hands-on, practical spirit who believes in loyalty to ideals, flexibility in the face of change, and introspection. A shrewd judge of national temperature and temperament, as Jamaica's greatest political organizer he revisits the rough and tumble of rural campaigns, euphoric national victories and shattering defeats. As a lawyer, he reflects on the power of legislature to change people's lives. In politics there are always disappointments and personal hurts; in sharing these, P.J. Patterson exhibits an honesty, generosity of spirit, and sense of humour about political opponents and allies alike. He shares insight about history, historic figures and puzzling national events, the trade union movement, the role of our music, and the extraordinary personal and public life of the only person to serve three consecutive terms as Jamaica's prime minister. It is a riveting account of Jamaica's living history. Magnificent! This book matters."
—*Rachel Manley, author of* In My Father's Shade

"In this book P.J. Patterson's writing itself is another dimension of his respectful adherence to the Jamaican people. He is attractive and not intimidating in his expressiveness, always making the language appropriate and contributory to the mood of his narrative. There is the crystal clarity with which he clings to the identities of his childhood friends and neighbours and recalls the tiny but potent districts of his western Jamaica; the lyricism with which he sings the natural beauty of the Mona campus, where he found the love of his life and learned the beauty of academic rigour; the unimpeachably humane logic that informs the positions he takes as he ascends with integrity the tiers of responsibility."
—*Professor Emeritus Keith Ellis, Department of Spanish and Portuguese, University of Toronto*

"Were *My Political Journey* not memoirs obedient to modesty, an apt title might have been *The Best of the Caribbean*. For that is what P.J. has been and because of the values, the dreams, the efforts that guided that life, this candid account of them will influence generations of West Indians beyond the present to know that the best is attainable still."
—*Sir Shridath "Sonny" Ramphal, former Commonwealth Secretary General*

"P.J. Patterson's memoirs reveal a man of integrity, an outstanding organizer and strategist, and a true democrat, committed to promoting consensus. With decades of ministerial service and leadership among non-aligned countries and CARIFTA nations, Patterson is one of Jamaica's most experienced and skilled politicians. As prime minister, he guided Jamaica through its worst economic crisis, while promoting some of our most significant infrastructural developments of modern times."
—*The Honourable R. Danny Williams*

"This is more than an autobiography as it provides invaluable insights, information and, more importantly, the context of the issues that have consumed the attention of Caribbean leaders for the last fifty years. . . . Perhaps the most significant aspect of this memoir is P.J.'s keen sense of the changes that were occurring and the need for new strategies for successful governance and leadership in the age of globalization."
—*The Most Honourable Sir Kenneth Hall, former Governor General of Jamaica*

"The volume covers the reflections and experiences of the Most Honourable P.J. Patterson, as they pertain to the regional and international issues to which he devoted a very substantial part of his career. . . . It is no exaggeration to say that the depth and quality of his involvement with these issues are probably without precedent among the leadership in the CARICOM countries since political independence."
—*Sir Alister McIntyre, former Vice Chancellor, the University of the West Indies*

"This book opens a window through which the reader can peer into the past to understand what agitated the author's passion to work with like-minded politicians and progressive members of civil society and the public sector, to redress the inequalities that disfigured Jamaica, especially in the 1960s. . . . Above all, after reading this book, readers will understand why we are such a divided society perpetually at war, despite unification efforts; despite examples from history that unity is vital to bring about fundamental societal changes; despite a shared history of struggle for upliftment from slavery and colonialism and towards black empowerment."
—*Professor Verene A. Shepherd, Professor of Social History, the University of the West Indies, Mona*

"A scintillating account of the growth and development of a Caribbean icon who has devoted his life to public service. In delightfully readable prose, P.J. Patterson describes a career watered initially by regionalism that flowed from the fledgling University College of the West Indies at Mona, matured in the hurly burly of national politics and coming to full bloom as a successful politician/prime minister who used his formidable talents for the benefit of his country and the region as a whole. This book is essential reading especially for those, wherever they may be who call the Caribbean space their own."
—*Sir George Alleyne, Chancellor Emeritus, the University of the West Indies*

"A fascinating memoir. Prime Minister Patterson, as a real statesman, shows how the English-speaking Caribbean became a unique player at the regional arena, enlarging its influence in the Latin American region, and at the world level."
—*Ricardo Lagos, former President of Chile*

"*My Political Journey* is simply one of the most incisive and elegantly written autobiographies by any political personality from the Americas and the Caribbean. Patterson offers us facts, wisdom and understanding on comprehensive bundles of issues over the past fifty years, which have defined Jamaica, our Caribbean, and their relationships with the rest of the world. His erudition, caring philosophy, humanity and strength of character shine through. *My Political Journey* is a magnificent testament to the life and work of a Caribbean man of the highest quality."
— *Dr the Honourable Ralph Gonsalves, Prime Minister of St Vincent and the Grenadines*

"For many decades Jamaica stood out in our eyes as an outstanding example of valuable and moving solidarity. This was significantly because of the eminent and principled position which the late Prime Minister Michael Manley took in support of the struggles for the liberation of South Africa and Africa from apartheid and colonialism. We were fortunate that as we entered into the post-apartheid period we could still count on Jamaica to continue to serve as a reliable comrade-in-arms, thanks to the support and wisdom of P.J. Patterson as we grappled with the new challenges at home and abroad which came with our liberation."
—*Thabo Mbeki, former President of South Africa*

"*My Political Journey* tells this important story of the power internationalist solidarity has to change the world. . . . This book provides a universal awareness that integrates free, state and community economic vision which points us in the direction of peace, prosperity and a meaningful life for all of God's children. Seeing the world through the Jamaican soul allows you to really believe that 'One Love' is truly an attainable realty."
—*Ambassador Andrew J. Young, former US Ambassador to the United Nations, Mayor of Atlanta*

"It is a pity that politics took P.J. Patterson away from his successful exploits as a barrister in our courtrooms, as politics deprived a generation of my colleagues of the opportunity to witness and experience his brilliant legal mind in full flight. . . . This book outlines his many achievements, his challenges and illuminates his selfless service to our nation."
—*Jacqueline Cummings, President of the Jamaican Bar Association*

My Political Journey

JAMAICA'S SIXTH PRIME MINISTER

P.J. Patterson

The University of the West Indies Press
Jamaica • Barbados • Trinidad and Tobago

The University of the West Indies Press
7A Gibraltar Hall Road, Mona
Kingston 7, Jamaica
www.uwipress.com

A catalogue record of this book is available from the
National Library of Jamaica.

ISBN: 978-976-640-701-8 (cloth)
978-976-640-702-5 (paper)
978-976-640-703-2 (Kindle)
978-976-640-704-9 (ePub)

Cover photograph © Maria LaYacona
Cover and book design by Robert Harris
(E-mail: roberth@cwjamaica.com)

Set in Scala 11/15 x 30

Printed in the United States of America

For my beloved mother,
INA MIRIAMNE JAMES,
to whom I owe everything,
and for my lodestar,
NORMAN WASHINGTON MANLEY

CONTENTS

CONTENTS

PART 2: THE PRIME MINISTERIAL YEARS

ACKNOWLEDGEMENTS

On retirement from public life in March 2006, I had a firm intention to proceed immediately to write my story, from the Hanover days of infancy at York View to Jamaica House.

As often happens to those in public life, my retirement turned out to be something of a misnomer. Numerous institutions, organizations and civic groups, alongside a range of regional and international colleagues, felt I had all the time in the world to devote to their particular request for speaking engagements or expert studies. No longer bound by the constraints of national demands, they viewed this as the perfect interval for me to devote my energies exclusively to various initiatives and projects and to make my experience available for the emerging challenges in spheres of common interest.

It is a tribute to a number of colleagues and influential scholars that after twelve full years as a private citizen I finally completed this manuscript. They never failed to remind me of an obligation to the people of Jamaica and our Caribbean to write these memoirs. Whenever I faltered, their urgings and confidence renewed my desire to share the narrative of my career in the law and write the tale of my leadership engagement in Jamaica and our Caribbean.

The exercise commenced with a series of interviews: Violet Neilson, Simon Clarke, Nathan Richards, Fay Pickersgill, Hartley Neita, Don Mills, Herbert Walker, Dr Winston Dawes, R. Danny Williams, Dr Matthew Beaubrun, Douglas Saunders and Dr Winston Davidson provided reminiscences of my childhood, student days, the period of apprenticeship in politics, practice in the law and eventual induction in government.

A work of such wide range required extensive research and the CHASE Foundation contributed a financial grant to undertake the initial phase. Maxine McDonnough was engaged and received considerable assistance in probing background sources from Delano Franklyn, Arnoldo Ventura and Byron Blake, who proceeded to assist in portions of the drafting.

ACKNOWLEDGEMENTS

I called upon a number of my special advisers and technocrats who had worked with me in the public service on the evolution of policies and design of innovative programmes and were therefore able to identify and sift through what had been accomplished in their respective fields of endeavour: Carlton Davis, Marjorie Henriques, Jacqueline DaCosta and Wesley Hughes offered substantial inputs.

Maxine Henry-Wilson, Omar Davies, Burchell Whiteman and Paul Robertson rendered invaluable support in the chronicle and analysis of the national priorities during our administration and responded to my plea to offer their observations and review in areas that fell within their ministerial and political competence.

Without the inputs obtained from Curtis Ward, Kenneth Hall, Richard Bernal, Delano Franklyn and Byron Blake for the Sir Arthur Lewis Institute of Social and Economic Studies Lecture in 2011, which offered prime ministerial reflections on Jamaica's fifty years of independence, the nation's exciting role in the global arena would not have been adequately summarized.

I was able to draw on a trove of correspondence with Rex Nettleford in areas of our cultural heritage and with Alister McIntyre in areas pertaining to international trade.

I am especially grateful to Arnold Bertram, Daphne Innerarity, Judy Raymond, Patsy Robertson and Hilary Beckles for their helpful suggestions as to the contour, format and tone of the final product.

Very special commendation is fully deserved by that tireless team who persevered to the end, who kept pushing and prodding – always there to promote and assist to make this happen:

- Mirven Tait, a zealous gatekeeper in the control of all the material flows and the only person who could decipher my scribble.
- Maxine McDonnough, whose work expanded well beyond research to serve as principal editorial liaison.
- Debra Hamilton, special assistant, as a reliable resource for providing the exact dates and details during the many years she managed my engagements and for sourcing the photographs.
- Delano Franklyn, former chief of personal staff, who was most familiar with my accumulation of speeches and helped to pull together the outcome of extensive involvement in the regional and external arena.
- Daphne Innerarity, for making available the required communication expertise and for her insistence on a clear, precise and intelligible script.

- Maureen Vernon, for effectively coordinating the right linkages between the separate periods in office.

I am heavily indebted to all the persons previously mentioned and a cadre of close friends who were a constant source of encouragement in the moments of doubting my capacity to complete the task.

While all of these people have tried to keep me honest in writing, I accept full responsibility for all expressions of opinion and any errors and omissions.

Due respect is extended to the *Gleaner* and the Jamaica Information Service for access to their archives for photographs and news reports and to my publishers, the University of the West Indies Press, and Shivaun Hearne and Judy Raymond for their professional scrutiny and execution.

Thanks to all those who encouraged me, the courtesies and kindness so many extended, and the inspiration that my mentors at every phase, my colleagues in the struggle and any extended family provided throughout the entire political journey.

Let the conversation begin!

ABBREVIATIONS

ACP	African, Caribbean and Pacific Group of States
ACS	Association of Caribbean States
ALGAJ	Association of Local Government Authorities of Jamaica
CARICOM	Caribbean Community
CARIFTA	Caribbean Free Trade Association
CCJ	Caribbean Court of Justice
CIA	Central Intelligence Agency
CIF	cost, insurance, freight
CSME	CARICOM Single Market and Economy
DLP	Democratic Labour Party
EEC	European Economic Community
GDP	gross domestic product
IDB	Inter-American Development Bank
IMF	International Monetary Fund
JAMAL	Jamaican Movement for the Advancement of Literacy
JLP	Jamaica Labour Party
JTB	Jamaica Tourist Board
NAFTA	North American Free Trade Area
NCST	National Commission on Science and Technology
NHT	National Housing Trust
NIR	net international reserves
OPEC	Organization of Petroleum Exporting Countries
PNP	People's National Party

ABBREVIATIONS

PNPYO	PNP Youth Organization
PRIDE	Programme for Resettlement and Integrated Development Enterprise
QC	Queen's Counsel
SIA	Sugar Industry Authority
UDC	Urban Development Corporation
WHO	World Health Organization
WIFLP	West Indian Federal Labour Party
WTO	World Trade Organization
YMCA	Young Men's Christian Association

PART 1
THE EARLY YEARS

CHAPTER 1
YORK VIEW, HANOVER

I WAS BORN ON 10 APRIL 1935, JUST three years shy of the one hundredth anniversary of the abolition of slavery.

My mother, Ina Miriamne James, born on 15 June 1898 in Dias, Hanover, was one of two children. Her elder brother, Richard, succumbed, before the age of puberty, to a severe case of crab poisoning. She attended the Mount Moriah Baptist School in Hanover. She was an excellent student and went on to become a teacher herself. At the age of twenty, she joined the staff of the Mount Peto Elementary School, where her aunt's husband, Daniel Henry, served as principal.

It was while teaching at the Churchill Primary School, near Green Island in Hanover, that "Miss I", as my mother was affectionately called, met my father, Henry Patterson. He had served as an overseer on the Eaton Estate, referred to by the surrounding communities as Santoy, owned by the Sanftleben family. Some would call him "Busha", but he was also known as "Mas' Hen", which he greatly preferred. He built a house, May Park, from which we often watched cricket being played on the playing field across the road. He also owned several parcels of land that had been sold by the colonial government for land settlement in the nearby village of Logwood. One of these was the source of water that the National Water Agency bought in 1954 to supply the needs of tourism development in Negril. It became known as Patterson Hole.

During school holidays, I enjoyed many visits to my father. I helped to milk the cows; tend to the dogs and the chickens in the yard; I learned how to ride a horse and a bicycle; I particularly enjoyed travelling in a buggy to church.

Henry Patterson loved horse racing and went to races at the Willie Reid Race Course in Cave Valley. As a trained farrier, Mas' Hen offered his services freely to anyone who had an injured animal and sent for him. He had a stallion that bred the horses within his own stable. He was generally up at the crack of dawn and rode out every day to tend to his farms, where he grew sugar cane, rice and bananas and saw to his cattle and pigs. Although active and otherwise healthy, he limped with his right foot, which was ascribed to an overdose of quinine to treat typhoid.

He was regarded as a benefactor to the community, especially the poor. He was kind, considerate and jocular. He would send milk for children and old people who could not afford it. He enjoyed good music, which was played on the HMV gramophone from his fine collection of vinyl records. But on Sundays, only sacred music was permitted.

He was a deacon in the Anglican Church and sat in the family pew every Sunday. He was not given to smoking or drinking alcohol. My father had nine children – Florence, John, Reginald, Daisy, Fred, Vida, Percy, Merle and Monica.

On my earliest visit to Nigeria as a university student, I listened with fascination to stories of the bitter disputes which had arisen in several tribes as to the rights of succession when a vacancy occurred in the chieftaincy. Among the cardinal rules was a requirement for the "navel string" – umbilical cord – to have been buried within the tribal borders. It was not where you first peeped at the light, but where your navel string was buried that determined your ancestral home. Mine was buried under the otaheite apple tree in the Mount Pleasant yard of the Dawes family, at Kendal in the parish of Hanover, from where I come. In every respect and by any measure, I am a true Hanoverian. I was taken by my godparents, Cyprian and Greta Dawes, and christened at the St Luke's Anglican Church nearby.

I got a good start in the rudiments of learning at an early age. This was hardly surprising, coming from a family of teachers. I was the sole pupil of my elderly cousin Rosa Carter, who had been well trained by my grandmother, Eliza James, and was widely regarded by the community as one of the finest infant school teachers around. My Sunday school teacher was Mrs Ursula Dilworth, at the Mount Moriah Baptist Church. She also served as the organist.

Whenever adults were engaged in "big people" conversation and did not want me to understand, they would use aphorisms or engage in parables. At other times, they would resort to spelling the key words in the sentences. This continued until the day I corrected a visitor to the house who had spelled a word incorrectly. Eventually, whenever they wanted to share anything that was secret they moved to another part of the house or sent me out to play.

In reflecting on my childhood, I realize that any successes I achieved in my academic and professional careers are unquestionably the product of the family and communities which nurtured me. Everyone in that small village of Dias was there to protect the infant Baby P., who lived in the house on the hill, York View, my maternal family home, and to extend a caring hand at every step of the way.

THE ANCESTORS

My great-grandfather Richard Carter, who lived in Wait-a-Bit, Trelawny, was an ardent member of the Baptist Church and held a position of leadership within it. Born into slavery, Richard Carter and his wife, the former Julia Dalrymple, migrated from Trelawny to Westmoreland soon after emancipation. Their first child was Eliza Matilda, my maternal grandmother.

Eliza Matilda grew up to become a formidable woman who devoted herself to her family and her career as a teacher. As a young girl, she attended the Baptist Training Institution in Savanna-la-Mar, which had been established soon after emancipation by Mrs Mary Ann Huggins, the wife of Baptist minister the Reverend John Huggins. Eliza Matilda excelled in her studies and was particularly proficient in music, the love of which she passed on to her students. After graduating from the institute she married William James, another teacher, who came from Glen Islay in Westmoreland. The family eventually moved to Hanover.

William James served as headmaster of Cacoon Elementary School. Among his pupils was William Alexander Clarke – whose surname later became Bustamante. My mother and his younger sister were in the same class. My grandmother became the principal teacher at the Cadbury School, until she eventually joined the staff at Cacoon. Later, after her husband's death, she retired from the public school system and opened a finishing school for young ladies, who came from far and near. From her home, Aunt James imparted knowledge and skills in music, drama and housecraft.

The significant role played by the Baptist Church in laying the foundations for the development of a free society in post-emancipation Jamaica is universally acknowledged. My great-grandfather Richard Carter and his family were among the beneficiaries of the sterling foundation the church had laid in the field of education. Consequently, I was raised as a proud descendant of generations of teachers and lay preachers, grounded in Christian beliefs and the imperatives of moral behaviour and social responsibility.

❧

My home in the Hanover hills was less than ten miles away from Frome, where the first eruption by the masses was taking place for better working conditions and the right to have their voices heard in the affairs of the land. The struggle for the grant of universal adult suffrage and self-government began in earnest in 1938, which unequivocally marked the beginning of a new Jamaica; the first step along the path to independence. As a child, I could sense that something unusual was happening around me – there was a lot of noise and movement all over the place. Unusual fires were burning and men with batons suddenly appeared.

The years after emancipation had not realized the dream of a better life in which the newly freed could pursue a path of self-improvement and citizenship, but instead were years of dire hardship which found the majority of Jamaicans eking out a meagre living on the marginal hillside lands they had captured. By the 1920s, decades of struggle in rural Jamaica had sent hundreds of Jamaicans into the urban centres, primarily Kingston, to try and earn a living. This merely placed additional pressure on the urban infrastructure, which could not accommodate the increased numbers in terms of shelter or employment. As a result, thousands of jobless and low-paid workers lived in sprawling slums.

Discontent was rife, even as the desire for better became more pervasive and insistent. More and more black Jamaicans recognized that they deserved a better deal in terms of education, housing, land ownership and increased opportunities for improving their quality of life. The seeds were sown by forward-thinking, educated men such as Dr Robert Love, who advocated improved social and working conditions and recognition of the rights of the ordinary Jamaican. It was a time of fervent political and social action; it was a time which would come to be recognized as the dawning of a new era when the ordinary Jamaican, the peasantry, sugar workers and dock workers and the working class, generally, revolted against the oppressive colonial system which had prevented them from pursuing any avenue for self-improvement.

The decade of the 1930s represented a major watershed in the history of Jamaica and the Caribbean. In March 1935, the avowed father of the modern political movement, Marcus Mosiah Garvey, had left Jamaica for the last time. He announced his intention to pursue political ambitions in England, where he would live until his death in 1940. It marked the end of Garvey's political career in Jamaica, but it was the beginning of an era that, influenced by his activism and writings, would culminate in the birth of modern Jamaica. For the first time, the issues of the mass of Jamaicans would take centre stage. We were about to witness the emergence of a new breed of leaders in Jamaican politics and the workers' and nationalist movements.

Garvey expanded on the teachings of Dr Robert Love to create the philosophy of pride and upliftment that would change the perspective of black people internationally. From his base in Harlem, he built the Universal Negro Improvement Association, which spawned branches across the globe, wherever there were communities of black people. His work was phenomenal and garnered for him admirers and critics alike. His success in galvanizing black people made him a target for the white establishment, which engineered his imprisonment and deportation to Jamaica in December 1927. Jamaicans had been keeping abreast of his activities and gave him a hero's welcome on his return home. According to a report in the *Daily Gleaner* of 12 December 1927, "deafening cheers were raised" when his ship arrived in Kingston Harbour.

He continued his seminal work in Jamaica, "taking his message of Black nationalism to all who would listen and read".[1] He spread the word on national pride and political awareness through his journals the *Blackman* (later the *Black Man*) and the *New Jamaican* and through his many meetings, debates and lectures. Thousands of Jamaicans thronged weekly to his cultural headquarters, Edelweiss Park in Cross Roads, to hear his messages of enlightenment and inspiration.

His own political ambitions were not realized in Jamaica, as the supporters of his People's Political Party were not able to meet the voter registration requirements. The manifesto of the party would, however, provide the main planks on which future political parties would build their constitutions. In it Garvey called for social and economic legislation, the promotion of native industries, minimum-wage legislation, the establishment of a Jamaican university, the establishment of a legal-aid department to assist the poor in the courts, legislation to protect voters, and land reform.

Decades would pass before Jamaica caught up with Garvey's vision. He consistently campaigned for social reform which would see the improvement of the ordinary Jamaican. He fought relentlessly against injustice and oppression, advocating for schools, better working conditions, improved wages and other benefits for the majority of Jamaican workers who toiled in the banana and sugar industries. He was prophetic when he warned that if their situation was not improved, working-class Jamaicans would rebel against the status quo.

While Garvey may have spoken specifically of Jamaica, his words would ring true for the entire Caribbean, and the mid-1930s would see labour uprisings protesting the unspeakable poverty and arduous conditions faced by the majority of people in the region. The unrest brought to the fore men who would lead Caribbean labour movements – the first successful political movements – and whose names are now recorded in the annals of Caribbean political history.

In St Kitts, sugar workers, led by Robert Bradshaw, struck for higher wages; in British Guiana sugar workers rioted and set fire to cane fields; in St Lucia coal

---

1. Philip Sherlock and Hazel Bennett, *The Story of the Jamaican People* (Kingston: Ian Randle, 1998), 308.

workers went on strike; and in Trinidad and Tobago Uriah "Buzz" Butler led a march of the unemployed into Port of Spain. Barbados also experienced stressful times, with Clement Payne's demand for the recognition of trade unions. Grantley Adams fought against his subsequent arrest and incarceration.[2]

In British Honduras, workers at Stann Creek staged a strike; in St Kitts, workers on the Shadwell sugar plantation struck; there was a public riot in St Vincent which forced the governor and legislature to seek refuge; and here in Jamaica the port workers of Falmouth and Kingston went on strike.

Garvey's work had increased the awareness of the people and proved the wisdom of the old Buddhist maxim which claims, "When the student is ready, the teacher will appear." Jamaica's readiness was indicated by the impressive cadre of conscious Jamaicans, at home and abroad, who came to the fore with a determination to effect change. These included St William Grant, A.G.S. Coombs, O.T. Fairclough, Adolphe Roberts, Sandy Cox, and Ken and Frank Hill, to name a few. The most outstanding were Alexander Bustamante, who styled himself the "lonely warrior", and Norman Washington Manley, a lawyer who had already gained a reputation for community-building through the Jamaica Social Welfare Commission. Launched in June 1937, Jamaica Welfare was funded by the United Fruit Company, through the efforts of Manley. Both leaders came to the workers' struggle through different portals, but were equally influential in their contribution to the birth of the new Jamaica.

Alexander Bustamante was a dramatic, larger-than-life figure who fought aggressively in defending the rights of the workers. He caught the imagination of the people and soon gained their confidence and loyalty. Along with St William Grant, an ardent Garveyite, he criticized the deplorable conditions of the masses, which included low wages, limited education, landlessness, and lack of adequate shelter and health care, resulting in malnutrition, malaria, typhoid, yaws and tuberculosis. Bustamante was fearless in leadership and his many letters of protest to the press and fiery rhetoric at meetings across the island brought him to the notice of the government. Like Garvey before him, he was considered a troublemaker and was closely monitored by the authorities. Bustamante's short-lived partnership with Coombs saw the formation of the country's first effective trade union – the Jamaica Workers and Tradesmen Union.

The years leading up to 1938 were tense ones, charged with the discontent of the people and the perpetual expectations of violence and unrest. The first salvo was fired on 4 January 1938, when workers at Serge Island Sugar Estate in St

---

2. Ibid., 364.

Thomas struck. The tension and unrest continued, with the threat of further violence, and on 1 May, twenty-one days after my third birthday, the riots at Frome Estate erupted as workers protested the failure to honour promised increases and improved benefits. Several rioters were killed. The situation further intensified, with workers staging strikes on the Port of Kingston, and protests soon spread to other equally disgruntled workers of the Kingston and St Andrew Corporation.

The immediate result of the workers' action was the formation of the Bustamante Industrial Trade Union, a vehicle that could effectively organize the workers' movement and give voice to the issues which plagued them. The formation of the union strengthened the fledgling workers' movement and ensured that it became a permanent element of the Jamaican workplace. While new trade unions would develop over time, Alexander Bustamante would continue to be regarded as the leader of the nation's working class.

It was natural that Norman Manley's legal background would see him approaching the political movement from the perspective of constitutional change, focusing, initially, on gaining a voice for the people by doggedly advocating for universal adult suffrage. Manley's work was supported by several forward-thinking groups and individuals who believed that the status quo in Jamaica had to be changed and the society restructured to provide a place for the ordinary Jamaican.

Manley established a reputation as a brilliant lawyer, much sought after by major local and international firms that worked in Jamaica. It was through his connections with the United Fruit Company that he was able to gain funding for the work of Jamaica Welfare. Manley entered the fray when he undertook to represent Alexander Bustamante, his cousin, against the government. He soon identified with the struggles of the people and decided to devote himself to supporting the workers' movement by forming Jamaica's first successful political party, the People's National Party (PNP), on 18 September 1938.

The formation of the party was the result of the combined efforts of men such as O.T. Fairclough, who travelled the island explaining the concept of the party; W.A. Domingo, Adolphe Roberts and H.P. Jacobs, members of the Jamaica Progressive League; and Frank and Ken Hill and Noel Nethersole, members of the National Reform Association. The first committee comprised Norman Manley, O.T. Fairclough, Howard Cooke, H.P. Jacobs, Noel Nethersole, the Reverend O.G. Penso and W.G. McFarlane. Howard Cooke shared with me the feeling of those heady days: "When we got together, we felt almost a missionary urge. We wanted to change things, we wanted to go out and tell people they would have a better life."

CHAPTER 2
MY EARLY EDUCATION

WHEN IT WAS TIME FOR ME TO ATTEND elementary school, my mother decided that I should not go to the school at which she taught. She feared either that I might be spoilt by some teachers or that students might react adversely towards me when she had to punish them for one reason or another. So off I went to live with my aunt Doris Carter-Henry, who was the postmistress at Somerton, St James. It was the first time that I had left the parish of Hanover, and I looked forward to going somewhere new and to making new friends at school.

The journey took three days. In order to get to St James, we had to take the bus, Malta, which wound its way through the districts of Lucea, Jericho, Cascade, Pondside, then down to Flint River, Hopewell, Reading and ending in Montego Bay.

In Montego Bay, my mother and I stayed with a cousin, Ida Moodie, who lived on St James Street. Along that main street were the Hanna Store, where my mother purchased the school uniforms, and Henderson's Book Store, where she bought the books and other materials for school. We also made a stop at Mr Myrie's grocery store, at the corner of Union and King Streets, where she bought me various goodies and equipped me with all I needed before I continued on my journey to Somerton.

I could never forget that bus ride from Montego Bay to Somerton. Although the most direct route was no more than ten miles, the route taken by the bus extended for some eighteen miles through the districts, hills and valleys of St James. Every time the bus came to a small village it stopped to let off or take on passengers. It was a time for the men to refresh themselves at the nearest bar or even play a quick domino game.

I had been put in the charge of the driver of the bus, who was the owner's son. He was Carlton Beckford. I still recall the care and the kindness he extended to me on that ride. In later years, when he moved to Kingston and gradually built a large business on Spanish Town Road selling motor-vehicle parts, he was known to all and sundry as "Mo-Bay Beckford".

My most outstanding memory of the journey was the happy and friendly passengers. They sang Negro spirituals, most of which I had heard in church, but they also sang a number of songs that I was hearing for the first time, songs like "Hill and Gully Ride", "Sammy Dead", "The River Ben Come Dung", "Dip Dem Bedward", "Chi Chi Bud Oh" and "Run Mongoose". Everyone joined in the lusty singing, even those who could barely turn a tune. No wonder that one of our foremost singers and songwriters, Jimmy Cliff, was born and raised in Somerton.

When the bus arrived in Somerton, the final point was the road nearest to the post office, where I was handed over to the care and keeping of my aunt, known to everybody as Miss Dolly. She took full charge of me. The love and affection she showered upon me made me feel right at home. She was a caring and considerate aunt who made it clear what was to be expected by way of diligent study and good behaviour.

SCHOOL LIFE

I arrived in Somerton that Saturday evening in January 1943 and had to go to school on the Monday morning. The school was about three hundred yards away from my aunt's home. I was escorted to school by none other than Mr Wesley Hewling, then a senior member of staff at Somerton Elementary. He became a legendary figure in education, serving at various times in virtually every office of the Jamaica Teachers' Association. When he left to be headmaster of his own school, he was succeeded by Norman Bingham, also an outstanding educator, before he moved into the field of insurance and became head of National Life, one of the island's leading insurance companies.

In those days schools were divided into upper and lower school. Because of the foundation I had received, I was placed in what was then second book. My first teacher was Miss Hattie Green, who eventually became the wife of Mr Hewling. Miss Gwendoyln Beckford, who taught me in third book, Miss Beryl Brown in fourth book and Miss Holt in fifth book. These women, who eventually became principals of schools, were responsible for ensuring that I had a sound educational footing.

The headmaster, Ivan Newton Cocker, believed in preparing his students for life, so he used every opportunity to relate school subjects to what happened in life and to learn from practical example. Within the school, we had to do everything that was being done at the country level. When adult suffrage was attained in 1944, he sought to teach us about the new electoral process by conducting a mock election.

I was selected to represent the PNP and a student named Vinton Grey was the Jamaica Labour Party (JLP) candidate. We had to campaign vigorously to convince our classmates to vote for us and had time each day to speak to the students. I won the election, with the able assistance of my schoolmate and campaign manager Violet Stewart.

Somerton remained part of the East Central St James constituency, from which Violet Stewart Neilson was elected as member of Parliament in 1989, enabling her to serve as Speaker of the House from 1997 to 2002. In 1944, I swept the mock elections at Somerton Elementary, representing the PNP. When the real elections were held, the PNP lost in Somerton and that constituency. At the national level, the JLP gained twenty-two of the thirty-two seats.

Little did I realize then that I had taken the first irreversible step on my political journey. From that tender age, I became increasingly immersed in the process, reading avidly the Hansard reports of parliamentary proceedings, which the *Daily Gleaner* carried in full, and travelling in the front of the truck to nearby political meetings with Louis Keane, the local PNP representative.

Ms Beryl Brown, who was also a Hanoverian, eventually migrated to the United States. Some time ago, I got a letter from someone who brought it to my attention that she had died abroad. The correspondent said that Ms Brown told them that while I was in her class, the children had been asked to write an essay on what they would like to be when they grew up. According to Ms Brown, I had said that I would like to be prime minister. I cannot remember saying that, because we were still a colony and the office of prime minister did not even exist. Most likely, she formed that opinion as a result of the mock election run among the students at Somerton at the time of Jamaica's historic first election under adult suffrage.

I seemed to have been infected with a political virus from birth, but I had no early inkling of the amazing journey ahead.

In that firmly colonial period, education was generally available to children aged seven to fifteen. Average attendance was low, and that contributed to low levels of literacy. The curriculum stressed reading, writing and arithmetic, although there was some exposure to biology and geography. Friday mornings were devoted to gardening for the boys and sewing for the girls. All of these were at elementary levels, with no systematic provision for a student to continue his or her education in any of these areas. The vast majority were therefore left to fend for themselves and were ill equipped to obtain skilled employment upon leaving school.

Places in high school were confined to some 1.5 per cent of children and outside the income stream of the vast majority of parents. Elementary education to age fifteen was largely a preparation for work in menial services at low wages and for employment by the big landowners.

Mr Cocker gave us an excellent foundation. He brought about an awakening in Somerton. While he was there, people called Somerton Elementary School "The College". People started to send their children to Somerton School instead of the one nearest to them.

Ivan Newton Cocker was nothing like the quiet spaniel. He knew how to bark and bite. In a fiery meeting of the Jamaica Union of Teachers, he silenced a rival who tried to interrupt him. "Sit down, Hogg. Can't you see Cocker is on the floor?" The audience erupted in loud laughter and prolonged applause.

Mr Cocker was not married. His sister Olive took care of him. All the children were his children, but some were very special. I was one of the latter. He was a strict disciplinarian who had a strong sense of civic responsibility and put a lot of effort into developing character. He was a nationalist and had pride in his people and his country. He felt that education was not only about the subjects that were taught, but was important in building a rounded personality. He supported the Jamaica Welfare, which Norman Manley had established to help the development of better communities. His pupils were outstanding in every area of school life, and no one could beat us in examinations or sports. In fact, Somerton was a pioneer of the 4H Club Movement and we were always rated among the leading schools in the island. We used to sing, "We are out to build a new Jamaica through this Somerton School of ours."

My family did not subscribe to the celebration of Empire Day, a public holiday that perpetuated the cult of inferiority during colonial rule. Before going to school on Empire Day, I was forbidden to sing "Rule Britannia, Britannia rules the waves and Britons never, never, never shall be slaves". My aunt instructed me to refuse any food handed out to mark the event. This included ripe bananas, which were being distributed because shipments to Britain had been suspended during World War II and the authorities were still purchasing by the bunch. I dared to ask why and she did not hesitate to explain, giving me an unusually stern warning that I would feel the dire consequences of any disobedience.

In addition to what was on the curriculum describing the invincibility of

Britain and the glories of the empire, we had teachers at Somerton who made sure we learned about the achievements of our Jamaican people. They taught us about those who fought against slavery, as well as contemporaries who were making their mark in Jamaica, and always talked about our own role models.

The school day provided the opportunity for play as well as work, and during recess, like other boys at the time, I played cricket with a coconut bat and made and flew my own kite. I loved to play marbles and spin gigs. On Friday afternoons, the boys would disappear for "bush cooking" and go in search of rabbit feed.

Somerton was a pleasant community in which to live. Most of the people were farmers growing domestic food supplies, but the area also produced sugar cane for Hampden Sugar Factory and bananas for export, which were shipped out of Montego Bay.

The only way of communicating over long distances, other than by letters, was by telegram. In cases of emergency, the telegrams were dispatched and families were often notified through this medium in cases of illness or death. Telegrams had to be delivered to the banana farmers, some of whom lived three or four miles from the post office. Very often, young members of families who lived close to the post office served as messengers and would be paid porterage of threepence per mile. I would use every opportunity to accompany my school friends to deliver the telegrams as this allowed me to get to know the village well. The prospect of enjoying all the fruits that grew on the trees by the roadside was, of course, another strong motivation.

I soon developed many friends in Somerton. The outstanding families in the district then were the Stewarts, the Cookes, the Falconers, the Keanes, the Blairs and the Peterkins. One of my favourite places was the home of the Stewarts, as I would get hot bread straight from the oven when they baked bread on a Saturday afternoon.

I attended the Baptist Church at Somerton. The pastor was the Reverend Fergus Lewis, father of Rupert Lewis, renowned professor of political thought at the University of the West Indies. He later moved to Port Antonio and then to the William Knibb Baptist Church in Falmouth. When I was at school at Calabar later I would sometimes go to visit the Lewis family in Port Antonio.

Around this time, World War II was coming to an end. We still had to observe the blackout periods, during which there were to be no lights at all; it was a security precaution to have total darkness. It did not affect us too much in Somerton, as there was no electricity in the district.

In those days the avenue to higher education for those students who did not go to secondary school was through a series of examinations called the first, second and third Jamaica Local Examinations. They were of an extremely high standard and passing all three qualified you to enter teachers' colleges – Mico, Shortwood, Bethlehem and St Josephs. Teacher Cocker taught English to first-, second- and third-year students together. My friends Joel Stewart, Ouida Stewart, Keith Falconer, Hazel Kerr and I were among the thirteen students who took the first-year examinations in 1947. I took the scholarship exam in the same year. Children from the surrounding schools like Sudbury, Chatham and Adelphi all sat exams at Somerton.

In those days scholarships to secondary schools were very few. There was only one per parish, as well as a few special scholarships donated for selected schools. I sat that exam at the Barracks Road School in Spanish Town, where my uncle, the Reverend Joslyn Carter-Henry, was the minister of the Phillippo Baptist Church and then returned to Somerton. Those students who did well enough to be considered for a scholarship would be called for an interview by the principal of the school at which the scholarship was tenable.

It would be another two months before I would be relieved of the suspense over whether I had made the grade. One Friday, just before midday, my aunt sent a message to me on the playing field to say I had to go to Spanish Town the following day to be taken to Calabar High School on the Monday morning for an interview by the principal.

To reach Spanish Town one had to walk about four miles through Cedar Valley to catch the Nathan's bus that would reach Adelphi at seven o'clock in the morning. Luckily, the bus stop was close to the home of Mrs Austin, one of the teachers at Somerton – I remember she used to ride her horse to school – so I was able to stay there and wait for the bus.

I left home early, while it was still dark. I found the route the bus travelled interesting: it went through Dumfries, Wakefield, Falmouth, Duncan's, Clark's Town, Stewart's Town and Jackson Town, a circuitous route. There were not many buses plying the country routes, so they had to drive that way to pick up and drop off their passengers. We stopped in St Ann's Bay around one o'clock for lunch and arrived in Spanish Town at about seven o'clock in the evening. I stayed with my uncle and his wife, Pearl Carter-Henry, at the Phillippo Baptist manse. She was the sister of Barry Ford and we became close friends from school days.

The following Monday morning I was taken to Calabar, where I was interviewed by the Reverend David Davis, an Australian, who had succeeded the Reverend Ernest Pryce, the second principal of Calabar. You can well imagine an eleven-year-old going in fear and trembling to be interviewed by the principal who would determine his fate. He asked me questions; I had to read; I had to answer mental arithmetic questions; and I was asked to recite a poem. I chose Wordsworth's "I Wandered Lonely as a Cloud". The interview, or rather interrogation, lasted for nearly an hour, and at the end of it I had no idea whether the principal had been sufficiently impressed. So I left and returned to the country none the wiser. I had done my best and I was hopeful.

About two weeks later, I received another telegram telling me I had won the Purcell Scholarship and should prepare myself to enter Calabar in January 1948. That scholarship had been created by a donation of one thousand pounds, which an elderly lady, Ms Purcell, had given to Calabar at the time of its construction. Through every succeeding phase of my life, I have never failed to appreciate the difference that winning this scholarship made. It created a solemn obligation to open the door of opportunity for boys of my kind.

CALABAR: THE UTMOST FOR THE HIGHEST

I recall only too well my first day at Calabar High School on 5 January 1948. It was then located at the corner of Slipe Pen and Studley Park Road, downtown Kingston, and the enrolment was 128. I was among twenty new boys. I came to school as a country boy – a proud scholarship winner – placed in second form to learn the mysteries of Latin, Spanish, algebra and geometry, which were not taught in primary school.

Calabar owes its name to that port in southeastern Nigeria from which thousands of enslaved Africans were forced to sail the treacherous Middle Passage to their eventual destination in the Rio Bueno Bay on Jamaica's northwest coast. The origin of the school's name spoke to our international vocation and training; and our destiny to be connected beyond our shores. It spurred inspiration in a culture and tradition that now transcends the school's own history of a hundred years, in both time and space. The founders' aim was to provide "a thoroughly modern education in a definitely religious atmosphere". The whole purpose of the school life was to develop self-reliance, honour and courage.

From the moment you passed through the hallowed school gate, you could not escape Calabar's insistence on strengthening the moral fibre of one's character; acquiring a sense of curiosity that would question the conventional wisdom; honing individual creativity and competitive skills to optimize personal goals while still accepting the value of service beyond self. What we were taught according to the syllabus in the classroom was only a part of what motivated us.

The preceding decade was a period of intense migration outflows, as the mobile Caribbean people sought work in the construction of the Panama Canal; on the sugar estates and the tobacco fields of Cuba; in the mines of Venezuela; in Costa Rica for establishing banana plantations and building the railway; and when they travelled between Haiti and Jamaica by sea it was on vessels of dubious seaworthiness.

Many of these emigrants were parents who sought schooling for their children back home in Jamaica, and a boarding institution offered additional advantages. One of the first boys I met was Simon Clarke, later United Nations Educational, Scientific and Cultural Organization director and education advisor for the Caribbean. He had come from Panama, where he was born to Jamaican parents, to attend Calabar. He never fails to remind me and my friends with a grin on his face of what I was wearing on my arrival at Calabar: "P.J. was dressed in grey knickers (pants), grey shirt, black shoes, black cap and grey knee socks. I was impressed. He was nattily dressed. Before that I only recall seeing anyone dressed like that in magazines."

I lived at Miss Olive Spence's boarding house on North Street, alongside boys who attended other first-rate high schools of the day – Kingston College, Excelsior, Kingston Technical High School. The boarding house was beside Steele's Bakery, renowned for its patties, sugar buns and meat loaves. In those early days in Kingston most of my weekends were spent at the Spanish Town Baptist manse with my uncle, the Reverend J.J. Carter-Henry, as he travelled from the Phillippo pulpit to preach at Old Harbour Bay, Hartlands, Kitson Town, Sligoville, Spring Village and Gregory Park, which were part of his circuit.

Our form teacher, Mrs Woodyatt, had a great influence on us. Her husband, the Reverend Cecil Woodyatt, the deputy headmaster, was a mathematician and taught physics to sixth-formers who also attended neighbouring high schools.

Given the sound foundation I had acquired at Somerton Elementary, I was off to a good start. On learning of my progress, Principal Ivan Newton Cocker of Somerton wrote to my aunt Dolly: "I was indeed thrilled to hear of Percy's success. The boy is doing things. He is certainly not little Percy any more. He is big Percy and will be bigger too. Great boy, I tell you. I imagine how you feel and how his mother feels and you know how I feel. Damn proud I tell you."

Before the end of my first year, the events at the London Olympics in 1948 confirmed the enormous prestige of the institution of which I was now a part. Two old boys, Arthur Wint and Herb McKenley, had won Jamaica's first gold and silver medals at these games. Our feeling of pride at Calabar cannot be adequately described. When these two alumni brought further glory to Jamaica at the 1952 Helsinki Games by establishing a new world record in the 4 × 400 metres relay, the headmaster was so delighted that at prayers the following morning, he ordered a school holiday for the rest of the day.

In the process, both took Jamaica to the world. They established the foundation from which this small island state has emerged as a superpower in track and field Olympic events. That victory in the Olympics was the only one for the British Empire on the track, and as the British anthem was played, the two Calabar old boys on the podium must have reflected on the journey they had travelled and the role that Calabar had played in that remarkable journey.[1]

There was no doubt about the excellence and commitment of the Calabar staff. Among them William Murray-White stood out. At full height he was five foot four, and simultaneously managed to inspire confidence, pride and respect! To his face he was, of course, "Headmaster". Elsewhere, he was "Dopey".

He had a biting wit and sarcastic tongue. In an algebra class a student once responded to a question by scratching his head before attempting the answer. Murray-White's comment was, "Young man, never scratch your head, you will only get splinters in your fingers." To another, on the result of a mathematics exam, he remarked, "In geometry you failed to disturb the scorer; you did infinitely better by getting one in algebra, and in arithmetic you did twice as well."

In school examinations, which took place every term, I had resigned myself to coming second every time, as my classmate Hugh Folkes would, deservedly, score 90 per cent in art and my mark was never more than 30 per cent. I could never make up such a huge gap. I only came first in fifth form when art was no longer compulsory. Classmates like Garth Martin, Karl Francis, Lester Chin and Alexander Hall were always running us close. By fourth form I had become somewhat distracted by other pursuits and dropped to fourth in the midterm exam. Mr Murray-White summoned me to his office and reprimanded me strongly for the slippage. He admonished me, "When you came to Calabar we thought you were a student of promise, but now you have become just plain and ordinary." During that stern scolding, I stood in complete silence and begged the

---

1. See Arnold Bertram, *A History of Calabar High School* (Kingston: Calabar Foundation, 2014).

floor to open and take me in. I walked slowly back to my classroom and moved my desk and chair to the front of the class without hearing a word of disapproval from the Reverend T.A.M. Grant, who was conducting the Latin lesson. Duly chastened, I revved up for the top in fifth form and onward.

⚓

Calabar's location in close proximity to the working-class community, its strong religious connections and the liberal influence of intellectually stimulating teachers combined to broaden the social perspective of the early students and encouraged an interest in the labour movement and its importance in a working democracy.

While Calabar was identified as having a special attraction for boys belonging to a "class on the rise", it made sure to welcome all social classes and every colour, so that the student body would be multiracial and start building friendships that would prove lasting and transcend the barriers of race and class.

To find room for the eleven boys who were consigned to second form in 1948, the classroom was in a tiny space between the classrooms for 5A and 5B. Whenever there was a debate among the fifth-formers I would take every opportunity to listen. On one occasion when the debate was opened to the floor, I dared to put forward my opinion. I was summarily chased out of the room by the seniors, who would not tolerate such audacity from a second-former in short pants.

In due course, I became a formidable debater and represented Calabar in inter-school competitions. This helped to boost my successful campaign for president of the Sixth Form Association. We met every Saturday at either Wolmer's or St Hugh's High School for Girls. We sought to insert our views in the national discourse and to engage in a wide range of community projects. It also provided an excellent opportunity for socializing.

In the scout movement, I rose from being a tenderfoot to patrol leader and later troop leader. This was another opportunity for leadership training. As part of my test to gain the first-class badge, I was required to take three boys with me and set up camp at the Red Hills property which the Baptists had acquired. In the bushes and ruinate we had to contend with rats, snakes and mongoose and we were only able to survive there for a single night.

My sixth-form experience was enhanced by close association with the Young Men's Christian Association (YMCA). Wesley Powell, founder of Excelsior High School and distinguished educator, was active in the club, and most of the island's prominent businessmen were YMCA members. It sponsored an

19

annual summer day camp for three weeks at Doncaster (Boy Scouts' headquarters). Counsellors were drawn from the high schools and lived at the YMCA at Hanover Street for the three weeks of the camp. I was one. We formed a special bond and developed a strong social conscience.

Each counsellor was given full responsibility for ten boys for the three weeks. I took my boys on a hike to Wareika Hills one day. We took the route across from Rockfort and back down to the University College of the West Indies. One of my charges fell and broke his ankle, and I had to carry him from the campus down to Hanover Street, some five miles, in the merciless Jamaican sun.

With the increase in student numbers, Calabar had outgrown the space at Studley Park Road and the buildings were crumbling. Hurricane Charlie in 1951 had torn off the roofs of several classrooms, so we had to sit our Senior Cambridge Exams in the open air. In the school's move from Studley Park Road to Red Hills Road in 1952, we senior boys had to help the younger ones to cope with the change of location and our new surroundings.

Among the outstanding members of staff was Neville Dawes, who taught me English literature as his special student. He had a strong impact on me, and to a large degree influenced my choice of an English major at the University College of the West Indies.

Calabar was spawned to remove the vestiges of slavery; to challenge the social status quo; to liberate the mind; to fashion the aptitudes and the disposition of young men to enable them to make their own distinctive mark on the contours of our nation and the horizons of our region and the world.

I owe a great deal to Calabar, which opened the door of opportunity and enabled us to prepare fully to take our place in life and our community. When Calabar celebrated its centenary in 2012, I was asked to serve as patron and honorary chair. It gave me a welcome opportunity to express my indebtedness in the foreword to Arnold Bertram's *History of Calabar High School*: "From the very start, we learned that Calabar was created for a very special purpose: to enable those of us who came from families of limited financial means to transform our own lives, and in doing so, to point the wider society towards the direction of freedom in the country and full respect for its people."[2]

---

2. Ibid., ix–x.

CHAPTER 3
THE MONA MOON AND THE REGIONAL CRADLE

FOLLOWING THE WIDESPREAD LABOUR UNREST AND SOCIAL UPHEAVAL throughout its Caribbean territories in the 1930s, Britain established a West India Royal Commission (known as the Moyne Commission) to enquire into the causes. The Commission on Higher Education in the Colonies (known as the Irvine Commission) was the direct result of its approved recommendations.

That report of the Irvine Commission gave birth to the University College of the West Indies. Its motto, "Oriens Ex Occidente Lux" (A Light Rising from the West), embodied the realization that the people of our region were all victims of a bitter human experience that had exposed them to displacement, fragmentation and exploitation. The University College of the West Indies, as Sir Philip Sherlock explained in his support of the Irvine Report, was intended to foster a special partnership between many peoples. This West Indian collaboration stood in opposition to the divisions imposed on the region by the rivalries of distant powers.

On the old Mona Sugar Estate stood the Gibraltar Camp, a relic of World War II, where Jews who sought to escape the ravages of Nazism were sheltered. These buildings were used to provide housing for some of the earliest students when the university opened its doors, and in September 1948 the first students, ten women and twenty-three men, moved into Gibraltar Hall to enter the medical faculty.

I entered the University College of the West Indies in October 1954 and joined the last group of those displaced from Gibraltar Hall, despite our resistance, to join a select group of freshmen who were assigned to the brand-new Chancellor Hall. By then, the old Mona estate had been transformed into "a functioning University and Teaching Hospital that were becoming internationally known.

The 302 students in residence included 138 doing medicine, 65 science, 85 arts, 16 education. Of these, 39 were from Barbados, British Guiana 35, British Honduras 3, Jamaica 130, the Leeward Islands 15, the Windward Islands 20, the Turks and other territories 5."[1]

When we awoke on the first morning, Mona was a wonderful place to behold. Many of us, even the Jamaicans, had never been able to admire those beautiful surroundings before. But especially for those who came from the islands with flat terrain, there was a special enchantment in the marvel of it all – the gentle slopes which gave way to the verdant hills around and the majesty of the distant mountains, covered by an azure sky.

I entered Block A of Chancellor Hall, with the chairman of the Guild of Undergraduates, Vincent "Bungo" Brown, from Montserrat, in the room next door. On the floor below were Woodville Marshall and Mervyn Morris, who later became professors of history and English. By 1955, I enjoyed the privilege of sharing a balcony room as block representative with Don Brice, the incumbent hall chairman. My room soon became known as the "music headquarters" because of the large Telefunken radio that I owned.

In those days all students were required to attend formal dinner, when we were mandated to wear our red gowns. Every night after dinner, we trekked to the Students' Union on a path ablaze with fireflies and the twinkling stars. The lure of the Mona moon was irresistible. Romance was in the air and lasting friendships were spawned. We dared to dream of a future extending beyond the borders of our separate colonies, to embrace the peculiar genius of the sons and daughters of a wider Caribbean.

It was in 1955 that the ritual of initiation for freshmen was introduced. It began as a prank which involved a notice being sent out that all students were required to participate in a rehearsal for a matriculation ceremony at the Undercroft. They were to be robed in their scarlet gowns, with the men in ties and blazers and the women in white dresses. The rehearsal was scheduled to start at three o'clock in the afternoon, which was the hottest period of the day. Of course, when they gathered at the Undercroft there was nobody there to receive them. To this day, no one has admitted responsibility. After that, every succeeding group of freshmen was subject to some form of initiation ritual.

Among that group was Shirley Field-Ridley, who had won a scholarship from British Guiana. I summoned the courage to invite this bright, attractive young

---

1. Arnold Bertram, *P.J. Patterson: A Mission to Perform* (Kingston: AB Associates, 1995), 34.

lady to be my guest at the national pantomime *Anancy and Pandora*. From that moment on, Shirley was the love of my life.

I was an active member of the Drama Society and served as treasurer under Slade Hopkinson's presidency in 1955. I took part in several productions, such as *King Lear* and *Oedipus Rex*, but am best remembered for being one of the faithful who stayed behind with Rex Nettleford to remove the chairs from the Dramatic Theatre before going home.

I had the opportunity to hone my public presentation skills through the Debating Society. Among the more memorable debates was one against the Oxford University debating team members Alec Grant and Roy Dickson, a Jamaican Rhodes scholar, who had just completed a ten-week tour of American colleges and universities. The honours were evenly divided: Robert Moore and I were voted the better speakers, while our opponents were considered more convincing.

No doubt the skills I developed through debating stood me in good stead when I was invited to participate in a live interview on BBC radio. The corporation had requested the university to invite two of its undergraduates to do an interview and I was selected, along with Ramsay Blackwood. After the interview, the BBC called from London to protest that it had not expected the students to be given the topics in advance and allowed to read their responses from a prepared script. It required the intervention of Sir Philip Sherlock, then director of the Department of Extra-Mural Studies, to convince the BBC that the students had been interviewed without any prior notice and had spoken without written notes.

❧

Among the offices I held in the Guild of Undergraduates was treasurer of the Students' Union. It was during my tenure that carnival was introduced to the Mona campus and I organized the first J'Ouvert fete in 1956 with the help of those to whom carnival was a natural art. We danced all the way from Ring Road to the Students' Union, with the pulsating rhythm of Lord Kitchener and the music of John "Buddy" Williams coming from our own University College steel-pan players. It was that year the Mighty Sparrow released "Jean and Dinah" and his lyrical joustings with Lord Melody soon began. They were the masters of *picong* and those calypsoes reflecting sexual exploits were laced with *double entendre*.

The students from Trinidad and Tobago had sensitized the rest of us to carnival. That, combined with the strong regional spirit, and love of calypso and dance, created a natural progression to starting our own carnival. That, in turn, resulted in the formation of a steelband. We came up with the brilliant idea of spreading Caribbean culture through the channel of the steelband and planned a concert tour in Europe. We booked the players' fares, but they were supposed to meet their needs for accommodation and subsistence from the concerts. But it was holiday time in Europe and, with schools closed, the audiences were too small to generate sufficient funds. I had to quickly organize some local festivities at the Students' Union to raise the funds to bring them back home sooner than anticipated.

In 1955, the Guild of Undergraduates established the External Affairs Commission to handle international student affairs. We had begun to appreciate the common issues we shared with other educational organizations globally and saw the need to establish relationships with other institutions through the world body. I became the first chairman of the commission.

The commission became active in international student affairs and resulted in my taking on an extensive itinerary. In the summer of 1956, I travelled to Germany as the guest of the German National Union of Students. I spent seven weeks touring educational centres, giving talks on student life in the West Indies, and visited the Berlin Wall, which demarcated East from West.

In 1957, I represented the University College of the West Indies at the Sixth International Student Conference in Ceylon (now Sri Lanka). The burning issues of academic rights, student freedoms, the threat of a nuclear holocaust, the evil system of apartheid, the anti-colonial struggle and hegemonic domination were on our agenda.

As we played our role in helping to promote international understanding, I was elected in 1957 to serve on the executive committee of the International Student Conferences. That year I travelled to Accra, Ghana, to attend a seminar of world university representatives on the role of students in Africa. This was my first step onto African soil, and part of that memorable journey was my visit to Ibadan, Nigeria, for the Seventh International Student Conference. Apartheid in South Africa and the situation of students in Hungary dominated our agenda. Our delegation took a strong stand in support of coloured students in South Africa and joined with other students globally to condemn the South African government's decision to introduce apartheid into open universities. We wrote to the National Union of South African Students expressing sympathy and wishing them well in their struggles. We also supported Hungarian students and endeavoured to assist them morally and financially. While travel to these conferences was funded entirely by a Cold War foundation in New York, we often found ourselves in sharp conflict with US positions that supported right-wing dictatorial regimes all over the world.

The Cold War was at its most intense, and the rigid separation between East and West was reflected in the ideological polarization between the International Union of Students and the International Student Conference.

There were times when my schedule conflicted with my academic work. One such was my visit to Nicaragua to investigate the abolition of academic freedom by the Somoza dictatorship. I recall having to seek permission to travel abroad during the academic term from my tutor, Robert LePage, of LePage and Cassidy's *Dictionary of Jamaican English* fame, who then lectured me in English literature. At that time Ralph Bunche, who had won the Nobel Peace Prize in 1950, was being celebrated for his work with the Jews and Palestinians. LePage asked if it was my intention to become an international civil servant like Ralph Bunche, or a lecturer in English like himself. I could not help wondering how he dared to place himself on the same scale as the black Nobel laureate. I thought it imprudent to reply that he was not in the same league as Ralph Bunche and simply urged him not to withhold consent for me to undertake the mission.

Once we had completed our assignment, we were advised that for reasons of personal security we should leave Nicaragua and write our report from the safety of Mexico City. It was in Mexico that I first had a direct and personal exposure to racial discrimination. As this was my first encounter, I did not immediately discern why my room reservation could not be found in the hotel where the Coordinating Secretariat of National Unions of Students had previously arranged lodging for the delegation, while there was no such problem for my white colleagues. It was the following day that I realized the hotel had lots of empty rooms.

The guild paid close attention to political affairs in the region. We felt that the student body should associate itself with the acceptance of federation for the West Indies, and forwarded a special memorandum to the London Federation Conference. It was also involved in trying to help students meet their financial obligations, and promoted the creation of self-help projects. Even then, we recognized the need for a students' loan fund and made a presentation to the Standing Federation Committee in February of 1957 asking for such a fund to be set up.

Until the start of the University College of the West Indies, most leaders of previous generations had become West Indians in wintry-cold Britain. Our group became regionalists by living in an environment which taught us that we had much more in common than the differences we had imagined.

Hopeton Gordon, Handel McFarquhar, Roy Johnstone and I formed the Political Club. I was the first president, and Woodville Marshall the secretary/ treasurer. Members of the executive committee included Erskine Sandiford, Daphne Pilgrim, Yvonne McCalla and Thelma Lawrence. The objectives of the club were to provide "education in the principles of the major political ideologies", and to display "an active interest in the political development of the British Caribbean area by expressing the opinion of the club as a whole on any matter of current interest".

Very soon after our launch, we pulled off a coup by being able to present the distinguished historian Eric Williams. He had been fired from his position at the Anglo-American Caribbean Commission in August 1955 and decided to visit Jamaica to meet with Norman Manley, who had won the elections here earlier that year.

On hearing of his visit in December, the Political Club seized the opportunity to invite him to speak at a special meeting in Arts Lecture Room 3. He readily consented. I was privileged to preside at the lecture he delivered that memorable Thursday afternoon. Because of the limited space, many were seated on the unyielding turf outside, with only their scarlet gowns as a slight shield from the damp grass.

I vividly recall the spellbinding eloquence and erudite analysis of this celebrated Caribbean thinker and visionary, which mesmerized the overflowing crowd, consisting of virtually every student and lecturer on the entire Mona campus. He set out his vision of a Caribbean which would be united across the barriers of language and imperial conquests, mobilizing its resources to create a new dynamic and forge a strong political and economic unit. He asserted that the best prospects for the transformation of Caribbean society were to be found in changing the mindset and expanding the mental and psychological horizons of the young. His closing words still resound in my ears: "I shall return to my homeland for the awakening and upliftment of my people and to rid the country at once and forever of political rascality and corruption."

Chairing that meeting served me well in later years, when he and Michael Manley were not seeing eye to eye on a number of issues. He had occasion to visit Jamaica during this time to open a ministerial meeting of the African, Caribbean and Pacific Group of States (ACP) and I was given the task of meeting him at the airport. I was apprehensive and dubious about what his reaction to me would be. On the way to his hotel, he said to me, "Patterson, I remember you. You presided over my first meeting at the university. You don't understand what this thing is all about, so I won't take it out on you." I said, "Thank you," and breathed a sigh of relief.

The speakers at our meetings were of a high calibre. Among them were: the deputy Speaker of the Indian House of Assembly, who spoke on India's march to freedom and its federal constitution; Douglas Manley and George Cumper, who presented on West Indian migration to Britain and its effects; Gordon Lewis spoke on the West Indies Federation; and a senior lecturer in history from the University of Natal, South Africa, enlightened us on the Education Act of 1953 and the pernicious plan for separate universities for blacks and whites in the land of apartheid.

The members of the Political Club travelled around Jamaica to give talks on the federal agenda. None of us had a car and we generally prevailed on Simon Clarke, who was one of the few students with one, to take us to meetings out of town. On a trip to Manchester, there was just enough gas in the car to get us to and from Mandeville. On reaching Mandeville, we discovered that the meeting was actually at Port Kaiser. So off we went, giving no thought to the fuel situation.

Our hosts put on a fantastic spread, and after enjoying an excellent repast we started on our journey home. After midnight, on reaching Gutters, St Elizabeth, the water hose in the car burst. We taped up the hose, found water and continued on the journey. As we approached the steepest portion of the Spur Tree Road, Man Bump, on our way to Mandeville, at around two o'clock in the morning, the car ran out of gas. We remembered having passed a gas station at the bottom of the hill, so we cruised back down and tried, unsuccessfully, to awaken the attendant. Eventually, a truck towed us up the hill to Mandeville. We got into Kingston at dawn, covered in mud, and reached campus just in time for breakfast.

The members of the Political Club took a keen interest in the federal agenda and we were certain that we had devised the most effective plans for the region. We drew up a model constitution for the West Indies Federation. When it was not accepted and the federation collapsed, we had no doubt that it was the direct result of ignoring our sage advice.

Arising from an article on the placement of the federal capital that I wrote in 1956, which was published in most national newspapers, the *Trinidad Guardian* invited me to become its university correspondent. My reward was a pile of its newspapers, which invariably arrived a month after they had been published, brought by the *Federal Palm* or the *Federal Maple* – two ships plying the

Caribbean Sea. Nevertheless, they were eagerly awaited, and the students from Trinidad and Tobago would come to my room in droves to catch up with the news and opinions from their homeland whenever a batch of the *Trinidad Guardian* arrived.

In addition to the activities already described, I was an active member of the editorial board of the *Pelican* magazine, the voice of the students. I served at different times as the news editor and sports editor. Among the other editorial members and contributors during my time were James Lee Wah, editor in chief, and such outstanding individuals in the contemporary literary field as Edward Baugh, Mervyn Morris, Burchell Whiteman, Jean Creary and Woodville Marshall. The humorous column written by Dunstan Champagnie called the "Book of the Dead" was compulsory reading in every edition.

Roy Augier, recruited as a fellow of the Institute for Social and Economic Research at the university, offered a number of young students employment to cover the election campaign of 1954–55. It provided the opportunity for us to meet the leaders of the PNP and the JLP.

During the holidays I earned some useful pocket money as a sports reporter for the *Daily Gleaner*, in the sports department led by L.D. "Strebor" Roberts and Basil "Baz" Freckleton. That assignment facilitated contact with the formidable editor, Theodore Sealy, and a wide range of fine journalists like Jack Anderson, Percy Miller, Ulric Simmonds and Barbara Goodison (Mrs Gloudon).

I majored in English with a minor in history. I enjoyed both subjects immensely, but my history lecturers claimed that history should have been my main course of study. The insightful lectures on West Indian history were not to be missed on any account. I recall particularly the tutorials, which had no more than four or five students in a group. Many of our lecturers chose to conduct their tutorials in their flats, and these had the extra benefit of refreshments. Those lecturers who were not "with it" served lemonade or orange juice, while others were known to serve things that loosened the tongue but dampened the intellectual input. The most delightful tutorials were those of Barbara Rooke, who always served sherry and exquisite canapés.

A love of literature points to a passion for reading and I certainly did not confine my reading to my textbooks. The period was one of great literary ferment. We were no longer confined to English and American authors. We took delight in reading C.L.R. James, Frantz Fanon, Roger Mais, V.S. Naipaul, Vic Reid, Martin Carter and George Lamming.

My study schedule was much determined by music programmes on the radio. There was a programme put on by the *Voice of America*, which recognized jazz as one of the major weapons of the Cold War. Initially the programme, with the booming voice of Willis Conover, famed as a musicologist, was aired between two and four o'clock in the afternoon, so it was convenient for me to study at that time. Later, it was shifted to two to four o'clock in the morning, so I had to change my routine to having dinner, going to the Students' Union, then returning home early to sleep and wake up in time to hear the programme. I learned then how to listen to music and get on with work.

⁂

In those early days, no matter the country of origin or the faculty to which one belonged, we were all one big family. The professors, lecturers, registry and hospital staff shared with their children on the campus and the entire student group one common space and fellowship. Within a short time, most of us became devout regionalists, not by any process of indoctrination, but by intuitive acceptance that destiny had brought us together to fashion a dynamic, vibrant Caribbean identity.

Few among us then would have discerned the latent propensity for political leadership which was revealed by medical student Kennedy Simmonds, who plunged into the political arena and was later elected prime minister of St Kitts–Nevis. The same cannot be said of Erskine Sandiford, whose scholarly pursuits did not conceal his intention to engage actively in the political arena in Barbados.

For reasons best known to him, there were three students on whom Philip Manderson Sherlock lavished his special guidance and erudition – Ramsay Blackwood (guild president 1955–56), Rex Nettleford and P.J. Patterson. We spent much more time in the precincts of the Department of Extra-Mural Studies than within our respective departments of natural science, history and English. He sought to impart his conviction that the Caribbean man and woman needed not only to achieve the highest levels of intellectual pursuit, but also to be served by consummate professionals who were creative and committed.

For many of my 1958 graduating class, the University College of the West Indies will be remembered forever because it helped to shape our character and determine our mission in life.

It was for me the best eventual retort to Robert Le Page when, on 19 April 2006, the chancellor of the University of the West Indies, Sir George Alleyne, conferred on me the Chancellor's Medal. To follow in the footsteps of Sir Philip Sherlock and Sir Alister McIntyre was honour enough. It was an additional source of pride that I became the first graduate of the institution to receive that accolade.

I quote from my response on conferment:

> Tonight's award reflects a summons to exert our own capacity within this region to make a decisive difference to the future of our own people and to make an impact on the Commonwealth, the region and the multilateral organizations in their mission to create a more just, stable and equitable community of nations.
>
> And I make no apology for seeking in different ways to keep these two objectives in balance. Given the history of the world in which we live, unilateralism is a decreasing option, even as we recognize the importance of preserving our cultural and national identities.
>
> We must be able in the words of one of the distinguished honorary doctoral graduates of this university, the Honourable Louise Bennett-Coverley to "dance a' yard" before we can dance abroad.
>
> For dance we must.
>
> We cannot allow ourselves to be swept by the tide of a passive acceptance of globalization or ignore the real opportunities to tell our Caribbean story and assert our Caribbean rights in various international organizations to which we belong.
>
> Your award of this Chancellor's Medal is a reminder to all of us who share this space as beneficiaries of the work of this university and contributors to regional development, that we have a responsibility to nurture the spirit of Caribbean regionalism and to build Caribbean self-confidence as we face the future together.

There is no reason for a change of my view, expressed in a gathering of alumni in April 1995, at which I noted that the University of the West Indies "remains the most creative gift we as a people have given to ourselves and persists as part of the hope of a future worth having. For integral to the great university traditions of teaching and research, is the empowering of the graduate to transform principles into further action in an unending cycle of knowledge-generation application, testing and representation which are the special attributes of all of humankind."

CHAPTER 4
THE FEDERAL EXPERIMENT

WHEN I ENTERED THE UNIVERSITY COLLEGE OF THE West Indies in 1954 as a Jamaican student, my knowledge of our region stemmed from the snippets of its history and geography taught in the traditional colonial grammar school, and my interest in the Caribbean was largely fuelled by the rising fortunes of the West Indies cricket team.

As students, we envisioned a future where the peculiar genius of Caribbean men and women would be spread throughout the region and extend across the globe into the corridors of international power. By the time of my graduation, I had been incurably infected by the regional virus. Pride and loyalty to the land of my birth have never deterred me from becoming and remaining an unrepentant regionalist. What may admittedly have been a largely emotional attachment then, has during the succeeding years hardened into a firm conviction that regional economic integration is an imperative. The assertion of our united voice as sovereign nations singing from the same hymn sheet is the only way for any of us to be heard in the global din. Today's international environment continues to validate the wisdom of those visionary pioneers who envisioned a full-fledged political and economic West Indies Federation.

To find the deepest roots of the consciousness that shaped a sentiment of "West Indianness", one needs to revert to the extended era of resistance and revolt by the enslaved in the Caribbean. In various places within the region this stubborn and persistent "no" to dehumanization came to a spectacular head at times: from Boukman and Toussaint in Haiti to Tacky in Jamaica and Cuffy in British Guiana. These resistant slaves were not conscious that they were laying the psychological foundation of a Caribbean movement. Yet that was indeed the objective lesson of their determination to confront their subjugation.

The post-emancipation decades of the nineteenth and twentieth centuries saw this psychological foundation being extended and consolidated, with indentured Indians striving to ameliorate their lot, as whole societies in the region struggled against the exclusion, marginalization and impoverishment perpetuated under crown colony government. A strong intellectual and political leadership was emerging to give systematic articulation to decades of subterranean rumblings and resistance.

The "Froudacity" of imperialist assumptions and impositions came under relentless attack by a long line of nationalist luminaries, starting with the landmark contribution of J.J. Thomas, followed by the work and voices of numerous others such as A.A. Cipriani, Cecil Rawle, Albert Marryshow, C.L.R. James, W. Adolphe Roberts, W.A. Domingo and George Padmore. Their cumulative impact, building on the psychological foundations of the preceding decades of resistance, was the forging of a national consciousness. While anchored in the specific conditions of individual societies in the region, this national consciousness was West Indian in scope and unbounded by territorial limits. Decades of spontaneous struggle and resistance eventually shaped and gave direction, by conscious intellectual and political leadership, to a cross-border consciousness of mutual belonging. In essence, this comprised the effective roots of a West Indian social and cultural collective.

As early as the 1800s, the British had discussed the idea of governing the then British colonies as one administrative unit. In fact, the Federal Colony of the Leeward Islands had been governed by the British in an administrative federation from 1871 to 1956.

The leaders of the indigenous labour movements – men like Grenada's T.A. Marryshow, and Trinidad and Tobago's A.A. Cipriani – were the strongest advocates of regional federation. Their ideas, however, differed significantly from those of the British, who were interested in administrative tidiness for their convenience. The regional pioneers had a vision of a union of countries centred on a constitution crafted by and for West Indians enjoying the rights and freedom of independent peoples, with leaders elected under universal adult suffrage.

With the labour unrest which characterized the region during the period 1934 to 1938, the calls for freedom grew louder. In an effort to get to the root causes of the unrest, the Colonial Office set up the Moyne Commission to examine what had triggered the combustion and propose the necessary steps to avoid further convulsion. Among the recommendations was one from the Caribbean Labour Congress, which proposed the establishment of a federation of the West Indies on the basis of full internal self-government with adult suffrage.

In September 1947, a large cross-section of West Indian leaders – in politics, labour and community development – met in Montego Bay to discuss the future of the region. Although the ideas discussed there were not as far-reaching as those of the Labour Congress, the meeting agreed in principle on the need for a federation.

Guided by Britain, negotiations began in 1953 to set up the Federation of the British West Indies. These negotiations were conducted solely between West Indian political leaders and the colonial power. They were held outside the region (in Britain) and did not continue the widespread involvement of various groups and non-state actors, as had been the case up to the 1947 Montego Bay Conference. During those six years, the Jamaican delegation to the negotiations would have been determined by the colonial governor and the chief minister, Alexander Bustamante.

On the Mona campus, we engaged as students, including those from British Honduras and British Guiana, in vigorous debates which resulted in our draft proposal for a federal constitution.

The appointment by the Colonial Office of Lord Hailes as the first governor general, and the selection of an elite group of federal civil servants set the stage for the first and only federal elections in 1958. By the time the final agreements were reached, two federal political parties had been spawned – the West Indian Federal Labour Party (WIFLP), led by Norman Manley, and the Democratic Labour Party (DLP), chaired by Alexander Bustamante. Both Manley and Bustamante decided, however, not to be candidates. So, from the start, the federal vessel was imperilled by the absence of its political captains.

The federal elections were held on 25 March 1958. In Jamaica, the JLP, as part of the Democratic Labour Party, won twelve of the seventeen seats – Robert Lightbourne, Morris Cargill, Kenneth "Ken" Hill and Lionel Densham were among the more notable. The PNP, allied with the WIFLP in the federal elections three years after its convincing 1955 general election victory, could muster only five winners – Ralph Brown, Howard Cooke, Pat Delapenha, A.U. Belinfanti and Frank Ricketts. Edith Dalton James, Aubrey Russell, Dudley Thompson, Vivian Blake, Leacroft Robinson and Balfour Barnswell were among those to bite the dust.

The West Indies Federal Labour Party, however, won twenty-five of the forty-five seats in the federal parliament. Norman Manley, the president of the party, and Eric Williams chose to remain at their national levels. Grantley Adams of Barbados was appointed the first prime minister of the West Indies Federation and Robert Bradshaw of St Kitts–Nevis–Anguilla was appointed minister of finance.

The lukewarm support for those who preached the federal gospel in Jamaica should have been an early hint of things to come and a clear warning from the electorate that enthusiasm for federation was marginal. It was, however, submerged under the more compelling and obvious message – the urgency of reorganizing the PNP and reconnecting with its voter base to regain the confidence of the Jamaican electorate by the time general elections would be due.

It was in that environment that I was lured into the active arena by none other than O.T. Fairclough, who, after inviting me for dinner at his home on East Avenue in Camperdown, persuaded me to serve as a party organizer for the PNP and defer my law studies. Before taking up the assignment, I was a frequent visitor to Headquarters House whenever the House of Representatives was in session.

One afternoon, the "Chief" (as Alexander Bustamante was popularly known) summoned me and said, "Sonny, come here. I have just discovered who you really are. You come from the James family but are masquerading under the name of Patterson. Your grandfather was my headmaster at Cacoon. You come from good family stock. What are you doing in my cousin's party? I hear you are very bright and aspiring to be a barrister like my cousin Norman. Let me give you sound advice. Go and study well – If you are half as good as my cousin Norman at the Bar, you will succeed as he is twice as good as all the others put together. But if you want to learn about politics, then come sit at the feet of Gamaliel."

It was the urgency of reorganizing the party that drove my recruitment to the organizing team. Led by Allan Isaacs as the national organizer, it included Ernest Peart and Eustace Bailey. That is how I came to work in the political field with the likes of Howard Cooke, Ralph Brown and A.U. Belinfanti, who devoted all their time to the rebuilding of the party whenever their presence was not required in Trinidad and Tobago. It was a learning experience that later proved of incalculable value.

I was able to set up the microphone and arrange lights for outdoor meetings, and also to dismantle them in a hurry when stones were falling all around. You had to know how and when to speak on the platform – but you also had to master the art of listening when interfacing with group members.

The federation faced several problems. These included: the governance and administrative structures imposed by the British; disagreement among territories over policies, particularly with regard to taxation and central planning; unwillingness on the part of most territorial governments to give up power to the federal government; and the location of the federal capital.[1]

Among the many issues which polarized the region were two which proved insoluble and on which the leaders appeared intransigent – the power of taxation and the freedom of movement. Jamaica resisted any fetter on the scope and pace of development within its borders. Trinidad and Tobago feared a wave of immigrants from the islands of the Eastern Caribbean. When Grantley Adams was lured over drinks at Up Park Camp by *Gleaner* reporter Ulric Simmonds into discussing the imposition of retroactive taxation, gale-force winds blew across the entire region.

Robert Lightbourne had resigned his federal seat to beat Ken Clarke of the PNP in West St Thomas during the 1959 general elections in Jamaica. A by-election was called to fill the vacancy in St Thomas and the PNP assigned me as the organizer for that campaign. Edwin Allen, who had lost his Clarendon constituency to Alphonsus Malcolm, was the JLP candidate and David Moyston, a lawyer, was the PNP's choice.

I remember too well walking down the main street of Morant Bay on the Monday morning of the nomination day. Coming from the other end was a crowd led by Sir Alexander himself. I ducked into a corner, not realizing he had already spotted me. As he got to me, he beckoned: "Sonny, what are you doing here? I thought you had followed my advice and gone off to study law and follow in my cousin's legal footsteps, as I advised you over a year ago. Instead Norman have you running up and down the country like mad ants. Soon, you can see, it will all come to nought."

I only realized the true meaning of his remark on hearing the radio news that night of Bustamante's decision not to contest the by-election and the JLP's declaration that it would take Jamaica out of the federation on returning to office and seek independence on its own.

That prompted Norman Manley to announce his decision the following day to revisit the federal arrangements and secure a new federal constitution: "When that is concluded, we will hold a referendum so that our people may decide." As Manley sought to exert the political leadership which would permit this, there were cracks in both the WIFLP and the PNP. He was now prepared to take the federal helm as leader of the WIFLP, but by then the rescue operation was much too late.

During the early months of 1961, West Indian leaders, their ministers and

---

1. CARICOM Secretariat, *CARICOM: Our Caribbean Community – An Introduction* (Kingston: Ian Randle, 2005), 38.

officials were all engaged in a frenetic series of conferences, consultations and workshops to devise the legal framework, the institutions, policies, social programmes and economic projects which could advance the growth and welfare of the countries and people of our region.

When G. Arthur Brown retired for the second time as governor of the Bank of Jamaica, he shared with me one of the reasons he felt impelled to write his memoirs. As they prepared for the final federal conference with the Colonial Office in London, Egerton Richardson and Brown, two of the brightest and most trusted public servants in Jamaica, were tasked with preparing a special document which Norman Manley entrusted to a safe and confidential pair of hands for personal delivery to Grantley Adams with the message: "I believe we can find a solution to our conundrum. If you as Premier of the Federation propose it, I will be the first to give my full endorsement. I believe this document provides the only way out." To Manley's total dismay, Grantley Adams never once mentioned at the conference any of the ideas or suggestions he had received. Manley concluded that the omission was deliberate and constituted a betrayal.

"You can hardly imagine my consternation when years after Adams's death his devoted secretary invited me to visit her on my next trip to Barbados. There she handed me an envelope, still with its original seal. I realized Grantley Adams had never opened it and hence was unaware of its contents," Arthur Brown related.

Unfortunately, within a few weeks of that conversation on the veranda of Vale Royal, Arthur Brown suffered a recurrence of his cancer, and so history can only conjecture as to the outcome if the envelope had been opened and the letter had been read and introduced by Premier Adams in the Lancaster House Conference.

At the time of the federal conference in London, I was a law student there, and on his way to Heathrow Airport, Manley invited me home to assist in the referendum campaign. I did not hesitate, as the campaign would fall during the summer holidays and provided a welcome opportunity to join in the thrills of a campaign which would decide the future of the federation.

The Jamaican legislature had to approve the enabling law and regulations to permit the holding of a referendum. The traditional election symbols – the head for the PNP and the hand for the JLP – were barred. The tree was chosen for those voting to remain and the bell for those opting to leave.

I wrote an article, "Jamaicans Abroad and Federation", for the YES campaigners which was published in the *Daily Gleaner* of 31 August 1961:

Most of the Jamaicans who live abroad are ardent supporters of the Federation. The reasons for such overwhelming support by workers and students alike are not hard to find. Although they explained their attitudes in a variety of ways, certain ideas were shared in common.

I approached one person who has been resident in Britain for seven years, but he was almost indignant when I asked him what he thought of Federation. "With my experience of living here, how could I be anything else but a Federationist?" he asked me. This response was fairly typical of others, for when West Indians live together they soon discover a unifying bond. Thus, it is no coincidence that members of the University College community are such vigorous exponents of the Federal idea.

By living together, they soon learn that the accidents of birth do not produce any real difference of upbringing or outlook. Our tastes for food and drink are similar, but in many respects unique. We share a common cultural background, not yet fully developed but clearly emergent.

While Trinidad and Tobago boasts of Beryl McBurnie, Jamaica has Ivy Baxter, The Mighty Sparrow is as well received here as is Louise Bennett in the Southern Caribbean. One steel band record during a New York party is enough to get every West Indian on his feet. There is the same rhythm and a sense of gay abandon that is peculiarly West Indian.

Such qualities are seen in our cricket. Not for us is the dour determination of the English nor the steady application of the Australian.

The sunny climate of our shores is reflected in the brightness of our cricket, a certain spontaneity in our laughter and our love of colour and spectacle. While these attributes need not in themselves create a nation, they are sure to prove invaluable as a unifying force and are sufficient answer to those who ask "What have we in common?"

Yet, important as these qualities are, there are more compelling reasons why so many Jamaicans abroad wish us to remain in Federation. In England, the natives make no attempt to distinguish between the Jamaican and the Antiguan, or the Guyanese and the St Lucian. All are regarded as West Indians and treated alike. We are victims of discrimination and subject to the same difficulties.

In adversity, we turn to each other for comfort and determine to seek our fortunes together. Experiences of this kind serve as a strong cohesive force. As time passes and more Jamaicans travel to the nine islands and we welcome in our island visitors from the other territories, we are bound to realize the extent to which our salvation depends on full cooperation.

On leaving home, the Jamaican appreciates even better how small this island really is. The city of London has six times the population of Jamaica and our whole country could fit easily between the banks of one Nigerian river. The individual wealth of many Americans far exceed the entire national income of the island. These facts are not intended to hurt our national pride, but are an avenue through which to view in proper perspective our country and the world in which we live. It is especially true in this space age that no island is a world.

What other course?

How can the West Indian migrant be anything but a Federationist when he lives in Britain, which is being forced to join the Common Market of Europe for her own economic survival despite centuries of splendid isolation and differences of language, religion and political system? Any West Indian who studies American history is bound to appreciate the extent to which the national prosperity is due to the success of a federal experiment.

These are some of the reasons why hundreds of Jamaicans abroad regret so much their inability to vote in this grave national issue. It is left to those of us who have the solemn responsibility on September 19 to show that we too are aware that no man liveth unto himself.

Ken Hill, who had been expelled from the PNP as part of a leftist purge, returned happily to the party to support Norman Manley and those in the leadership who were genuinely committed to the federal cause. The six-week campaign was arduous and exhausting. The opponents did not confine their main arguments to whether or not Jamaica should remain in the West Indies Federation. Their propaganda ranged from the state of roads and water supplies to the high cost of living. Towards the end they invented the bizarre story of Russian ships in Kingston Harbour with chains to take the Jamaican people back to slavery. The PNP lost because there was division in our own camp. For me, it was a lesson on the fatal consequences for a party that is not united.

In that referendum 61.78 per cent of the electorate went to the polls and by a margin of 38,895 voted to secede. It is now history that the federal adventure became unstuck after Jamaica's secession, and the exasperated declaration of Eric Williams that one from ten left nought.

Determined to pursue their vision vigorously, Premiers Errol Barrow of Barbados and Forbes Burnham of then British Guiana, and Vere Bird Sr, chief minister of Antigua and Barbuda, met in July 1965 to discuss the establishment of a free-trade area among their countries. By December of that year, the three leaders had signed the agreement at Dickenson Bay, Antigua, to set up the Caribbean Free Trade Association (CARIFTA). They decided to delay implementing the agreement in order to give other countries of the region the opportunity to join.

By 1967, the University of the West Indies had completed three studies on various aspects of integration, namely regional trade, economic development and air transport, which would guide deliberations on a new form of regional cooperation.[2] In October of that year, the fourth conference of heads of government was held in Barbados.

At that meeting, the heads of government decided to proceed on the basis of the 1965 Dickenson Bay Agreement and to form the CARIFTA Secretariat and the Caribbean Development Bank. Acknowledging the different stages of development of the member countries, two categories were established: the more-developed countries – Barbados, Guyana (formerly British Guiana), Jamaica, and Trinidad and Tobago – and the less-developed countries –Antigua and Barbuda, Dominica, Grenada, Montserrat, St Kitts–Nevis–Anguilla, St Lucia, and St Vincent and the Grenadines. William Demas, CARIFTA secretary general from January 1970, worked assiduously with the existing political leadership to ensure that the movement gained strength under their direction and guidance.

In addition to the trading arrangements at the core of the agreement, there were other important areas of cooperation which have proven invaluable to the region. They encompassed legal affairs; shipping and air services; meteorological, health, broadcasting and information services; technical assistance; standards; and industrial research. In mid-1962, a common services conference was held to decide on the maintenance of some of the federal initiatives, mainly the University of the West Indies (successor to the University College of the West Indies) and the Regional Shipping Council. By 1973, other regional institutions were serving the region well, including the Caribbean Development Bank and the Caribbean Examinations Council.

---

2. Havelock Brewster and Clive Thomas, *The Dynamics of West Indian Economic Integration* (Kingston: Institute of Social and Economic Research, University of the West Indies, 1967); Alister McIntyre, Norman Girvan, George Beckford and Eric Armstrong, *Possibilities for Rationalizing Production and Trade in the West Indies* (Kingston: Institute of Social and Economic Research, University of the West Indies, 1967); Steve De Castro, *Problems of the Caribbean Air Transport Industry* (Kingston: Institute of Social and Economic Research, University of the West Indies, 1967).

CHAPTER 5
MY LEGAL CAREER

SHIRLEY FIELD-RIDLEY, MY FIANCÉE, had taught history at Rusea's High School in Lucea, Hanover, for one year before preceding me to read law at the University College, London, in 1959. When I took her to embark on the SS *Golfito* at Port Antonio for the voyage on the banana boat to Southampton, we had agreed to end our relationship, as she would be returning to British Guiana and I to Jamaica. But during our correspondence while apart, we agreed to settle in Jamaica and made all arrangements for the wedding. Angela Lewis (later Mrs Hudson-Phillips) was bridesmaid and Woodville Marshall the best man as, surrounded by a throng of family and friends, we were married at the Kentish Town Methodist Church on a bright and pleasant Saturday afternoon in August 1960.

In September 1960, I entered the London School of Economics and enrolled as a law student in Middle Temple.

As a student at Middle Temple, I was required to dine in hall for six nights in each term. For those of us enrolled at university, the requirement was reduced to three nights. These occasions gave judges and Queen's Counsel (QCs) a golden opportunity to interact not only with fellow students but with benchers of the Inn. It was during the campaign for the federal elections in 1961 that the results of my first year were published. I was delighted to learn that I had won the Sir David Hughes Parry Prize, awarded to the student gaining the highest marks in the law of contracts. I also received a Leverhulme Scholarship, which is given to the top three students of the class of that academic year.

Student life was heavily intermingled with my involvement in Jamaican politics. I had special access to the critical events of the period, despite living in faraway London. Having lost the referendum on the Federation of the West Indies, Premier Norman Manley led the team that travelled to London for discussions with the UK government on independence for Jamaica. His favourite London hotel was the Howard, a small hotel at which he had stayed since the days when he appeared before the Privy Council as an advocate. Fortuitously, the Howard was near the Inns of Court and the London School of Economics. He expected me to visit the hotel each morning on my way to classes and again each evening after his delegation had returned from meetings with the Colonial Office.

At this time, he shared with me the ongoing discussions. I was only too happy to be afforded this unique opportunity to be kept abreast of the exciting and historic developments which were taking place. It gave me a personal insight into an exercise which entailed negotiating with the Colonial Office and resolving differences between the government and opposition delegations. These discussions formed the basis for the first constitution of its kind. This was taking place at a time when neither the JLP nor the PNP could be certain which party would prevail in the polls to follow.

Three things stand out in my memory. These were special provisions, geared to deal with the peculiar circumstances of the time. First, the Privy Council, as our final court, was deliberately not entrenched in order to permit a replacement for that body which would assume the judicial functions being performed then by the existing West Indian Federal Court of Appeal. In a short time, that federal court had established a reputation as one of the finest in the Commonwealth, but it would fall to Caribbean governments to decide later whether it would continue. Second, the chief justice was head of the Judiciary. J. Leslie Cundall, then attorney general, who became the first president of the Court of Appeal, prevailed in ensuring that the chief justice could only sit in the Court of Appeal by special invitation. Third, the government members of the delegation proposed 1 August 1962 as the date for independence. The JLP delegation opposed any link with Emancipation Day. It was Ivan Lloyd, PNP member of Parliament for South East St Ann, who came up with the compromise suggestion of the first Monday in August, which was accepted.

At the end of the talks, Norman Manley announced his intention to hold national elections to allow Jamaicans to choose the government of their new nation. During our journey to Heathrow Airport, he asked me whether I would be prepared to return home to help organize the party for the election campaign. This, unlike the referendum, was during term time, and I would therefore require permission from the London School of Economics to be absent from classes. I approached the dean, Professor Gower, with the request. He said I had been identified by the faculty as a future professor of law and I was jeopardizing my prospects for academic advancement. He would have none of it. Disappointed at his reaction, I enlisted the support of my tutor, Professor

Griffith, who interceded on my behalf. Professor Gower, with great reluctance, finally conceded. He said as a graduate student, I was expected to be mature enough to take my own decision. He then pronounced: "You go with my leave, but not with my blessing." And so I returned home for the campaign.

I arrived home in February 1962 and returned to classes at the London School of Economics in the middle of April 1962. Exams for part one of the law degree were scheduled for June, so I needed to study full-time to catch up. During the following academic year, I concentrated on meeting the expectations of my tutors in jurisprudence; conflict of laws; and industrial, administrative and family law to sit the final LLB exam.

It is rare for students who complete their LLB degree in June to take the Bar exams in September, as usually they want to enjoy a holiday break. In addition, there are subjects for the Bar finals which are additional to those taken for the law degree. But I was determined not to be in London for another winter of days-long fog, burst pipes and scarcely any central heating.

To make matters worse, the West Indies team, led by Frank Worrell, was touring England. Woodville Marshall and I went to the test matches at Lords, Old Trafford and Edgbaston. The final match, at the Oval, ended the day before the Bar exams began. I was there to see the West Indies win. "Strebor" Roberts, with whom I had worked on the *Gleaner* sports desk, declined an invitation to dinner at my home when he discovered I had to write my Bar finals the following day.

As I prepared to leave for the exam, my wife Shirley asked me why I was wasting my time, since there were not likely to be any questions in the exam papers about the West Indies victory over England, but I was determined to escape the rigours of winter, Having given up the lease on our flat, I went to Fleet Street to collect the morning papers with the final exam results and wondered where I would live if I were not successful. Shirley had left two weeks earlier for home in British Guiana, as our first child, Richard, was on the way and she wanted the care and support of her mother and family. We also thought it would give her an opportunity to give something back to her country before joining me in Jamaica.

I suffered some moments of anxiety, as the banana boat's arrival in Southampton was delayed because of the Hurricane Flora rains in September 1963 which had devastated the island. I was a happy man as I boarded the SMV *North Star*, which would take me to Jamaica.

The eminent barrister Vivian Blake, QC, moved for my admission to the Jamaican Bar on 20 December 1963 before Mr Justice Moodie.

In the 1960s, the legal profession was divided between barristers, who had the right of audience in all the courts, and solicitors, who appeared in the resident magistrates' courts, but were confined to instructing counsel in civil matters in the Supreme Court. Only counsel could appear in divorce cases, whether these were contested or uncontested, and that provided a good income for many a young counsel. All appeals from the resident magistrates' courts to the appeal court had to be represented by counsel.

Although I knew all the heads of the leading chambers well, they were all overcrowded, so I had to find my own office space from which to practise. Noel Silvera, a solicitor, and his wife Mavis Sutherland, an optometrist, had constructed a new building at 39½ John's Lane for their professional practices. I rented an office there for the princely sum of £13.10 a month. My initial staff consisted of a single messenger, Gladys, who would run errands and take messages.

Norman Manley had an office in the Myers, Fletcher and Gordon building on Duke Street, where he confined his legal work to writing opinions and drafting pleadings. I was honoured to receive from him the keys to his locker, number 1, in the robing room for counsel at the Supreme Court. I took from his cubicle and delivered to Jamaica's most eminent and successful counsel his wig and robe, and received from him the tenets which should guide me in my legal career. It was my privilege to "devil" for him on a wide range of pleadings and legal opinions for which he was retained – and you had better go well prepared. He gave me letters of introduction to a number of firms – Brian Nation in Montego Bay, Munair Hamaty in Savanna-la-Mar, Delapenha and Iver in Mandeville, and F.M. Grosset in Port Antonio.

I was really excited when, within a week of my admission to the Jamaican Bar, the distinguished David Coore, QC, enquired whether I would serve as his junior in a murder case to be heard at the Supreme Court before Mr Justice William Douglas, later to become the chief justice of Barbados.

Apart from being my first appearance in court, the case stands out in my memory because the depositions disclosed, apart from an alibi, every conceivable defence for a charge of murder. The incident complained of, involving our accused client, had taken place on the high seas, and raised issues of jurisdiction, the lapse of time before death, causation, self-defence and provocation. Lloyd Barnett, then crown counsel in the Department of Public Prosecutions, was vigorous in prosecuting the case. But from the start, the jury was mesmerized by Coore's brilliant conduct of the defence, and the acquittal came as no surprise.

My first solo circuit court appearance was in a case of murder. Huntley

Munroe, QC, then deputy director of public prosecutions, warned me before Mr Justice Douglas took his seat: "I have heard of you. Young sprats like you, I eat before lunchtime. Remember, I am the last of Her Majesty's counsel who successfully pursued in her realm a case of treason felony."

It was some time before the first words could come out of my mouth when I stood to question the witnesses, but my confidence steadily increased with every question I asked. When the jury rendered a guilty verdict of manslaughter and the judge, after my plea in mitigation, imposed a sentence of three years, Munroe reluctantly muttered, "Counsel, it looks like I will have to pay you a bit more attention."

The case to follow was one of carnal abuse. Dudley Thompson, QC, had asked me to impanel the jury, as he was going to Hanover in order to apply for a change of venue before Mr Justice Small. Two days after, he still had not returned to Savanna-la-Mar, but Mr Justice Douglas was anxious to proceed and refused to accept my indication that I had no *locus standi*. I would have to make other arrangements for a case in Mandeville, since that was a court of inferior jurisdiction. "I will adjourn for lunch and give you a chance to read the depositions during the interval," he concluded before rising.

That was on a Wednesday. I did not see or hear from Dudley Thompson until the following Friday afternoon, after the jury had already retired. When a verdict of "Not guilty" was returned, Dudley leapt from the front bench to release the prisoner in the dock and take him outside to a jubilant crowd, who shouted, "You gone again, Dudley T."

That baptism was but the first of many immersions to come. The word was spread by the jurors, who sat in camera, that the case had been conducted brilliantly by a "young counsel who was stinging like a wasp". Barristers were not allowed to advertise, but the epithet served to attract many future clients.

The private Bar had brilliant leaders such as Vivian Blake, David Coore, Leacroft Robinson, Harvey DaCosta and Dudley Thompson. All had taken silk. Richard Mahfood, Raymond Alberga, Winston Frankson, Emile George, Carl Rattray, David Muirhead and Norman Hill were demonstrating their mastery of civil law. Ian Ramsay had already established a formidable stable of younger counsel in criminal law. The robing room of the Supreme Court was always abuzz. There was keen rivalry while sharing precedents and techniques for dealing with different judges and juries. Collegial relations and friendships that would last a lifetime were formed.

The solicitors who frequented the resident magistrates' courts made it clear to all young counsel that they would give no quarter in the legal contests in the courts below. If you were up against H.O.A. Dayes, Ross Livingston, Sydney Phillips, Newton Willoughby or those of like ilk, one had to be in top gear or run the risk of being totally demolished in open court.

Going out to the courts in rural areas had its special appeal. Balaclava in St Elizabeth, Gayle in St Mary, Cottage in Mile Gully, Manchester, Manchioneal in Portland, Ulster Spring in Trelawny, Cave Valley in St Ann, Frankfield in Clarendon, Bluefields in Westmoreland, were typical of these courts. Some were scenic, some on rough roads, many on the upper floors of police stations in need of repair. At each of them and so many others, lunch had to be arranged with local people and this inevitably meant the best of fresh, spicy Jamaican country cuisine – a special treat for visiting lawyers. The after-court sessions at local venues were equally delightful and could last well into the night. Opposing counsel often travelled to court in the same vehicles, sometimes much to the suspicion of their different clients. But that soon dissipated when the cases were called up and the attorneys went at each other hammer and tongs.

It was rare for large legal firms to brief single counsel in civil cases before the Supreme Court. The induction usually began with going in as junior to a QC and using whatever limited avenue was open to be heard and not only to be seen. A breakthrough came for me in a civil case brought by fisherman Egbert Jackson (aka Charlie Mattress) of Matthews Lane fame, who sued the attorney general for malicious destruction of his hut at Back-o-Wall – a sprawling slum in west Kingston – when it was bulldozed by the government to make way for the construction of Tivoli Gardens. In addition to all the equipment he lost, there was a claim for loss of earnings, as it was a long time before he could go back to sea. The award of special and general damages exceeding five thousand pounds brought me favourable professional attention and opened the gates for briefs from many law firms.

New ground was broken when Leacroft Robinson, QC, and I appeared in a suit versus the attorney general of Jamaica on behalf of Gladys Harrison, a retired principal of Oberlin High School, for a breach of her constitutional rights when she was wrongfully omitted from the voters' list for the general elections of 1967. It was a glaring case of electoral malpractice, for which she won a tidy sum.

I appeared in a series of election petition cases and for people charged with various breaches of trade union law. Lloyd Tate, union delegate, was one such. He had been charged with breaches of trade union law for protests organized at Delisser's Banana Plantation in Lottery, St James. This required me to travel from Kingston on three occasions to the Spring Mount resident magistrates' court without even reimbursement for travel expenses.

Michael Manley and Hopeton Caven saw to it that I was kept busy, all pro bono, between the resident magistrates' courts in St Andrew and Portland, as they sought to assert their places on the industrial battlefield. They were locked up repeatedly for breaches of peace and unlawful assembly, but the success of the Crown was rare.

When Reg Ennis formed the Port Supervisors Union, I spent weeks preparing the case for recognition of that category of middle management to obtain the right to collective bargaining. And so the Union of Technical Administrative and Supervisory Personnel became the first group of supervisors to emerge on the Jamaican trade union landscape.

MANAGING THE SKATALITES

In 1966, Anthony "Tony" Spaulding moved to share chambers with me at 39½ John's Lane. Our secretary Grace Powe (subsequently Mrs Duncan) ran the operations. We were extraordinarily busy in the circuit courts and the Supreme Court.

Of all the murder cases we did, the one which evokes most interest was that of Don Drummond, legendary Jamaican trombonist and composer, who was charged for the murder of Margarita Mahfood, his paramour.

That story begins with the formation of the Skatalites in the summer of June 1964, two years after Jamaica's independence. The group persuaded the jazz tenor saxophonist Tommy McCook, who had only returned to Jamaica two months before independence, to lead that most accomplished group of musicians. Band members included fellow tenor man Roland Alphonso, Lester Sterling on alto saxophone, Johnny "Dizzy" Moore, trumpet, and Jackie Mittoo on piano and organ. Jah Jerry Haynes played guitar, Lloyd Brevett string bass and Lloyd Knibb drums. In this most formidable aggregation of musical giants, the genius on the trombone, Don Drummond, stood at the pinnacle, alone.

The naming of the band reflects the space race during the Cold War era. Names thrown out suggested sputniks, rockets and satellites before Tommy suggested Skatalites, explaining the emphasis should be on the music they were creating. They also played popular clubs and nightspots around the city and a number of out-of-town gigs, but the Bournemouth Club in East Kingston was the home base of the Skatalites. There they played a couple of nights each week, with a Sunday matinee dance proving most popular.

The duels on the tenor saxophone between Tommy McCook and Roland

Alphonso had often to be broken by the persistence of Lloyd Knibbs on the drums, so that Lester Sterling on the alto saxophone or Johnny Moore on the trumpet could get their chance. Wherever they went, we were there – Tony Spaulding, Roy Hylton, Hopeton Caven, Ralph Fisher, Lance Johnson and I – suitably accompanied. Our friends at Monymusk and Frome would ask me to engage them for the annual cropover dances on the West Indies Sugar Company estates.

One Friday after another, Margarita would turn up at our John's Lane office to complain that there was no money for their household expenses. Don was never one to get some money for himself after each engagement of the band. At first, we would give her some cash from the office, until it was decided that the money distribution had to be put on a sound footing. It was obvious that someone would have to take charge and so I came to assume the role and functions of manager of the Skatalites.

Don Drummond spoke through his music, which moved in an instant from a haunting melancholy to an exciting ecstasy. One memorable Friday night at the Glass Bucket Club on Half Way Tree Road, Don and Ernie Ranglin, who had just landed from a stint in the Bahamas, had a showdown for seventy-five minutes, playing "Indian Summer". The great pity is that it was not recorded.

Don Drummond, a poetic trombonist, had a sage-like personality. He was an introvert and yet lyrically expressive, as every note carried meaning, resonance and melody. Drummond brought to mind the Shakespearean comparison of the lunatic in *A Midsummer Night's Dream*:

> The lunatic, the lover and the poet,
> Are of imagination all compact:
> One sees more devils than vast hell can hold,
> That is, the madman: the lover all as frantic
> Sees Helen's beauty in a brow of Egypt.

Spaulding and Patterson were joint counsel who undertook the defence when a murder at the home which Drummond and Mahfood shared was reported to the Rockfort Police Station in early January 1965. We were unable to obtain any statement or account from the prisoner. The pathologist's report revealed that the nature of Mahfood's stab wounds was inconsistent with self-infliction. There was no evidence to suggest the presence of a third person, and so the defence had to call witnesses, one of whom was Dr Matthew Beaubrun, to testify as to the criminal responsibility of someone afflicted with insane delusions, according to the McNaughton rules.

Following several exhausting days of trial, submissions by counsel and the directions of Mr Justice Fox, a special verdict was returned that the accused was "not guilty by reason of insanity". Don Drummond was ordered to be held at Her Majesty's pleasure and confined to the Bellevue Mental Hospital, where he unfortunately died in 1969.

CHAPTER 6
ENTERING THE FRAY OF POLITICS

WHEN I JOINED THE PNP AS A MEMBER of the organizing staff in 1958, I was assigned to the parish of St Elizabeth, where the PNP candidate, Dr Aubrey Russell, had lost the seat to Lionel Densham of the DLP in the federal elections of 1958. The parish was vital to the PNP, which had won both seats in 1955, as it was intended to increase the number of constituencies in that parish from two to four for the 1959 general elections.

Since I had no relatives in the parish, arrangements were made for me to lodge with the Bardowell family – Lionel and Philippine – in Black River for a month until I found my own digs. Once I arrived, there was never any thought of leaving, as I became a member of the family and elder brother to their four children – Merlene, John, Linda and Anthony.

I shared space with J.A.G. Myers in the National Workers Union Black River office and got involved in all the issues and operations of the sugar industry, the port workers and clerical staff within the parish. The possibility of my running for a constituency was raised as early as 1959, when the boundaries were drawn for four new constituencies. Portions of the old North St Elizabeth and the old South St Elizabeth constituencies were merged for the North East constituency, which lumped the Retirement, Siloah and Balaclava divisions from the old north together with Braes River and Santa Cruz from the previous south. Seven PNP candidates were vying for that new seat. Five of them came from the north, which was the more populous and enjoyed stronger support for the PNP. It included the sugar belt of Appleton, which was extremely fertile for the party, with the trade union movement extending back to the time of the Trade Union Congress with Ken Hill, Frank Hill, Richard Hart and Arthur Henry. There still remained, in that part of the constituency, some activists who were extremely upset at their expulsion from the party in 1952 because of ideological differences. Significant portions of the working class had to be convinced that the PNP remained a vehicle worthy of their support and Claude Jarrett was a main contender.

There were difficulties in choosing a candidate for the North East constituency because the ones who had strength in the north were not well known in the south, and vice versa. We did not have election polls then, but took soundings by having trained workers go through the area to find out who had what degree of strength and support. Emerging from the north as the front-runner was Oswald "Ossie" Parnell, of the renowned Parnell family, who represented the Balaclava division.

Party leader Norman Manley convened a meeting of constituency delegates in Santa Cruz at which he ordered all seven candidates to make a pledge committing themselves to support whichever candidate emerged the victor. Parnell refused to take the pledge and so was immediately disqualified by N.W.

Parnell's influence was extensive, particularly in the Balaclava and Roses Valley areas and the people in that area rebelled over his rejection. As organizer, I was required to deal with the situation and there were many who suggested that the person best suited to restore unity and bring everybody together was none other than the organizer – P.J. Patterson. I was then twenty-three years old and rejected the clamour. After considerable effort on my part, the supporters in that stronghold accepted Sydney Pagon, who then proceeded to win that constituency in five successive elections.

The success achieved in the 1959 election in St Elizabeth, under my organizing stewardship, was spectacular. We won three out of four seats, including North West St Elizabeth, where we defeated the well-beloved Neville "Cleve" Lewis. We lost South West St Elizabeth on a magisterial recount by thirteen votes, owing largely to disappointing returns from boxes where our canvassing had shown stronger support.

After that tremendous showing, Michael Manley made a strong attempt to persuade me to become directly engaged in the labour movement rather than studying law. He tried hard to convince me to join the exciting National Workers Union team he was building, but my determination to enter the Bar never wavered.

When I returned in December 1963, I once again became active in the party, helping to repair the organizational structure. I was in great demand as a platform speaker all over the island and was fully engaged in the 1967 elections. As a member of the Bar, I provided representation in the courts on a range of cases from violations of labour legislation to election petitions.

Burnett "B.B." Coke indicated that he would not be running again, and I was gearing up to become the party candidate next time around in South East St Elizabeth. Coke became seriously ill with cancer and unfortunately died within a year of the 1967 election. That sudden vacancy had to be filled in a by-election.

After the party's 1967 defeat, I was instrumental in persuading Vivian Blake that he should return to active politics, and his membership of the Senate provided a good start. When the parliamentary vacancy suddenly occurred in South East St Elizabeth, I immediately proposed that Vivian Blake should be the one to go forward and I would wait. He asked me to become his campaign manager and I took charge of assembling his victorious team in a constituency which I knew intimately. We beat Glen Mitchell, a favourite son of St Elizabeth and my colleague at the Bar, by less than four hundred votes in a vigorous campaign.

I was greatly disappointed when I was omitted from the slate of eight opposition senators whom Norman Manley appointed in 1967, and so was much of the party rank and file. But I did not allow this to deter me.

With the successive losses in the 1961 referendum and the general elections of 1962 and 1967, Norman Manley regarded it as a compelling duty to review and rebuild the structure, organization, outreach and financing of the party. He handpicked me to chair the newly formed Reappraisal Committee, which comprised party stalwarts, professionals and representatives from interest groups which had supported the PNP since its birth.

We recommended the separation of the post of party president from that of chairman, so as to relieve the leader of chairing the weekly meetings of the executive, the monthly meetings of the National Executive Council and the many sessions of annual conference. To obtain the best choices for serving the party, the new tiers of vice presidents allowed the delegates to choose four of equal rank instead of separately electing the first, second, third and fourth vice presidents, which did not always result in the best pick of the crop.

We recommended a youth organization and women's movement as arms of the party, and the National Workers Union to formally become an affiliate. The party organization was decentralized and six regions created with specific functions and authority. The party secretariat was strengthened in order to support the general secretary with the appropriate skills to raise funds, research, communicate and recruit. For the first time, there was a post in the secretariat for a national organizer, and Courtney Fletcher was assigned to lead the fieldwork.

When I presented our report to the annual PNP conference in 1968, it was approved by acclamation. Norman Manley observed, "The future of our party is secure and I can now depart with the confidence that our vessel is in good shape for the journey ahead."

On Manley's imminent retirement as member of Parliament for East Central St Andrew, I was invited by a majority of the party executive in that constituency to offer myself as his successor. I began extensive activity there, meeting with party groups and building a strong network of support. I wrote to the constituency executive to confirm my interest and availability. Dr Kenneth McNeil, who had been an unsuccessful contender for the seat in the Linstead/Ewarton area of St Catherine, threw his hat in the ring for East Central St Andrew.

N.W. confirmed in a letter his desire to avoid any contest for the seat until he had retired as party leader.

13th November, 1968
P.J. Patterson, Esq.,
Chambers,
39½, John's Lane,
KINGSTON

Dear Patterson,

Since Kenny McNeil has been back I have spoken with him about your letter to the Executive of the P.N.P. and your interview with me.

He does not think, and I agree with him, that any useful purpose would be served by having a conference between us, and I have decided, since I do not wish to be involved, on the eve of my retirement as Party Leader with any contention of this sort, and feel that I have a right to be protected from it to act as follows:

I will advise the Executive of the East Central St. Andrew constituency that they have a duty to reply to the Party Circular of 8th April, 1966, and I will also advise them of your contentions and of your desire to be considered as a Candidate for that Seat. I will suggest that they say that following on the circular they had decided to name you as an acceptable candidate for the Constituency since I do not propose to stand as a candidate in the next Election. They will then go on to say that they have learnt that you would like to be considered as a candidate.

As far as the constituency executive is concerned this will completely discharge their responsibility.

I propose myself to address a document to the Secretary of the Party to be placed before the Executive.* In that document I will set out concisely how it came about that Kenny McNeil was brought into the constituency and how I became, through your letter, aware of your contention.

I will also express the view which I firmly hold that any good candidate known to the constituency who proposes to stand on behalf of the Party should have no difficulty at all in being elected.

When the time comes this will be the issue squarely in the lap of the Executive. I propose, incidentally, that these matters should be put on the Agenda for consideration by the Executive after I have retired as Leader. I can see no harm to be done by delaying the matter till some time after February. However I will await your views on these suggested procedures before I do anything.

Yours sincerely,
N. W. Manley
*You will have an advance copy
NWM
NWM:fec

I thought long and hard before deciding that N.W. should be spared the trauma, as he left the stage, of penning such a document to the secretary of the party. I enjoyed a close relationship with Kenny, who had contributed to building the party over a substantial period. I withdrew my name from consideration.

The party decided that in the next elections, I would stand as the candidate for Central Westmoreland, because Matthew Henry, the incumbent member of Parliament, would not be running.

RECEIVING THE CALL

Lunch at Winston Chung Fah's International Chinese restaurant on Barry Street was quite an event. One kept wondering whether Maurice Tenn's appetite was truly insatiable. It was a special menu prepared by Winston himself before he got involved in football coaching. A close-knit group of counsel – Churchill Neita, Ian Ramsay, Tony Spaulding, Maurice Tenn, Howard Hamilton and I – were engaged in defending five people charged with a murder committed at a dance in Waterhouse, St Andrew. We had given our closing addresses to the jury before lunch and were returning to court for the summing-up.

On our way back to court, as we were passing the flower vendors, who were in their usual spot on the sidewalk on King Street, before the General Post Office, a man in the crowd shouted to me, "Mr P., your time come." Surprised, I asked, "What do you mean?" The flower vendor said, "Didn't you hear?" I said, "Hear what?" This total stranger had just said the words that would change my life forever. Maxie Carey, the PNP member of Parliament for South East Westmoreland, had suffered a massive heart attack while driving back that Friday morning to Kingston from Savanna-la-Mar, where he had attended a parish council meeting. In 1970, members of Parliament were ex-officio members of the parish council. Maxwell Carey had always taken his attendance seriously, as decisions taken at the parish council level had such a direct bearing on the state of every rural constituency, particularly our roads and domestic water supplies. His death was totally unexpected, and certainly I had never envisaged that the summons for me to run would come under such tragic circumstances.

Tony Spaulding said to me: "P.J., you must go straight to Garth Road," where party leader Michael Manley resided. My colleague counsel agreed and assured me that they would manage things at court in my absence. "Don't worry, we will take care of your clients." I went to the robing room to shed my robe and wig, and headed for Garth Road. The moment had arrived. It was now my turn to get involved in the heart of party political representation.

By the time I got to Garth Road, the officers of the party had already assembled. My heart was beating wildly, but I managed to present a reasonably calm exterior. As I entered, the response and the demeanour of everyone in the room confirmed what the stranger on the street had said. It was really true. The party leader said to me, "It is no longer Central Westmoreland; it is South East Westmoreland. Saddle up!" Dudley Thompson shared with us that G.G. Blackwood, vice chairman of the constituency and headmaster of New Works School, had already sent him a telegram – "I am relying on your support to replace Maxie Carey," to which he had replied: "Provided the undertakers have no objection."

I had no hesitation in accepting the challenge to contest the seat for a constituency I knew well. I had visited my eldest brother John Patterson, who was the overseer of the Robins River property in the constituency. He had actually been a candidate for the PNP in the parish council Whitehouse Division, and on many occasions my mother, after she had retired, worked as a teacher at Kings Elementary School in the constituency. At that time the headmaster was Desmond Gascoigne, a well-respected figure in the Jamaica Teachers' Association. He was also active in political circles and had been a chairman of the South East Westmoreland constituency. As a party organizer in St Elizabeth, I had spent a lot of time in the adjoining areas of Kilmarnock, Berkshire, Newmarket, Pisgah, New Roads, Carmel and Fustic Grove, which shared a common border; so I was already well known in many areas.

There were other local aspirants for the seat. The one who was most entitled to serious consideration was Ralph Anglin, principal of the Chantilly Moravian School, who had served for years as secretary to the constituency of Eastern Westmoreland – a comrade to the core. He was the first to express full support for my candidacy and immediately became the leader of the team that would see to my selection as the candidate, and an architect of our future success.

Soon after I arrived in the constituency, everybody joined the campaign. Apart from their knowledge and regard for me, they had supported the party continuously since F.L.B. Evans, known to all as "Slave Boy", had won the constituency as an independent in 1944 and chose to join the PNP from then. His resignation from the House in 1951 was to protest the failure to provide water for the people. He won the by-election comfortably, beating Ms Gladys Longbridge, a daughter of Parson Reid, in the hills of the constituency.

When Slave Boy left to win Western Westmoreland for the first time against C.C. Campbell, Maxie was victorious in 1955, 1959, 1962 and 1967. In accepting the nomination as the PNP candidate on 15 February, I pledged to build on the foundation laid by Maxie Carey. The constituents asserted that the time had come for them to have a member of ministerial timbre, and one whom they regarded as their own. I promised:

> I accept today, with a feeling of humility and pride, the nomination to bear the standard of the People's National Party in SE Westmoreland. . . . I say humility because today marks a turning point in my own life and career because I am being called upon to meet a new phase of challenge and adventure and I accept this nomination with a feeling of pride . . .
>
> My youth, talent and belief are at your command, and as Ruth said to Naomi: "Entreat me not to leave thee, nor to return from following after thee: for whither thou goest, I will go, and where thou lodgest I will lodge: thy people shall be my people and thy God my God."

The by-election campaign was exciting and both parties went all out to secure victory. I chose Keble Munn, who was then deputy general secretary of the party, as director of my campaign.

Ralph Anglin was the local campaign manager and led the charge in organizing on the ground within the constituency, which he knew inside out. He remained my campaign manager for all subsequent elections. He was a man given to painstaking detail, an invaluable quality in an organizer.

Then there were my councillors. We had five divisions in the constituency, all held by PNP councillors, who gave me their full support – Ivan "Bob" Pinnock in Whitehouse, Arthur Crooks and Lynford Stone in Darliston, Herbie Green in Lamb's River and C.C. Jones in the Leamington Division. I was also able to bring in a number of personal friends from other areas of Westmoreland. Howard Cooke, who was in charge of western Jamaica, rallied that part of the island.

Ernest Peart and Winston Jones from Manchester took charge of parish council divisions. In addition, my closest friends, Hopeton Caven, Wesley Wainwright, Tony Spaulding, Ruddy Lawson, Herb Rose and Reginald Ennis, moved in to help me. These were all experienced campaigners who had good organizational skills and were great team players. Everyone was assigned different areas of responsibility, whether it was a number of polling divisions or a particular community. We also had a cadre of trained constituency workers, experienced and knowledgeable in election organizing and campaigning.

The support of my colleagues in the legal community was invaluable. I had to give up my practice to focus on the election, and they handled my cases while I was on the campaign trail. Carl Rattray, Maurice Tenn, Clarence "Billy" Walker and David Muirhead saw to it that my legal practice did not suffer and my clients were well served.

My non-local team and I lived at the Whithorn home of Spurgeon Stewart and his wife Rita. In Darliston, Mrs Maud McLeod's house was our home and in the Whitehouse area Reggie Parchment and Aunt Birdie hosted us. With virtually three places of residence, we were provided with three lunches or three dinners, which courtesy constrained us to consume. Luckily, there were some people in the team who could give a good account of themselves when it came to eating. It was a win-win situation for hosts and guests alike.

Michael Manley, party leader, gave me his full support. On nomination day, after I handed in my nomination papers at Darliston Primary School, he joined me in a tour of the constituency. It was some time in February, well into the dry period, and at that time the constituency did not have more than twenty miles of asphalted road. We drove on hundreds of miles of dirt roads and as we travelled through the Big Woods area, through Content, New Works, Bog, Beeston Spring, Long Hill, Petersville, Whitehouse, Culloden, Hopeton, New Roads, Ashton, Berkshire, Pisgah, St Leonard's, Amity and Belvedere, we had to stand up in an open-topped vehicle. By the end of the day, we were covered with dust and grime – white, red and brown. Towards the end of that journey Michael gave free rein to his propensity for colourful language and I had to coax him to complete the tour.

As with any political campaign, slogans were important in engaging the interest of the people. "We say P.J." was printed on all campaign material. Nina Simone's recording of the song "Young, Gifted and Black", as well as Bob Andy and Marcia Griffiths's local version, was extremely popular. The people of the constituency grabbed on to this as the slogan and campaign song. It caught on like wildfire. But the "Young, Gifted and Black" theme did not sit well with

Michael Manley, and he told my campaign people so in no uncertain terms. He and Hopeton Caven had some harsh words before he accepted that it was never intended to exclude him and that his leadership in the fight for human dignity was not in question. But by then, the song had taken on a life of its own and the campaign could not stop it.

In any political campaign, important elements of equipment were vehicles and loudspeakers for the divisions. An effective presence had to be maintained in the town squares – Darliston, Lamb's River, Whitehouse. It is a deeply rural constituency; at that time few places had electricity and the main method of communication was the telegram.

There were a number of people, friends and professional colleagues, who were prepared to contribute, some with money and some in kind. We also put on three major fundraising activities: one at my Shortwood Road home in Kingston and the other two in the constituency.

The 1970 by-election was easily my most challenging. It was hotly contested. It was my first time in the field and I had to make myself known through the entire constituency. We had to travel into every area and go house to house, because the people wanted to see you and talk with you. The terrain was difficult, with hills, valleys and narrow walking tracks. I walked miles to get to some places where there were only a few families. But you dared not ignore them.

The campaign was intense because both parties had all their top brass out. The JLP's candidate was Euphemia Williams, head teacher of Beaufort Primary School in Westmoreland. She had the advantage of living in the constituency and was a formidable opponent. She was supported by Hugh Shearer, who was then prime minister and leader of the JLP, and Cleve Lewis, who was then the minister of communications and the member of Parliament in the adjoining constituency. All the officers and ministers of the party and the Bustamante Industrial Trade Union, which supported the governing party, were fully involved. The Revere Bauxite Plant at Maggotty was in operation and union workers were all brought into the constituency to help in my opponent's campaign.

There were some pockets within the constituency that were still predominantly JLP – places like Seaford Town, Cairn Curran and Beaufort. Some years later, Shearer himself shared an amusing story with me: one day he was coming down from Berkshire and saw some children leaving school. He gave them the JLP's "V" sign and they gave him the sign in return. He stopped his motorcade and came out and said, "I am meeting you bright and intelligent children for the first time." The children formed a ring around him as he said to them, "You children seem to be very well informed." The leader of the group looked up at him and said, "We say P.J.!" They kept him there for about five minutes with the incessant refrain. He said to me, "You set the children on me!"

During the campaign, one of the JLP councillors from Montego Bay decided to take up a group of people to terrorize the residents in Bronte, which is on the way to Kilmarnock, a mountainous area where the road is full of curves. A few of the invaders had guns. But they had made a serious mistake and had not taken the terrain into account. When they passed the first curve and started to intimidate the people, community members shouted to those above, "Dem a come!" The people at the bottom blocked the road after they had passed and the people at the top blocked the road before they could reach them, trapping them in between. The area was rocky and the people started pelting the gangsters with stones. I got a telephone call asking me to send someone to rescue them, so I did. They never made that mistake again.

There were also some agonizing experiences. One unpleasant incident occurred when I was travelling from Savanna-la-Mar to Whitehouse. I had received advance information that a JLP motorcade was coming to Whitehouse via Long Hill. By my calculation, if I went along the Culloden Road to White-house, I certainly did not expect to run into the motorcade. However, the motor-cade passed Whitehouse and went on down to Ackendown, then turned back, passing through Whitehouse and Culloden on its way into the hills of St Eliza-beth. It was at this point, just as I approached the New Hope School in Culloden, that I met the tail end. I pulled off the road and parked to allow the motorcade to pass. Luckily, I was not driving a campaign car but a private car, and, also fortu-nately, I was alone, as under those circumstances nobody could get the impres-sion that I was trying to be disruptive. Some of the JLP supporters recognized me and came over and tried to overturn the car – with me in it.

Fortunately, I suffered no harm: two members of the protective services who were travelling with Shearer came out and stood before my car to fend them off, and the children from New Hope School across the street ran over and stood in front of the car to protect me. We had a meeting in St Leonard's that very night and my theme was: "Yea, though I walk through the Valley of the Shadow of Death."

The election took place on 24 March 1970. The polls opened at seven o'clock in the morning and voting took place without any mishap. After the polls closed at five o'clock in the afternoon, the eighty-one boxes were counted. I was declared the winner, with 4,575 votes to Mrs Williams's 3,659 votes, a margin of 916. The people hoisted Michael and me on their shoulders and carried us into the schoolroom with singing and rejoicing. We thanked the many individuals who had played a role in bringing about the victory.

The *Gleaner* reports of the following day noted that I had increased the margin of victory for the PNP over that achieved by Maxie Carey in 1967. This became important, as the victory reflected a massive vote of confidence in the PNP and its leadership. The result was a repudiation of violence for political ends.

I was, naturally, elated, proud and fulfilled by the results. I was immensely grateful to my large, hardworking and dedicated campaign team, who had made this victory possible.

As I rejoiced that night, I remembered my promises to the people of South East Westmoreland and prepared to meet a new phase of challenge and adventure.

CHAPTER 7
THE 1972 ELECTION CAMPAIGN

AFTER MICHAEL MANLEY'S OVERWHELMING VICTORY against Vivian Blake for party leadership in 1969, every member of his team knew there would be no easy way to win the local-government elections that were pending and we had to ready ourselves for the fight immediately.

We were celebrating his election and mine as a vice president that Sunday afternoon at Karl Hendrickson's Courtleigh Manor Hotel when the afternoon newscast carried the story that Dr Ivan Lloyd had resigned from the party and had retired as a member of Parliament for the South East St Ann constituency. Michael immediately announced that I would, as vice president, take over his previous vice-presidential responsibility for party organization. Dr Lloyd's announcement of his resignation as member of Parliament brought a sudden end to our celebrations.

The first order of business was to identify the best candidate to run in a constituency that we had won in every election since the granting of universal adult suffrage. I was in Claremont the following morning to meet with Foggy Mullings and contenders for the seat.

There were a few among the older ranks of the party who wondered whether I was up to the assignment. Allan Isaacs, who had been in charge of island organization when I was in St Elizabeth, and supported Blake's candidature, felt he was being shunted from the spotlight.

Ulric Simmonds, senior political reporter, expressed grave doubts in the *Sunday Gleaner* of 16 February 1969:

> I cannot for instance see Messrs. Blake, Coore and Patterson filling the party-building role among the mass of the Jamaican people that has been carried out by their old front-liners of the People's National Party, carrying on the grassroots politics that is necessary to political survival in Jamaica. Perhaps they can

and they will surprise me, but for now Mr. Michael Manley in my opinion, is carrying a ton of weight on his shoulders as he assumes leadership of his party. The only viable lieutenant he has among the Vice-Presidents in the old dynamic sense of the term is Mr. Glasspole.

Wills Isaacs, Florizel Glasspole and Howard Cooke, with whom I had worked over the years, displayed their confidence in my skills.

We lost no time in preparing ourselves for the challenge. The party, having already accepted the recommendations of the Reappraisal Committee to ensure that the new party structure would be effective against any JLP challenge, charged me with their implementation. We strengthened the secretariat of the party with the incorporation of Robert "Bobby" Pickersgill, Leroy Cooke, Patrick "Pat" Cooper and Kenneth "Ken" Chin-Onn. David Coore had been chosen at our February 1969 meeting as the first chairman of the party other than the party leader. That allowed Michael time to travel around Jamaica, meeting with groups and communities, while still discharging his responsibilities as president of the National Workers Union. Carlyle Dunkley had the task of organizing a youth arm and Mavis Gilmour of helping to build a women's movement.

In October 1969, Michael Manley, Robert "Bob" Saunds and I went to Africa, on a tour of Ghana, Nigeria, Tanzania, Zambia and Ethiopia. Michael's brother, Douglas, was then working with the United Nations in Ethiopia. Michael, with the aid of his mother, Edna, persuaded him to come home and run for the South Manchester seat.

We returned from Ethiopia with "the Rod of Correction", which would play a major role in engaging the interest of the electorate during the campaign. The Rod of Correction was a symbol of the command of Emperor Haile Selassie I, Elect of God, Conquering Lion of the Tribe of Judah, King of Kings of Ethiopia. The rod was a symbol of his mission to correct what was wrong and to connect with the homeland of Africa. Our election campaign started on our return from Africa. We did not wait for the announcement of the election date, but immediately went into the field.

Michael first presented the rod at a campaign meeting at Mill Bank, Portland, in December 1969. The crowd went wild for this gift from Emperor Haile Selassie. The rod was so enthusiastically received that the JLP decided to get in on the act, and by early February, Edward Seaga announced that it was now in his possession, as Manley had dropped it when he "fled" a meeting at Coronation Market the previous week. Manley responded by showing the rod and assuring the people that the rod was still with him.

The Rod of Correction was only one element of a well-executed campaign. Michael Manley ran for a constituency, Central Kingston, for the first time in 1967. Up to then, he was primarily seen as a trade union leader: he led the National Workers Union and Hugh Shearer led the Bustamante Industrial Trade Union. When he became the leader of the party, he quickly stamped his mark. He had massive public appeal, based on a number of factors, not least of which were his undoubted charisma, his star quality, his passionate commitment to the cause of the poor and his gift of oratory. His trade union activities had made him well known as a seeker of equality and justice for all. Among his earlier supporters were those who at one time embraced him because of his family origins. Many of these, in later years, were to express their disappointment that his commitment to the poor, to the masses, to the underprivileged in the quest for social justice were his paramount considerations, and not perpetuating privilege, as they seem to have expected. His popular appeal was immediate: to the young, whom he inspired; to the ladies, for whom he had a particular attractiveness; to the intellectuals, with whom he could engage in meaningful discussion. He had a capacity to speak to crowds in ways that they could easily understand and could relate to. His speeches were always dramatic presentations, and, of course, he had the added tool – the Rod of Correction.

There were people, corporate groups, who had traditionally given to both parties. Some gave more to one than the other, depending on their preference. Certainly in the campaigns of 1962 and 1967 the PNP had received decidedly less than the JLP. In addition to the traditional fundraisers, the new infusion of business people in 1972 helped immensely in opening doors and providing additional funds. We could not wait until the announcement of the election to start collecting for the campaign. We used to have house parties and dinners, and also received support from the overseas communities, particularly the Jamaica Progressive League in New York. Some funds came also out of the Jamaican community in Canada and the United Kingdom. But the bulk of funds was raised in Jamaica. Much of our contributions came from people who gave what they could in kind, but most precious of all was the time people gave freely to break down the social barriers of class and colour.

THE TEAM

By 1972, wanting to deal with the predominant concerns of the various elements of the society we sought to unite, we had put in place working groups under each shadow minister. I was responsible for youth and community development. Out of the recommendations of those groups and with the clearance of the shadow cabinet, we were able to put forward a platform to which everybody in the party could subscribe and which was both pragmatic and had national appeal.

By then, we had also put in place a new organizational structure. The general leadership of the party was confined principally to the administration. Courtney Fletcher was brought in as the national organizer. We appointed a number of parish or regional organizers: comrades Wynter, Durrant, Bascoe and Francis, who reported through me, as chairman of the organizing committee, to the party leader. Once established, the party leader himself presided over the National Campaign Committee and, as the national campaign director, I spearheaded the organization of the election campaign.

I severely curtailed my law practice from August 1970, dealing only with those cases in which I was already involved, in order to spend time out on the campaign trail. I acquired a Volvo, because of its reputation for safety and durability, and employed a driver so that I could focus on planning and strategizing even as we covered the hundreds of miles over hill and valley across the island. We set up a campaign office on Waterloo Road separate from the party office. Owen Karl "O.K." Melhado and Peter Rousseau were important elements of the office machinery. Hope Wilson was my secretary.

I did not have the responsibility then of giving the closing address, so after speaking on the platform, I could go into the crowd and enjoy myself. I was free to mingle and enjoy the revelry of a wonderful and invigorating campaign. It allowed me to hone the organizing skills which I had acquired since 1958 from the field in St Elizabeth, Westmoreland, western Jamaica, St Thomas and the corporate area.

I was over in the west end of the island when Michael Manley called and said, "Go and find Desmond Leakey, wherever he is, and tell him he is going to be the candidate for North Trelawny." I went and found him on Burwood Beach, near Glistening Waters, and told him, "Come, you have to pad up." We had never won North Trelawny before and that was an achievement. There were Derrick Rochester in St Elizabeth; Owen Sinclair in Westmoreland; and Anthony Capleton and Horace Clarke, who were coming on board in St Mary. The Reverend Roy Robinson, Aston King, Upton Robotham, Mel Brown and Francis Tulloch were among our fine, energetic and confident candidates.

I was planning the itineraries of all the leaders, including Michael Manley. I planned for Florizel Glasspole, Wills Isaacs, David Coore, Keble Munn, Winston Jones, Howard Cooke and myself. Nobody could plan the route for a motorcade better than I, who knew Jamaica well from my previous exposure. Before the election was actually announced, as campaign director, I was everywhere, including, of course, in my own constituency, but once the date was announced, things changed. I spent the early period in the corporate area and in the east, then moved into the centre and then the north. In the last seven or eight days of the campaign, I confined myself to western Jamaica.

We also received the support of a number of professionals, including attorneys and doctors. The support cut across all social groupings. We sought to involve business leaders. In addition to the traditional core of PNP leadership, a number of young businessmen had come out in support of the leadership of Michael Manley. There were the local executives in major insurance companies, who included people like Danvers "Danny" Williams, Manley McAdam, Patrick "Pat" Rousseau, Karl Hendrickson, Cecil Chuck, Eli Matalon, John Marzouca, Frank Pringle and Douglas Graham.

Aaron Matalon, who was an outstanding business leader and marketing genius, worked closely with us. Most of the meetings on marketing and communications, which involved Michael, the public relations and communications teams and myself, were held in the basement of Aaron's house on Tyndhurst Avenue. Marketing and communications were integral elements of the 1972 campaign, so his guidance as a genius of packaging for the marketplace was invaluable.

The party had always had a public relations and communications arm. But we realized that for the 1972 elections we had a political product that had to be sold. That product comprised Michael Manley and the quality of the people we had brought into the shadow cabinet and the representative ranks for constituencies; and projecting the idea that we were a party committed to change. We benefited from the services of outstanding professionals, such as Gerry Grindley of Grimax Advertising and Desmond Henry, Ralston Smith and Ken Jones of Public Relations Associates, one of the pioneer firms in the field. One of the promotional vehicles was our adopting orange as the party colour instead of red.

THE BANDWAGON

As part of the strategy of connecting with the people, we put together in 1971 what we called the bandwagon.

> Bandwagon brought together the popular artistes and the political leaders on an island-wide tour and emerged as a major factor. Some of these artistes were

64

already in the forefront of the revolt against the JLP regime. Reflecting the popular sentiment, the Ethiopians started in 1968 with "Everything Crash" to be followed by Alton Ellis' "Lord Deliver Us". Justice Hinds and the Dominoes in "Carry Go Bring Come" asked "How Long Shall the Wicked Reign Over My People". Then there was the late Delroy Wilson voicing the expectations of the people with his hit song which became the anthem of the campaign, "Better Must Come". Junior Byles was a crowd favourite with "Beat Down Babylon"; while Clancy Eccles came on strong with his chartbuster, "The Rod of Correction". The lyrics from this song which sought liberation from the biblical villain King Pharaoh and equated Michael Manley with Joshua, the biblical hero of the battle of Jericho were immensely popular.[1]

We first took the bandwagon into the capitals of the parishes and after that moved into strategic locations that would bring together people from neighbouring constituencies. There was hardly any artiste of note who was not playing in the bandwagon. As national campaign director, I had overall responsibility for the planning and execution of the entire programme. Two of the people who made a major contribution and assisted with the professional and physical arrangements were Paul FitzRitson and "Buddy" Pouyat. They arranged the movement and accommodation of the artistes, who did not ask for full entertainment fees, but we had to take good care of them on tour. These songs expressed the discontent which existed in virtually every sector of the society.

For the first time in Jamaica, popular culture was used effectively as a tool in the art of mass communication, identifying the slogans that would embrace the call for national unity. We were trying to create a new Jamaica. We envisioned a land in which differences of class, race and material wealth would be superseded by the shared national pride of being Jamaican. In short, we wanted to break down the rigid social and class divisions that persisted even in the late 1960s and early 1970s.

Once the date for the 1972 elections was announced, the bandwagon had to cease, because the electoral law prevented the use of live music at campaign activities. Why was this? It was ingrained in history that the British, who fashioned the original laws during slavery, attempted to protect themselves against the enslaved by outlawing music in order to prevent messages being sent by the drums from one plantation to another in our fight for freedom.

---

1. Bertram, *P.J. Patterson*, 66.

VICTORY

On that fateful election day of 29 February 1972, after I left my constituency, members of the western campaign team met at what was then the Bay Roc Hotel, now Sandals, Montego Bay, to celebrate.

I woke up the next morning to the reality that Jim Thompson, our candidate in North Eastern Westmoreland, had won by about one hundred votes. His opponent was Esme Grant, a former parliamentary secretary in the Ministry of Education. I realized that my responsibility that morning was to get out to Whithorn, where the votes were being counted, to ensure that there was a proper count. As I travelled from Montego Bay to Whithorn, everywhere along the road – through the town of Montego Bay, through Anchovy, Reading, Montpelier, Knockalva, Ramble, Whithorn – the people were out with their brooms and tree branches, symbolically sweeping out the JLP. Expectations were high.

I thought to myself that this must have been how people felt when slavery was abolished. The tears were running down my face on the twenty-mile journey from Anchovy to Whithorn. I kept saying to myself, "The people have put their faith in us and we can't let them down." The people had been determined to effect irreversible political change that would create a society rid of the baggage of colonialism, colour discrimination and class prejudice and that would see the people who had been neglected and taken for granted assert their rights to recognition and respect. They voted for a movement that would uplift them and their children.

I did not get back to Kingston until two days after the elections. The celebrations were in full swing. Michael Manley's BMW was smashed beyond repair by the tumultuous crowd as his car entered the victory meeting at East Race Course.

A proud moment for me was the first press conference that Michael gave, as prime minister–elect, in the foyer of the parliament building, Gordon House. As we were getting ready to take our seats, I was going to sit somewhere down the line when Florizel Glasspole, who was the senior parliamentarian, insisted, "Come here, sit beside Michael on his right-hand side. You have earned the right to be here, through your performance in spearheading the organization to ensure this victory." It was a significant moment for me. I had proven to be up to the task of organizing a successful national campaign.

The year 1972 marked a whole new approach to electioneering. It became more scientific, prolonged and professional. The fact that the ordinary people had proven that by working together, each person, by participating, could make a difference, meant the people did have power to choose their government. And so a spirit was awakened in the electorate for which the PNP, as the nationalist party, deserves full credit. The Jamaican people felt more self-confident, more self-assured, more secure in their cultural identity and assertive of their rights as citizens of Jamaica.

In looking back, we realized that there were notable shifts towards the PNP in two particular areas. We were able to attract as much, in fact more, rural support than the JLP, including in the sugar areas and areas peopled by the working class, like those in bauxite communities. We were able to enjoy more support than we had done previously, among the very poor, the masses.

In the 1972 elections we still enjoyed considerable support in a predominantly middle-class constituency such as Northwest St Andrew, which comprised Cherry Gardens, Russell Heights, Graham Heights, Armour Heights, Grosvenor Heights and Havendale. Although the JLP candidate was Herb McKenley, an Olympic gold medallist and a popular national figure, he was defeated by Allan Isaacs, who garnered 10,610 votes in a constituency with 17,892 registered voters and with a turnout of 13,565 (75.9 per cent). As a result of this resounding victory, Isaacs was dubbed "Mr Ten Thousand". The trend was also reflected in constituencies in St Ann, Manchester and St James, where it was not just the middle class who had come out in support, but citizens of every social and economic stratum.

That 1972 campaign was the most exciting campaign of all in which I participated. It was devoid of political violence and set the standard by which other campaigns came to be judged. As was the case in 1938, when the protests of workers from the cane fields of Frome to the Kingston waterfront marked the start of democratic nationalism, the election of a PNP government for the first time in independent Jamaica began our journey of social liberation.

By 1972, the PNP had momentum going for the party in the island generally, and my constituency was part of the general campaign. Of course, by then many of the people who had helped me in my 1970 by-election had their own constituencies to deal with, and as the national campaign director, I had to be present everywhere. It followed only a year after my first victory and benefited from all the residual goodwill of the first campaign. It was certainly not as strenuous as the first one, however, as the national public relations machinery, slogans and publicity all spilled over into the constituency.

The 1976 elections, however, presented a unique situation that had to be handled with the appropriate strategy. My opponent in that election was a Reverend Captain Granville Davis, who was also reputed to be a "scientist", or obeahman. I remembered that we had lost South West St Elizabeth in 1959 to the Reverend C.D. Wright, who was generally known as "Poco", because he would jump Pocomania and work obeah. One of the lessons I learned then was that many of the people of whom you would never have thought it indulged in or believed in the power of the obeahman. When the PNP failed to perform as well as expected in areas of South West St Elizabeth, where we knew the party support was strong, we decided to carry out a review, and many people shamefacedly admitted that they had, in fact, voted for "Poco". When asked why, they explained that they had been to him for treatment and burning of candles, and so if they did not vote for him he would know. I said to them, "But how was he going to know? It was a private ballot." But they were convinced that he had the power of divination and would know if they had not voted for him.

In 1976, I decided that I was not going to take this Poco man lightly. We had torrential rains after opening the new Maud McLeod High School in Darliston, as is usually the case whenever I go to Westmoreland, but nevertheless, that night we had a meeting in New Roads Square, close to Captain Davis's house. I put on an African robe and my Ethiopian cap, and carried a matching staff which I had acquired on a visit to Africa. Others on the platform were dressed in similar attire and we distributed candles among the crowd. Captain Davis and his household could hear everything that was said. During the programme, we sang "Lion of Judah Shall Break Every Chain". We had a lively and well-attended meeting and it was declared that we had a higher level of "science" than the captain had.

On the Tuesday morning, I was in the constituency office when some of Captain Davis's relatives came to see me. "You have to help us," they said. I asked, "In what way?" They said he had taken flight from his house nearby during our meeting the previous night. He had disappeared through the banana walk and had not been seen since. So would I send a hailer, a van, through the area to tell him that it was safe to come back home? I did, and he eventually returned on the Tuesday night.

We won a resounding victory.

CHAPTER 8
JAMAICA'S EXTERNAL TRADE NEGOTIATIONS

DURING THE 1950S, JAMAICA EXPERIENCED IMPRESSIVE GROWTH IN the bauxite and tourism industries, and significant spread of industrial development. It was felt, however, that the economic growth that continued during the 1960s was not helping the broad spectrum of society. Bauxite accounted for half of the country's export earnings and a quarter of the government's income, but the industry only provided employment for a small percentage of the working population.

The divisions of colour and class in the society were clear and strong. Senior positions in the largest companies were the province of foreigners and included only a few Jamaicans of colour. There was, undeniably, an urgent need for change; hence our slogan, "Better must come."

Michael Manley's commitment to economic equity and his passion for social justice served as the main planks for our entire campaign. Workers and poor families should no longer be denied the basic requirements of health care, education and housing. The dominant message was about building a society that offered better opportunities for everyone.

The challenge was gargantuan. We had inherited a society in which the unevenness in the distribution of wealth was among the worst in the world. There were high levels of unemployment, just under 25 per cent, and the distribution of income among the employed was grossly inequitable, with the large black majority earning depressed wages.

My portfolio assignment in 1972 as minister of industry, tourism and foreign trade was a dynamic, challenging and absorbing combination that demanded ingenuity, diplomacy and energy. The entire ministry had to become integrally involved in activities relating to our trading partners, as industry is invariably affected by issues that relate to export and the earnings we derive from it.

The primary commodities in which Jamaica traded at the beginning of the 1970s were the traditional export products of sugar and bananas. With the impending entry of Britain into the enlarged European Economic Community (EEC), we were particularly vulnerable where these were concerned. There was no certainty that the terms of the Commonwealth Sugar Agreement would be maintained under this new arrangement. Robert Lightbourne, the previous minister of trade and industry, had already embarked on the groundwork to prepare how Jamaica and other members of the Commonwealth would relate to the EEC. He had dispatched one of the country's most astute negotiators on trade from the ministry, Frank Francis, to open our embassy in Brussels.

Our new regime proceeded to build the framework on the belief that, despite our small size and status as newly emerging sovereign nations, we had a responsibility to play our full part in world affairs. We had a responsibility to focus international attention on the grossly unequal distribution of the world's wealth and to force movement towards a more equitable distribution. We promoted a new order which would ensure a better standard of living for all the world's people.

We agreed with Julius Nyerere, the first president of Tanzania and one of Africa's most respected leaders, on what he described as the need for a "trade union of the poor". We believed that the poor nations should band themselves into a collective, coherent body that could make reasonable demands on the rest of the world. To pursue our trading arrangements, while creating this trade union of the poor, it was our aim to build the regional economic process; promote Latin American and Caribbean cooperation; and increase cooperation among Commonwealth countries, with the overarching purpose of bringing collective bargaining strength to bear in the international market while maintaining traditional friendships.

Three broad principles summarized Jamaica's objectives relating to international trade in the 1970s. First, we intended to change the terms under which goods and services between developed and developing countries were traded, to generate an expanded flow of real income to developing countries. We believed countries with mineral resources were entitled to secure maximum benefits from the sale of these resources to develop their own economies, but they should be sensitive to the needs of those developing countries without essential resources such as energy.

My first external engagement was at the United Nations Conference on Trade and Development in April 1972 in Santiago, Chile. Presidents Luis Echeverría of Mexico, Fidel Castro of Cuba and Salvador Allende of Chile were the stars on parade.

My presentation focused on the problem of commodities, particularly the disadvantage faced by developing countries in regard to prices for primary export products. Several of our primary commodities were facing severe handicaps in relation to preferential treatment. We pointed to the urgent need for commodity agreements to counterbalance plunging prices on the world market. Commodity prices were then barely at the rate of the late 1940s, despite the fact that production costs had risen significantly over the intervening years. Prices no longer bore any relationship to producers' costs. The developing countries of the so-called Third World should not be asked to accept that the principles of a modern agricultural support policy were applicable only to benefit the rich, while the fluctuating fortunes of a free market economy were rigorously applied to the agricultural commodities of the poor.

We asked for concrete recommendations from the secretary general of the UN Conference on Trade and Development and hoped that the issue of reverse preferences would not become an obstacle. Jamaica highlighted the intrinsic problems associated with the development of the economies of small island states such as limited land space, limited natural resources, small domestic markets and dependence on external markets. These issues would be raised again and again in various forums over the ensuing years in an effort to redress the imbalances inherent in the global economy.

THE CARIBBEAN FREE TRADE ASSOCIATION

With the collapse of the federal experiment and the advent of the JLP as the government, it was the Ministry of Trade and Industry, under Robert Lightbourne, which had spearheaded our regional engagement and enabled our membership in CARIFTA. The new PNP government of 1972 saw CARIFTA as an opportunity to build technical cooperation and economic growth. Our role was not to be a passive one but to actively build the regional economic process.

We were intent on exploring the deepening of CARIFTA. At my first meeting of the Council of Ministers in Dominica, we discussed issues relating to a common external tariff; harmonizing fiscal incentives; localizing industry; a common protection policy; and considering the economic viability of the less-developed member territories.

The meeting decided that the more-developed territories should provide assistance and expertise to the smaller territories. Within the limits of our resources, Jamaica was prepared to participate in any special efforts to enhance the viability of the economies of the less-developed member territories. This participation would have to be of mutual benefit to Jamaica and the CARIFTA partners.

By April 1973, we had declared our commitment to regional economic integration and announced Jamaica's participation in the Caribbean Common Market, a regional venture aimed at creating a more meaningful economic entity capable of negotiating from a stronger position with countries or blocs of countries outside the region. On 4 July 1973, Jamaica became a signatory to the Treaty of Chaguaramas establishing the Caribbean Community (CARICOM). The treaty required, among other things, harmonizing fiscal incentives throughout the region, preventing undue advantage being enjoyed by some territories which would then attract industrial development at the expense of others.

Throughout my first term as minister of industry, my team had to grapple with the tension created in the attempt to balance domestic and regional interests. I recall Jamaican manufacturers expressing the justifiable concern that our CARICOM partners were taking advantage of us, as while our imports from the region had increased in 1975, our exports had declined. While Jamaica was rigorous in observing the policy on trade with third countries, some of our partners were merely paying lip service to it, particularly in relation to imports of raw material and intermediate goods. Many were still permitting the canning of third-country agricultural inputs, which were able to qualify for CARICOM tariff treatment and to compete throughout CARICOM and on the Jamaican market against Jamaican products. This called for a review of the policy as well as pursuing a system of full reciprocity among the more-developed CARICOM member states.

No doubt other ministers of industry in the region faced similar issues. Whatever the internal problems, the gains to be had from solidarity far outweighed individual concerns. The increased cooperation among member states facilitated a unified approach to the anticipated change in our relationship with Britain on its impending entry into the EEC. Our primary concern was how this would affect the quantity, price and terms under which sugar would be bought by the enlarged community. Sugar was, then, the pillar on which our collective economies depended, and this subject would claim much of my attention over the ensuing years.

❧

Before the United Kingdom successfully applied for membership of the European Common Market in the early 1970s, a special trade relationship existed between Europe and the former French colonies in Africa (the Yaoundé Convention), and, with Kenya, Tanzania and Uganda in East Africa, the Arusha Agreement. Britain had made several attempts to enter the EEC before, but had been vetoed by President Charles de Gaulle of France; the Common Market was dominated by France and Germany, which provided the bulk of the funds. However, Ted Heath, the British prime minister, was finally able to secure the agreement of the other members. One challenge for Britain was how to deal with former and newly independent British colonies. It was accepted that some accommodation would be required.

The countries of the Caribbean, led by the trade ministers of CARIFTA, discussed the type of relationship they wanted and how best to attain it. At a meeting in Roseau, Dominica, in May 1972, the relationship with the EEC was a dominant item on our ministerial agenda and it remained so until the Lomé I Convention was signed in Togo in early 1975. In the conference room were four sovereign nations – Jamaica, Trinidad and Tobago, Barbados, and Guyana. St Kitts, St Lucia, St Vincent, Antigua, Dominica and Grenada were still dependent territories.

As indicated earlier, the existing models of association were the Yaoundé Convention, which applied to the francophone territories; and the Arusha Agreement, which existed in East Africa. There was also the option of a Part 4 Relationship, which applied to countries that were still colonies of the United Kingdom. This was influenced by the French pattern, where colonies were departments of France.

Minister Ronald Armour of Dominica contended that there was no need for the dependent territories to look beyond a Part 4 Relationship. Barbados, Guyana, Jamaica, Trinidad and Tobago were not content with either the Arusha or Yaoundé model, as neither could accommodate our interests fully. We also did not wish to have two different arrangements for CARIFTA members. We wanted to negotiate a new model, a *sui generis* arrangement. A great deal of effort was put into establishing a common Caribbean position which could unify the independent countries and the remaining colonies. Varying points of view were essential ingredients in the discussions on the new model.

Arriving at a common position in the Caribbean would prove easier than for our colleagues in Africa. Their difficulty was due to stark differences between the francophone and anglophone countries. Fortunately, both the Arusha Agreement and others within Yaoundé, which entered into force on 1 January 1971, were due for renegotiation. The Caribbean persuaded them that the best chance of securing what we all wanted would be to try and establish an umbrella approach that could embrace the Caribbean, Africa and the Pacific as one.

On the occasion of the ministerial meeting of the Non-Aligned Movement, in Georgetown, Guyana, Shridath Ramphal, foreign minister of Guyana, convened a meeting of Caribbean ministers with their African counterparts, on 9 August 1972, to pool our diplomatic and technical resources to pursue the negotiations. We also sent a number of ministerial delegations to Africa, and received similar delegations in Georgetown. The high quality of Caribbean leadership and technical expertise was quickly acknowledged. Geographically, the Caribbean was in a good location between the other two regions. The Caribbean was also at the centre of the initiative in two respects: the effort to bring everybody in; and conceptualizating the operational framework. Errol Mahabir and Branford Tait, the ministers of foreign trade from Trinidad and Tobago and Barbados, joined me and Shridath Ramphal in the intensive negotiations, which included those Caribbean countries which were not yet independent.

It was, of course, necessary to visit the European capitals to sensitize them to the new approach, the specific interests that we wanted to protect and the objectives we wanted to secure. Between 17 and 30 November 1972, I visited Britain, Belgium, the Netherlands, France and Italy to seek their full understanding and support on areas of special mutual interests. The question of sugar was of particular importance in view of reports from France that the Lancaster House assurance on Caribbean sugar, which guaranteed access to the enlarged European Community, was not being accepted as a binding commitment.

In the United Kingdom, I met with the Right Honourable John Davies, chancellor of the Duchy of Lancaster and newly appointed minister for Europe, and Lord Campbell of Escan, chairman of the Booker Group of Companies. In Belgium I met with Andre Fayit, secretary of state for foreign trade in the caretaker Belgian government, and with Monsieur Jean Dennau, who had special responsibility for negotiations leading to the accession of candidate countries and the agreement with non-candidate European Free Trade Association countries. In Italy I met with Mauro Ferri, minister of industry and commerce, and Matteo Matteotti, minister for foreign trade.

Before we met in Brussels in July 1973, the Commonwealth Sugar Exporters had gathered at Lancaster House in London. Britain at that time had a keen interest in what was happening in sugar. First, its refineries were supplied by Commonwealth sugar; second, the British were significant consumers of sugar; third,

British businesses had significant investment in sugar production throughout the Commonwealth, for example Booker Tate in the Caribbean.

At the end of our meeting the prime ministers of Mauritius and Fiji proposed that the minister from Jamaica should be the spokesman for the group. I was chosen by acclamation. When we first gathered in Brussels in July 1973 the ACP group presented three statements. We had worked hard to get everyone to accept the concept of only one representative from each of the three regions. Wenike Briggs of Nigeria was the spokesperson for the African grouping, Shridath Ramphal for the Caribbean and Ratu Kamisese Mara, prime minister of Fiji, on behalf of the Pacific.

At the core of the negotiations was the call by the EEC for reciprocity. We made the critical breakthrough when Cameron Tudor, foreign minister of Barbados and a Greek scholar, reminded us of the Aristotelian dictum which we inserted in the Caribbean Statement on 28 July 1973, "Justice requires equality between equals but proportionality between non-equals." To that philosophical grounding, Shridath Ramphal added, "This must surely mean that between those who are unequal in economic strength, equity itself demands non-reciprocity." The European Community was never able to refute Aristotle.

After the July 1973 meeting we decided to have one spokesperson for the group. Wenike Briggs, trade commissioner of Nigeria, was selected. Africa was the most populous, and Europe was most interested in Africa because of the size of its market and its mineral resources, including petroleum.

We were collaborative, allowing all views to contend in order to arrive at a common position which all could accept. Linkages between sugar, trade and financial institutions were created. Shridath Ramphal was appointed to lead the trade negotiations and different leaders were designated for other spheres. We formed a bureau, consisting of the chairman of the ACP and representatives from the various regions. Together we became a formidable and united force to maintain ACP solidarity and stay on course for a victorious outcome.

At the following meeting, in October 1973, the Caribbean proposed the presentation of one statement on behalf of the entire ACP Group. That statement was made by Nigeria, but the Caribbean crafted the most substantial inputs. We were sensitive to the fact that while our focus might have been on bananas, sugar and rum, other countries had other specific considerations which had to be accommodated. The ACP Group, headquartered in Brussels, acquired an intercontinental identity when the Georgetown Accord was signed in June 1975.

The Caribbean ministers attending the meeting in Brussels in October 1973 were well supported by the secretary general of CARICOM, William Demas, and Edwin Carrington. Included in our ranks were Robert Bradshaw, premier of St Kitts–Nevis–Anguilla, and James Mitchell, premier of St Vincent. East African Community trade minister Robert Ouko and the chairman of the African group, Zaire's trade minister, Joseph Mobutu, worked closely with us.

Very little progress was made at this meeting, as the EEC failed to translate its promises into reality. While the community had given a guarantee that 1.4 million tons of Commonwealth sugar would be accommodated annually in the European market at a fair and reasonable price, the question of the quantity was now being stubbornly resisted by the French. Sugar was a major factor in social and political stability in the West Indian region, and an industry which would perish if its future was not assured. It was evident that the EEC had not arrived at any common position on trade, price stabilization and sugar, subjects that were at the core of the negotiations.

They were completely surprised at the unity displayed by the ACP group and their inability to manipulate the anglophone and francophone countries. The forty-six countries resisted the Yaoundé and the Arusha models. We insisted on an umbrella-type agreement which could accommodate the vital interests of all countries, while permitting variations to accommodate the peculiar positions of each of the three regional groups. We wanted to create a new relationship model.

Several discussions at the ambassadorial level failed to bring about a common stand within the European Community. We proposed a meeting in Kingston at which either side could freely express its views and at which we would be able to bargain on important points of principle so as to achieve agreement.

The meeting in Kingston in August 1974 was the first of its kind on non-European soil and was responsible for bringing about a significant shift in the way Europe viewed the ACP. Eric Williams, prime minister of Trinidad and Tobago, was invited to open the meeting of the ACP ministers and Prime Minister Michael Manley opened the ACP/EEC meeting.

New ideas emerged that had been in gestation but which were now clearly and firmly articulated. The establishment of a regime for the stabilization of export earnings emerged from our deliberations during that meeting. At the Kingston conference, the European Community finally accepted that there would be no reverse preferences. Reciprocity was thrown out of the window. Barriers arising from rules of origin and tariffs which threatened to restrict ACP goods appeared insurmountable. In future negotiations, ambassadors were instructed to ensure that free access would not be prejudiced by either of these rules of access or tariff barriers.

The Kingston meeting was not without some level of intrigue. By that time the chairmanship of the ACP had moved from Nigeria to Senegal. The minister from Senegal and I were co-chairs of the Kingston meeting. On one occasion we were waiting to start but could not find the co-chairman from Senegal, nor the chairman of the EEC. We soon discovered that they had convened a meeting of their own, and I had to break it up. We made it clear that all negotiations would have to be in the open and we were not going to accommodate any secret deals.

The next meeting was in Brussels in January 1975. Sugar and beef were the most difficult to negotiate. The sugar negotiations were fierce. In addition to the British interest, because of the common agricultural policy, members of the EEC were determined to prevent Caribbean sugar from coming in. Our goal was to secure a commitment from the EEC to provide a guaranteed market for 1.4 million tons of refined sugar. As a result, we had to negotiate separately with the United Kingdom and the EEC, with the former on price and the latter on guaranteed quantity.

We insisted that (1) the price was not to be imposed by a pricing system determined solely by the EEC or European circumstances; (2) price was not to be limited by the prevailing price structure; and (3) the price system should take account of inflation.

In the closing days, the divide was wide and the tension was high, so much so that my counterpart, the commissioner for agriculture, Pierre Lardinois, and I almost came to blows. We were shouting at each other so heatedly that Claude Cheysson, the European commissioner from France, had to come from next door to make sure that we were not about to fight. After we had concluded and initialled the entire agreement, we were all together for a social celebration when Lardinois proclaimed that if Europe had to negotiate and it was not against the ACP, he would like me to be their principal negotiator.

The last item on the agenda at the Brussels meeting was rum. We had nego-tiated a package, but it could not be approved because of a veto imposed by the French which only their president could lift. The veto had been imposed a few months before when he met with the US president, Richard Nixon, in Guade-loupe, at which time he had given Guadeloupe and Martinique the assurance that their rum would not have to compete with rum from our Caribbean islands when we completed the new trade arrangements. Giscard d'Estaing, president of the republic, could not be disturbed between midnight and six o'clock in the morning. We had to await his return to the Elysées Palace to have the veto lifted.

The final agreement achieved duty-free access to Europe for fresh grapefruit, grapefruit segments, some other forms of fruit, and tobacco. While there would be limitations on the trading in sugar, it would be far more beneficial than anything in force with Europe before. Cigars had duty-free access provided that 70 per cent of the raw material and labour components were of ACP origin. All rum entering the EEC was to be duty-free; the export earnings from critically important crops such as sugar, bananas and citrus were to be stabilized by drawings from a special fund if, over a period of four years, there was a fall in the level of these earnings.

In addition to grants, loans were to be available, at special interest rates, from the European Development Fund. Expertise from the developed countries was promised to help develop technology.

We were, justifiably, proud of the new arrangements, which were of real historic importance. The outcome really represented the first time that the countries of the continent of Europe and the countries of the developing world, many of which historically were colonies, entered a new arrangement characterizing the changed status between them.

The agreement was signed on 28 February 1975 in Lomé, capital of Togo in West Africa. No one can claim that the ACP Group achieved all that it sought, but no one can deny that the Lomé Agreement broke new ground, and at the time was expected to serve as the template for a fair and mutually beneficial partnership between the developed and developing world. It was a solid foundation on which to build.

Shridath Ramphal and I enjoyed great respect and affection within Africa and the Pacific, because we were fighting for all the members of the group. Our historic contribution to Caribbean-European cooperation was recognized by the European Commission when a special Patterson-Ramphal room was named in our honour at the Brussels headquarters of the commission in February 2009. The technical support assembled by the Caribbean, led by William Demas, Alister McIntyre, Frank Francis, and "Scotty" O'Neil Lewis, of Trinidad and Tobago, was invaluable to the entire ACP.

THE IRAN SUGAR DEAL

From the outset of our administration, we declared our intention to diversify our exports and broaden the sale of our commodities wherever a viable opportunity was presented.

In regard to sugar, 1974 was rife with uncertainties brought about by Britain's impending entry into the EEC and the need to establish a new trading regime with the enlarged market. We were well aware that, despite Britain's eagerness to accommodate the 1.4 million tons negotiated under the Sugar Industry Authority (SIA), several EEC countries were reluctant to admit so large a volume. These fears strengthened our resolve to seek alternative markets and broaden trading options by giving favourable consideration to third countries which were interested in purchasing sugar from Jamaica.

In keeping with this stance, in 1974 we sold 50,000 tons of sugar to China as part of the process of market diversification. We were also looking at the possibility of selling sugar to Africa and the Middle East without abandoning our commitment to the United Kingdom and the EEC. It was in this context that one of the most problematic and challenging foreign trade and diplomatic situations emerged, in 1975.

In mid-1974 the SIA received proposals from two North American companies – Joseph Kell Enterprises Incorporated and McAdam Properties Incorporated – to buy 350,000 tons of sugar for sale to Iran over a seven-year period. In the proposed agreement, Jamaica was offered a price of US$330 a ton – more than the world price – for a shipment of 50,000 tons of sugar in 1975, and an agreement to sell was negotiated. Both companies negotiated a corresponding agreement of sale with the Government of Iran to supply the sugar they were purchasing.

Under the arrangement Kell/McAdam would have purchased the sugar and could have resold to Iran at US$1,040 per ton. For 1975, their profit would be of the order of US$700 per ton. The gross value of the contract to Jamaica in 1975 would be approximately US$52 million CIF. The SIA negotiated an amendment of the settlement with Kell/McAdam under which a substantial portion of their compensation would be paid in 1975, giving them a lump sum of US$10 million; and they would receive an annual retainer of US$500,000 between 1975 and 1981. However, in order to receive US$10 million in 1975, they had to give a discount of over 13 per cent per year on future payments. Thus the total settlement would have been US$13.5 million, and not US$17.5 million, as originally contemplated.

Subsequently, we sent a negotiation team to Iran to finalize contractual arrangements and to explore the possibility of a government-to-government agreement. We regarded the contract as an opportunity to open the door to a broader relationship with Iran not confined to sugar. In addition, Iran was a significant oil exporter and we were looking for a secure source of crude oil and natural gas for the oil refinery and petrochemical plant in Luana, St Elizabeth, which was then in the pipeline. We also wanted to explore the possibility of exporting bauxite to Iran. Furthermore, a long-term sugar contract with Iran would prove a fillip in our negotiations with the EEC.

Our team, led by chairman of the SIA Richard Fletcher, found the Iranian authorities not only willing to negotiate on a government-to-government basis but to offer a higher price for the sugar than the US$330 per ton previously negotiated with the middlemen. The existence of the agreements with Joseph Kell Enterprises Incorporated and McAdam Properties Incorporated, however, prevented the completion of negotiation, as, in the absence of a satisfactory solution of all legal claims, the Government of Iran was not prepared to conclude a contract with Jamaica. We therefore had to negotiate compensation to them for loss of profit as well as for their expenses and efforts. Before long, it became obvious that they had powerful backing, in the family of the Shah of Iran. Whenever progress was made within the formal negotiations, instructions attributed to the imperial palace would make it clear that no deal could be consummated without payment to the Kell/McAdam Consortium.

For compensation, the Americans were looking for a margin of US$150–US$160 a ton. We got them down to US$110 including shipment, or US$50 per ton excluding shipment, of the first year's proceeds, bearing in mind that after the first year there was not likely to be another bonanza.

During that time the price of sugar on the world market was US$1,400 per ton and so the team was able to negotiate a first-year price high enough to provide for the entire amount of compensation to the Americans, as well as shipping costs. This price on the world market could not be considered stable and this was to be a long-term contract. The deal was consummated at US$1,040 per ton.

The memorandum of understanding signed with the Iranian authorities was for the supply of 300,000 tons of raw sugar to be delivered at Iranian ports at a rate of 50,000 tons annually from 1975 to 1981 at a price of US$1,040 per metric ton. The rules governing the agreement were the rules of the Sugar Association of London.

The contract was hailed as a "great breakthrough" for Jamaica and Iran and a positive move towards establishing new relationships between the two countries. The deal was reported in the London *Times* and generated worldwide reactions. This was a formidable weapon in our armoury as we continued our negotiations with the EEC on a brand-new sugar protocol.

During this period, the price of sugar shot up on the world market. We were able to obtain the highest prices for firm quantities of supply. Fred Peart, the minister of agriculture in the United Kingdom, flew to Brussels for a meeting to beg us to provide a sufficient quantity for the British refineries and their domestic market and avoid political injury to the Labour government.

The SIA opened a current account at the Manufacturers Hanover Trust Company of New York because it was convenient to deal with one institution in financial transactions relating to Iran, thereby reducing confusion, delay and costs. A company known as Tenecas was established in Iran to undertake representations for us in Iran at US$125,000 per annum; the English agents were paid US$40,000–$45,000 per annum.

The first shipment of 50,000 tons, in 1975, went smoothly. In 1976, however, the Iranian government failed to fulfil its obligation to send a letter of credit to the bank in New York, and no further shipments of sugar were made to Iran. Some staff in the Ministry of Commerce in Iran had been charged with fraud in relation to a sugar deal with Tate and Lyle and so all contracts were being scrutinized, including the Jamaican contract, which was examined and cleared. Sir Egerton Richardson was appointed to resolve the issue.

The contract with Iran was the most favourable any government of Jamaica had ever negotiated for the sale of sugar up to that time. In relation to earnings from the deal, agricultural exports for 1975 were J$182 million, and sugar contributed 80 per cent of this. The contribution to the Consolidated Fund was J$22 million and in that same year J$5 million was allocated to workers' housing programmes and an increase of 100 per cent in wages to workers in the industry. The Iran transaction would have contributed about 25 per cent of the total sugar export earnings.

Headley Brown, then the chief economist in my ministry, Hans Priester, a renowned expert on sugar who had been recruited by Robert Lightbourne, and Richard Fletcher constituted a formidable team of advisors who ensured Jamaica got the best deal.

As minister of foreign trade, I was responsible for the negotiations of the sale contract and had discharged my responsibility in full when the entire contract was sent to the board of the SIA. I was not responsible for nor involved in any of the subsequent discussions or negotiations between the SIA and the Iran signatories on the implementation of the agreement. Be it remembered that the SIA fell within the portfolio of the Ministry of Agriculture. It was the board of the SIA, with the approval of the Bank of Jamaica, which decided to purchase up front the sum of US$10 million from the Americans in 1975. I neither directed this nor was I ever consulted on a commercial decision made by the SIA board. I knew nothing about the arrangement.

Following that, questions were raised relating to the payment made to the Swiss Bank on behalf of the American agents and the alleged failure of the SIA to pay the requisite taxes of US$3.58 million.

When wide and malicious allegations of corruption were made to implicate me, I insisted that a forum which could pronounce authoritatively and credibly on the allegations be established, otherwise I would leave the cabinet to clear my name.

The Honourable Kenneth Smith, chief justice of Jamaica, was appointed the sole commissioner to conduct an inquiry into the allegations. After I had given my evidence in chief, lead counsel for the JLP, Frank Phipps, QC, conceded there was no question to ask of me. There was no evidence to support the allegations of corruption against me or the SIA. I was never involved in the discussions to buy out the payments which would fall due. Not surprisingly, the chief justice concluded there was no ministerial impropriety and dismissed any allegation of misconduct. There was not even a faint sign or smell of smoke, because there was never any fire.

It is high time that history record the probity of the Iran Sugar Agreement and my absolute vindication.

CHAPTER 9
TOURISM: THE NEW FACE

TAKING ON THE TOURISM PORTFOLIO IN 1972 WAS not something that I immediately embraced. That portfolio was originally intended for Wills Ogilvy Isaacs, known as "The Bishop". He was a spellbinding platform speaker and a political tactician who had contributed immensely to the strength and success of the PNP and one for whom I had the greatest respect and affection. He had declined the tourism portfolio, as he felt it would be too strenuous for a man who was now winding down his active political career, and suggested that I, being young and energetic, should take it on instead. I was hesitant, but eventually accepted Wills's wish for a lighter burden. I realized the likely effect on the political image of one who had been the shadow minister for youth, but concluded that it would give me the opportunity to change what was wrong with the image of the industry.

Anthony Abrahams had taken over from John Pringle as director of tourism and assured me, even before I had taken the oath of office, that he was fully on board to effect the changes that would reflect positively on our product as well as our marketing efforts. Handling the challenges of the industry would call on all the considerable resources of the team as we sought to alter the face of Jamaica's tourism.

I was privileged to enjoy the major benefits of working with the members of the top-quality team that I inherited in the Jamaica Tourist Board (JTB) in tackling the anticipated challenges. They included Slade Hopkinson, outstanding Caribbean writer and theatre personality; Winnie Risden, one of Jamaica's premier communications professionals; Marcella Martinez; and Fred Wilmot, veteran Jamaican journalist – a veritable who's who in the Jamaican communications and public relations arena. The Planning, Research and Statistics Unit was led by Rupert Mullings, supported by Ainsley Elliott. Both were subsequently elevated to the position of deputy financial secretary. Fay Pickersgill was a rising star in that department and worked her way to later becoming a director of tourism.

The modern tourist industry had its genesis under the Norman Manley–led administration during the period 1955–59, when the institutional framework for the encouragment of the industry was instituted. With the advice of tourism guru Abe Issa, now acknowledged as the father of Jamaican tourism, the government had passed the Tourism Board Law in 1955 and established the JTB under Issa's chairmanship. The industry experienced immediate growth, a trend which continued into the 1960s. By the mid-1960s it was clear that tourism had become an important source of foreign exchange for the country.

While the economic benefits were undeniable in terms of the country's balance of payments, the benefits were neither perceived nor felt by the ordinary Jamaican. Most of the assets were foreign-owned and managed. Jamaicans did not enjoy the facilities provided for our visitors, as the class and colour barriers that persisted isolated them from the industry. In addition, many people objected to the way Jamaica was promoted in the marketplace. It was no wonder, then, that the attitude of the general populace to tourism was negative.

Further complicating the problem were several other issues such as the absence of a clear national policy on how to handle the industry; the cost factors arising from high airfares to Jamaica; discriminatory regulations restricting charters coming into Jamaica; high internal transport costs; mediocre service in important areas of the sector; and, perhaps most daunting, the prevalent harassment of our visitors.

Total transformation of the industry was an imperative – from servitude to service, from exclusion to inclusion, from benefits confined to hoteliers only to broader levels of social participation. My ministerial mandate was clear and compelling.

I spent many hours with the team as they briefed me on the complexities of the industry. My first official act as minister of industry and tourism was a meeting with executives of the JTB on 16 March 1972. I took the opportunity to assure them that under my watch I would seek to ensure that tourism play a much wider role in national development. I emphasized that while I respected their knowledge and experience and was receptive to new ideas, nothing would be accepted simply because that was the traditional way of doing things. Of course, it also provided the opportunity to share the thinking of the government on the way forward as we proceeded to revolutionize the industry.

It was our intention to move away from the old pattern of a tourism industry that was elitist and remote from the ordinary Jamaican people. We intended to involve them and spread its benefits through a number of strategies. I pointed to the tremendous opportunities tourism offered for interlinkages with other sectors. For example, links with agriculture would provide work for farmers and food for hotels, and links with the entertainment industry would see local creative talent channelled into hotels.

We also intended to break down the local attitudinal barriers which were hampering the growth of the industry and, in so doing, sow the seeds for the generation of a sustainable industry.

The industry then was riddled with prejudice. During my early days in office, I had paid a three-day visit to Montego Bay in order to meet with leaders and workers in the tourist industry. In an effort to establish a better link with the wider community and the promotion of sports, I had persuaded the hotel owners to sponsor a football match at Jarrett Park. Peter King, then my personal assistant, had arranged accommodation at the Half Moon Hotel. I did not know that he had tried to place me at the Tryall Club until I got a message from the union delegate that the workers at Tryall were about to call a strike and my intervention was necessary to prevent it.

When I arrived at Tryall, I learned that the manager of the housekeeping department had asked whether I did not know that Tryall Club was not for black people. The workers were furious that a son of Hanover and minister of tourism would not be welcome there. I found the situation particularly perplexing as the lady in question was one whose house I had frequently visited during the 1972 election campaign. I spoke with the hotel employees and secured their assistance to restore industrial calm and refrain from damaging the property. The chairman of the Tryall Hotel Owners Association was furious when he heard what had happened, and called me to insist that I spend the pending Easter weekend in a cottage he owned.

Not only have my subsequent visits to Tryall throughout the years been incident-free, but I have always been made to feel completely at home and comfortable with the home owners, the management and every member of staff.

Before the Jamaica Hotel and Tourist Association's August 1972 annual general meeting, I felt it was time to share the new vision for the industry with the people of Jamaica, and so we called a press conference to highlight the major issues that the ministry would be tackling. I put forward our vision for the development of an industry that welcomed Jamaicans and in which Jamaicans embraced visitors with traditional Jamaican hospitality.

One of the first initiatives was to ensure that all Jamaicans had access to beaches without creating inconvenience for visitors; another was the development of Negril, not only as a tourist resort but also as a national recreation centre. Other attractions to be developed with local patrons in mind were Irwin Gardens, Cornwall Beach Bathing Club and Montego Bay Craft Market. We would also be encouraging Jamaicans to vacation at hotels in the off-season periods. In keeping with this, an intensive public relations programme would have to be mounted to educate the public about the facilities available. We also wanted to maximize cooperation and collaboration among the ministries and agencies which had an impact on the industry, such as the Urban Development Corporation (UDC), which was responsible for developing tourist centres such as Ocho Rios and Negril.

We also wanted to change the people involved in the management of the industry to reflect the Jamaican face. Up to that point, management and senior positions had been reserved for foreigners. The JTB was mandated to mount a training programme to bring about this change. Staff were to be recruited from overseas only if no Jamaican was available to fill the position.

In that first year we used every opportunity to promote the new directions the government would take in not only revitalizing but revolutionizing the country's tourist industry. On one point we were very clear. Discrimination would not be tolerated in Jamaica's tourist product. The Jamaican people, at all levels and of all races and combinations of races, insisted that the only sort of tourism they would tolerate was one devoid of all forms of racial discrimination or social snobbery.

I had personal experience of this situation and was determined to erase it. When I taught at Cornwall College, after leaving Calabar and before entering the University College of the West Indies, there were weekends when, as the master on duty for the boarding students, I had two specific assignments. The first was to escort the boarders to Doctor's Cave Beach for swimming, and the other to take them to the St James Parish Church for evensong on Sundays.

Doctor's Cave Beach was a members' club. Its trust deed had provided this special privilege for boarders at Cornwall College. Its rules excluded residents of Montego Bay from entering as temporary guests. This meant that except for a select and privileged few, the people of Montego Bay were barred access. This, in effect, resulted in segregation, which was a cause of understandable resentment among the people of St James. It was also anathema to several of its members, led by Herbert Morrison, who had fought against racism all his life.

My appointment as minister of tourism made it possible to join forces with Dr Morrison and open the beach for all to enjoy. In this spirit we welcomed visitors of all races and targeted non-traditional markets such as the ethnic communities in the United States.

Specific programmes on which we immediately embarked included tackling crime and violence by increasing police patrols in tourist areas; rigorous staff training; improving standards in hotels and monitoring service levels by introducing a "Man of Standards" (quality control officer); designating October Tourism Month; planning infrastructural programmes such as improved landscaping of the tourist belt and better street lighting in Montego Bay city centre; and upgrading airport facilities as well as regulating U-drive operators, visitor attractions and in-bond shops. Our efforts were welcomed by the major industry players.

In 1973 we were proud to announce a 13.5 per cent increase in tourism earnings over the previous year, bringing in over US$100 million in foreign exchange, and visitor volume rose to 493,000, a 10 per cent increase over 1971 and the largest increase since 1968. Stopover visitors increased by 13.5 per cent. This encouraged us to press on with our plans, and we announced our intention to fill ten thousand rooms in 1973 and to double the number of rooms over the next five years.

While this was a promising start, there was no denying the many problems which beset the industry. It continued to be plagued by the perennial problems of theft, touts and periods of low occupancy. The government was blamed, for increasing the number of rooms, and we had to point out that the performance of individual hotels was determined by their operational efficiency and individual marketing programmes. We had previously made the point that the JTB's obligation was to market Jamaica as a destination, but hoteliers were responsible for marketing individual properties.

The government came under heavy criticism for having acquired hotel properties. The critics felt we had no business owning and running hotels. The fact is, we had no desire to be in the hotel business, but we had to protect the government's investments. The loans made to the previous, foreign owners of the hotels had been guaranteed by the government, and so when they were unable to service their debts, the government was forced to take over the debt obligation and the liabilities of the hotels. We had no alternative and became owners of the hotels by default.

Cabinet had put an embargo on any further purchase of hotel property and we wanted to buy the Royal Caribbean, which was originally being sold for US$3 million, but had been successful in negotiating the price down to US$1.5

million. At that time the government also needed to buy furniture, beds, linen and cutlery to equip the newly established nursing quarters at the Cornwall Regional Hospital and the Sam Sharpe College. We struck a bargain with the Royal Caribbean for sale "as is", including everything in the hotel – furniture, linen and so on. In advance of the cabinet meeting, I obtained the support of Kenny McNeil and Howard Cooke to convince our colleagues that we could source the items needed for both institutions at a cost of US$1.5 million. Thus we saved the hotel and provided the equipment needed for the school and hospital.

National Hotels and Properties was set up to administer and manage the new hotel acquisitions. It was managed by qualified Jamaican nationals, such as Hugh Dyke and some others who were previously employed in the hotel industry while they were still under foreign management.

The fact that local investors, particularly the Issa Group, seized the opportunity to invest in the industry was an added boon. With the shortage of foreign exchange, importers needed to find independent sources of earning foreign exchange. Several Jamaicans subsequently entered the hotel business, initially in an effort to earn foreign exchange to run their other ventures. It soon became evident to an entrepreneur like Gordon "Butch" Stewart that the business of tourism offered the greatest scope for earning foreign exchange and for corporate growth. His Sandals chain has become the most powerful enterprise in our Caribbean hospitality trade.

It was a real challenge trying to restructure and redevelop tourism. The high-end tourists were no longer coming to Jamaica. We had to look increasingly to group bookings and expanding conference facilities. In keeping with this, the Groups and Conventions Department was created, targeting Europeans and minority ethnic groups in particular.

Then there was the issue of a culture change among hotel employees – to underscore the difference between service and servitude. Scholarships were offered to train Jamaicans in hotel management, including scholarships from the German government, the Pringle Scholarship and the Maybelle Ewen Scholarship. In this way we were able to accomplish the Jamaicanization of the hotel management.

Our efforts paid some dividends, as visitor statistics showed a small but steady increase up to 1975, even while global travel was on the decline, with visitors to major destinations in Europe and the Caribbean also down, the exceptions being Bermuda and Jamaica. The number of cruise-ship visitors to Jamaica also increased.

By then the government was the largest investor in the industry. I took every opportunity to point out the role of the workers in the sector in keeping the industry operating at the highest standards. I outlined some of their responsibilities, demanding that hotel employees treat the properties as their own. There was, among some sectors, the mistaken notion that the government was an external body and, as such, its holdings could be treated carelessly. I told them the property of the government was the property of the people and, therefore, the workers were expected to be vigilant in protecting their jobs and hotels. They had to undertake increasing responsibility in the administration and shaping of the industry.

From then on, approval for all visitor accommodation construction had to be sought from the ministry to prevent haphazard development. We also had to have a say in the fixing of hotel rates. We did not forget the smaller cottage-resort subsector, which represented 20 per cent of the hotel sector and was primarily owned by Jamaicans. The JTB allocated additional funds to assist the Jamaica Association of Villas and Apartments. We also looked at major refurbishment of the two international airports with the assistance of a World Bank loan.

In 1975, we introduced several initiatives to increase the effectiveness of the ministry and its agencies, including new legislation, restructuring the JTB and setting up new units. These included the Tourism Product Development Company, to administer quality control and licensing, as well as developing attractions for the foreign and local tourist markets.

This allowed the JTB to focus on research, marketing and planning. A Tourism Planning and Implementation Unit was created within the ministry, staffed by economists and professionals in travel and tourism. A company, Jamaica Vacations, was set up to facilitate charters coming into the island and encourage group travel by making the best use of Air Jamaica's and Air Canada's bulk rates and spearheading the development of air/cruise/hotel packages. Yet another organization, Jamaica Resort Hotels, was formed to market the hotels. These ventures would be supported by an intensive marketing and advertising programme in North America mounted by the JTB. In October 1975, the amendment of the Jamaica Tourist Board Act gave the JTB borrowing powers. This was intended to make the organization more effective in enhancing visitor attractions.

As we approached the end of our first term, we were able to report that tourism had maintained its position as second only to bauxite and alumina in foreign exchange earnings up to 1975.

I was proud to share the following data in the parliamentary debate on tourism policy in the House on 17 March 1976. In the period 1965–75, total visitors per year increased from 302,000 to 553,000 and earnings had grown from US$46.4 million to US$116 million, with the gross foreign-exchange earnings representing an annual average of 18 per cent of total foreign-exchange earnings. Some twelve thousand people had been directly employed and another twelve thousand indirectly employed in the industry.

Even then, however, the signs of the downturn that would overtake us in 1976 were evident. We could no longer avoid the inflationary wave which had swept over the world in 1974. Deep recession had spread from the industrial countries to other parts of the world. The steep rise in oil prices had a negative impact on the global travel industry, and we experienced a drastic reduction in visitors from our traditional US market. We were fortunate to have additional visitors from Europe and Canada, but these were not enough to offset the fall-off from the United States.

In 1976 foreign-exchange earnings fell by 17.7 per cent and employment by 12.3 per cent. The number of visitor arrivals fell from 553,258 in 1975 to 470,714 in 1976. In 1977 it would fall to an all-time low of 386,514.[1]

These negatives, however, helped to drive the Jamaicanization of the industry. The JTB placed emphasis on a programme to get Jamaicans to vacation at home and to rediscover their island. We promoted places like Folly, Lovers' Leap, Edinburgh Castle and Port Royal as interesting historical places to visit. We prepared five-minute dramatic pieces on these sites, performed by people in Jamaican theatre like Leonie Forbes and Charles Hyatt. The JTB took travel agents on tours to the various spots and played the relevant tape on approaching a particular destination. They were all impressed. The stories were also placed as advertisements in newspapers. We focused on introducing Jamaica to Jamaicans. We told local people about places in their own communities that they did not know about. For example, few residents knew that the Dome in Montego Bay was founded to provide the first water supply for that township.

Perhaps the most influential programme mounted to introduce Jamaicans to the hotel industry was the one through which the government provided paid holidays at local hotels for civil servants. This was a positive variation on the previous practice of paying for senior civil servants to holiday abroad.

We had started the Discover Jamaica Programme in 1976, and by 1977 the hotels were overflowing with Jamaicans on weekends. In 1977 over 131,000

---

1. Planning Institute of Jamaica, *Economic and Social Survey of Jamaica 1975* (Kingston: Planning Institute of Jamaica, 1976).

Jamaicans vacationed in the island's hotels. In order to help the sector to adjust to the many local visitors, the JTB reoriented hotel staff by helping them to understand that they also had to regard Jamaican guests as tourists. Shirley Fletcher was in charge of that programme.

Another fascinating project was mounting signs at various beauty spots across the island over a designated weekend. The effect of this was remarkable.

The "Meet the People" Programme, which had been started in 1968, came under Hartley Neita's umbrella. Jamaicans were invited to host visitors in their homes and to introduce them to interesting facets of Jamaica. Hartley invited a broad cross-section of Jamaicans he knew to become involved. He asked Lady Josephine Glasspole, wife of the governor general, to be the patron, and she hosted a tea party once a month for about twenty visitors, who were brought in from Ocho Rios and Port Antonio to King's House, the governor general's official residence in Kingston. These were all extremely successful.

However, a viable tourist industry had to include foreign-exchange earnings, which would contribute to a healthy balance of payments in addition to economic growth. Emphasis on bringing in overseas visitors had to be strengthened and sustained. In presenting the tourism aspect of the 1977/78 production plan, following our victory at the polls in December 1976, the strategy was to reorganize the ministry's agencies to pursue a more deliberate and targeted marketing strategy in order to increase foreign-exchange earnings and employment in the sector.

Tourism remained within my portfolio as minister of foreign affairs, foreign trade and tourism. Jack Stephenson, as minister of state, took charge of the tourism section.

The roles of the agencies were enlarged. The JTB, for example, was charged with stimulating demand overseas for the Jamaican product; coordinating the activities of the various market sectors; and disseminating the Jamaican image overseas. In so doing the agency would direct its efforts in three main directions: groups and conventions, tours and charter developments, and retail and special markets.

Jamaica Vacations was expected to concentrate on charter developments, while the Tourism Product Development Company would be expected to be more rigorous in implementing quality control and play a greater role in setting and enforcing standards in keeping with our cultural and national aspirations. It would also have increased responsibility for licensing resort cottages and attractions.

The National Tourism Council, chaired by the minister and comprising representatives of the JTB, Tourism Product Development Company, Air Jamaica, Jamaica Vacations, National Hotels and Properties and Martin's Travel, would ensure maximum coordination among the agencies involved in the industry. A planning unit for tourism was established in the ministry to help increase the industry's net foreign-exchange earnings.

Our hard work and strategizing paid off. In 1978 we started to see a turnaround, and visitor arrivals again climbed above the half-million mark, with 532,864 arrivals. The main growth areas were the United States, Canada and West Germany. The sector contributed US$44 million to foreign-exchange earnings, and restored buoyancy in the sector was evident in increased employment – 11,850 directly and 14,820 indirectly. The growth trend continued into 1979, which proved the best year ever up to that point, with visitor-arrival statistics of 593,671.

I was extremely proud of our performance and must record my admiration for the team that allowed us to realize this success in the face of great odds. In addition to the unfriendly global economic climate and increasing political violence which led to a prolonged state of emergency and a general election, we had to contend with many negative reports in the foreign and local press. There were several media advisories coming out of the United States strongly recommending against travel to Jamaica.

One writer on Jamaica's tourist industry, Frank Fonda Taylor, noted: "In the era of the cold war, the diplomacy of non-alignment and relations with Cuba that Manley opted for was hardly compatible with the strategy of tourism development that his regime supported."[2]

There is no denying that our ideological position was one that the United States overtly opposed. These factors served to influence the North American market in deciding where to spend their holiday budget. There were also a few wholesalers who were not comfortable with the balanced positions we took consistently on the conflicts between Israel and Palestine, and who sought to divert their customers to other destinations.

On an Air Jamaica flight from New York – after my final address as foreign minister to the UN General Assembly in 1980 – I had engaged in pleasant conversation with a honeymoon couple, and told them I was returning home to Jamaica. "Jamaica is too dangerous, and going communist," they said. "On no account would we ever come there. We are going to Negril instead." When

---

2. Frank Fonda Taylor, *To Hell with Paradise: A History of the Jamaican Tourist Industry* (Pittsburgh: University of Pittsburgh Press, 1993), 184.

they disembarked in Montego Bay, I made them none the wiser. I wished them a pleasant stay in sunny Negril and they expressed the hope I would enjoy the rest of my trip home to Jamaica and be safe.

Democratic socialism meant social justice and economic opportunities for all: tourism, as a creator of jobs and earner of foreign exchange, was vital to those goals. Ideology had not prevented Yugoslavia from enjoying the greatest growth in tourism globally. I underscored the fact that what visitors were most concerned about was feeling safe while vacationing.

The new director of tourism, Desmond Henry, worked with Peter Martin and my former personal assistant, Carmen Tipling, in developing a new appeal: "Jamaica is more than a beach – it is a country."

CHAPTER 10
A NEW INTERNATIONAL ECONOMIC ORDER

THE SHARP RISE IN OIL PRICES AFTER MAY 1973 threatened a convulsion through-out the entire international economic system and institutions.

In December 1975, just before the UN Conference on Trade and Develop-ment, representatives from the developed and developing world met outside the UN forum to grapple with issues relating to international development. The Conference on International Economic Cooperation, also referred to as the Paris Club, was originally intended to be a conference on energy involving the mem-ber countries of the Organization for Economic Cooperation and Development. The Organization of Petroleum Exporting Countries (OPEC), however, refused to discuss energy to the exclusion of other matters fundamental to the restruc-turing of the world economic order. Consequently, the scope of the conference was widened and the number of participants increased.

We were honoured that Jamaica was chosen to be one of the group of nineteen countries selected to represent the interests of the Third World in negotiations with the EEC, Canada, Sweden, Japan, Switzerland and the United States.

The Jamaican delegation chosen for the deliberations was regarded by friend and foe as formidable and top class. Sir Egerton Richardson was outstand-ing, and at the technical level he demolished the self-serving presentations by technocrats from the G7 developed countries. The developing countries were advocating for a new approach to issues facing the developing world, the New International Economic Order. We considered the conference to be a forum for managing change in the economic relations between rich and poor nations. One of the areas on which we placed priority was the needs of the least developed countries and those most affected by the recent changes in commodity prices.

The negotiations, which lasted from January 1976 to June 1977, were organized under four commissions: energy, raw materials, development and finance.

The Energy Commission was primarily concerned with energy prices and the purchasing power of energy export earnings. OPEC wanted a mechanism in which oil prices would not be eroded by price increases for items imported from the North. This assurance of indexation was not forthcoming from the developed countries, but there was a measure of agreement on the availability and limits of oil supplies which would suggest the value of international energy cooperation.

The Raw Materials Commission sought the establishment of a mechanism to ensure price stability and increased export earnings. It was proposed that this matter be addressed through a compensatory financing facility. Although such a facility already existed at the International Monetary Fund (IMF), it was a component of the borrowing arrangements within this institution, and loans from the IMF were linked to the members' quota allocation. Amounts available to developing countries were inadequate, as the eligible amount was dependent on the members' quota and drawing rights. This compensatory facility proposed by the developing countries was necessary for commodities which could not be stockpiled, such as bananas.

The developing countries argued that the way forward to achieve price stabilization and protection against export-earning shortfalls was by establishing a common fund for commodities. Indexation was not supported by the developed countries.

Discussions in the Development Commission focused on encouraging the developed countries to help bring about growth in the developing countries. One position was that the developing countries should be able to use their raw materials to enhance their production capabilities by improving processing facilities as well as their marketing thrusts. Another was that the transfer of resources to the developing countries should be achieved by increasing levels of official development assistance and a critical look at the debt problems which were obstacles to the provision of government capital for infrastructure and production capabilities.

A few developed countries, including the Scandinavian countries and Holland, had agreed to increase their official development assistance to 0.7 per cent of their gross national income in keeping with the demands of the developing countries. The Commonwealth Heads of Government Conference hosted by Jamaica in 1977 endorsed the expert group's proposal that official development assistance should be increased to 1 per cent.

It was generally agreed that trade between industrial and developing countries should be markedly increased. The developing countries, however, posited that in arriving at a level playing field to fix trade concessions, the measure that should be referenced was unemployment levels, rather than gross domestic product (GDP). This proposal was rejected by the industrial countries.

The Finance Commission focused on issues relating to the availability and conditions of loans. Debt relief and debt burden varied among the developing countries: the very poor and the most seriously affected were those countries with large balance-of-payments deficits and which were in dire straits in meeting external debt payments. The other group comprised countries which had relied on commercial borrowing. It was proposed that compensatory finance balance-of-payments support to the non-oil developing countries needed to be expanded.

The developing countries represented at the Conference on International Economic Cooperation did not present a united view, as they were at varying levels of economic, social and financial development. This was a major constraint to successful negotiations by the G77 group of developing nations. Argentina, Brazil and Mexico, for example, would not discuss the "Debt Problem", as they were already accessing the international financial markets. In addition, in terms of suppliers, credits and loans, these countries were competing with developed countries which were recovering from recession and therefore needed loans themselves.

THE UNITED NATIONS

The government that Jamaica elected in 1972 shared the philosophy and intent to pursue the restructuring of the world economic order to effect a more equitable distribution of international resources.

Until 1980, we used one session after another of the UN General Assembly and all its agencies to call for the establishment of the New International Economic Order, founded on the principle of a just and equitable relationship between the prices of raw materials, primary products, manufactured and semi-manufactured goods exported by developing countries and the prices of the capital goods and equipment they imported.

The concept of the New International Economic Order arose from the need to integrate international political and economic relations into a single conceptual framework for global development from which benefits would accrue to all countries and all peoples. The New International Economic Order had to take place within the context of the UN system.

Three areas were identified for new approaches by the United Nations. First, the transfer of resources from developed to developing countries should have been implemented by the Seventh Special Session of the General Assembly; the flow of concessional financial resources to developing countries should be made "predictable, continuous and increasingly assured". Instead there were arguments over the definition of official development assistance and the failure of one or another donor country to maintain the promised level of aid. There was the need to keep watch on the movement of resources on concessional as well as non-concessional terms, and to be prepared to work towards establishing a commission on the transfer of resources.

Second, international monetary reform was delayed by the slow pace of the reform of the Bretton Woods system. There was continued delay by those countries which had the power to place narrow national or group interests above the interests of the global community. I called upon the General Assembly to establish an ad hoc commission on international monetary reform charged with calling for reports on measures under consideration in the IMF, assessing the progress of implementation and promoting and guiding international monetary reform.

Third, in terms of the effective conservation of oil and natural gas there was need to explore new energy sources; ensure that investment choices in developing alternative energy reflected rational strategies in developing countries; research solar, wind and other renewable sources/forms; provide financial and technical assistance for high-risk investment in energy exploration; develop known resources; and provide diversification programmes. We also proposed an institution to provide technical cooperation between developed and developing countries in energy exploration, diversification and technology transfer.

The issues highlighted included the economic relationship between developed and developing countries and the production and use of raw materials in that relationship leading to unequal income distribution. The prevailing patterns restricted real returns enjoyed by developing countries for the exploitation and use of their resources, and real income was transferred in favour of rich nations.

We recommended that current mechanisms needed to be replaced by a more equitable system, such as enabling developing/producer countries to take steps to ensure a just return for their raw materials. This did not have to result in price increases in manufactured goods, but would have brought about a narrowing of the profit margins of the capitalists. We empathized with oil-exporting countries and saw the increase in oil prices as part of a larger issue of restructuring the world economic order.

In the global discussions on the need to establish a charter of economic rights and duties, there was a sameness to the agenda from one year to the next. Identical issues were debated but no consensus reached on approaches to the international development strategy which we recommended be formulated within the framework of the New International Economic Order. Our emphasis that failure to achieve a relevant world economic policy would make a mockery of plans was largely ignored or only paid lip service by the developed world.

Six years later, in 1980, there had been little or no change in international affairs. A recurring theme in our presentations had been the need to complement political independence with economic independence; decolonization with economic liberation. Even political gains made by developing countries in the post-colonial era were now under assault, and the international political climate was undergoing most significant deterioration at precisely the time when international economic conditions were at their worst and the need to restructure the international economic system was most compelling. Developed countries showed indifference and hostility to proposals and continued resistance to changing the structure of the world economic system.

I was firmly of the view that economic problems of the North could not be isolated from the South. There was a need to overcome the separation of issues such as money and finance, which, along with energy, represented the centrepiece of international concerns at that time. The international monetary system had to be urgently brought into line with the complex realities of the prevailing international economic concerns and needs of developing countries.

The recommendations of the Independent Commission on International Development Issues – the Brandt Commission – on alleviating poverty and promoting international peace and unity did not represent the full measure of the call for the New International Economic Order.

The 1970s contributed to the understanding of the basic problems in money, finance, trade, industrialization, technology transfer and other issues. A review of the 1970s showed that the early promises of the decade had not been realized and the challenge of the 1980s would be a reassertion of principles of sovereign equality, territorial integrity and non-interference in internal affairs.

At one time, there was a hope that the 1980s would be a watershed decade for the international community. There was an intention to launch the global round of negotiations in 1981 and to approve an international development strategy for the decade. But already there were signs that industrialized countries were resisting an effective global effort.

And so, in my closing statement as foreign minister of Jamaica to the United Nations at the General Assembly in 1980 I asserted:

> As we have met in forum after forum to address the major political and economic problems of our time, the cascade of words has brought forth but a trickle of deeds. A verbal avalanche has yielded a veritable mound of inaction. Success continues to elude our grasp.
>
> But we must persevere. We must remain undaunted. We must stand for peace. We must stand firm against the exploitation of nation by nation, of man by man. From our achievements, though few, we must recognize the measure of the possible.
>
> Mr President, our obligation to history and to succeeding generations must be to redouble our efforts *now* to effect *now* meaningful political and economic change even as the obstacles increase.
>
> The United Nations is the cornerstone of all our hope. It is here we must lay foundations for the future.

CHAPTER 11
FROM CARIFTA TO CARICOM

ON 3 JUNE 1972, THE GUILD OF GRADUATES held a luncheon in my honour as the first alumnus of the University College of the West Indies to become a cabinet minister in the Government of Jamaica. In this respect, Jamaica had lagged behind our sister territories.

I expressed my pleasure at being Jamaica's representative on the CARIFTA Council of Ministers:

> Long before the Caribbean Free Trade Association (CARIFTA) was ever conceived I, like all my friends gathered here today, had the unforgettable experience of living in a West Indian community and of learning at first hand of the problems and aspirations of the region.
>
> The new Administration has made it clear that Jamaica intends to play her full role in regional economic cooperation and in declaring this as our policy we see no incompatibility between pursuing a policy of enlightened self interest and that of securing for the Commonwealth Caribbean as a whole a better quality of life for all its people.

Early that year, the CARIFTA Secretariat, under Secretary General William Demas, produced a forward-looking book, *From CARIFTA to Caribbean Community*. The focus was on the membership of CARIFTA, which had been collaborating for almost five years. It was grounded in the observed reality that the "free trade integration" process was quickly reaching its limit. Furthermore, the gains from the process were concentrated in a few member states. This was leading to increasing tension, especially between the less-developed countries and the more-developed countries. Jamaica was in this latter group and was a main beneficiary of CARIFTA. The timing of that publication was opportune.

Michael Manley was also an unequivocal regionalist. He had published an article, in the October 1970 edition of the journal *Foreign Affairs*, entitled

"Overcoming Insularity in Jamaica", in which he expressed strong sentiments in favour of regional economic integration. Further, two of his associates from his student days in London, Errol Barrow of Barbados and Forbes Burnham of Guyana, were two of the three original signatories to the CARIFTA (Dickenson Bay) Agreement.

Jamaica, at the policy level, was ready for the challenge of deepening the integration process. Up to that point the country had been kept in the process mainly by my predecessor in the Ministry of Trade and Industry, Robert Lightbourne, and by members of the local manufacturing sector – Aaron Matalon, Ray Hadeed, Vin Bennett, Charles Henderson-Davis – who continued to support it. But there was a political divide in the country over the relationship with members of the erstwhile federation. It was our challenge and responsibility to galvanize, direct and coordinate the development of Jamaica's position. There were different perceptions across the government and we had to convince many of the senior advisors and administrators that they need not fear a deepening of Caribbean integration.

The seventh meeting of the heads of government of the Commonwealth Caribbean was convened in Chaguaramas, Trinidad and Tobago, in October 1972. The main issue for discussion was the deepening of the Caribbean integration process on the basis of the documentation and recommendations submitted by the CARIFTA Secretariat. The key substantive proposals related to (1) economic integration through a common market; (2) greater functional cooperation in areas such as health, education, sea and air transport, culture, science, technology, agriculture, mines, finance and labour; and (3) coordination of foreign affairs. Issues of the organizational, institutional and decision-making arrangements were never far from the surface.

Jamaica organized and drew on resources and skills across the various ministries and in the private sector. Our delegation to Port of Spain was organized to reflect the broad range of issues. It was led by Prime Minister Michael Manley, who was kept fully informed at all stages of the preparations and was involved in all the key policy issues.

The conference was to be chaired by the host prime minister, Eric Williams. In light of the history of disagreement between Jamaica and Trinidad and Tobago over matters of economic integration and the relationship between Michael's father, Norman Washington, and Eric Williams, we were extremely apprehensive as to how the "Doctor" would receive Norman's son. As was the emerging practice, meetings of officials and ministers preceded the meeting of the heads of government. I arrived in Trinidad and Tobago in advance of

Prime Minister Manley to pave the way for the personal contact between the two prime ministers, which would be vital to the outcome of the conference. The notoriously difficult Williams was known to be an amiable and gracious host, supremely charming whenever he chose. To the great relief of all, the relationship between the two bloomed so positively during the conference that Williams, uncharacteristically and informally dressed, visited Michael in his suite at the Hilton Hotel late the night before he was scheduled to depart to bid him goodbye in person.

The work of negotiating and structuring a Caribbean Economic Community was complex. The arrangement had to accommodate, inter alia: (1) countries of differing economic sizes, economic endowments and development potential; (2) countries of different political status, with the majority having no competence either to enter into a treaty relationship with the other members or to take part in negotiations involving foreign policy; and (3) countries like the Bahamas which had no interest in economic integration or cooperation.

The overriding sentiment among the leaders, however, was the need to move forward. The conference took the policy decision that the region would establish the Caribbean Community and Common Market. It set a timeframe for negotiating the detailed arrangement by scheduling its next meeting for April 1973 in Georgetown, Guyana. It charged ministerial bodies and technical working groups to work through the policy, legal (treaty) and technical issues. The trade and industry ministers (the CARIFTA Council) had to work through the economic integration issues, while the attorneys general and legal affairs ministers had to structure the legal framework. A special committee of customs experts had to develop proposals for the Common External Tariff and the Rules of Origin. These were the bases on which the heads of government triumphantly left Port of Spain. But the work was just beginning.

Individual member states had to structure their internal arrangements to bring together their contending interests and develop national positions which they could advance and defend in the region-wide negotiations. The West Indies Associated States/East Caribbean Common Market members had to bring their national positions into a subregional position.

Mine was the responsibility for coordinating the development of Jamaica's position on the economic side, as well as several of the areas for "functional" cooperation, and for taking these into the region-wide negotiations.

These negotiations did not take place in a single meeting. In reality, between January and March 1973, we perfected the art of "shuttle diplomacy". I made numerous "official" and "unofficial" trips to Port of Spain, Bridgetown and

Georgetown and to the capitals of the Eastern Caribbean islands. The work advanced, but ministers arrived in Georgetown at the beginning of April with much work still to be done. Among the most intractable issues was the balance between the interests of the less-developed countries and the more-developed countries. This was not strictly a technical issue or an issue where the balance could be demonstrated. There was deep fear and suspicion, which were seldom articulated.

The differences in political status, idiosyncrasies and differing temperaments of prime ministers, premiers and chief ministers did not make for easy resolution of outstanding issues. Yet the heads of government, led by the wily Guyanese president Forbes Burnham, were determined that an agreement had to be struck before the end of Thursday, 12 April, as they did not intend to conclude on the supposedly unlucky Friday the thirteenth.

Negotiations proceeded in the main conference room at the Georgetown Pegasus Hotel among the heads of government and in subcommittees at ministerial and technical levels on particular issues. Progress was discernible, but slow in the context of the timetable.

This was clearest in the work of the legal committee. By Thursday, they were proving the adage that "a committee cannot draft". The chairman dispatched a committee of two – his own attorney general, Shridath Ramphal, representing the more-developed countries, and Lee Moore, the attorney general of St Kitts and Nevis, representing the less-developed countries, to produce a "working draft agreement". They emerged late that evening with a "consensus" document, later dubbed the "Moore–Ramphal Effort". This became the basis for further negotiations. The negotiations continued mainly among ministers. At minutes to midnight on Thursday 12 April 1973, the conference stopped the clock in the main conference room.

The plenary remained in suspended session. A break-up fete, at the nearby Umana Yana (a conference centre built in indigenous style), which was to double as a birthday celebration for all those who had had birthdays during the week, including me, became a feast for the guests only.

In the main conference room, heads, ministers and officials milled around awaiting the outcome document. The chairman made available his best brandies, whiskies and wines. The decibel level of the banter increased, and some succumbed to the lateness of the hour on the stationary clock, while one notable head slipped conspicuously under the conference table to the floor, boots and breeches first. But all remained within calling distance for the resumption, which took place in the early hours of the morning, when the agreed outcome, the Georgetown Accord, emerged as the document to be refined for signature.

The clock on the wall could now be reset. Outside, daylight was approaching. Some delegates and staff of the secretariat went directly to breakfast in the dining room of the Guyana Pegasus Hotel. Other delegates, including heads of government and ministers, prepared to make the thirty-mile trip to the Timehri Airport and to convene in Chaguaramas for the signing.

THE ROAD TO CHAGUARAMAS

The Georgetown Conference had agreed on the principle for the deeper integration process. A treaty must reflect details and be consistent with international laws and principles governing treaties. There would really be no agreement until countries were ready and empowered to sign the treaty. In the circumstances of the Caribbean in 1973, eight of the thirteen eligible states listed in paragraph 1(a) of the treaty had to receive specific permission or entrustment from the United Kingdom to sign any treaty even with their British Commonwealth neighbours.

We had to re-engage the process of shuttle diplomacy, small group negotiations and liberal use of the telephone. The date for the signing of the treaty was a parameter. An early determination was to structure the treaty in such a manner that it could be signed and become operational among those who possessed the necessary competence. It had been agreed that the treaty would be finalized and ready for signature in Chaguaramas on 4 July 1973, to honour the birthdate of Norman Washington Manley. It provided, innovatively, in article 22 that "The Treaty shall be open for signature on the 4th July, 1973 by any State mentioned in paragraph 1(a) of Article 2 of this Treaty." It further provided in article 24, on Entry into Force, that the treaty "shall enter into force on 1st August, 1973, if Instruments of Ratification have been previously deposited in accordance with Article 23".

Article 23 simply required ratification by Barbados, Guyana, Jamaica and Trinidad and Tobago. This device was coupled with provisions which allowed, *inter alia*: the CARIFTA Agreement to subsist along with the CARICOM Treaty until each member had signed the new treaty; the treaty and the annex to the treaty to be signed separately; and that only members with the competence to deal with matters relating to foreign policy could participate.

With will and determination we met the deadline and so the Treaty of Chaguaramas, establishing CARICOM, and its annex establishing the

Caribbean Common Market, including the Common External Tariff, were ready for signature by the four competent member states on the appointed day. I was a ministerial witness on 4 July 1973, when Michael Manley signed the two agreements for the Government of Jamaica. Prime ministers Errol Barrow of Barbados, Forbes Burnham of Guyana and Eric Williams of Trinidad and Tobago also signed the treaty.

The next challenge was to get the agreements ratified by these four states, including Jamaica. We had less than a month to complete the national constitutional processes and to submit the instrument of ratification to the secretariat, which had to transmit certified copies of each instrument to the government of each member state. There were neither emails nor reliable overnight delivery services in those days. But the processes were completed and the new treaty became effective among Barbados, Guyana, Jamaica and Trinidad and Tobago on 1 August 1973.

The other eight members of CARIFTA listed in article 2, paragraph 1(a) completed the process and became members of the community and common market on 1 May 1974. The CARIFTA Agreement technically ceased to exist on that date, but in practice persisted until 1 August 1974, when all members had acceded to the new treaty. The Bahamas signed the CARICOM Treaty in July 1983, on the tenth anniversary of the original signing.

The signature and implementation of the Treaty of Chaguaramas were preceded in May by the first of several major exogenous shocks which would create an unimaginable international environment for its operationalization.

In May 1973, OPEC increased the price of crude petroleum fourfold, from US$2.50 to US$10.00 per barrel. This historic decision posed a major economic and international relations challenge for progressive, primary (raw) materials-exporting countries such as those in the Caribbean. All the CARICOM/CARIFTA member states, with the exception of Trinidad and Tobago, were totally dependent on imported crude petroleum or petroleum products for almost 100 per cent of their energy. The OPEC decision would affect both our production and consumption adversely. No one could escape.

On the other hand, as producers and exporters of primary commodities such as bauxite, sugar and bananas, we were also victims of the power of the industrialized countries.

As trade and foreign ministers, we were conflicted as to how the new CARICOM arrangements would allow us to seek and cooperate in finding the right solutions when all member states, except Trinidad and Tobago, were energy deficient.

We developed an operational "strategy" to (1) support OPEC in the international debate; (2) seek to negotiate with the OPEC members for easement or transfer; and (3) use the "opportunity" to negotiate better prices for our commodities. It was the environment of commodity price instability generated by the May 1973 OPEC decision that facilitated our negotiation of the sugar, banana, rice and rum protocols with the EEC.

There were some major developments within CARICOM as the region struggled not just to adjust to the external environment but also to take advantage of its new arrangements for collaboration to find avenues for growth and development. Ministers of trade agreed that where a member state had been forced to reduce or restrict imports, it would apply this only to imports from third countries. Trade within the common market would only be restricted as a last resort.

The conference, at a special meeting in April 1976, decided to establish a Caribbean multilateral clearing facility by widening the bilateral facilities which had existed since 1969. It also decided to increase the credit within the facility and lengthened the period for settlement.

The special meeting of conference established a balance-of-payments support facility to assist member states which might run into difficulties. The rationale was that this would remove the need to trigger the balance-of-payments provision in the treaty. Unfortunately, Guyana and Jamaica ran into serious balance-of-payments difficulties at the same time and before the fund had built up significant reserves.

The conference, at the special meeting, agreed to implement a regional plan aimed at increasing food production and trade in the region. In order to implement this plan, the conference established a regional corporation (the Caribbean Food Corporation), which had as one of its remits the establishment of the Caribbean Agricultural Trading Corporation. All member states contributed to its equity.

In spite of these initiatives, the increasingly hostile international economic environment, mounting economic difficulties in some member states and clear ideological polarization had begun to take a toll on the fledgling movement. The supply of energy to the oil-deficient countries in the Caribbean required the utmost sensitivity. Eric Williams kept Burnham, Barrow and Manley waiting before their meeting in Port of Spain began. They left greatly disappointed at the level of support for CARICOM colleagues in the face of continued high oil prices.

However, Mexico and Venezuela established the special San José Accord in 1980 to mitigate the adverse impact on member states. Furthermore, the World

Bank's mishandling of Williams's proposal for a multilateral Caribbean Group for Cooperation in Economic Development to mobilize resources resulted in his virtual withdrawal from the process. Ideological tensions had intensified to dismantle all the prospects of combining regional energy and mining resources for an aluminium smelter in the Caribbean.

Ministers, including trade ministers, continued to search for ways of enabling the process, but there was no movement at the highest level of policy. Robert Bradshaw presided over the conference of heads in Basseterre, St Kitts, during November 1975, without Eric Williams. There was no meeting at the level of conference after that until November 1982.

Subsequently, there were other developments which were not favourable to the integration process. Among these were: (1) the second oil-price shock and global economic recession of 1979; (2) the revolutionary change in government in Grenada in 1979, followed by the ideological divisions and the counter-revolution and the US-led intervention in 1983; and (3) the coming into prominence of the Washington Consensus, with its focus on structural adjustment and economic dependency.

These developments led to a retreat from fundamental principles on matters such as collective sovereignty, the joint development of the natural resources of the region to that end and the primacy of the regional market for regional producers. The combination of these factors limited the achievement of the objectives of the Treaty of Chaguaramas.

At the tenth meeting of heads, 3–7 July 1989, the chairman, Prime Minister Herbert Blaize of Grenada, spoke to the question of CARICOM, "in view of today's international trends", almost a quarter of a century since the search for Caribbean unity had begun at Dickenson Bay. Prime Minister A.N.R. Robinson of Trinidad and Tobago suggested the time was propitious for a re-examination of where we had reached in our efforts at integration and where we wanted to go.

As a sort of "new boy/old boy" Michael Manley was warmly welcomed back to the starting blocks. Manley, a founding signatory, asked his colleagues to impose a "certain discipline of performance and ensure that the major specific injunctions of the Treaty of Chaguaramas would be put in place by 1992". Jamaica supported the call to rekindle the regional flames and to move economic cooperation from a common market to a single market and economy.

The 1989 Declaration of Grand Anse sought to create a revised treaty with the objectives of (1) deepening the economic integration process by advancing beyond a common market towards a single market and economy; (2) widening the membership and thereby expanding the economic mass of CARICOM (for instance, Suriname and Haiti were admitted as full members in 1995 and 2002 respectively); and (3) progressively inserting the region into the global trading and economic system by strengthening trading links with non-traditional partners.

It was there that a West Indian Commission was established, under the chairmanship of Sir Shridath Ramphal, to review the Treaty of Chaguaramas after extensive consultation. It also decided to convene a tripartite conference involving heads of government, the private sector and labour to determine strategies and policies to meet the challenges of economic development and integration likely to face the region in the twenty-first century.

Jamaica was assigned the responsibility of overseeing the technical work on the feasibility of a Caribbean investment fund and work towards the creation of a Caribbean capital market, beginning with a CARICOM stock exchange. This would begin with linking the existing exchanges in Barbados, Jamaica, and Trinidad and Tobago. As minister of finance, development and planning, most of this fell under my portfolio.

Two teams led by the Bank of Jamaica advanced and coordinated the technical work and negotiations to secure decisions, so that I was able to advise the conference in 1992 that Jamaica had successfully discharged the mandate within the timeframe set.

THE KINGSTON SUMMIT, 1990

At the tenth meeting of the conference, in Grenada in July 1989, Jamaica offered to host the eleventh meeting in Kingston in July 1990. Plans were well advanced when Prime Minister Manley became ill. As host he would be the chairman, so in deference to him, the other heads of government decided to postpone the meeting until the end of July, in the expectation that by then he would be back at the helm. As it turned out, he had not recovered sufficiently and the heads agreed that the meeting should proceed with Michael as the new CARICOM chair; as the acting prime minister, I would preside over the eleventh summit.

As was the custom, the conference itself was preceded by two weeks of ministerial and official-level meetings. I had gone to the parish of St James on the Friday before the summit, for a series of official engagements which would culminate in taking part in the national church service to launch our annual celebrations of Emancipation Day and Jamaica's independence.

When the news broke in the early afternoon of the attempted coup d'état in

Trinidad and Tobago, I had to fly by helicopter back to Jamaica House (the Office of the Prime Minister) for verification and regional consultation. It was quickly confirmed that the prime minister and most of his cabinet, as well as other parliamentarians, were being held in the Red House (the parliament building) by the heavily armed Muslimeen group. The group had also taken control of the television station, from which the coup leader had announced the takeover. The staff, including the news director, who appeared on television with the coup leader when he made the dramatic announcement, was being held hostage. The main police station, which was near the parliament building, had been firebombed.

The army quickly mobilized and surrounded the parliament building and the television headquarters. The security forces, on the command of their wounded but courageous prime minister, prevailed and took the captors into custody and freed the hostages.

As a result of immediate phone calls with heads, CARICOM issued a statement of unreserved condemnation of this treasonous assault on constitutional democracy. We deplored any usurpation of the rule of law and insisted that the sanctity of the Parliament of the Republic of Trinidad and Tobago be restored. We roundly condemned the holding hostage of the prime minister, members of his cabinet, parliamentarians and other people.

For a brief period, it was doubtful whether the eleventh conference of heads could convene in Kingston. Prime Minister Robinson, once released, implored us to ensure the conference was held and instructed his foreign minister, Sahadeo Basdeo, who was in Miami, to return home via Kingston. That ensured the presence of a high-level Trinidad and Tobago delegation, which was duly authorized to participate in all the caucus decisions pertaining to that country and other weighty items on a heavy agenda.

It was a sobering experience that placed the vulnerability of small states in stark relief. The conference agreed in its resolution on the incident to review the existing arrangements to support regional security.

Despite the ominous scare and the sombre mood, the experience of that 1990 meeting convinced me, beyond any doubt, that the conference had the capacity to multitask. The entire agenda was fully addressed and major decisions taken, as any reading of the Kingston Communiqué will attest. We ended our meeting with the clear instruction that the work and reports commissioned at Grand Anse would be ready for the next conference of heads in Port of Spain.

I was prepared and equipped for whatever was to come.

CHAPTER 12
THE CUBAN RELATIONSHIP

ONLY NINETY MILES TO THE NORTH, CUBA IS our nearest neighbour. We do not share the same language, but in all essential ways there are many ties that bind us. I have said it often: "We did not make Cuba a Caribbean country – God and nature ordained it so."

Historically, the experiences of plantation society, slavery and colonialism have made us brothers and sisters all, as today there are thriving communities of Jamaican descendants in Cuba. During years of dire hardship, thousands of Jamaicans went to Cuba at the turn of the twentieth century to work in the booming sugar industry there. This wave of migration continued up to 1929–30 when the Great Depression set in and the price of Cuban sugar plummeted.

The links which continued throughout the decades were strengthened when our PNP administration reached out to our closest neighbour and embraced our commonalities, while celebrating and learning from our differences.

Michael Manley lost no time in championing the establishment of diplomatic relations with Cuba through the Cuba-CARICOM Accord signed in December 1972. Jamaica was joined in this initiative by the three other independent Caribbean states – Guyana, Barbados and Trinidad and Tobago. It was a courageous step of fraternal solidarity which Cuba has treasured abundantly. This brought Cuba into the Caribbean fold and opened avenues for establishing missions and bilateral cooperation. We seized the opportunity to cooperate in areas such as tourism, education, medicine and culture.

As minister of industry, tourism and foreign trade, I had to interface with Cuba in all three areas of my portfolio and deal with my ministerial counterparts there. My first ministerial visit to Havana was to meet President Osvaldo Dorticós and Deputy Prime Minister Carlos Rodríguez on the expansion of trade and cooperation between the two countries. El Comandante, Fidel Castro, with whom I also met, had chosen then to remain as head of the Communist Party, and apart from the formal structure of the Cuban government.

Our initial overtures, through visits by Michael's cabinet to Cuba as well as those by Cuban missions to Jamaica, engendered much controversy and criticism. In many quarters there was a feeling that any relationship between Cuba, a self-professed communist country, and Jamaica must mean that we intended to follow a similar political path. Our declaration of democratic socialism was seized, at every opportunity, by hostile forces to fan the communist flame. The Cubans expressed moral support and solidarity with the Jamaican government's effort to create an equal and just society and a self-reliant mixed economy.

Our several visits allowed us to appreciate the commitment and the creativity of the Cuban government's efforts to diminish the impact of decades of oppression and exploitation of the Cuban people. It was a real pity that more Jamaicans did not have the chance to visit Cuba and see conditions for themselves, rather than simply accepting the reporting of the Western press, much of which sprang from ignorance and a lack of understanding. They would have seen the benefits of the *brigadistas* (volunteers in the literacy campaign) and the micro-dams, and been impressed by the programmes to eradicate illiteracy and vastly improve health conditions.

Of course, on my return to Jamaica, I had to address the criticism. At a meeting with various representatives of the travel industry, I pointed out that it was the sovereign right of every independent country to maintain relationships with any country of its choice. In the 1960s the idea of a Republican president visiting China, as Richard Nixon did in 1972, would have been startling. Even then, Jamaicans were innovative and independent-minded enough not to slavishly copy another political system.

The Cubans had left no doubt as to their intention to redevelop their tourist trade. With many modern tourist complexes being built throughout that country, and existing facilities being renovated, Jamaica expected to face formidable competition, and it was in our interest to explore joint marketing ventures with Mexico, Venezuela and Cuba to determine the most profitable and saleable package.

Socialist principles were not inconsistent with tourism, and the country with the greatest tourism growth was Yugoslavia, which had been in the forefront of socialist advance. In Cuba the political philosophy of the government had not prevented the growth of a tourist industry, and one that was fundamentally different from what it used to be during the days of Batista. So, as in our case, their tourism was not predicated on exploiting their citizens or compromising their national pride and dignity. Visitors to Cuba felt safe, they felt welcome, and the quality of what they received was acceptable.

Jamaica and Cuba continued to discuss cooperation in tourism and even looked at the possibility of package tours for tourists from the United States in the event the US government lifted its ban on travel to Cuba. The Jamaica Hotel and Tourist Association endorsed the liberalization of travel to Cuba and we signed a bilateral air transport agreement.

Tourism was only one of the many areas in which the two countries established partnerships. Jamaica's health sector benefited significantly in the 1970s from assistance from Cuba through the many health professionals – doctors, nurses, technicians – who boosted our resources. At that time, too, the opportunity was opened up for Jamaican students to study medicine in Cuba. Today there are hundreds of Cuban-trained doctors serving in our nation's health sector.

Jamaica was privileged to host the Cuban leader in October 1977, when he returned Manley's visit of 1975. He came not by air but by sea. On 17 October a crowd estimated at over a hundred thousand descended on Sam Sharpe Square in Montego Bay to hear the Cuban leader first hand. The people were mesmerized by his oratory, but his rhetoric was measured. He was careful to avoid any statement or single word which the opposition could weaponize.

Fidel Castro spoke with passion on the struggle for liberation and was determined that his visit should reflect a victory by spawning a number of educational institutions which would link Cuba and Jamaica by the disciplines they imparted and the students they taught. It was during this visit that Michael and Fidel agreed on the construction of the José Martí Secondary School in St Catherine; the Garvey Maceo Comprehensive High School in Clarendon; and the G.C. Foster College of Physical Education and Sports, also in St Catherine. Michael went down in the helicopter, so mine was the privilege of travelling with Fidel to Frome on a Jamaica Defence Force fixed-wing plane and to point out during the flight the locations which Fidel himself chose as the best sites for those schools.

Today we are reaping the benefits of these institutions. Year after year, the G.C. Foster College equips each graduating class with a mastery of the techniques and skills that ensure that the outstanding talents in all our infant, primary and secondary schools benefit from trained physical education teachers. Our specialists geared to train athletes are no longer confined to the traditional schools, but also come from the districts and villages where they live. It has, unarguably, contributed to the success and quality of our locally trained athletes on the world scene.

I will never forget being with Fidel Castro, in my role as foreign minister, at his press conference wrapping up that historic visit to Jamaica in 1977. After answering all the questions, he turned to me and gave me a warm *abrazo*. "Thank God my stay is over and I never put a foot wrong, nor made an offensive remark during all of it," the Cuban leader smiled.

The combination of foreign affairs and foreign trade in one ministry in 1976 had allowed me to continue my collaboration with Cuban foreign trade minister Cabrisas in the UN Conference on Trade and Development and the UN Industrial Development Organization and to embark on a close working relationship with *El Canciller* Malmierca in the Non-Aligned Movement.

Our two nations were in the vanguard of the anti-imperialist struggle to liberate those countries which sought to achieve political independence and exercise full sovereignty in the ownership and control of their natural resources. At ministerial meetings in Santiago, Manila, Nairobi, for the UN Conference on Trade and Development or Non-Aligned Movement gatherings of foreign ministers in Algiers, Belgrade or New Delhi, Cuban and Jamaican voices were heard in unison, clamouring for a change in that global order, where the fight for freedom was inextricably linked with the arrogation of economic power.

Jamaica's close ties with Cuba during that period attracted the hostility of the United States. The Cold War was at its height and the United States looked unkindly at relations between Jamaica and a self-declared communist country. The JLP capitalized on this and exploited the communist bogey with tremendous effect.

It was Fidel Castro's decision to confront the racist hordes of South Africa with Cuban troops on the battlefields of Angola that finally brought the abhorrent regime in Pretoria to its knees. Henry Kissinger was disgusted and threatening when, on a tourist visit here, he asked Jamaica to denounce the intervention. Michael Manley bluntly told him no, and earned Kissinger's wrath. We were irrevocably committed to the presence of the Cuban Army in Angola, that heroic force which defeated Jonas Savimbi and repelled the fascist South Africans. No price was too high, no sacrifice too great for the Cuban people as they struck that fatal blow against the evil and pernicious system of apartheid. The name Fidel Castro will be etched in letters of gold in the annals of history for his courage in finally shattering the walls of apartheid.

The Central Intelligence Agency (CIA) was active in Jamaica leading up to the 1980 elections, and pursued a deliberate programme of destabilization. Michael Manley compared the events in Jamaica during those months to the situation in Chile just before Allende's overthrow: "The rampant crisis, insidious, intangible and invisible"; "the enemy advancing in disguise"; "the lack of identifiable enemies or targets" could all have applied to Jamaica at any time from 1976 to 1980".[1]

In response to repeated denials by the United States of any CIA involvement in Jamaica he had this to say: "They deny it to this day, but I prefer the judgements of the heads of the Jamaican security forces at the time. Police, army and special branch concurred that the CIA was actively behind the events. My common sense left me with no option but to agree."[2] The subsequent release of CIA documents reveal irrefutable evidence to concur with this view.

I assert, categorically, that any fallout from our principled relationships with Cuba – local, institutional or global – was never Cuba's fault. At no time whatsoever did Cuba seek to impose or seek to influence us to adopt the Cuban political system or economic model. Time and time again, Fidel Castro and Carlos Rafael Rodríguez would share with me and numerous party delegations how post-revolutionary Cuba was forced to chart its own course following the exodus of its top professional cadres, the hardships it suffered as a result of the US embargo, how the Cubans defeated the Bay of Pigs invasion and the measures they were forced to take thereafter in protection of their sovereignty.

They had taken the path their requirements dictated. They expected us to determine our own course. They entertained no doubt as to our progressive credentials in the fight for liberation and social justice, but respected the inherent differences in our system of parliamentary democracy. Fidel Castro never demanded that we share and apply the same political ideology or construct of the Cuban system. His was a formidable vision of that brotherhood in the Third World, exploited for centuries, which had to be formed as an impregnable bulwark to fulfil the single purpose of making a better life for the poor and disadvantaged people on planet earth. In all the years that followed, Fidel remained irrevocably committed to that single endeavour.

---

1. Michael Manley, *Jamaica: Struggle in the Periphery* (London: Third World Media, 1982), 211.

2. Ibid., 140.

CHAPTER 13
MY PARLIAMENTARY CONSTITUENCY

FOR ANY READER UNFAMILIAR WITH THE INTRICACIES OF the Westminster parliamentary system, it is necessary to explain the critical importance of winning the right to represent the people of a constituency at each election, whether you are the prime minister or the deputy prime minister. Managing it successfully requires close personal attention and a sound organization to maintain solid support.

Managing a constituency 120 miles from Kingston presented several challenges that come with distance. My visits to the constituency, mostly on weekends, were scheduled so that my state or national party-related engagements could be carried out either on the way to or from the constituency, and often in the west. It was important to maintain a political office that was well staffed, fully equipped and properly serviced so that every member of the constituency would be welcome and properly assisted.

The needs of people fall into two broad categories. Most come to the constituency office for help in getting jobs. There are those who need assistance with health-related matters, who may be referred and guided to public facilities. I placed great emphasis on opportunities for education at every level, and all our scholars in my constituency could rely on my full support.

During the first phase of my representation, I had always given great responsibility and authority to my councillors, sometimes to the chagrin of people who were not always happy with the attitudes and responses of particular councillors. We had a close relationship, always working as one team. The one who was generally regarded and often described as "miserable" (a Caribbean expression for one who is overly fussy and nitpicking in all things) was Bob Pinnock. He was not fazed in the least by this description. The two things that stood out most about him were his integrity and his loyalty. He insisted on performance for money spent. When there was a contract in his division, if the contractor did not perform, there would be hell to pay. Whenever he made a request of me and he was not getting the right response quickly enough, he reserved the right to curse and abuse me. But should anybody agree with him on any negative opinion he expressed about me, he would turn on them and spring to my defence, usually asking, "Who authorize you?"

Ralph Anglin, the mayor and constituency secretary, was invaluable. He always followed through and would ensure that in working with me he received a response to matters to do with the constituency. My portfolio, foreign affairs, foreign trade and tourism, entailed frequent and prolonged periods of absence from the constituency. Senator Noel Monteith, vice chairman of the constituency, was a formidable source of strength, especially in presiding over meetings of the constituency committee. These were held religiously once a month, whether I could attend or not. I received full reports on constituency matters; any complaints raised and important matters were all brought to my attention. My treasurer, Hortense Evans, could account for every dollar received and every cent spent.

THE 1980 ELECTIONS

In 1979, we experienced a major disaster in the island. A tropical depression had resulted in rains that caused severe flooding in western Jamaica. Newmarket, a township in my constituency in St Elizabeth, was partially submerged for some six months. I was on my way home, via New York, from a meeting in Geneva when I received a call from Michael instructing me to mobilize what assistance I could through the United Nations before coming home. Having disembarked at the Donald Sangster Airport in Montego Bay on my arrival in Jamaica, I had to go to my constituency by military helicopter. Owing to the flood damage, all one could see when we flew over Darliston were the tops of the telegraph poles. Nothing was visible in between.

While standing at the courthouse in Newmarket one Saturday afternoon, we heard the sound of an engine and looked up, thinking it was a helicopter or small plane; it was a boat on the water coming from Leamington, below the point at which we stood, about eight hundred feet above sea level.

On another occasion, while travelling in a Jamaica Defence Force military helicopter that was delivering food to isolated communities, I nearly lost my life.

One of the districts that nobody had been able to reach was Petersville, so I went in with the military staff to deliver food and medical supplies. As we were leaving, we heard that Beeston Spring, a nearby community, had also been cut off, so I asked the pilot to let us touch down there to see what the situation was like. As we were taking off from Petersville, I saw to my horror that we were heading straight into the electricity transmission lines. I shouted, "Down!" Thanks to the skill and quick reaction of the pilot, Captain Lance Shearer, the helicopter dropped about fifty or sixty feet, thus avoiding the high-powered tension lines. He belonged to a Jamaica Defence Force Air Wing of experienced and capable pilots who, throughout the years, have been of the highest calibre. No matter how bad the weather or treacherous the terrain, a truly impressive team of aviators undertook impossible missions as urgency required.

There was no official disaster-response mechanism in the island then. And it was out of that disaster that people like Franklin McDonald, former executive director of the Natural Resources Conservation Authority, which was later subsumed under the National Environment and Planning Agency, emerged as a leader in disaster-mitigation preparation. Gloria Knight, general manager of the UDC, mobilized all the available resources to assist the recovery programmes. Colonel Trevor MacMillan was seconded by the Jamaica Defence Force to manage the operations in that part of the island. They did a tremendous job.

As part of an extensive rebuilding programme, funds were distributed to citizens in two tranches to repair damaged houses and to help with the recovery. Some of the money became available just when the elections were announced. But, instead of being a boon, it was almost the worst thing that could have happened in some of my stronger areas. Why was this so? Simple enough. Those who got said they had not gotten, and those who did not get – even though they had not suffered any damage – were upset that they had received nothing. Their disaffection was reflected in a number of ballot boxes.

In the 1980 elections, an extensive and well-orchestrated propaganda campaign, with the support of external intelligence, had spread fears about communism. The party had not successfully managed to counter these fears, and I was among those who lost my seat.

During the 1980–83 period, many things seem to have turned on tragic events. Jack Stephenson died in a road accident in his constituency (North St Catherine) near the alumina plant in Ewarton. He was minister of state for tourism, my professional colleague at the Bar and my close personal friend as well. He was an only child and his father, Dr Frank Stephenson, was most distraught and so I had to take charge of organizing Jack's funeral.

Jack had also lost his seat in 1980. While I was making arrangements in his former constituency, many comrades said to me, "Look at how ungrateful the people in Eastern Westmoreland are [for not returning me to Parliament in the elections]; why don't you run in this constituency? We are so much nearer to Kingston."

I gave them two responses: "You all can't talk about ingratitude, because the same thing that the people in Westmoreland did to me is exactly what you did to Jack Stephenson, so you don't have any record of gratitude. But I made a commitment and I am going to honour that commitment. If I return to active politics, I am going back to where I came from – South East Westmoreland." I was pleased to introduce Robert Pickersgill to the people of North West St Catherine for the 1989 elections, and they have held firm since then.

By the time I decided to return, the people in the Whitehouse Housing Scheme, which I had built and where I had lost badly in the 1980 elections, had renamed the main street, without my approval, Patterson Boulevard. From every section of the constituency there was an outpouring of welcome when I announced my decision to remain.

MY CONSTITUENCY

On becoming party president and prime minister in 1992, I explained to the people in my constituency that while I remained their member of Parliament, my responsibilities and obligations as prime minister were not only to them but also to all the other fifty-nine constituencies in the island. They had to understand that my time and attention would be shared. Of course, they were entitled to the benefits of national programmes geared to improve the quality of life for all our people and meet their basic needs for food, health and shelter. I also made clear to them that, contrary to the Jamaican saying "Parson christen him pickney first", they would have to accept that many other constituencies needed my urgent attention, so they would have to share in the general development that was taking place. I emphasized the role they would have to play in community development at the local level and the value of self-help projects and the spirit of self-reliance.

Curtis Evans served in the constituency office to respond directly to the most urgent needs. His sudden death created a yawning gap, but the rest of the team rallied and we continued to move forward.

Another formidable source of strength was Mrs Mavis "Pinkie" Bowers. I could not have run that constituency without her. When I became prime minister, given my tight schedule and foreign travel, driven by Junior Lambert, she went down to the constituency at least once a week to respond to specific issues that needed my personal attention. People soon came to realize that even if they did not see me in person, once they had seen Mrs Bowers they would get the response they needed.

I will never share the view that a member of Parliament should be denied the competence and resources to respond to the needs of constituents, no matter how small. There are some things in any constituency to which the member of Parliament must be able to respond and which the central system will never regard as being of sufficient importance for the national budget. There might be a wall in a community that is going to fall down on somebody's house, or water that needs to be guided through a proper drain but which is flowing along a course that might destroy somebody's house or little plantation. That concept led to our creation of the Constituency Development Fund, which subsequent administrations have substantially expanded.

Such funding programmes have to be well structured: there has to be accountability, and they should not be used for partisan purposes. There should be as much community involvement as possible, especially in social development programmes. In the Lift Up Jamaica Programme, we made sure that the decisions were inclusive, but the political representative should not be denied an input.

The annual constituency conference was always an enjoyable experience. There was, first of all, the private session, confined to delegates and group representatives. What did we do? First, we made sure that the delegates attended, so we had to provide their transport. Second, we allowed them to participate fully in the discussion. There were reports from the constituency about their needs, their organizational structure and what they had achieved. In fact, we developed a healthy rivalry between the councillors as to who could present the report that best represented what was taking place in the divisions.

The public session was the big one, held in the open, and more of a political rally. This was not confined to delegates, but all supporters and friends of the constituency were welcome. The selection of a guest speaker would depend on particular issues of interest to the nation or the constituency – education, agriculture, community development; whatever message you wanted to get across.

The major anxiety we experienced was over the weather. If we tried to hold the session indoors, it was often too packed. When we moved outside, it invariably rained. In accordance with the party's political timetable, the constituency conference would be scheduled for August or September, sometimes coinciding with threats of a hurricane, so we would have to postpone it. But usually, no matter when we decided to have it, there would be rain, which we accepted as a blessing.

My constituency was one of the best-run. I came into the party at the organizational level, not as a bigshot, so I knew the elements of building a sound political organization, and brought those skills to the management of my constituency. When I was party leader, I had an obligation to set high standards so the finger could be pointed at poorly organized constituencies.

Many of the things that needed to be done for the constituency could not be done with public funds and exceeded what my ministerial income would allow. So my constituency, like several others, ran a foundation, Seawest, that arranged fundraising activities and permitted us to contribute to particular areas of educational advancement, creating small enterprises, and community and sports development, to highlight a few areas. Most of the members of the foundation were external to the constituency, but were supportive and helped secure the necessary funds.

Several programmes were implemented under my regime that were geared towards constituency development. There were Lift Up Jamaica (referred to earlier), umbrella organizations like the Sports Development Foundation, and programmes of the Social Development Commission.

When I went in 1970, some ardent JLP supporters in Cairn Curran, one of the districts in my constituency, who had never voted for my predecessor, Maxie Carey, were hostile. In one of his fits of temper, Maxie had told them: "If you want water you have to cut pitch pine!" When I gave them water, everything was hunky-dory. Despite varying political views, you have to treat your constituents well. Some will never change, no matter what you do. But once you treat them well, they will respect you, even if they do not vote for you.

The constituency that I left in 2006 was totally different from the one I had entered in 1970, with regard to the educational facilities, training facilities, the roads, the electrification programme, the telephone system. The advent of the cellular phone made all the difference.

In the hills of New Roads, Kentucky and Content the people are farmers – tomatoes, vegetables, fruits and so on, which they sell within the constituency and as far as Savanna-la-Mar. We boosted that activity. We did a great deal for the fishermen by setting up a fishing complex. The quality of the housing stock was substantially improved. I regard the delivery of water to the hills of Darliston as a fulfilment of Slave Boy's (F.L.B. Evans's) dream and among my most far-reaching accomplishments.

By the time I retired, the main roads had been upgraded and miles of parochial roads asphalted, patched and regularly bushed. Water supplies had been extended and catchment tanks repaired. The Rural Electrification Programme had brought light to all but a few remote areas. Playing fields and sports facilities had been upgraded and competitions were ongoing in football, cricket, volleyball and netball. The Darliston Health Centre had an ambulance and a full-time doctor to cover the centre and visit other clinics.

The proudest legacy of all is what we were able to achieve in building human capital by expanding education and training facilities for the young people of Eastern Westmoreland. This equipped them with the skills for successful engagement in agriculture, small-scale industries, the hospitality trade, home economics, entertainment and the service sector.

At my departure, the constituency had been mobilized to improve its lot by dint of hard work and geared to face the future with the confidence that it is for the youth to shape for their own generation and for posterity.

CHAPTER 14
REFLECTIONS ON THE 1970S

MUCH HAS BEEN SAID ABOUT THE 1970S. There can be no debate about the social gains achieved, but, equally, one has to accept that there were economic and political challenges arising from both external and internal factors. At the beginning of the period, there was a society rife with discrimination, prejudices and inequity.

Among the major problems was the huge deficit in literacy, which led to a severe shortage of skilled personnel to drive the expansion of production and economic growth. One of the first priorities was to improve the nation's human resources. An island-wide literacy campaign was launched under the auspices of the Jamaican Movement for the Advancement of Literacy (JAMAL), established in 1974. A number of non-governmental agencies, church groups and community groups had run adult literacy classes before, but this national effort was unprecedented. It engendered a strong spirit of voluntarism, as people from all walks of life participated, giving classes in community centres, church halls and empty classrooms. It was widely supported by the populace, who wanted its services.

The "free" places available in secondary school more than doubled between 1972 and 1980. We increased tertiary education at the University of the West Indies as well as at the technical level at the College of Arts, Science and Technology, doubling enrolment to over fifteen thousand by 1980. Michael Manley's announcement of free education in 1973 enabled the children of many poor families to benefit from tertiary education. It changed the human-resource landscape, paving the way for a modern nation in which the average Jamaican could contribute to national development in any sphere.

A two-year compulsory placement within various government entities for secondary-school students not going on to university provided technical, vocational and on-the-job training. The young people were placed in the Jamaica

Defence Force, libraries, schools, media houses and ministries. While there was some initial resistance to the National Youth Service, the benefits soon became apparent, as participants were introduced to new fields and many made lifetime careers out of these placements.

The raft of social and industrial legislation which created new equity in the status of women, children and workers was unprecedented. We attacked social inequity at its root by examining the legislation that had subjugated the majority of our population. Oppressive laws were removed from the books and a raft of new ones were introduced to build a just social order. Among the most significant were the Status of Children Act, which gave all children equal rights under the law, whether or not they were born out of wedlock; the Minimum Wage Act, which ensured all workers – particularly domestic workers, who had long been taken advantage of – a basic salary; the Employment (Equal Pay for Men and Women) Act, as acknowledgement of the invaluable role Jamaica's women played in nation-building; and the Maternity Leave Act, which gave all female workers three months' leave, two with full pay, to care for their babies after birth.

The Bureau of Women's Affairs was established in 1975 to address the problems that confronted women, such as high rates of unemployment, and violence against women in various forms such as spousal abuse, rape, incest and sexual harassment. The bureau, led by Beverly Manley, started with a desk run by Lucille Mathurin Mair, and remains an important legacy of the 1970s. We made tremendous strides in changing the status quo in terms of national pride and self-worth. Rex Nettleford described this period as the days of "smadification" – those who were hitherto regarded as nobody had gained recognition, for the first time, as being somebody.

In August 1975, as the impact of spiralling oil prices became more severe and inflation was rising sharply, the government announced several measures, including price controls, stabilization of fees by professional groups, and foreign-exchange controls, and provided incentives to encourage production.

Long before we entered a formal agreement with the IMF, we were being pressured by the lending institutions to introduce wage restraints and freeze allowances. Not surprisingly, there was strong resistance, and any such shift in the pay guideline would require that the unions obtained, in return, some benefit for their membership.

We set out to forge a national consensus. We established an economic stabilization commission, made up of representatives from the private sector, public sector and the trade union movement, to explore ideas on how to stabilize the economy. Out of these meetings, the idea emerged of mobilizing savings on a mass basis and utilizing them to meet one of the most urgent needs of our society – housing.

Negotiations among the chief stakeholders – government, trade unions and employers – were long and, at times, even acrimonious. The final breakthrough came at Jamaica House at a Saturday-afternoon meeting which the prime minister had to turn over to me to complete the tough negotiations, as he was suddenly called away to return to his office upstairs to resolve another pressing aspect of our ongoing discussions with the team from Washington. When Michael returned to the banquet hall, I was privileged to report that we had concluded the deal with the trade unions and the private sector for the establishment of the National Housing Trust.

It was with great enthusiasm that Prime Minister Michael Manley stood up in Parliament on 8 October 1975 to introduce the National Housing Trust to the House of Representatives. He described the initiative as "one of the very great steps forward this country has ever taken". The National Housing Trust would be funded by mandatory contributions from employers, employees and self-employed people between eighteen and sixty-five. Employers were required to contribute 3 per cent of their total wage bill and employees 2 per cent of personal gross earnings. Depending on their job, self-employed people could contribute 2 or 3 per cent of their earnings. In allocating loans, priority would be given to the lowest-paid members of the trust. The National Housing Trust was operational by January 1976 and the first set of Jamaicans to receive benefits was announced in August 1976.

As with any new idea, the concept was not embraced by all and a passionate public debate raged as the pros and cons were examined. However, we had the support of the unions, and the advantages soon became apparent as people started to collect the keys to their homes. Because of the homes the National Housing Trust has provided for thousands of Jamaicans, it remains one of the most outstanding legacies of the 1970s.

On the economic front, we were too heavily dependent on imports. We imported a large percentage of the food we consumed. We imported inputs for all the major industries – building materials, agricultural inputs, fuel, machinery and household appliances. In short, many of our industries relied on imported raw materials, which constrained our ability to compete. Our foreign-exchange earnings were dependent on sugar, bauxite, bananas and, increasingly, tourism.

The first big shock was the increase in oil prices. When oil moved from US$1.70 to US$12 per barrel, it severely affected commodity prices and indeed the entire economic chain. Compounding the effect of the global recession was the significant decline in demand for bauxite and sugar, our main exports. During this global recession, we were tied to a prevailing system and would, inevitably, be affected by the problems that beset it.

We had to seek new solutions. After intensive negotiations led by Mayer Matalon, Pat Rousseau and Alister McIntyre, a new tax regime and mining rights were finalized with the alumina companies. The bauxite levy in 1974 imposed a tax that was charged to companies operating in the bauxite sector. This helped us set up the Capital Development Fund to finance capital and development projects in designated areas. Three institutions were created under the fund: the Jamaica Bauxite Institute, Jamaica Bauxite Mining Limited and the Bauxite and Alumina Trading Company. The Jamaica Bauxite Institute was formed in 1976 as an arm of the Jamaica National Investment Company. Its role was to monitor, evaluate and do research on the bauxite/alumina industry, and to protect the interest of the Jamaican government in the industry. It also provided technical support to the other two institutions.

The requirements of the national budget have forced successive governments to dip into the Capital Development Fund and they have failed to restore the fund to use it for the purposes for which it was originally intended.

The overall contraction in the economy, with limited exports and foreign exchange, caused us to impose exchange-control mechanisms and import restrictions. This led, naturally, to a widespread black market for foreign currency and the over-invoicing of imports and under-invoicing of exports. This severely affected government revenues, which were insufficient to carry out the regular administrative, interventionist and social programmes. This caused a decrease in carrying out government capital works, and when these works were implemented, external assistance had to be sought. During this period, Jamaica also suffered a contraction in foreign assistance from the traditional donors who disagreed with our focus on social programmes. There were, however, other countries, such as Holland and Norway, that were sympathetic to Jamaica's approach to development and helped fill the gap.

We intended to wrest ourselves out of a repressive system and to ensure that our economy would not return to total dependence on the capitalist system.

Perhaps the area which most blatantly demonstrated the inequity in Jamaican society was land tenure. In 1961, the year before independence, 10 per cent of the population owned 64 per cent of the land, a pattern that continued into the 1970s. In an effort to ameliorate this situation, we embarked on a limited agricultural/rural reform programme. This was carried out primarily through Operation Grow, a massive food-production drive to help create food self-sufficiency. The initiative was intended to marry "idle hands with idle lands" and had three components. One saw government farms set up to provide jobs for out-of-work agricultural workers. Hounslow in St Elizabeth was one such farm.

Another initiative was the Land Lease Programme, under which large land-owners were encouraged either to utilize their land for food production or to lease it to small farmers, who were given technical advice, inputs such as fertil-izer, and access to credit. The programme helped more than twenty-three thou-sand farmers to cultivate eighteen thousand hectares. It is estimated that 14 per cent of idle land was redistributed through this programme.

The third aspect of Operation Grow was the Self-Help Programme, which provided loans of up to ten thousand dollars to farmers with between five and twenty-five acres. These loans were available at low rates of interest.

The government was forced to become involved in the management and oper-ation of several areas to ensure the provision of services and products needed to keep the economy operational. The National Commercial Bank was acquired from its former owners, the British-based Barclays Bank. Barclays and other corporate entities such as Cable and Wireless and Tate and Lyle were no longer prepared to continue their local investment and were insisting on implementing policies that would inhibit development.

❧

In 1974 Michael Manley announced the government's philosophy of democratic socialism. He made the case for it as a morally superior vehicle of social organ-ization: "The Socialist believes that every individual . . . is entitled to an oppor-tunity in life and believes that the wider family, that wider community we call the nation, that family that is the nation, owes an opportunity of life with income and security to all its members."

This egalitarian approach, while embraced by the many who had long suf-fered under the yoke of capitalism, earned the wrath and hostility of entrenched groups in business and media and our political opponents.

From the beginning and throughout the 1970s our philosophy of democratic socialism was committed to the concept of the mixed economy, comprising public, private and cooperative societies. But soon after the declaration of this philosophy, fissures within the party became apparent. Allan Isaacs, who joined the cabinet as minister of mining and natural resources, made a public state-ment about his disaffection with the party and alleged the government was going communist.

This was the same Allan Isaacs who in 1967 had been a most vigorous proponent of the party's campaign document espousing democratic socialism, perhaps the most radical of all the party's policy documents in its history. His was not so much a change of heart but a change of standing within the party hierarchy. He had lost his influence and command.

This incident signalled the cracks which soon became more evident in the edifice of the PNP. The unity of the party was damaged and too much of its internal debate and processes became fractious. The rational discourse which was the hallmark of the PNP too often descended into vitriolic exchanges and suspicion of the motives of others who held contending views. Frequently, the differences had more to do with the rhetoric and utterances on issues rather than the substance of policies, to which all of the cabinet and party executive were fully prepared to subscribe. There was genuine support for the policy thrusts and programme initiatives of the Michael Manley administration, but differing approaches as to how they were to be communicated.

The lessons we learned from this scathing experience on the management of the state and political engineering would prove of inestimable value in the 1989–92 Manley administration and mine of 1992–2006. Our reflections on the period helped to create the template for the proper blend of technical competence and political idealism, as well as an inclusionary approach and defusion of conflicts.

By 1979, with an upcoming election, negative responses to democratic socialism had reached fever pitch. The country suffered from the emigration of large numbers of the upper middle class, the business class and the intelligentsia.

Violence and threats to the security of the nation raged and led to a state of emergency. From the date of the declaration of the state of emergency to this day, there are those who have persisted in questioning its legitimacy and wrongly ascribed partisan political motives. They do so by deliberately distorting the clear findings of Chief Justice Kenneth Smith after receiving all the complaints and evidence from affected parties.

I have no intention of re-litigating the issues, but reflect, for the sake of history, on his findings in paragraph 18 of his summary, relating to the allegations of Albert Robinson.

> Evidence given at the enquiry that Mr. Robinson and his activities were not factors in the decision to advise the declaration of the State of Emergency in June 1976 was not challenged and was uncontradicted . . .

Admittedly, the decision to advance the date of the declaration of the state of emergency from June 22 to June 19 was made because of the Albert Robinson affair. He had told lies at Turtle Towers about Dr Duncan and the SDC. The evidence is that it was believed that the lies had been recorded on tape by members of the JLP and it was feared that the contents of the recording might have been published by the JLP at their conference on Saturday June 19. By bringing forward this date of the declaration to coincide with the date of the conference, it was hoped to prevent the damage to the public interest which, it was believed, publication of the false story would cause.[1]

In the concluding section of volume 2, the learned chief justice categorically denies any notion that the declaration was corrupt and made purely for political gain:

> The constitutional authority for advising the declaration of a state of public emergency is vested in the cabinet. The uncontradicted evidence before me was that the Robinson affair influenced the decision to advise the declaration of the 1976 state of public emergency in one respect only, namely, the date on which the declaration should be made. An explanation was given for the decision being influenced in this respect. There was no valid reason before me for doubting this evidence. Though the bringing forward of the date was intended to have a direct effect on the proceedings at the JLP conference being held that same date, the ultimate objective was stated to be for the general public benefit. There is, therefore, no valid ground for finding that the decision of Cabinet was in any sense a corrupt use of authority.

We must not allow the perpetuation of a lie or distort what Chief Justice Smith so correctly decided.

In the 1976 election campaign, the PNP was able to boast about its wide range of major accomplishments. It was best captured in the lyrics composed by a young balladeer, Neville Martin from Lottery, St James. To the strum of his guitar, we first heard "My Leader Born Ya", conveying a message to "those people who no love progress". The crowds went wild as they listened to the lyrics:

---

1. Summary of the *Report of the Commission of Enquiry into Allegations of Corruption in Government; Allegations of Albert Robinson*, volume 11, 487.

Juck them with land lease,
Juck them with the pioneer corps
Juck them with JAMAL
Juck them with free education
Equal pay for women
Juck them with the minimum wage
No bastard no dey again
Everyone lawful
Juck them with the Cuban schools
Juck them with the micro-dams
Juck them with the basic schools
Juck them with housing
Juck them with the Impact Programme

Our opponents could find no answer to our exciting musical campaign as we swept through the hills and valleys, along the highways, the city streets and the dusty country roads of the whole island.

Among the issues we had to tackle head-on was our precarious foreign exchange shortage and the conditions for forging an agreement with the IMF. Our preparations began with some level of intrigue, as our position paper, which was supposed to be a top-secret document, somehow got into the hands of Leader of the Opposition Edward Seaga and was broadcast on a local radio station – RJR – before the government had settled its negotiating stance. Allan Isaacs and his permanent secretary were initially found guilty of breaking the Official Secrets Act and thereby breaching their trust. They were later acquitted on appeal.

As indicated earlier, Jamaica's economy was battered by the global crises that began in 1973 with the increase in oil prices. Our import bill increased despite measures such as price and exchange controls. We had to ensure that the available foreign exchange went towards importing priority items such as food and drugs. In addition, public expenditure had been considerably increased as we invested in education, health and agriculture and tried to stimulate the growth of smaller industries by encouraging the development of small businesses.

It became clear that we would not be able to cover our foreign-exchange expenditure without external help. The country had lost some US$260 million in foreign-exchange reserves and the situation was compounded when foreign concessional loans dried up. This was further aggravated by the loss of export earnings in the tourist (US$22 million), bauxite (US$119 million) and sugar (US$92 million) industries.

One of the first steps under the first IMF agreement in July 1977 was devaluing the dollar and instituting a dual exchange-rate policy, which saw a higher rate imposed on imported items categorized as "non-essential". Other conditions were adopting a more restrictive incomes policy and reducing the fiscal deficit from 18 to 6 per cent.

Despite our valiant attempts at compliance, the IMF suspended the agreement because the net domestic assets of the Bank of Jamaica had exceeded the agreed ceiling by some 2.6 per cent, and this was considered a technical breach. The screws were further tightened and Jamaica had to agree to a 10 per cent devaluation even before any further negotiations began. One condition of the three-year extended fund facility mandated the unification of the dual exchange rate. This actually meant a 47 per cent devaluation on the basic rate that had been applied to basic items, plus a 15 per cent crawling peg devaluation each month over the next twelve months. Other requirements included J$180 million in taxes; removal of price controls; a 15 per cent ceiling on wage increases; ceilings on loans to the public sector; restrictions on the role of the State Trading Corporation; and the promotion of foreign investment and private-sector activity.

We managed to satisfy the IMF in the short term, but the vagaries of the world economy soon took their toll as we grappled with the effects of oil-price increases and international inflation, which pushed up prices generally. During 1979, we had torrential rains, resulting in flood damage that led to a shortfall of some US$20 million in agricultural exports. In addition, we had to put in place J$35 million to cover the cost of rebuilding.

As with all loans, several conditions were attached and these marked the beginning of Jamaica's experience of structural adjustment. This meant that we had to subject ourselves to the dictates of the IMF in terms of the policies we pursued.

The demands made by the IMF contradicted our administration's policies of expenditure on social development, strategies aimed at poverty eradication and increased public-sector involvement in the economy. It called for liberalization and privatization of the economy; increased foreign investment; a decrease in public spending, particularly on social programmes; and further foreign-exchange controls. The discussions within the government and party about the IMF path were laden with tension and disagreement over the prudence and even the necessity of pursuing such a course. The terrible diminishment of our coffers offered us no alternative but to seek external assistance.

Unfortunately, the only route open to us was to approach the IMF, as accessing funds from commercial entities also required the IMF's seal of approval. The discussions became more contentious and the internal divisions went deeper and deeper as the IMF conditions brought increasing hardship for the working classes whose lives we had promised to improve.

The conditions prescribed for Jamaica were based on the IMF's analysis of the Jamaican situation, which concluded that the instability of the country's balance-of-payment situation was due to uncompetitive exports caused by high labour costs; an over-valued exchange rate; printing of money; excessive imports; and state intervention in the economy, resulting in lack of business confidence and flight of capital.

These views were countered by Norman Girvan, then head of the National Planning Agency, who saw in the IMF's diagnosis the implication: "That the root of the problem was the shift in balance of advantage in favour of labour at the expense of capital, and in favour of the public sector at the expense of the private sector, both local and foreign. Thus, behind the concern for 'sound economic management' there lay underlying opposition to the class and ideological content of the PNP government's policies."[2]

The Emergency Production Plan of 1977 was an attempt to find an alternative path to the IMF. We called on the expertise of senior party members and economists at the University of the West Indies, led by Norman Girvan, to weave together policies and programmes that addressed the needs and concerns of the people against the backdrop of the principles of democratic socialism. We hoped that this would be transformed into a course of self-sufficiency and economic independence.

The plan was revolutionary in many ways. It required Jamaicans to change attitudes towards work and consumption and the many taste patterns developed through centuries of colonial indoctrination. In recognition of this, the Ministry of National Mobilization was created in January 1977 to provide the impetus to energize the society to work towards the desired goals.

Among the taste patterns we hoped to change were basic food habits. Slavery and colonialism led to tastes for food that we do not and in fact cannot produce, such as flour, rice, saltfish and sardines. We produce cassava, and yet cassava flour is used in relatively small quantities. It was the aim of the mobilization programme to encourage Jamaicans to eat what we grow and grow what we eat. Our drive for self-sufficiency was criticized, and even ridiculed, by many. So it

---

2. Norman Girvan and Richard Bernal, "The IMF and the Foreclosure of Development Options: The Case of Jamaica" (paper presented at the Second Congress of Third World Economists, Havana, Cuba, 26–30 April 1981).

is quite ironic that three decades later, an almost identical programme is being promoted by many of those who were among our most ardent critics. The concept of self-sufficiency in food, regardless of which party or group promotes the idea, is always deserving of full national support. The same concept was applied to clothing, housing, tourism, manufacturing, construction and so on. There was a place for mobilization in every area of the plan.

Under the Emergency Production Plan the government established the State Trading Corporation under the umbrella of the Trade Administrator's Department. An important component was the mechanism for monitoring and controlling the implementation of the plan – the Emergency Plan Implementation Control Unit – based in the Ministry of National Mobilization. An important initiative was upgrading the National Planning Agency to departmental status as the technical secretariat to the Emergency Plan Implementation Control Unit.

Between December and March, the concentration on the pros and cons of an IMF programme diverted some of the considerable energies which should have been channelled into strengthening our organizational capacity to replace the scurrilous propaganda about a communist takeover. Following a vote by the National Executive Council of the PNP, the cabinet accepted by early 1980 that the IMF was not the way forward, and so in March we discontinued our relationship. But the party and government were unable to recover from the effects of the IMF's structural adjustment programme.

CHAPTER 15
THE TURNING TIDE

THE ECONOMIC CRISES OF THE 1970S DEPLETED the nation's resources. There was a marked deterioration in the terms of trade, and foreign-exchange inflows dropped to such an extent that not even the foreign exchange raised from the bauxite levy could offset the steep increases in the price of oil. The government was forced to resort to a borrowing programme with the IMF.

The World Bank imposed conditions for structural adjustment loans which resulted in deep cuts to social programmes. Economic challenges were intensified by the crawling peg system of the foreign-exchange rates, lifting price controls and introducing wage ceilings.

The shortages of basic food items consumed by the majority of the poor caused considerable hardship. Discontent was mounting. The IMF programme was translated into the slogan: "It's Manley's Fault." A tax increase on gas imposed in 1979 brought the country to boiling point. There were riots across the island over four days and the country was virtually shut down.

Then came the momentous decision by the National Executive Council at a meeting in Ocho Rios to avoid the IMF straitjacket and to pursue a non-IMF path. This led to Michael Manley's announcement that the government would seek a new mandate from the people. The debate was intense and the final vote reflected that the party was split right down the middle. The minister of finance, Eric Bell, and the minister of state for planning, Richard Fletcher, felt they had no option but to resign. Both were quickly recruited by the Inter-American Development Bank.

By the following week, I was on a plane to the Middle East in our efforts to plug the foreign-exchange hole which our departure from the IMF had left. Despite the unfolding of our Emergency Production Plan, there were severe tremors in both the economic and social arena. Michael Manley, Dr D.K. Duncan and I were united in the view that there was no option, in a democracy such as ours, but to seek a new mandate from the people. This led to the prime

minister's decision to hold general elections two years before they were consti-
tutionally due.

The elections could not be held for eight months, as the recently created
Electoral Advisory Committee had not completed an updated voters' list, and the
accompanying regulations were still outstanding.

After the electoral sweep of 1976, the JLP had simply refused to accept that
in the first-past-the-post system, they had gained only thirteen seats to our
forty-six in the House, despite winning 43 per cent of the popular vote, and
wrongly attributed that to dishonest practices. For our part, the government,
through leader of the House Keble Munn, stated that it was "determined to
establish an electoral system in which every citizen can have total trust and
complete confidence".

On 31 October 1978, the House began debate on a private members' motion
brought by Alva Ross, member of Parliament for South East St Mary, deploring
the failure of the Special Select Committee which had been established a year
before to make recommendations on electoral reform. His resolution proposed
that no further by-elections be called under the existing system.

When that motion was defeated, I gave notice of the following resolution:

> Whereas there is need to implement a process of electoral reform as well as
> the need to secure meaningful changes in other vital areas of the country's
> constitution;
>
> Whereas parliamentary democracy is based on the fundamental right of
> people to secure effective representation which requires that by-elections should
> be conducted without undue delay;
>
> BE IT RESOLVED that this House recommends the establishment of a Joint
> Select Committee of both Houses of Parliament consisting of an equal num-
> ber of Members of the Government and of the Opposition with the Speaker as
> Chairman; and that the Terms of Reference of this Committee be to resolve
> the outstanding differences between the Parties and to determine the precise
> form and content of the Constitutional Amendments, both with respect to an
> Electoral Commission and other aspects of constitutional reform;
>
> AND BE IT FURTHER RESOLVED that there should be established in the interim
> an Electoral Committee consisting of 5 Members to be agreed by both Parties
> which shall act as an Advisory Committee to the Minister responsible for elec-
> toral matters;
>
> AND BE IT FURTHER RESOLVED that this Honourable House endorses the need
> to hold by-elections as vacancies occur so as to ensure that the democratic rights
> guaranteed to all Jamaicans under the Constitution are preserved.

It was crafted after a stormy meeting at Jamaica House the previous Sunday night. The relationship between the two leaders, Michael Manley and Edward Seaga, was too tempestuous to achieve agreement and so they both decided that Hugh Shearer and I would lead the teams from the government and the opposition in order to obtain concrete results.

We were able to reach consensus that electoral reform should be part and parcel of constitutional reform, but in the meanwhile other arrangements would have to be found in accordance with existing provisions of our constitution. This led to the creation of the Electoral Advisory Committee, which removed ministerial portfolio responsibility from all electoral matters and required the chief electoral officer to act in accordance with the directions of the committee.

Prime Minister Manley, after announcing his decision to seek a new mandate, sought, by letter of 16 February 1980, a realistic estimate from the Electoral Advisory Committee of the time it would need to put the appropriate machinery in place to honour his undertaking.

In his reply of 25 February, chairman Gladstone Mills expressed the committee's views that the system should contain two features: a photograph as an integral part of the identification card and equipment to identify those who had already voted.

He concluded:

> As regards the time frame, as we have indicated on the basis of the system recommended, it may not be feasible to complete all the relevant processes by October, 1980. Indeed, an estimate suggests early December as a realistic completion date. It is important to emphasize that any delay occurring in any of the processes is likely to affect adversely the timing of the entire system. Further, the effectiveness of any system adopted will depend to a great extent on the effectiveness of the security forces in eradicating or at least minimizing the incidence of violence and intimidation.

On 29 April, the leader of government business, Seymour Mullings, was able to advise that "the Committee considers that these objectives could be met by two mechanisms. The first, by the inclusion of a photograph as an integral part of an identification card both to be completed during the enumeration exercise conducted on a house-to-house basis; the second mechanism would involve the use of equipment which is guaranteed to identify persons who have already voted up to a period of 48 hours after having done so."

The ensuing prolonged period of campaigning was marked by political violence on so vast a scale as to threaten the cohesion of the nation itself. It was the most ferocious that Jamaica had ever witnessed. It was ideological warfare. The JLP, supported heavily by entrenched business interests and the media, created widespread fear that Jamaica was about to go communist. Meanwhile, Seaga was promising that under his renewed leadership "money would jingle in people's pockets".

A few months before the October 1980 elections, all opinion polls pointed to a sweeping victory for the JLP. When Paul Robertson announced at a PNP meeting the results of a survey which indicated that the PNP had only seven safe seats, there were howls of disbelief, as the party held a majority of thirty-four in Parliament.

One Carl Stone poll after another revealed a massive swing against the party which was enough to engulf constituencies with margins like my own. Both Michael and D.K. tried to persuade me to move from South East Westmoreland to a safer constituency in St Andrew that would allow me greater mobility in the national campaign and alleviate the disadvantages of my portfolio, which entailed extensive foreign travel. My preference for a rural constituency and the pledge to my constituents prior to the by-election were sufficient reasons to decline.

When the date of the elections was announced at Sam Sharpe Square, Montego Bay, referring to the size of the crowd, party president Michael Manley proclaimed: "A hundred and twenty thousand strong cannot be wrong." But wrong we were. On election night, only nine PNP candidates escaped the wrath of the people. Until the results began to come in from my own constituency, I still entertained hopes of retaining my own seat. I did not.

After I consoled those in the constituency office, most of whom were weeping, I thanked them for all they had done in the campaign and assured them of my determination to rebuild our political fortunes. I left in a private, unmarked car, driven by my friend Bobby Miller, to escape the anti-PNP demonstrations which had erupted along the route to Montego Bay.

It was difficult to maintain party morale after a disastrous meeting in Spanish Town where attacks of high-powered artillery caused the front line of the party to wonder whether they would get home alive. The murder of our candidate, Roy McGann, in Gordon Town spurred a feeling of despondency among our ranks on the eve of nomination day. I felt it the more severely as Tony Spaulding and I had been the ones who recruited him as a member of the PNP and watched his work as junior minister in the Ministry of National Security.

By nomination day, it was clear that hostile elements were seeking to introduce violence in an otherwise peaceful community. After my own nomination in Darliston, we had gone to lend support to Jim Thompson at his nomination centre in Whithorn. On the way back, our motorcade came under gunfire in the vicinity of the JLP stronghold. The open-top Mercedes Benz, owned and driven by my close friend Milton Weise, was hit by four bullets. We managed to get back safely to our campaign headquarters, where a group of my stalwart supporters sought to convince me that they needed arms to respond and defend. I told them bluntly that they would get nothing like that from me – "not even a slingshot".

At a later date in the campaign, my caravan came under severe gun attack on the road between Albert Town and Warsop. Our security escorts forced us to take cover at several points when gunshots barked from the hills and the corners of the Cockpit Country.

❦

In the sweeping electoral victory of 1976, our defeat in the northern belt of St Andrew revealed that we were losing ground within portions of the professional middle class, which was not dispensable. Certainly, one major strike against us in 1980 was the loss of even more of the middle class.

However, the situation was far more complex. The prevailing economic environment was also an issue. You can have a sound economy and still lose the political battle. But it is always more difficult to win the political battle when the economic engines are sputtering. There was also the business of ideology and the fear whipped up by the JLP and the media in that regard. If people outside had been aware of the vigorous debates within the party to buttress and promote democracy, the fear that we were about to surrender our gains in building a participatory society would have dissipated. The commitment of Michael Manley and the stalwarts of the PNP to democracy was cast in stone.

Whatever our individual opinions on the reasons for our defeat, we appreciated that we had to carry out a thorough analysis of the factors contributing to it. The party's executive created an appraisal committee on 3 November 1980 to investigate the causes of our loss in the recent general elections. The committee, chaired by Paul Robertson, included Paul Burke, Horace Clarke, Omar Davies, Carlyle Dunkley, Norman Girvan, Maxine Henry, Seymour Mullings and Hugh Small. That group, in planning the way forward, undertook to produce analyses of the electoral data and identify the pattern of the swing and examine the party's preparedness for the elections, the role of the security forces, and the electoral system itself. The committee also looked at the JLP campaign and media strategy employed.

Not surprisingly, the reappraisal report concluded that the communist bogey was a major factor motivating voter behaviour. The communist scare and the rapid deterioration of the economic situation after 1977 were fertile ground for the anti-communist propaganda to flourish. The loss of respect and confidence within the security forces made it even more difficult to control crime and violence.

Disunity within the party, which was reflected within the cabinet and government, made it impossible to govern effectively, manage the economy and deal with the mounting challenges to the government's authority. Finally, party workers and supporters became demoralized and this also limited the effectiveness of the PNP's election campaign.

The reappraisal report pointed the way forward, enabling the PNP to transcend the bitter divisions that arose from the debates, allowing them to heal so that the PNP would be the preferred electoral party for 1983 and beyond. The challenge for the future was to regain political power, govern effectively and carry out the PNP's historic mission.

For this to happen, the party had to unite around a clearly articulated and commonly shared ideological position. The leadership had to be exemplary in displaying public and private conduct consistent with that ideological position and in performing in the service of the people. Finally, the party's organization, political education and mobilization activity had to serve as an effective link with the majority classes in the country that formed its natural constituencies.

RATTRAY PATTERSON RATTRAY

When I retired to bed that night of the 1980 defeat, I had given no thought to the next stage of my career. The following morning, after a good sleep, I woke up with an absolute sense of clarity. Thank God I had remained in sound professional standing throughout my ministerial years.

After breakfast, I telephoned Carl Rattray, who had also been an unsuccessful candidate, in South East St Catherine, and told him we would be forming a partnership with Alfred "Freddie" Rattray, who was our ambassador to the United States and the Organization of American States. The moment I hung up, I called Freddie in Washington, DC. Without hesitation, he was ready and eager to join us. He was trained and qualified as an accountant and had practised as a partner in one of our most eminent law firms, Myers, Fletcher and Gordon, before being appointed ambassador. His mastery of intricate corporate affairs was renowned. His political sympathies and allegiance were no secret. Carl and I believed Alfred would be the ideal managing partner and one unlikely to get too fully immersed in the political arena.

In that judgement, we were proved entirely wrong. From the moment he returned home he became totally involved in PNP fundraising, research and recruiting. For a time, he was the most politically energized of the group. He quickly became a member of the executive of the PNP, as well as chairman of its External Affairs Commission.

After a careful search, we rented an office building on Caledonia Avenue. Freddie, the managing partner, ran a tight ship. Mrs Cynthia Small was recruited as the office manager. In effect, she was more like the fourth partner. A company, Patriarch, was formed to manage our business operations, but no partnership agreement was ever prepared or signed by the trio; we operated on the basis of trust and honour.

Carl and I had no intention of returning to the courtroom. We contemplated becoming more involved in arbitration proceedings, drafting pleadings and writing legal opinions. Things did not work out that way.

The Rattray Patterson Rattray office at 13 Caledonia Avenue, in Kingston, opened for business on the second Monday of February 1981. Just as we were about to leave office, thirteen workers who had been fired earlier that day by the government-owned television station, the Jamaica Broadcasting Corporation, descended on our offices and retained us to represent them for wrongful dismissal. We spent the rest of that evening and most of the early Tuesday morning preparing to file an originating summons which sought an ex parte injunction to restrain the corporation from filling the vacancies and a declaration that the contract of service of the dismissed workers still subsisted, as the alleged redundancies were not genuine. Thereafter, any hope of being spared active court appearances was dashed. From then on we were to be involved in a myriad of similar cases. Our legal services were sought in Jamaica and throughout the Caribbean.

The ruling of Chief Justice Kenneth Smith, granting the ex parte injunction, created a legal precedent which was the subject of an appeal by the Jamaica Broadcasting Corporation, and so the hearing of the originating summons was adjourned pending the hearing of the appeal. Mr Justice Theobalds accepted the arguments from Carl and me that the ruling of the Court of Appeal would have a crucial bearing on the final outcome of the substantive issues to be heard in the originating summons. The appeal was heard by president of the court the Honourable Edward Zacca, Mr Justice Kerr and Mr Justice Rowe over five days.

The appeal was dismissed, as the judges held that workers could not be summarily dismissed by way of redundancy from positions which would still subsist in a corporate entity under the disguise of different job descriptions.

That ruling brought to an end the Jamaica Broadcasting Corporation's resistance to our legal claim. The old master and servant relationship had been abolished in law and the Labour Relations and Industrial Relations Act now reigned supreme. With the consent of our clients, who no longer wished to return to the employ of the corporation, we negotiated on their behalf and got financial compensation for their dismissal. Every one of the eleven has since reached positions of eminence in their subsequent professional careers, including one in the law.

There was a heavy stream of clients whose cases required litigation. Some were unions, civil associations and members of the public service who sought redress from government action. On a regular basis, we were in chambers or before the full court. Our frequent appearances before the Industrial Disputes Tribunal often kept us hopping from one panel to another.

There were also many criminal cases, which saw me back in the circuit courts. In Westmoreland, five people were charged for murder, resulting from a dispute over land boundaries on the Leamington property which had been acquired by the government for resettlement of tenants and farmers. I led a successful team of Headley Cunningham, Fred Hamaty and Leonard Greene in securing their acquittal.

Hugh Small and I formed the legal team to represent Michael Manley and R. Carl Rattray, QC, who were defamed by an article written by John Hearne in the *Daily Gleaner*, alleging they knew of the illegal detention and torture of detainees at Up Park Camp. The narrative and intricacies of those two cases will, hopefully, be the subject of detailed legal analysis in due season.

Having been admitted to the Bahamian Bar, I enjoyed once again the stimulating flights of advocacy in the Supreme Court and before commissions of enquiry with counsel from Britain and Australia and the renowned American counsel F. Lee Bailey.

Our vast experience was harnessed through the international consultancy group Interconsults. As president, I assembled a team with the expertise to do a study and advise the ACP on the implications for the group of the membership of Spain, Portugal, Ireland and Greece in the European Union.

The Commonwealth Secretariat procured the services of Carl Rattray and myself as advisors to the Honourable George Price and the Government of Belize in the search for a resolution of the age-old border dispute with Guatemala. Under a technical assistance programme, we worked with the Office of the Parliamentary Counsel and the attorney general to draft a constitution for Belize. We were honoured to be special guests of Prime Minister Price on its first independence day.

RESTORING CONFIDENCE

In 1980 two of our nine seats were won in St Mary by Horace Clarke and Terry Gillette; hence the first meeting of the National Executive Council was held in Highgate, St Mary. The mood was sombre but defiant. The only way to stop the demoralization was to stem the blame game and begin the process of rebuilding and unifying the party.

We started a number of parish dinners, not only to raise funds but to bring comrades together again. Lively discussions about party policy were encouraged at the levels of groups and leadership. It was generally accepted that while we would have to operate within a market economy, our fundamental objective of giving opportunity to the widest cross-section of the people could not be compromised.

After his massive victory (fifty to nine), Seaga might have thought it would be easy to turn things around. Before long, he came to realize that life with the IMF would not be a bed of roses. Despite his being the first head of government to be received by President Reagan after his election, and the sub-sequent creation of the Rockefeller Group to spur investment, the promise of money jingling in people's pockets was not realized, and the euphoria quickly evaporated.

In the referendum of 1961 and the general election of 1962, I had tasted defeat, but nothing compared with the agony of our devastating loss in 1980. Much of the damage had been self-inflicted and we were largely to blame for exposing ourselves to punches and blows which weakened our resistance. The factions within the party were quick to point the finger at each other without accepting that the blame game would not restore our fortunes. Given my dual functions as vice president of the party and deputy prime minister in the government, I had a responsibility to remain engaged until the report of the reappraisal committee was completed, no matter my despondency.

We had launched the thrusts for social engineering in our communities, schools and workplaces to promote self-respect and widen participation by our students, workers and citizenry. We had conferred equal rights on our women and children; provided land for our small farmers; lifted the living standards of household workers and the poorest; exercised the influence and outreach of Jamaica as a sovereign nation.

And yet we were booted from office. Like so many other members of Parliament who had worked to improve the network of schools, clinics, roads, water supplies, housing, in their constituencies – Sydney Pagon, Keith Rhodd, Ruddy Lawson, O.D. Ramtallie, Dr Percy Minott, Desmond Leakey, Winston Jones, Carmen McGregor, Derrick Rochester – I was unceremoniously kicked out by voters in areas where we worked the hardest. It was time for deep introspection and recalibration. I declined to return as a member of the Senate, owing to my strong view that the upper house is not the place for defeated candidates.

❧

When my wife Shirley returned to Guyana for the birth of our son Richard in March 1964, we never intended or contemplated that it would have resulted in our separation. In retrospect, the outcome was predictable. She joined the legal practice of Carter and Martin, linked with chambers led by Forbes Burnham, and, not surprisingly, became increasingly immersed in the politics of the People's National Congress. During my visits to Guyana and hers to Jamaica, along came Sharon in January 1966. We quickly reached and maintained full accord on their care and upbringing in Guyana.

Richard, as he moved from St Stanislaus College in Georgetown, Guyana, and prepared to enter university, had come to live with me while Sharon was completing her O levels at St Rose's High School in Georgetown.

Shirley's sudden passing on 26 June 1982 was a stunning blow to all of us. Richard left immediately and I followed for the funeral in Guyana's National Cultural Centre. I had to bring my daughter home. It was a blessing that the children's maternal grandmother, Anna Bertha Field-Ridley (Moms), came to spend a few months in Jamaica with us to help in the process of a painful loss and the adjustment to a new home and school environment. The hiatus from public office enabled me to devote time and attention to bonding as a single parent with Richard and Sharon.

My return to the law also enabled me to earn an income sufficient to fund my children's higher education, as they had elected to pursue fields of study not then offered by the University of the West Indies.

Among the swirling rumours about the accumulation of wealth by people in political life, it is a cause of great pain when being in office serves to deplete one's previous savings and results in only a trifle when compared to the monetary rewards of professional practice. No one compels a politician to make the sacrifice, but it is hurtful that when you do there are groundless accusations smearing your reputation.

Moreover, I had begun to enjoy the intellectual stimulus of the law and the rewards which success brings the second time around. It was a proud and satisfying day when in 1983 I was admitted to the Inner Bar – Queen's Counsel.

After his libel case had been settled, Michael Manley asked to meet with Carl, Freddie and me. A sumptuous lunch of good food and fine wine was arranged in the conference room at our Caledonia Road offices. We enjoyed it to the fullest and for two hours engaged in humorous banter and friendly conversation on every imaginable topic – except the one for which Michael had come.

As the afternoon wore on, Freddie Rattray spoke: "Michael, I know your purpose. You can depart in peace. It is simple and obvious. P.J. is returning – you will need a good attorney general – and Carl will also come through the Senate, as he will not be running for a seat. I am remaining to manage the firm, but intend from here to give whatever political help is necessary."

Carl and I were flabbergasted. Alfred Rattray had sealed our fate without one word of discussion. Michael was as happy as a lark, thanked our managing partner profusely and dashed through the door to keep his next appointment. We both asked Freddie, "Who gave you the authority?" With his usual broad smile he replied, "The nation needs you both. The firm has to make the sacrifice."

We realized that the die had been cast and we had to get ready for the fray.

CHAPTER 16
THE PEOPLE'S FORUM

IN 1982, THROUGH MY LETTER TO THE PARTY'S PRESIDENT, I had advised the annual conference that I had decide to opt out of the contest for a vice presidency and allow a period of reflection and renewal. In August 1983, Michael and general secretary Paul Robertson came for breakfast at my home to convince me that the time had come to end the sabbatical. I was elected chairman at a meeting of the National Executive Council in Ocho Rios on 9 October by 124 votes to 23 for Paul Burke, the chairman of the PNP Youth Organization (PNPYO).

It had been a stormy interlude during which the ideological tensions threatened to escalate into an unbridgeable divide. The PNPYO had issued a document which warned of exacerbating the internecine warfare by my return to the party's leadership. The PNPYO was properly censured by the council for its refusal to withdraw the document.

My acceptance speech on 9 October 1983 emphasized the imperative of restoring unity and discipline within all the organs and structures of the party: "The time has come to intensify the organising activities of the party and work on the social and economic policies we need to implement when we are called once again to be the government of Jamaica."

By then, disillusion was widespread among the people and cracks were becoming evident in the government. The situation was becoming desperate on the social front and the promised economic miracle had not occurred.

When Maurice Bishop was murdered in Grenada on 25 October 1983, Seaga saw his chance to capitalize on that tragedy. He revived the communist bogey, saying the bloody coup in Grenada was a mirror of what would have happened in Jamaica but for the PNP defeat at the polls three years before. A statement by Paul Robertson, PNP general secretary, calling on him to resign as minister of finance because of poor economic management, was used as his justification for calling general elections.

By then the political stocks of the PNP were soaring so high that we were confident of regaining power, but for an outdated electoral list that would exclude the considerable number of young people who had recently come of age. To hold the snap elections, Seaga was prepared to renege on the solemn agreement between the two parties that no elections should be held until the electoral lists were properly updated. Data from pollster Carl Stone showed that the PNP would win with an electoral list including the young voters who were entitled to be registered, but lose by a narrow margin with the outdated list.

On 27 November, Seaga called snap elections for 27 December 1983.

I chaired the meeting of the National Executive Council on the Sunday night at the East Street office of the National Workers Union. In the midst of loud and constant barking of enemy guns from the surrounding Fletchers' Land, the vote, after long debate, split down the middle, was to reject the Seaga double-cross. To boycott the election was a tough decision, and there were strong views for and against. But once taken, in accordance with the party's democratic principles, the decision was respected by all and the healing swiftly accomplished. The party resolved not to slide down the precipice and a line was drawn in the sand to rule out a dangerous precedent that would have permanently undermined our democratic tradition.

We named representatives for each of the sixty constituencies, but they were ordered not to sign nomination papers. Among them were the likes of Edgar Watson, Clayton Morgan, Horace Dalley, O.D. Ramtallie, Owen Sandeman, Ken Witter, Frank Pringle, Douglas Manley, Ginard Barrett and Manley Bowen. The voters' list included 100,000 people who had either died or migrated, and wrongfully omitted 150,000 young people who were not eligible for the 1980s voters' list. The few independents who ran all lost their deposits and the JLP candidates were returned in all seats.

Our decision was one of the most far-reaching in party history. In these uncharted waters, the party was forced to strengthen its organization and find new ways of communicating with the people outside of Parliament. To resist, within the law and our constitution, the establishment of a one-party state, the People's Forum was born.

Without a voice in Parliament, the party maintained an effective voice in the nation's affairs by organizing itself along the pattern of a formal opposition and assigning specific portfolio responsibilities to individuals. The forum moved from parish to parish to permit wider participation and to be an organ for mobilization. Carl Rattray presided as would the Speaker, and Terry Gillette was the forum coordinator or chief whip. The responsibilities of the spokespersons were to monitor the government's performance; analyse bills, legislation and ministry papers; help develop political options; work closely with various task forces which had been constituted; articulate party positions; and maintain regular contact and dialogue with major organizations and individuals in related sectors. We invited members of the diplomatic corps, the clergy, the trade unions, the private sector, the media, professional organizations and the public at large to attend our sessions, and they responded well.

The PNP also made its presence felt by street activity such as protest marches, demonstrations, night vigils and public meetings.

Jamaica's constitution is based on a bicameral legislature, with clearly prescribed functions for the prime minister and leader of the opposition. The PNP took a firm stand and refused to participate in any sham of naming eight members of the opposition to the Senate, as the constitution requires. This had to be done instead by Seaga, who appointed eight "independent senators".

In all other areas which involved a role for the leader of the opposition, Seaga took the necessary steps to introduce amendments to the constitution and legal provisions which made Michael Manley the unquestioned leader of Her Majesty's opposition.

The first People's Forum took place at the Jamaica Pegasus on 2 February 1984. Held on the first Thursday of every month, the forum was designed to enable the PNP to continue to vigorously represent the broad interests of the people through representation for improved quality of life at the national and community levels; represent and promote the party's point of view on legislation; scrutinize the government's economic and social performance; and assess the state of the economy, cost-of-living concerns and, very importantly, the conditions of the working class. The People's Forum provided the opportunity for the party to interact with the public and for organizations and members of the public to express their views on topical issues.

Michael and I were not assigned any specific portfolio duties, but were expected to address matters of overwhelming national importance, foreign relations and regional affairs. Paul Robertson, a nominated member of the Electoral Advisory Committee, was expected to report at each forum on the ongoing preparations for the local and national elections.

Spokespersons were expected to help develop political options, work closely with the various task forces, articulate party positions and maintain regular contact and dialogue with major organizations and individuals in related sectors.

Organizations such as the church, Press Association, Jamaica Manufacturers' Association, Master Builders Association and members of the media had access to the forum. Through the People's Forum, the voices and viewpoints of the party were heard and articulated with no less force and clarity than would have been the case had the party remained in Parliament. The shadow cabinet met regularly, not merely to consider and pronounce on pressing issues, but also to deliberate on policy papers well prepared by the various task forces as we sought to identify options and modules for our return to office.

The forum called upon the government to heal the wounds inflicted on CARICOM after the Grenada invasion. It was felt that the focus should be on the deepening of the CARICOM market, rather than enlargement, and priority should be given to restoring bridges of diplomatic contact within a true acceptance of ideological pluralism. We proposed the coordination of policy positions in international forums to enable CARICOM states to present a unified and consistent approach in the search for new markets.

The emerging pattern in the 1980s showed a growing impatience with any concept of ideological pluralism and so we strongly deplored "the intrusion of external factors devised to fracture the unity of the Caribbean".

On the eve of our twenty-third anniversary of independence, we were in full flight at the Oceana Hotel. As party chairman, I propounded that there would be no cause for celebration and no money with which to celebrate. Instead of jingling pockets there were gnashing teeth.

I reflected that the bold visions of our founding fathers had been replaced by a spirit of doubt that questioned our own capacity to save ourselves. Our forefathers had been compelled to recognize the physical limitations of slavery – but never accepted it as a necessary, desirable or permanent condition of life. I emphasized that we were in danger of losing our will as a people to survive and of returning to a system which enslaved not merely our bodies but, even more dangerously, our minds.

I spoke of the assault on our institutions, seeking to demoralize our nurses; attempting to humiliate teachers; dividing the church; emasculating the trade unions; and the excessive use of Jamaica's military:

> The conflict between the Government and every single sector and institution in the country can no longer be seen through a narrow focus or in separate compartments. It has not come about by accident but by the deliberate decisions of Mr. Seaga and his supine Cabinet. The intention is to emasculate the Unions, stifle the voices of protest and impose a stranglehold which saps all strength to resist.
>
> It is amazing how muted today are the voices which were so loud five years ago in speaking about the virtues of democracy. Where are the thundering

editorial front pages? Where are the calls from the Private Sector to lock down the country? We hear instead of the need for strong Government. When the Unions demand the right to meet with the Prime Minister and are bluntly refused it is they who are accused of taking the path of confrontation. When the people engage in peaceful protest we hear from the very people who preached the language of overthrow and underthrow of the dangers of political anarchy.

We were all in high spirits as I concluded:

In law, a situation of redundancy exists when an employer ceases to carry on the business for the purposes of which the employer was employing him.

In national life, a situation of redundancy exists when a Government ceases to fulfil the functions for which it exists or to carry out the functions for which it is elected. Using this yardstick, the Government of Eddie Seaga is not just the Government of redundancy – it is also a Government in redundancy.

Abraham Lincoln defined democracy as a Government by the people, of the people, for the people. Seaga defines Government as a system of redundancy, for redundancies and by redundancies. The Government of Edward Seaga is REDUNDANT – it is high time for them to go.

LOCAL-GOVERNMENT ELECTIONS

Local-government elections, having been twice postponed, could no longer be delayed beyond 1986. They turned out to be a referendum on Seaga and the government. By then, he had been forced to break temporarily with the IMF because of its insistence on harsh conditionalities and his own urgent need to craft a budget that could reverse the fall in popular confidence.

He imposed an increase in gas tax. The people were ready. Once again, this decision led to the eruption of riots all over the island. The country was turned upside down and the Seaga administration was forced onto the defensive.

A number of new PNP candidates had been victorious in the local-government elections. The new mayors took charge of the parish councils, but found that the local-government system had been emasculated. New candidates Ben Clare, Calvin Lyn, Manley Bowen, John Junor, E. Ginard Barrett, Carl Marshall, Phyllis Mitchell and others began to gear themselves for the anticipated parliamentary elections. The movement of the political pendulum was unmistakable. The PNP had to prepare for taking office whenever the next general elections were held.

I maintained responsibility for the preparedness of the election machinery as campaign director. I chaired the Commission for Communications and Outreach, which was charged with conveying the party's message to the public and with recruitment of membership. Paul Robertson, as general secretary, anchored the organizing committee. Michael Manley and I had a lot of work to do with the world outside, international institutions and interest groups. We devoted considerable time to examining the structures of government in the light of our previous experience in office and how best to fashion an administration that met the needs of Jamaica's unique needs and psyche.

In September 1988, Hurricane Gilbert struck Jamaica with savage force. It was a full-blown category 4, with howling winds and torrential rains that battered the island from sunrise to nightfall. The Seaga government made restoration a first priority and did a good job on this. It effectively mobilized international support, and we relied on the tradition of our people to cooperate and support each other and the worst-affected communities to, once again, expedite recovery.

The convincing victory of the PNP in the 1986 local-government elections foreshadowed what was to come in the next general elections. The JLP was not about to go down without a fight. But we were not prepared to surrender ground. New energies – Headley Cunningham, Errol Ennis, Dr Karl Blythe, Carl Miller, K.D. Knight, Burchell Whiteman, Derrick Kellier, Easton Douglas, Violet Neilson, Sam Lawrence – were beginning to make their presence felt in constituencies we needed to recover. The campaign momentum had to be maintained and the groundwork prepared for the next PNP administration.

CHAPTER 17
FORWARD TOGETHER AGAIN

NORMAN MANLEY, AFTER A LENGTHY DEBATE AT THE PNP'S annual conference in 1940, declared that the party would become a socialist organization. It was seen as a counter to fascism, which was spreading in Europe as well as in other countries which border the Mediterranean. He said then that "socialism was not a rigid dogma . . . embodied in any finally revealed biblical text". He emphasized that democracy would be the hallmark of the party by virtue of how it organized itself. It would allow all to participate, mainly from the ground up; hence the group structure of the party. Socialism, as outlined by Norman, meant "we would be in the vanguard of our own progress", and as a democratic socialist party, "we would be progressive in our intentions, programmes and policies".

Not all party members shared Norman's perspective of "democratic socialism", and the result was the basis of constant debate and friction. The ideological battle came to a head in 1952, when the party expelled four comrades – Ken Hill, Frank Hill, Arthur Henry and Richard Hart, referred to as the 4Hs – who were deemed to be "communist".

The expulsion of the 4Hs did not halt the progressive thrust of the party. Norman set about developing programmes to uplift the masses. After he cauterized the divisive ideological debates and got the party to agree on a programme of action, the party won the elections in 1955 and 1959. During the period of government from 1955 to 1962, the party never waned in its intentions, but the ideological debates never reached the intensity of the early 1950s.

With Michael Manley at the helm, the PNP won the elections in 1972, and in 1974 its commitment to democratic socialism was once again emphasized. The party embarked on a suite of social reform programmes aimed at expanding social equality: free tuition for education at secondary and tertiary levels; the national minimum wage was introduced; labour laws were changed to bring about equal pay for women; maternity leave was introduced; land reform increased; a national literacy campaign was introduced; and the National Housing Trust was formed. The voting age was lowered from twenty-one to eighteen and student councils were formed.

From his election in 1974 as JLP leader, Edward Seaga decided that he would label Michael Manley and the PNP as communists. His aim was to conflate democratic socialism and communism. The close working relationship the PNP had developed with Cuba was grist for the propaganda mill and we failed to counter it effectively. The Workers Party of Jamaica, a communist party, declared that it would give the PNP "critical support" in its programme of social and economic reform and appeared at times to have infiltrated the PNP.

There was a pushback by the private sector against the party's democratic socialist position, resulting in a loss of productive capacity and an artificial shortage of consumer goods. The increased division within the party led to a loss of valuable leadership time, as we tried to hold it together while preventing its national agenda from being derailed. So a divided PNP lost the 1980 elections.

The party used the 1980s for introspection, while seeking to heal its internal divisions. A series of meetings were organized – including what became known as the "Palace Meetings", a number of meetings and discussions aimed at party unity which took place at the former Palace Theatre in Kingston. It was decided to reactivate political education within the party, and that effort became the centre of the rebuilding efforts. Out of it emerged the Vernon Arnett Party School.

In his budget speech of 22 May 1991, Michael Manley admitted that

> in the 1970s there was an attempt to create a model of development from within our own resources. The attempt tried to put heavy emphasis on self-reliance, which was correct. It involved a very substantial expansion of the state in the economy, in general, and in production, in particular, which turned out to be an error, a mistake. There was an attempt to secure economic justice by an even greater measure of economic regulation, which was a short-term convenience, but a long-term error.

The new world market system had begun to remove any option of an alternative economic model.

As the decade progressed new advances in technology permitted the instant transmission of information. This led to a citizenry that had become far more aware and the demand for state machinery that was far more inclusive, accountable and transparent. These developments had a profound impact on the party.

In light of the fundamental changes internationally, we found that with the dismantling of the East and West ideological praxis, the aims and objectives of the PNP would seek to retain the party's progressive construct, and its policies and programmes would become focused on uplifting the citizens of a more egalitarian society.

In preparation for the next general elections, the party set about rebuilding its organization and mobilizing the people. Returning as campaign director for the victorious team in the 1989 general elections, I took leave from my law practice in October 1988 to devote my time exclusively to ensuring victory. The campaign slogan "We Put People First" found resonance in urban and rural communities alike. After the campaign of 1980, the most vitriolic, violent and murderous Jamaica ever witnessed, I made a solemn pledge to my God and for my country to spare no effort in leadership to remove political warfare as a source or element of criminal violence. It should never be allowed to happen again.

At the beginning of the new administration in 1989, Michael Manley reappointed me deputy prime minister and assigned me responsibilities for development, planning and production. The country was battered by enduring spiralling inflation and the heavy national debt that had been accumulated. The Jamaican economy was "a heavily regulated economy" with price, import and exchange controls; heavy government ownership; and weak infrastructure. The immediate task was to rescue the economy from the inflation and national debt that had been accumulated by the previous administration.

The entire Caribbean region was facing the formidable challenge of finding its rightful place in a new global order of economic liberalization, deregulation and the imminent threats to existing preferential market agreements. With the advent of globalization and the overriding acceptance of the market economy, a new approach was inevitable. Our fixity of purpose, however, never wavered: to achieve equality of opportunity in a society and to use political action to under- write and guarantee social justice.

The world had become a colder, more unfeeling place and the leaders in the global marketplace had become even less tolerant of the idea of making accom- modations for the hardships faced by developing countries. Jamaica now had to compete strictly on the bases of price, quality and service. One of our greatest challenges was reconciling the requirements of a market economy with the party's commitment to equality of opportunity.

The guidelines on which we agreed to operate in the new era of globalization were published in *The Compass*. This party document addressed how we would remain true to our democratic socialist roots, while adopting economic policies and programmes to accommodate the influences of market forces. Authored by the party president, it was the subject of extensive discussion at the level of party groups and then full debate by the executive before it was finally approved by the National Executive Council.

In keeping with these guidelines, it was established that our mandate was to reform and stabilize the economy in pursuit of sustainable growth and focus on developing human capital through education and training. The party, as government, was also to ensure equal access to amenities, expand our physical infrastructure, and maintain law and order, while facilitating equal access to social justice for all the people.

The intention was to pursue greater liberalization to keep in step with global trends, including increased private investment. Regulations and controls would be used to put checks on market activities. The concern was to concentrate on human capital along with economic capital, emphasizing social development as well as economic production. We envisaged a state that was caring and responsible but not paternalistic.

Our economic programmes were predicated on earning our way through production. As minister of development, planning and production, I presented to Parliament on 31 January 1990 measures to address key obstacles in the productive sector and the outlines of a five-year development plan. I announced specific measures which were capable of early implementation and could make an immediate impact – medium- and long-term measures would be addressed in the five-year plan to follow. A national drive for production, coupled with a new, positive approach to the country's economic development, was the only way forward to reduce our dependency in overcoming the mighty odds we faced. I concluded, "To the task, Jamaica – Yes we can." We coined the slogan "Yes We Can" before Barack Obama's presidential run in 2008.

One week after my first cabinet appointment, Sir Egerton Richardson and I had lunch at the Casa Monte Hotel. He had come from his post in Washington to receive instructions from the new administration. He had spotted me, during his previous tenure as financial secretary, as one of Norman Manley's protégés. Among the views he imparted then was one on the essential traits of a minister of finance. He thought highly of David Coore, QC – "a fine intellect and a true gentleman, but far too amicable". He expanded on that: "No matter how brilliant or astute, the minister of finance must not be too pleasant. He must be a mean son of a bitch. When he says no, he must mean no. Even to the prime minister, his boyhood friend, he must not yield. The only person who can be meaner is the financial secretary."

By no stretch of imagination could Seymour "Foggy" Mullings ever fit that unusual job description. He was easily one of the most pleasant and humble people to enter the political field. Indeed, it was the time and keen attention he gave every constituent in South East St Ann which made him one of the nine to survive the political wipeout of 1980.

As the opposition spokesman on finance has to be a member of the House of Representatives, and with the loss of Hugh Small in East Kingston, the choice fell to Seymour Mullings, who undertook those rigorous duties as an able and loyal team player.

When Jamaica failed to clear another IMF hurdle in 1991, Michael Manley was insistent that the situation warranted a new minister of finance. If playing conditions warranted a change of ministry, Seymour St Edward Mullings was prepared to go, but he did not deserve humiliation. So long as he was being replaced by the deputy prime minister, my friend of many years would happily accept the replacement. My respect and admiration for Foggy's devotion to the PNP and his genuine commitment to service contributed heavily to breaking down my resistance. I finally succumbed to Prime Minister Manley's persistent pressure to head a reorganized Ministry of Finance, Planning and Development. Mullings was happy at his return to the Ministry of Agriculture, and the prime minister sent Horace Clarke to the Ministry of Mining and Energy on the transfer of Hugh Small to the Ministry of Industry and Commerce.

In January 1986, the Seaga administration had introduced a number of tax reforms which reversed previous measures of progressive taxation. With the intention of reducing that portion of tax revenue coming from income tax and easing the burden on pay-as-you-earn, a special unit was created in the Ministry of Finance to prepare the way for a value-added tax. It fell to my watch at the Ministry of Finance to implement a regime which would substitute a general consumption tax of 10 per cent for a range of sales, excise and consumption taxes.

To stimulate export, there was zero rating to permit the recovery of tax on earlier stages in production. The thorniest issue was how we could cushion the poor in a new system. I asked my minister of state, Errol Ennis, to preside at meetings of the Joint Select Parliamentary Committee and to engage in the widest consultations at the consumer level. The outcome was a list of exempt items for a basket of basic goods.

The budget for 1991–92 was presented in May, before the settlement of a letter of intent with the IMF to support a standby agreement. It was called "The Opportunity Budget". Why so? I explained in closing the debate that it presented an opportunity for the private sector to expand, as we reduced the public-sector deficit, so as to release more credit for private investment opportunity. We sought to increase production in all sectors of the economy, with special emphasis on export, tourism and agriculture. We stimulated job creation and relevant skills-training opportunities and the urgent improvements necessary in social sectors including education, health, water and shelter. We also opened wider the door for people to participate in the economic building of Jamaica by privatization, rewarding our workers for their labour, and by new programmes that provided a window of hope for our youth – creating an opportunity for all. I continued:

> For 12,000 households to own their own homes within the two-year period 1990–1992 – opportunity.
>
> For rural farmers to get their products to market, access to better roads through the Rural Roads Rehabilitation Project – opportunity.
>
> For improvement in the quality of life of inner-city youth through the implementation of the Socio-Economic Support Programme which will provide training and employment opportunities for a large number of persons;
>
> opportunity for 70,000 persons to receive increased benefits under the Food Stamp Programme;
>
> opportunity for some 6,000 persons currently on Food Stamp Programme to be taken off and given self-supporting grants as a start of productive activities;
>
> opportunity for workers to earn their just share through the removal of wage guidelines;
>
> opportunity for unskilled workers by an increase of the Minimum Wage to $140 for household workers and $160 for other workers;
>
> opportunity for 13,500 pensioners who will benefit from an increase in pension allowance;
>
> opportunity for persons who derive pensions from sources outside of Jamaica to be relieved of income tax;
>
> opportunity for an additional 100,000 students to benefit from the School Lunch Programme;
>
> opportunity for 2,000 children to benefit from a school bus service;
>
> opportunity for 7,000 needy students to benefit from Special Assistance Programme;
>
> opportunity for farmers to produce in the National Production Plan for Food Security;
>
> opportunity for the manufacturing sector by the granting of incentives on special encouragement;

opportunity for an additional 48,000 wage earners to be relieved of Income Tax;

opportunity for the Tourism Sector to have greater access to their foreign exchange receipts;

opportunity for workers in the hospitality industry to be relieved of paying tax on tips received;

opportunity for workers to be exempt from Income Tax for productivity related gains in approved schemes;

opportunity for Jamaicans who introduce foreign currency into Jamaica for productive purposes to repatriate such funds;

opportunity for persons to receive selected drugs or special drugs for special illnesses from special pharmaceutical outlets island-wide;

opportunity for persons who can now import cars, used cars, into the island;
opportunity for persons benefiting under the National Insurance Scheme – some additional 25,000 will benefit for the first time.

In view of what was to come, fate must have ordained how I closed the debate on "The Opportunity Budget".

On whatever side of the House we serve at present, the office that we occupy must be held in sacred trust for the people. It is to them we are accountable. Our democratic system gives no one the prescriptive right to any office.

I will repeat my remark, no one is ordained by some divine right . . . be it prime minister, minister of finance, leader of the opposition, or otherwise.

No party, no leader, no minister, no member of Parliament, should ever forget that the duty to serve comes first. It must, at all times, take precedence over the quest and ambition for power. We who are privileged to serve can only give the best we can. The times ahead are difficult and challenging. We require strength, courage, conviction – purpose for my part: neither personal abuse nor any attempt at political denigration will deter me from seeking to make my contribution, however small, however difficult, to the welfare to the people from whom I spring and of whom I am a part.

It is with a deep sense of humility and a keen awareness of the opportunity which history has afforded that I move for the adoption of the Appropriation Bill, this "Opportunity Budget", which will promote the destiny of the only country to which I have ever pledged and will always owe true allegiance, Jamaica . . . this land of my birth.

CHAPTER 18
I SHALL RETURN

JAMAICA'S HUGE EXTERNAL INDEBTEDNESS OBLIGED US TO SEEK to reschedule those portions which were eligible with our external creditors. The multilateral financial institutions were averse to any rescheduling, and the amounts due to our suppliers and vendors had to be paid on time. We therefore had to focus on the bilateral lenders and commercial banks which together accounted for 58 per cent of the total external debt.

As minister of finance, I led a team of officials from the ministry and the Bank of Jamaica to France, a mission which culminated in an agreement on 19 July 1991 that rescheduled an amount of US$140 million, representing principal and interest payments due by 30 June 1992.

I returned to Jamaica late on 21 July, only to be told that I should go directly to Ocho Rios, as Prime Minister Michael Manley wished to see me urgently before a cabinet retreat at the Ciboney Hotel. It was a mid-year retreat to address a number of burning national issues – the economy, crime, job creation, social policies and plans for physical infrastructure.

As the helicopter landed in the hotel grounds in Ocho Rios, I was ushered to the prime minister's suite, where Paul Robertson, general secretary of the party and a member of the cabinet, was already waiting. Michael greeted me warmly, but even before I had any chance to brief him on the outcome of the Paris Club, he launched directly into the issue foremost on his mind. He reminded us of the two serious health problems he had suffered the previous year – a nearly fatal bout of pneumonia and bronchitis, quickly followed by surgery in New York for cancer of the prostate. The most recent visits to his top-level medical team had disclosed signs of a recurrence of the cancer, and he had made up his mind to have the party select a new leader at the sixty-third annual conference in September, to relieve himself of further stress.

Robertson and I were both shocked at this sudden turn of events. While we both knew and accepted that Michael was likely to go before completing his full five-year term as prime minister, and were well aware of his health concerns, neither of us had anticipated this timing. Despite our attempts to persuade him otherwise, he remained adamant, and then proceeded to explore with us the best scenario for disclosing this decision to the party and the nation.

The party's constitution requires conferences to be held in each constituency before our annual party conference. These are customarily held between August and early September. The party leader's constituency, East Kingston and Port Royal, was always the last, as it was the best way to mobilize good attendance at the public session of the party conference in the National Arena by comrades from the adjacent constituencies.

Michael suggested a change in the customary sequence. He wished to bring his constituency conference forward, as he wanted to make the public announcement there. He suggested that I hold my constituency conference the following Sunday, at which I would launch my own campaign for what he expected would therefore be a smooth transition. We hugged each other, shared a drink, shook hands and pledged not to divulge any of this before the appointed day. Not a whisper was heard during the cabinet retreat. Our two constituency executives never learned the reason for the sudden change of dates, which had already been fixed, for our constituency conferences.

It was the custom for the party leader, chairman and general secretary to meet each Friday morning to discuss party business. After the East Kingston and Port Royal constituency conference, the following Sunday, there could be no turning back. At the outset of our meeting on the second Friday in August, I urged we take one final look. I stated that the party was totally unprepared for this thunderbolt. Throughout the ranks, it would be met with great consternation. The calls for Michael to reconsider would be vociferous and unceasing.

"Once you know you will reverse your position when the party's outcry begins, let us accept here and now that the timing is not propitious. I will be among those asking you to stay."

I made it clear that I would not allow myself to be a victim like Karl Hudson-Phillips in Trinidad and Tobago. He had become a casualty by sticking his head out, only for Eric Williams to recant on his decision to step down. That put paid to Karl's succession plans.

Michael, after Paul intervened in similar vein, was forced to concede that more time was required. "I will agree to postpone my departure this year until annual conference, September 1992, and not one day after," Michael proclaimed. We acquiesced and moved on to the other items on the weekly agenda.

We had to stick to the change from the normal sequence previously agreed, as it was too late to reverse, so his went first and mine followed. We did not disclose why. Both constituency conferences were held in good spirits. The PNP's fifty-third annual conference ended triumphantly, without a hint or murmur of the departure Michael had previously contemplated.

In 1984, Michael had had to have surgery for diverticulitis. It had weakened his physical frame considerably. In 1990, a new diagnosis disclosed prostate cancer and the need for extensive treatment. He was preparing for that when suddenly a severe attack of bronchitis put him in the University Hospital of the West Indies. After a special Sunday meeting of the cabinet to finalize the budget for the 1990–91 fiscal year, I visited him in his private ward to report on the decisions we had taken, only to realize how gravely ill he was. Although barely able to speak, he was resisting advice to seek medical treatment in Florida, as he did "not wish to do anything which could reflect adversely on our own capacity in Jamaica". I asked for a quick assembly of his top-class medical team, led by Professor Owen Morgan. They agreed that he needed early access to the most advanced diagnostic equipment, which was not available here.

Armed with their opinion, I said to the ailing Manley, "You left me in charge. I have decided that you must go abroad for treatment." Michael was visibly relieved. I headed to Jamaica House, with the full support of Paul Robertson, to arrange for him to be transferred to the Miami Heart Hospital in Florida.

The weather that night was awful: thunderstorms and lightning. In order to avoid the turbulence over Cuba, the air ambulance could not take the usual flight path, and took twice the normal time for both legs of the journey. If there was any doubt about how seriously ill he was, that disappeared as I watched Michael allow himself to be lifted and taken to the waiting air ambulance without any protest or resistance. Heather Robinson was the only one who noticed when I turned away to pray.

On reaching home that night, I remained awake until Robert Hart, who had been my Chancellor Hall colleague as a student at the former University College of the West Indies, called to say Michael had arrived "in bad shape but just in time. One hour later and it would be a different story".

When he eventually recovered from that life-threatening illness, he had to build up the strength and resistance for cancer treatment at Sloan Kettering Center in New York. As a consequence, I acted as prime minister for nine months. When he resumed duty as prime minister and party leader, Michael expressed delight and satisfaction with all that had been accomplished during his illness. Our standing in the polls had improved and we were all geared for the next round.

I will never forget the generosity of my cabinet colleagues, who took me for dinner at the then popular Blue Mountain Inn restaurant to express their appreciation of the way I had led the team and guided the affairs of the country during this challenging period.

Among the thorny issues that had come before the cabinet during Michael's illness was one relating to an appeal by Shell for a tax waiver on a cargo of unleaded gasoline it had imported. By then, the cabinet had already decided to allow unleaded petroleum into the domestic market, but the regime had not yet been gazetted and put in place. Shell had picked the starter's gun, and so its application for duty relief was brought to cabinet. After full deliberation, the waiver was approved.

Everything seemed quiet and normal until months later, when a subsequent application for a waiver from Shell was addressed to the prime minister, and copied to me, as minister of finance, and to Horace Clarke, who had by then become the minister of energy. As we were about to start cabinet that Monday morning, Michael pulled us aside and asked for the background of the letter. When we gave it to him, he said, "Now that you have brought me up to speed, P.J. and Horace, you both deal with this." It never appeared on any cabinet agenda, as there was no formal submission before the cabinet on the request from Shell. It was not mentioned by Prime Minister Manley to cabinet that morning and the letter was never an item for cabinet attention. We had no idea what was to ensue.

Acting on Michael's instructions, I convened two meetings with Horace Clarke and the appropriate officers from our two ministries, who examined the implications and agreed that a waiver was appropriate. At the end of the second meeting, Horace Clarke asked for a few days to make sure that all members of the energy sector, including the Petroleum Corporation of Jamaica and the Petrojam Refinery, were fully on board, and said he would thereafter convey the recommendations to me for appropriate tax relief. When I received his letter conveying the requisite support of the Ministry of Energy, I signed the document, in accordance with the authority and format required for the waiver of customs duties by the minister of finance.

In view of the way Michael had referred it to Horace and me, it never occurred to me that it was expected to secure specific cabinet approval. Immediately after signing the waiver, I boarded a plane at the Norman Manley Airport to attend a meeting of Caribbean Development Bank governors in Barbados.

During the week that followed, there were loud rumblings from the chairman of the Petroleum Company of Jamaica, Eli Matalon – and over the weekend, all hell broke loose about the granting of the waiver.

The following Monday morning, Michael hosted breakfast at Jamaica House. Having given him a full and accurate account of all that had happened, I stated my regret at my failure to inform him personally when the matter was settled and explained why neither Horace nor I had expected us to place the application before cabinet for approval. I went further, to say that if he felt there had been an unacceptable error of judgement on my part, my immediate resignation would be available. Michael rejected the offer completely.

By 1991, the PNP had slipped badly in the polls. The economic pressures were negatively affecting our standing. The bold moves to remove foreign-exchange controls and let the market determine exchange movements resulted in a rise in demand, a sudden devaluation and a surge in inflation. Comrade leader Manley called a meeting at the Oceana Hotel to tell us what we already knew: that the PNP was in deep trouble.

It was at this stage that I told him that in view of the danger to our political fortunes, there might be virtue in my taking leave from the cabinet. I indicated that it would also enable me, as party chairman, to work at the national level on restoring our political standing. Since he had already intimated his firm decision to retire at the next party conference in September, I said the interval would also allow me time to put my constituency organization on a sound footing.

I started to relish the prospect of going to the Olympic Games in Barcelona. Michael repeated his desire for me to remain but it soon became obvious to me that there were some palace guards around Michael who were seeking to stoke fire. In cabinet that Monday, there was tension in the air. The numerous meetings which followed – of cabinet, party executive and parliamentary group – only served to widen the gulf.

After countless hours and endless days of debate within the government and party, there was only one way out to avoid further disarray and disintegration. Cabinet members decided to offer our collective resignations to the prime minister and thereby allow him the freedom to choose.

I decided that it would be better for both the government and party to be excluded from consideration for appointment to the new cabinet. That decision was not taken lightly. Many of my relatives and close friends sought to dissuade me; within the party and huge portions of our political support, many were astounded. I was determined to clear my name of any wrongdoing, but to do so in a manner that would keep the party and government intact, as there was nothing to be gained by burning bridges. I would not defend myself to the detriment of the movement, and I therefore confined myself to using only those elements in the arsenal which were critical to my exoneration.

It is significant that a few weeks after my departure, the new cabinet sanctioned the introduction of unleaded petrol to the marketplace and by doing so never breached the terms of the US$30 million that had come from Venezuela, as had been contended by some as the ground on which the waiver should have been refused.

That period was by far the most hurtful and agonizing in my life. The pain was further compounded by the fact that my mother had been confined to bed and was no longer able to speak or respond in her customary way.

In her closing years, I had insisted on moving her from York View to my home in Kingston to ensure she got the best care. She knew it had to be, but she remained stubbornly resistant to the move. She used every device – even dubbing me "Squire" for locking her up in my "castle". She would appeal to all my friends, including Hugh Shearer, to "take her down". She would wait until my close friends, who all adored her, were present to shout, "Mi hungry" – but that only provoked their laughter.

Maybe it was divine reward for her abiding faith and strong political conviction that she was spared from knowing about the destructive forces which were at work to tarnish my name and portray me as disloyal, in stark denial of every value she had nurtured and instilled in me.

For a previously scheduled appointment at the party headquarters on Hope Road, the Mango Tree comrades were there to greet me. This was a group of party stalwarts who met daily under the huge mango tree at party headquarters to express their opinion and pass judgement on everything that transpired in the party. Their approval was treasured and disapproval feared. On my arrival the day after I ceased to be deputy prime minister, they greeted me warmly and expressed the hope that I would not abandon them. It was with confidence and a sense of mission that I announced to the press which had gathered: "I shall return."

So much of the sharp divide and partisan diatribe which followed could have been avoided if my offer and Horace's to go had been accepted at the outset.

On the second Sunday of January, I held a rally in the hills of Darliston for my constituency and a throng of comrades came from Negril to Morant Point in solidarity. My opening salvo came from Psalm 121:1–2, "I will lift up my eyes unto the hills, from whence cometh my help. My help cometh from the Lord, which made heaven and earth."

Easton Douglas was the main speaker, and a majority of the cabinet came to show their support. The resounding response of the huge crowd was clear evidence that at this time of trial and tribulation, perseverance, abiding faith and fervent prayers would see me through as I concluded: "The Lord shall preserve thy going out and thy coming in from this time forth, and even forever more" (Psalm 121:8).

MOTHER'S DEATH

My absence from the cabinet allowed me to spend a great deal of my time in the weeks that followed with my mother. When her condition appeared somewhat stable, her personal physician, Dr Matthew Beaubrun, approved my request to travel.

So I accepted a long-outstanding invitation from Emory University to deliver two lectures to a graduate class on trade and development hurdles and prospects for the Caribbean, in the first week of February. Having done so on Thursday and Friday, I travelled to Miami on the Saturday morning, planning to return home on Monday afternoon.

During the trip, I called every morning and evening to enquire about my mother's condition. Up to the Saturday evening there was no change. For some strange reason, I woke up on the Sunday morning with a compelling urge to catch the afternoon flight. It turned out that she had deteriorated during the night and someone had tried to reach me at the hotel by phone. I never got the message, as I had gone to pick up a few items from a nearby store. But when my household heard that I had cut my stay short, everyone thought I knew.

When I could not get a seat on the direct flight to Kingston, my impulse to come home was so strong that I took the one-stop Air Jamaica flight through Montego Bay. I could not understand why those who had come to meet me were hustling me out of the Norman Manley Airport – until I reached my driveway and heard the heavy breathing from the front room. I rushed inside, kissed my mother and could feel a gentle squeeze when I held her hand. She was waiting for me. Within fifty minutes, she had completed her earthly sojourn. I knelt down in prayer to give thanks to the Almighty for her life and that spiritual force which had brought me home to say my final farewell.

In her last jottings, she had written: "I am blessed with one son for whom

I praise the Lord. I have reached my limited age and now living by grace but praying that God will still guard and guide me to do my part in the best way till it pleases Him to say to me – 'I am ready for you. Your work is now ended. Enter into the joy of your Lord.'"

It is difficult to explain and not easy for people who know nothing about my upbringing and religious faith to understand the extent to which my mother was my compass in life. Throughout my entire life and in perpetuation of her memory, I would never betray the principle of honesty she embedded in me nor allow my integrity to be impugned.

She gradually overcame her disappointment that I had become a minister of government instead of a Baptist minister only because I managed to convince her it was my way of endeavouring to help God's children on earth. Although she had her favourite prospects, I was never quite as successful after my divorce in helping her overcome the disappointment that my marriage to Shirley had ended before death did us part.

To this day, I have always stopped to ponder whether any step I consider taking would make Ina James proud or ashamed. The answer determines whether or not a choice really exists. She taught me never to be afraid to pray for divine guidance in the most agonizing moments of life. As seemingly insurmountable problems came to be solved, her coterie of staunch admirers would often remind me: "It's because your mother is still watching over you from Heaven."

Once my mother had been laid to rest, I was about to embark on a course of activities with a deadline for the annual party conference in September, but by March, Michael's doctors had advised him that the stress was too much and he ought to make an earlier departure, owing to his failing health.

As deputy prime minister and party chairman, he had relied on me greatly for much of the heavy lifting during his final term. Although no longer in cabinet, I was required as a member of Parliament to attend a press conference at Jamaica House for an announcement that Beaches Whitehouse would be built in my constituency of Eastern Westmoreland. On arriving early, I found Michael in a towering rage, hurling one expletive after another and inventing some new ones. It turned out that the night before, the Brown's Town Market on Windward Road, near the asylum, had been bulldozed, destroying the goods of every vendor.

O.D. Ramtallie, Desmond Leakey and Ralph Brown were in the room. "P.J., what am I to do with these [expletive] people you have left me with?" he asked. I knew that none of what happened was the deliberate fault of any of those three ministers, who would have given their lives for Michael Manley. I could not let him go into a press conference in that state of agitation, so I calmly said, "Michael, go back upstairs. We will sort it out."

"Thank you, P.J.," he responded, and stormed out of the room to cool down. And so we did.

Two weeks later, Michael summoned a special meeting of the National Executive Council for 15 March 1992 and told the officers of the party, shortly before entering the main hall of the Jamaica Conference Centre, of his decision to retire. Expressions of gratitude flowed from members of the council at the impending departure of the man who had given such long and distinguished service as the second leader of the PNP. Emotions ran high.

He reminded everyone that the existing policies of the government had been unanimously approved by the party at its annual conference in 1991.

> The leadership contest will not affect the market economy path; will not affect liberalization; will not affect privatization; will not affect our export orientation; will not affect our commitment to tourism; will not affect the programmes of empowerment; will not affect our commitment to CARICOM and regional integration.
>
> What the contest will decide is who, in the opinion of the delegates, is the person to succeed me as leader of the party, but the choice will be between persons who have helped me make all the policies which now guide the actions of the government.

With the compass already clearly set, Portia Simpson and I met with the party leader and general secretary on the morning of 16 March to formally advise that we would be exercising our democratic right to seek the leadership. Guidelines for the election were agreed and we pledged to ensure a contest which would not be to the harm or detriment of the movement. The day of reckoning would be 28 March.

CHAPTER 19
AN APPOINTMENT WITH DESTINY

WHEN I ENTERED THE HALL OF THE CONFERENCE CENTRE, that Sunday morning of 15 March 1992, the prolonged applause and standing ovation of members of the National Executive Council left me overwhelmed and humbled. It was a clear signal from the party that my time had come. I was in no doubt of the eventual outcome. Portia Simpson had not been the original choice of candidate for those who did not support me. She was catapulted into running for the leadership when those who had backed another choice changed their minds about his electability.

My formidable campaign team, led by Carlyle Dunkley, Paul Robertson and Vin Lawrence, got to work. We were ready to roll.

But self-proclaimed pundits postulated that I would be "easy pickings" for Seaga, and some of his designated ministers started to choose their preferred official residences and plan how their offices would be refurbished. Many of my friends from the academic community and savvy pollsters advised me not to contest the internal election. The party was trailing badly in the polls and could not possibly win the next general elections. They feared the fortunes of the PNP were so low that I would be a sacrificial lamb and my tenure as prime minister would be short, as the JLP was bound to win when next we faced the polls. I told them there had never been a clear vacancy before, and it was now or never.

While voting at the special conference would be confined to delegates, the campaign would embrace the entire membership of the party and our traditional supporters. We hit the road and made a direct pitch to mobilize our delegates.

Thirty-seven of forty-five PNP members of Parliament openly expressed their support for me, and so too did all our mayors and chairmen of municipal and parish councils. I received the backing of the National Workers Union and the vast majority of party life members. A meeting of our women, organized by Donna Scott-Mottley, Sonia Gonzalez and Heather Robinson at the Sheraton

Hotel, was overflowing, and reflective of my earlier role in the formation of the women's movement and its growth. Paul Burke, who had twice run against me as party chairman, was unequivocal in his support, as my chairmanship had convinced him of my capacity to bring together the tendencies within the party.

The campaign team took nothing for granted. Horace Clarke, O.T. Williams, Minna Wilmot, Bobby Jones, Ralph Brown, O.D. Ramtallie, Arthur Jones, Marie Atkins and John Junor were among those assigned regional specific duties, and managed to secure the bulk of delegates in a number of seats where the members of Parliament and caretakers followed their own persuasion.

My previous involvement in directing Michael Manley's presidential campaign was invaluable. It is the delegates who matter most.

At the press conference to launch my campaign on 17 March at party headquarters, I pointed to a fundamental difference from the leadership contest in 1969: "In 1969, we had three years to prepare for state power. This time we are not permitted the luxury of a learning curve. We are in midstream. The present and future success of this administration cannot rest with personalities and slogans. It must rest on the ability to successfully implement the policies and programmes consistent with the course on which we have embarked."

We produced a four-page pamphlet, *Appointment with Destiny*, which set out in simple form the issues and factors which would influence the choice of a party leader and prime minister. It mentioned the critical role the PNP had played in cultivating a democratic way of life and the new frontiers it had consistently forged for comprehensive nation-building. The party had set the agenda for universal adult suffrage and self-government leading to independence, and accelerated mass education as a liberating force for individual development, social mobility and economic development.

The manifesto document spelled it out:

> The new Party Leader will inherit a fantastic and rich tradition. At stake was consolidating this mega legacy, this tapestry, a tried and tested formula to build a brighter future.
>
> The Party Leader will be expected to sustain the tradition created by its Founders and so ably entrenched by Michael Manley during his tenure.
>
> The elements of the PNP's VISION for the 1990s into the 21st Century are:
> - The irreversible thrust to Liberalization and the development of a truly competitive economy able to contend in the fast-changing international environment.
> - Social Justice.
> - Human Resource Development.

- Empowerment of the individual for participation in business and the economy and within the context of integrated community development.
- Protection and enhancement of the environment for the benefit of this and generations to come.

P.J. Patterson completely accepts this vision and will strive to implement it.

Among the personal attributes it listed were:

The ability to understand and distill the salient features of our legacy and the raison d'être of our movement in service to the people of Jamaica and the capacity for inspiring the nation.

P.J. Patterson's respect for and contact with the humblest in our land, as well as the economically powerful, the social worker, the cane cutter, the factory or hotel worker, the scientist, the student, the teacher, the farmers, the doctors, the nurses.

P.J Patterson as our Leader, will represent us locally, nationally in regional or international fora. As our standard bearer, the Leader and Prime Minister P.J. Patterson will command respect and be able to treat with persons at all levels.

In the current complex Structural Adjustment Programme, P.J. Patterson has the leadership skills to contend with multi-lateral organizations and treat with bilateral relations and our own broad-based private sector, which includes small, medium and large enterprises.

The position of Prime Minister needs P.J. Patterson's ready grasp of issues and speed of response to urgent imperatives at home and abroad.

The summary concluded:

The job is in the final analysis, a lonely job, colleagues, advisers and well-wishers can be of immense value and support, but in the final analysis with the Leader stops the buck!

The job of Leader and Prime Minister involves a time perspective, a duration of service.

The new Leader will have to see us through the 1994 elections, which will determine whether the PNP is re-elected or returns Jamaica, our Country, to a JLP stewardship under Edward Seaga.

In the attributes cited P.J. Patterson has no equal among all the possible contenders.

My record of performance and accumulated experience pertaining to both the party and the government were there for all to judge. No matter what the detractors said, the PNP was not prepared to deny me the right to take the helm of the party which built the national movement and had never failed to recognize the primacy of our people.

I insisted that the campaign, while vigorous, should be without rancour, and resisted all temptations to respond to personal, scurrilous attacks and attempts by the opposing camp to manipulate delegates. Knowing the circumstances which led to Portia's drafting made me order that anyone who had an ill word to say about her should keep it to themselves, as they would be immediately dismissed from my team if they uttered it. She was a political gem. It was my duty to protect her and ensure that, in due season, her time would come. I knew that the party's fortunes would rest on unity of purpose and vision in order to face the formidable challenges of securing a place in the new global order, and she had a vital role to play.

The contest was keen, but I never doubted the outcome. It was the evening of 28 March 1992, and my opening words from the podium were from Psalm 27:1–2, "The Lord is my light and my salvation; whom shall I fear? The Lord is the strength of my life; of whom shall I be afraid? When the wicked, even mine enemies and my foes, came upon me to eat up my flesh, they stumbled and fell."

The delegates exploded in tumultuous applause and a standing ovation, but I did not continue in that vein. Celebrations were in order, but we had to embrace those who were joyful in victory and yet comfort those who were experiencing the bitter disappointment of defeat. I was now the leader of the party and prime minister designate. As president, mine was the responsibility to lead the process of healing the wounds and mending the broken hearts. It is the winner who must be magnanimous and lead the way to restore unity.

This was a first-time experience for either of our two mainstream parties, as the choice went beyond the party presidency to make me the sixth prime minister of Jamaica. It was to prove a blessing that allowed me to obtain a democratic mandate rather than an automatic passing of the baton.

Before we left the National Arena, Terry Gillette, as chief whip, convened a meeting of the parliamentary group and my unanimous endorsement set the stage for the governor general to be so advised by the outgoing prime minister.

Never before had there been a leadership campaign played out in the full glare of national publicity, complete with paid advertisements and a televised debate between the two candidates. In both groups, those who had supported me and those who had not, were colleagues and friends whom I had known all my political life and with whom I had forged bonds while we worked together in the trenches. I was confident that the democratic tradition we had built would survive the internal rivalry, but it required thoughtful treatment at every step from that moment on.

I outlined the tasks of the party so that the delegates could grasp what was required:

> All of us are witnesses to the next step in the forward march of a party which is proud, which is united, which is jubilant, but most of all, a party that is ready to settle down to hard work. We have come a long way over the past fifty-four years and we have a long way to go. But we cannot get weary yet. We have to build on the foundations laid by those who have gone before us, all who have made a remarkable and outstanding contribution in their time.
>
> We have to carry on the fine tradition of sacrifice, of devotion, of commitment to country, and of impeccable integrity in all aspects of public life. I want you to know that I will give of my best. I do not pretend that I will have magic or instant solutions. I assert that I will be truthful, I will be frank, and I will always keep in step with my party and our people.

We had witnessed a passing of the baton and I showed how the imperatives of our national situation would determine the course of the next leg on which we were about to embark:

> We are a society going through a process of economic transition and social change. It has its difficulties, it has its pains, but it has its possibilities, and there is light at the end of the tunnel if we only have the will to persevere. I face this challenge with confidence, because in the past, the party has proven its capacity to rise to the occasion and provide our country with the leadership that it requires.

From then, I signalled the need for respect and discipline within the party. As leaders, we had to provide that leadership, we had to begin right here among ourselves. We had to command and extend the respect which is necessary for each of us as human beings, irrespective of our station in life. We had to restore a sense of discipline within the society, as no society could survive on indiscipline. I emphasized that discipline ought not to be secured by the slave master's whip or the bullet from any element of our society, but by our respect for each other as individual human beings.

I paid homage to my two predecessors – Norman Washington Manley, who had a genius for building the fundamental institutions on which an independent country must depend; and Michael Manley, who created a process of social liberation and an emancipation of the minds of all Jamaicans which remains an indelible chapter in our history. I acknowledged that following in their footsteps would be challenging. I prayed for the strength, wisdom, and guidance to make me worthy of the trust the party had placed in me.

The first signal that I sent to the party as the new prime minister was by way of the cabinet I appointed, which was essentially the cabinet that Michael Manley had chosen in January. At the King's House swearing-in ceremony, I announced "The team stays in place." The need for unity in the country included unity in the party. "We have just exercised our democratic right within the party and that is now behind us. We have to go forward together, united and strong."

During the campaign I was asked time and time again about the composition of the cabinet, but I decided that was not the right time to answer those questions. "I do not want to keep you in suspense any longer. Insofar as the cabinet is concerned, I can answer in a phrase: the team stays in place," I said.

No one was sacked because he or she had supported another candidate for leadership. The elections were over and we were now operating as one family. Party members who had not supported me in the leadership contest were not victimized.

I paid due tribute to Michael's contribution as "simply unrivalled":

> My very first act as prime minister relates to recognizing the service of my immediate predecessor. He has given leadership in many fields, but in one area I would say that his contribution is simply unrivalled.
>
> Jamaica, under his leadership, was raised to unprecedented international respect and importance. It is, therefore, because of the sterling contribution which Michael Norman Manley has made in this field that I have recommended to the governor general that the Order of Merit for distinguished service in the field of international affairs, be conferred upon him.

I have always been proud of my ethnicity, as a black man, visibly of African descent, who had emerged from a humble rural background through the avenue of education to become prime minister. My elevation to top leadership was seen as an acknowledgement of the validity and strength of African roots in the order of Jamaican society.

But the record will show that at no time did I campaign on the slogan "Black Man Time". I never said that, nor heard it from anyone who was part of the campaign. To have done so would be to destroy the cornerstone on which the party was built. As Norman Manley proclaimed at the Ward Theatre in 1938, on the naming of the party, "National because it insists on the development of Jamaica as a whole – without regard to colour, race, class or creed".

In that same breath, N.W. committed the party I was about to lead as one to "unswervingly aim at all those measures which serve the masses of the country, whose interest must predominate above and beyond all other classes". Hence I had always had a strong belief in opening the door of economic opportunity to wider participation by those who should no longer be impeded by the historic taint of colour. Our national motto says it best – "Out of Many, One People".

A letter I received from the "Burning Spear", Dudley Joseph Thompson, QC, who was by then our ambassador to Nigeria and western Africa, spoke to the historic significance of my mantle:

> Through the ups and downs of your political career, I have never lost faith in you or left your corner. It is truly a great achievement and one which I am proud of for many serious reasons.
>
> As a Pan-africanist writing (in exile) from the Motherland, I can say after half a century in politics, that Marcus Garvey, George Padmore, Kwame Nkrumah and all those I have worked with, would feel good today that a poor, black boy by his own bootstraps, perseverance and ability, have [sic] reached the top of the pile. We know it is an awesome and a lonely spot to occupy, but it is already symbolic that you should make this rendezvous with history. Michael bequeathed us all a great legacy. You will find his a hard act to follow. May God bless him with many years of happy life. He's earned it. We all owe our vision and our dedication to Norman Washington and Michael has not tarnished the image of that great Party.
>
> This is not the time to give advice. Your mail must be flooded with the hundreds who know how to run Jamaica better than you. I will not make such a claim, but suggest the following:
>
> – Keep to your vision. Give thanks to God often for putting you in the position as His instrument to help the poor and depressed.
>
> – Continue to be an outstanding member of your Race, so that those thousands and millions of our children, who will adopt your standards and repeat them meticulously in their own lives, will advance our people.
>
> – Make absolutely sure that no decision you make will bring shame on your son and daughter in this world.

To such wise brotherly counsel, one could only say a loud Amen.

On 15 July 1994, at the end of my luncheon address to the Canadian Club of Toronto, Ambassador Vincent McFarlane came rushing towards to me as I was leaving the platform. The Royal Canadian Mounted Police, not knowing who he was, tried to block him until my nod. He was a former permanent secretary in the Office of the Premier and our first high commissioner to Canada. He then embraced me, sobbing, for a full minute, before saying a word. Then he muttered, "Norman Manley's vision come to pass." I did not know what he was talking about and asked him to explain.

"When you came to see us off at Heathrow after the Independence talks at Lancaster House in 1962, Norman Manley said to us, after the BOAC VC10 had reached cruising height, 'We have just left a future prime minister on the ground.' I am delighted that his prophecy is now reality."

That story meant so much to me. During my worst travail, Norman Manley's constant reminder that "fixity of purpose" was an essential ingredient in political life had encouraged me to stay the course. I felt humbled to have followed the sage advice of my political mentor.

As I took the oath of office for the first time on Monday, 30 March 1992, I told the country:

> Today, after nearly 30 years of independence we are still in search of total national unity. We are still in the quest for developing a sense of national pride; of securing economic development and the spiritual well-being of the nation. In the context of Jamaica today and tomorrow's world the achievement of these goals calls for even greater commitment and compelling sense of urgency.
>
> For, if there is one recurring lesson from the past 30 years of independence, it is, simply, that, "a nation divided against itself cannot stand".
>
> Consciously or unconsciously, it seems that we are all guilty of contributing, even in some small way, to this division in our society – by party, by social class, by religious creed, by economic status, or by accident of colour. Against the reality of these divisions all expressions of national unity become empty rhetoric.
>
> Conscious of the sincerity and the sterling contribution of my predecessors in this high office, I have spent long hours of reflection and I have asked myself, "What difference can I really make? How can I, by example, as well as by precept, help to change our values and attitudes so that we can provide that sense of unity and action which is the only foundation on which national prosperity can be built?
>
> There are many who doubt that one individual can make a difference. Let each of us begin with the man, or woman, in the mirror. Let each of us choose to light a torch rather than curse the darkness. Then we will be well on our way.
>
> For my part, I intend, at all times, to act and speak with the level of dignity and decorum that befits this high office. We should never allow any exigency of partisan competition to lower our standards of expression. As we speak against violence, as we speak against indiscipline, those of us in political life must eschew verbal vulgarity in our political discourse.

I concluded with a vision shared:

> Jamaicans from all walks of life wish to see Progress that is in measurable terms, that is: that our people be able to afford a decent standard of living; that their incomes enable them to bring the prices of their basic necessities within their reach; that they have the prospect of owning their own homes; of getting a transportation system that is reliable and stress-free, and an environment which is sustainable.
>
> I do not believe that it is too much for us to ask a commitment from all of us to speak softly, to restore a sense of decency, to respect the good name of our neighbours, to exercise discipline, and to conduct our affairs based on the Christian principles of loving our neighbours as ourselves.
>
> I hope that during my tenure it will be possible to restore harmony and balance within the nation, as we strengthen our relationships abroad. I also hope that we will work together in ensuring that our country grows resilient, grows strong, and that the beauty which nature has endowed us with, is enjoyed by the people who inherit our country, as we work together for Jamaica – Land we love.

P.J. Patterson graduating from the University College of the West Indies in 1959.
(Patterson collection)

P.J. Patterson arriving at Gordon House on 7 April 1970 to be sworn in as the new member of Parliament for South East Westmoreland. © The Gleaner Co. (Media) Ltd

P.J. Patterson, PNP vice-president; Michael Manley, PNP president; Edna Manley and recently retired PNP president Norman Manley go to cast their votes in the 1969 Kingston and St Andrew municipal elections. (Patterson collection)

Minister of Industry, Tourism and Foreign Trade P.J. Patterson attending his first international assignment at the United Nations Conference on Trade and Development, Santiago, Chile, in April 1972. (Patterson collection)

Minister of Industry, Tourism and Foreign Trade P.J. Patterson on his first visit to Cuba in 1974. (Patterson collection)

Minister of Industry, Tourism and Foreign Trade P.J. Patterson holding a press conference on his return from Cuba in 1976. With him are Adrian Robinson (*left*), director of tourism, and Ben Clare (*far right*), Jamaica's ambassador to Cuba. © The Gleaner Co. (Media) Ltd

Minister of Industry, Tourism and Foreign Trade P.J. Patterson on an official visit to Los Angeles, California, in 1976. (Patterson collection)

Minister of Industry, Tourism and Foreign Trade P.J. Patterson (*right*) handing over copies of the revised laws of Jamaica to Alister McIntyre, secretary general of CARICOM (centre) and Edwin Carrington (*left*), CARICOM's director of trade and integration, April 1976. © The Gleaner Co. (Media) Ltd

Minister of Industry, Tourism and Foreign Trade P.J. Patterson signing the Canada-CARICOM Trade and Economic Cooperation Agreement, 20 January 1979. *From left*: Albert Mathew, Judy Allen, Denis Gregoria de Blais, Basil Pitt. © The Gleaner Co. (Media) Ltd

Minister of Foreign Affairs P.J. Patterson addressing the United Nations, c.1980. (Patterson collection)

P.J. Patterson with supporters at the annual PNP conference of the South East Westmoreland constituency, at Maud McLeod Secondary School, 21 August 1983. © The Gleaner Co. (Media) Ltd

PNP chairman P.J. Patterson with Sam Mahfood (*left*), president of the Private Sector Organisation of Jamaica, at the Jamaica Exporters' Association Conference/Marketplace, Wyndham Hotel, New Kingston, 23 June 1985. *Second from right and far right*: George Morgan and Claude Clarke. © The Gleaner Co. (Media) Ltd

PNP chairman P.J. Patterson (*third left*) speaking to the press on 19 April 1985, at the party headquarters, Old Hope Road. *From left*: Ralph Brown, spokesman on local government; Portia Simpson, vice president; and Paul Robertson, general secretary. © The Gleaner Co. (Media) Ltd

Deputy Prime Minister Patterson with President Nelson Mandela of South Africa during his visit to Jamaica in July 1991. © The Gleaner Co. (Media) Ltd

P.J. Patterson with his children, Richard and Sharon. (Patterson collection)

P.J. Patterson with his mother, Ina Miriamne James. (Patterson collection)

P.J. Patterson making his first budget speech as minister of finance, 10 May 1991, Gordon House. On *his left*, Prime Minister Michael Manley looks on. © The Gleaner Co. (Media) Ltd

PART 2

THE PRIME MINISTERIAL YEARS

CHAPTER 20
TAKING THE REINS

THE PNP'S RETURN TO GOVERNMENT IN 1989 TOOK place amid rumblings within the Eastern Bloc and, as the impending collapse within the Soviet Union itself signalled, a new phase in the Cold War. We were witnessing the end of alternative ideological models and the advent of the market economy as an essential plank of globalization.

This shift paved the way for a new decade when the force to free the economy, with its roots in the Margaret Thatcher–Ronald Reagan axis of power, became the ideological and philosophical guide for the policies of the international financial institutions and their satellites.

From this new direction emerged the Washington Consensus, which established the essential elements of "first-stage policy reform" that all countries should follow to spur economic growth. Any refusal would mean the denial of external financial flow. This neo-liberal view of globalization emphasized the importance of macroeconomic stability and integration into the international economy. The framework included strict criteria for limiting budget deficits. Public expenditure priorities had to move away from subsidies and social amenities towards previously neglected fields with high economic returns. Interest rates should be market-determined and exchange rates should be freed, or at least managed, to induce rapid growth in non-traditional exports. There would be a reduced role for the state.

Like so many other developing countries, there was a fall in Jamaica's human-development indices as a result of profound changes in the global architecture. The global economy in the early 1980s witnessed a major recession which saw the demand for Jamaican exports falling sharply. The bauxite/alumina sector was especially hard hit, with bauxite production falling from 12 million tonnes in 1980 to 7.7 million tonnes in the mid-1980s. The national debt ballooned during the period from "forced credit", as the country financed itself by building up payment arrears. Indeed, the country's net international reserves (NIR) averaged a negative US$489 million per annum between 1980 and 1989. The net reserves reached a low of negative US$807 million in 1983.

Jamaica's per capita GDP performance was weak during most of the 1980s. Using 1980 as the base year at 100, the per capita GDP index rose only marginally to 103.9 by 1989. GDP growth averaged 0.9 per cent per annum during the decade. The last three years saw some recovery of GDP as the price of oil on the world market fell precipitately by approximately 50 per cent from an annual average of US$31.02 per barrel (for the period 1980–85) to an annual average of US$15.70 per barrel between 1986 and 1989. This fall in oil prices was a major factor in the improvement in the economy during the latter part of the decade. This rate of growth was not, however, sufficient to wipe out the decline that had taken place in the earlier part of the decade. As a result, the GDP level at the end of 1989 was barely greater than it was in 1980.

This relatively poor economic performance occurred despite the tremendous diplomatic, political and economic support that was extended to the Edward Seaga administration by the Reagan-led US government. Extensive pressure was applied to the Washington-based multilateral financial institutions (the IMF, World Bank, and the Inter-American Development Bank [IDB]) to assist the Seaga administration. Between 1981 and 1984, the World Bank estimated that Jamaica had received approval of over US$2 billion in concessionary financing from these institutions.[1]

There were also special bilateral arrangements between Jamaica and the United States made to assist the growth of the economy. President Reagan authorized the purchase of 2.23 million tons of Jamaican bauxite for stockpiling. This represented, at the time, a significant injection of cash into the economy to support the balance of payments and to fund the import of crucial goods. There were also special interventions by US private sector–led groups to help jumpstart the Jamaican economy by private foreign investment. These extraordinary efforts failed to drive the economy onto a sustainable growth path. Indeed, Seaga was quoted conceding that "non-traditional exports of vegetables, seafood and apparel" for the years 1983 to 1995 under the Caribbean Basin Initiative arrangement were disappointing.[2]

1. Omar Davies, "An Analysis of the Management of the Jamaican Economy 1972–1985". *Social and Economic Studies* 35, no. 1 (March 1986): 73–109.

2. Patrick Bryan, *Edward Seaga and the Challenges of Modern Jamaica* (Kingston: University of the West Indies Press, 2009), 218.

In addition to the significant economic and financial assistance that Jamaica received from the US and UK governments and the international financial institutions, there were strenuous efforts to reform the Jamaican economy and public sector to achieve greater efficiency and economic growth. The overall effort was, nevertheless, adjudged to have been largely a failure by the US government bureaucracy and the multilateral financial institutions that all had major policy disagreements with the Seaga administration. For many in the bureaucracy of the Reagan administration, the Seaga administration was too statist in its approach to development. The acquisition of the Esso Refinery and the Alcoa Plant ran contrary to their capitalist model. They did not see a sufficiency of effort to break down the so-called socialist infrastructure that had been left in place by Michael Manley from the 1970s.

The Heritage Foundation, the Washington financial institutions and the local private sector all complained that the Seaga administration was not relying on the market enough and that Jamaica was too heavily regulated to be efficient. It was clear that the love affair between the local and international private sectors and Seaga was over after the mid-1980s. The demand of the IMF for a sharp reduction in the size of government and budget deficit resulted in an all-island strike by the labour unions in 1986.

Jamaica entered the 1990s with tremendous social and financial deficits following the lost decade of the 1980s. The "counter-revolution" of the JLP, defined around the slogan "making money jingle in your pocket", was a major disappointment for the majority of Jamaicans. The external historical and structural forces that were at work against small, open and vulnerable economies during the 1980s did not disappear with the change of administration in 1989. In fact, the global economy entered the 1990s in a weakened state. Global GDP growth was only 0.1 per cent in 1991 and 1 per cent in 1992. The unrelenting and disruptive forces of globalization were having a negative impact on both developed and underdeveloped countries.

❧

Assuming the leadership of Jamaica as prime minister in 1992 was a huge challenge but presented a great opportunity to make a difference. However, I was under no illusion about the difficulty of the task of transforming a largely underdeveloped and fractured society into a truly democratic and people-centred nation. The challenges in the economy were truly monumental as the global economy offered limited opportunities. This was made even more so by the unpreparedness of the local private sector to take on the challenges in the global marketplace.

The sector was built on extensive domestic protection going back to the colonial era and which was systematically extended in the post-independence period. Most firms were simply unprepared to face the onslaught of global competition. Yet, with the unrelenting forces of globalization bludgeoning the opening up of domestic markets for multinational corporations, there was not much by way of defence that the Jamaican state could offer. Indeed, the Jamaican state was equally subject to the unrelenting forces of globalization, through the demands of the traditional international financial institutions (the World Bank, IMF, IDB) along with the newly minted World Trade Organization (WTO). Access to resources for formulating national policies was largely based on the notion of adherence to the Washington Consensus. None of the multilateral institutions or any of the Western countries from which we obtained bilateral assistance was prepared to work outside the framework of the Washington Consensus.

The Jamaican government of the 1990s clearly recognized the need for deep reform of the Jamaican economy and society to compete globally. A major difficulty we encountered was the absolute insistence by the international financial institutions on the "one size fits all" approach, regardless of the stage of development of a country or institutional and cultural differences. One of the most egregious instances of its doctrinaire application was the IDB's insistence that small farmers borrowing from the Agricultural Credit Bank of Jamaica should face market interest rates, regardless of the consequences.

In order to stimulate agricultural production and encourage the small rural farmer, Jamaica devised a special programme which would allow a lower rate of interest for the sector. Since it required a special loan from the IDB, I paid a visit to Washington to discuss the rationale for our proposal. In the absence of IDB head Enrique Iglesias, who was abroad, I met with his deputy, an American, James Conrow.

When asked the reason for its rejection, he related the bank's experience in Argentina, where those loans were abused by the large owners of the *latifundia* (estates). He harangued me on the dangers and short-sightedness of the state becoming engaged in developing areas, and when I reminded him of Franklin Roosevelt's successful Tennessee Valley project, he turned as red as a cherry. My retort was: "I will waste no more of your time or mine. I have to catch a flight home from La Guardia."

Too often, valuable programmes and farsighted measures fall victim to myopic institutional doctrine. One of the challenges of managing the Jamaican economy in the early 1990s was the differential impact of globalization on various segments of the population. There were clear winners and losers from the reform of the economy as globalization took effect. Workers in previously protected industries that now had to face international competition were likely to lose, either in terms of jobs or lower real wage growth. In order to counter the harshest features of this new development, we started retraining programmes for new investments by the state and the private sector to improve efficiency. The state also had to pick up some of the slack while the adjustment process worked its way through.

One of the most unfortunate features of the approach of the international financial institutions was their disregard of simultaneously undermining the state and the domestic private sector though exposing them to the tsunami forces of globalization. The local private sector, even at its height, was never capable of facing full-fledged international competition without significant reforms and new investments.

The Jamaican state was itself in need of major reform and restructuring. Indeed, many in Western governments saw the main problem of underdevelopment as being "the government", and argued for a minimalist state as an essential element of the Washington Consensus.

My perspective on this issue was articulated in my first budget speech as prime minister in 1992: "To my mind, what our present resolve to empower our people and to rationalize and maximize their creative and productive capabilities implies is not so much less government but different, efficient and better government."

My budget speech of 1993 further outlined my general position on the role of government. I saw the need for greater clarity and guidance for all elements of the society and to communicate my views to our international partners. I noted that the role of government "is to provide leadership and political management. It is to set macro-economic and socioeconomic goals. It is to develop and implement strategies and programmes that enable us to achieve these goals. It is to inspire our citizens to unite behind all these goals and actively participate in them."

The 1990s was the most extensive period of institutional and policy reforms in Jamaica's post-independence history. To make the economy more globally competitive and modern, it was imperative that we build the modern infrastructure to support production and export. We had to move quickly to modernize our telecommunications network and physical infrastructure to prepare Jamaica for a new economy driven by information technology.

Within a few months, we realized the true depth of the long-standing balance-of-payments problem we had inherited. We discovered that the Bank of Jamaica, without the knowledge or approval of the cabinet, had been engaged since 1988 in the illicit purchase of foreign exchange on the black market, at rates exceeding those published by the central bank. That threatened the credibility of our foreign-exchange system and resulted in major changes at senior levels of the bank's management. A commission of enquiry, chaired by Horace Barber, made sound recommendations to prevent any future recurrence.

Gordon "Butch" Stewart stepped forward to help in stabilizing the rate by offering to sell portions of his tourism earnings at fixed rates. It was a notable and welcome gesture.

My career of serving at the most senior levels in the PNP and the government had equipped me with the technical and political competence to tackle the offices of party president and prime minister.

I attributed the quip of Bruce Golding, then chairman of the JLP, that the PNP had selected "a boy to do a man's job" to an outburst of partisan exuberance which would forever haunt him in the battles to come.

The third president of the party knew full well the awesome expectations of taking the helm after thirty-one years of N.W. Manley as captain and twenty-two years of his son Michael. Despite the changes of time and circumstances, N.W. and Michael had adroitly piloted the ship of state with distinct differences of style and articulation.

I knew full well that comparisons would be unavoidable and so it was necessary to stamp my authority and execute my official and political duties in accordance with my own judgement and style. While commitment, vision and integrity are traits of leadership to be emulated, a true leader is not a mere carbon copy. As Marcus Garvey had written, "Let us not try to be the best or worst of others, but let us make the effort to be the best of ourselves."[3]

Over my career, I had built up considerable knowledge of the business of government and assessing the political tide. In learning how to read the temperature of the country or the mood of a crowd, my teacher was none other than Edna Manley, who had the eye of a great artist. In my earliest campaigns, she

---

3. Amy Jacques Garvey, comp., *Philosophy and Opinions of Marcus Garvey, or Africa for the Africans*, 2nd ed. (London: Routledge, 2006), 24.

would call me to her side on the platform and would identify who would follow N.W. to the end and who was hostile, and point out who was listening but did not understand, or who was hearing but not accepting. I understood the value of being firm and settled in purpose, and this was best done by engaging the analytical mind and clearly articulating a steady vision in a sober tone.

The decision to keep in place the cabinet I inherited was mine alone. Unity was imperative. I assured Portia Simpson that my respect and deep affection for her was in no way impaired by our contest for party leadership. She deserved full support in being completely equipped for the next leg of our journey. Roger Clarke was immediately assigned the responsibility for the divestment of sugar lands to the cane-farming groups when huge tracts of state property became available.

The member of Parliament for South West St Elizabeth, Danny Buchanan, had adopted tactics that would prevent delegates from his constituency support-ing me in the presidential election, obviously forgetting that this was a constitu-ency where I had cut my teeth as an organizer. Later, the delegates accepted him for the next general elections only after I told them in a meeting in Black River that he was needed in my team for the future and pleaded for his return as the PNP candidate. His loyalty and splendid ministerial contribution paid back for my intercession in rich abundance. Donald Buchanan became an invaluable member of my team and was always there to watch my back. He was a formi-dable foe to the opposition in every parliamentary encounter. I asked Horace Clarke to concentrate his vast political acumen for the succeeding months in St Mary, Portland and St Thomas and restored him to the cabinet after our victory in the 1993 campaign.

New energies were recruited for my team at the Office of the Prime Minister and the statutory boards as Vin Lawrence, Kingsley Thomas, Nathan Richards, Maureen Vernon, Jacqueline DaCosta, Arnoldo Ventura and Raymond Reece all came aboard from the Ministry of Development Planning and Production. We revved up the communication team with Ralston Smith, Monica Campbell, Daphne Innerarity and Colin Campbell. Arnold Bertram and Maxine Henry-Wilson were among those who returned to the political frontline.

For my first meeting on 6 April, the Reverend Maitland Evans was invited to deliver a short spiritual exhortation, a reading from the scriptures and prayers. Listed on that agenda was a cabinet submission from the Ministry of the Public Service and Information in connection with a proposed increase in pension, the provision of support staff and other benefits for retired prime ministers and surviving spouses. The proposals, dated 3 March, which had been settled during my absence from the cabinet, sought approval to upgrade the prime minster's pension to the same level as his or her salary from time to time and provide a housing allowance equivalent to that payable to ministers. The cabinet approved and ordered that the chief parliamentary counsel should be instructed to draft the necessary amending legislation.

I had no reason to believe that the cabinet decision was never enacted by Parliament, as both retired prime ministers (Hugh Shearer and Michael Manley) had begun to receive the increased emoluments. It was eleven years later that I discovered that this change had slipped between the cracks, as that section of the Ministry of the Public Service, which had been merged with the Ministry of Finance, had never in fact sought the appropriate amendments to the Pension (Prime Minister) Act. The payments had been made by the legislature, with the authority of the Ministry of Finance, through additional funds which it had specifically provided for this purpose throughout succeeding years.

Neither Michael nor Hugh was married in April 1972 and when they did get married, to Glynne and Denise respectively, the provisions for surviving spouses would not have applied, as the existing law was confined to wives of incumbent prime ministers. Cabinet approved an amendment to entitle surviving spouses at the time of death of former prime ministers to receive pension benefits, whether or not they had been married during their tenure. When the bill was returned for cabinet to sanction parliamentary presentation, I was surprised to see that the Memorandum of Objects also included those which the cabinet had passed in April 1992, relating to the prime minister. Although it would have been unusual, I thought chief parliamentary counsel had on this solitary occasion made a mistake by including them. Seaga had also retired by then. My check with the clerk of the legislature, Heather Cooke, confirmed that the amendment had never been laid in either House and would therefore have to form part of the Bill to Amend.

This chronology will, I hope, put to rest any suggestion that the cabinet decided in late 2005 to increase former prime ministers' pensions because of my impending retirement in March 2006. Anyone who visits the recommendations of the prior Oliver Clarke Report on Parliamentary Salaries will realize that the differential stipulated between the salary of the prime minister and that of other cabinet ministers is predicated on the full pension attached to the office.

CHAPTER 21
THE GOVERNMENT

IN MARCH 1992, WHEN I ASSUMED THE LEADERSHIP of the party and the nation, the JLP was ahead in the polls. Spearheaded by the Ministry of Development, Planning and Production, the administration had begun to take the bold steps necessary to ensure our survival and find our rightful place in the strange new territory of economic liberalization and deregulation. By October 1992, the PNP had reversed the situation, taking over the lead and maintaining it until the general elections six months later.

A year afterwards, highly respected pollster Carl Stone remarked to me, in a private conversation at the prime minister's residence, Vale Royal, "I have never seen the pendulum swing like this before."

What had made this possible? I regard dialogue and adequate consultation as primary instruments of policy. The Live and Direct programme facilitated a close connection between people and their communities and allowed us to explain the policies; we were also able to reveal an impressive list of achievements that had made a noticeable and positive difference in the lives of our people by identifying the priority areas and pushing programmes on which we had embarked in a convincing way.

On 15 December, Michael Manley penned a letter which said everything:

My Dear PJ,

I am writing you at this time for reasons that will, I hope, become clear as you read it. It is a sheer coincidence that the letter follows your appointment to the Privy Council by a day and your poll results by about a fortnight. Nonetheless, my congratulations on the first and heartfelt bravo on the second!

I really write personally and would have done so if the Privy Council had not come through yet and if the poll had been more modest.

I regretted at the time the fact that three people who were close to me had opted to support Portia – not because of their decision but lest the number seemed too large to seem coincidental. I myself developed a genuine "neutrality of the mind" because I felt it to be my duty and because such is my nature if I once feel there is a clear path of duty.

I realized that you would probably have the detachment to understand that but doubted whether all the people close to you could do the same.

Be that as it may, you won and I felt there was a great historical justice in the outcome. I then settled down to be quietly supportive and to watch with genuine and, believe me, warm interest to see how you would tackle the transition, which was one question, and the job itself, which was another.

I want you to know I think you have done both superbly well. I say this as a sort of end of year comment based upon careful observation and analysis.

From the outset the touch of declaring your assets publicly and making integrity a central theme was inspired. The country thirsts for it – don't let up for an instant.

"Live and Direct" was a marvellous combination of the images of the contemporary culture, opportunity to "get to know" people, and the chance to listen and be heard. Add to all this, the calm style and judicious approach and you have created a complete image which will be sustained because it builds upon a truth of your personality. Incidentally, I have very much appreciated the courtesy with which my own departure has been handled.

Looking to the future, two comments may be obvious, but must be made. Next year is the one where the tough decisions will come to be made and the ugly and the unexpected will happen. I know you will be strong where you have to be and cool while you arrive at your decisions – as if you don't know!

Secondly, you have set a hell of a pace because you had to. But remember that the body has its limits. They vary with the individual but the limits are there. Learn to listen to the signals that tell you how to avoid those limits. I ignored them all my life and had to watch my body almost fall apart after 1984. I am sure you are tougher but still I sound the gentle caution.

Well – it's been a long journey from our safari in 1969. It has had its ups and downs. But the respect has never varied and the friendship never waned.

Good luck and God bless.

Warmly

Michael

I was overcome with emotion, and my tears flowed in solitude. We had indeed come a long way from our earliest acquaintance, when "Young Boy Michael" drove at frightening speed in the Studebaker sedan to address the sugar workers at Appleton Estate during my organizing stint in St Elizabeth. Politics apart, we shared a passion for music, sports and art. On so many occasions when we were seen in public apparently in earnest conversation, the fortunes of the West Indies cricket team or the performance of our athletes was the subject. Our five-nation visit to Nigeria, Ghana, Kenya, Tanzania and Ethiopia in 1969 had brought us close enough to confide in each other on intensely personal affairs. We had, indeed, gone through together the ups and downs which are features of political life. Whatever the issue, party organization, political strategy, national priorities, external policies, we were interlocked. He was the captain of the team and I knew I had to respect his call even when mine might have been different.

I never forgot Norman Manley's words when he launched the PNP: "The Party will be modelled on strictly democratic lines. With regard to every person who joins this Party he pledges himself to abide by and be loyal and faithful to the aims and objects of this Party."[1]

At all times, whether as vice president or chairman, I was prepared to stand up and fight internally to execute the purpose of the party and to help build our nation as a whole. Once a decision was made by the party in accordance with the democratic process, I was prepared not only to abide by it, but to insist on its enforcement. In that space, there is no room for intrigue. Personal ambitions had to be subordinated to loyalty for the national good.

Over thirty years of independence, Jamaicans had become more comfortable and self-assured in dealing with race, colour and class. They saw my elevation to top leadership as an acknowledgement of the validity and strength of African roots in the order of Jamaican society.

The party's official campaign slogan for the 1993 general elections, "The Best Choice", was based on its actual achievements and sound plans for the future. Jamaicans presented the PNP with 59.4 per cent of the popular vote and fifty-two of the sixty parliamentary seats. It was a record-breaking victory, with the largest ever majority in any Jamaican general elections.

The campaign focused on the economic issues. Fixing them remained the first item on our agenda for change. The government had inherited an unstable economy in 1989, one that was fraught with problems, but had been able to demonstrate by performance and intention the ability to take Jamaica out of the economic wilderness.

---

1. N.W. Manley, *Manley and the New Jamaica: Selected Speeches and Writings 1938–1968*, ed. Rex Nettleford (Kingston: Longman Caribbean, 1971), 17.

Despite the economic constraints, we managed throughout the life of my administration to produce positive results. With Omar Davies as minister of finance and planning, Shirley Tyndall as financial secretary and Derrick Lattibeaudiere at the Bank of Jamaica, we attained tight fiscal control and adjusted domestic interest rates, completing the Extended Fund Facility, passing twelve consecutive quarterly IMF tests between 1993 and 1996 and ending Jamaica's eighteen-year borrowing relationship with the IMF in 1995. We won the argument that our next step should be our own macroeconomic programme so that it would be responsive to domestic challenges. Particularly satisfying was the approval of the staff-monitored programme by the IMF, the World Bank and the IDB, which opened the way for the country to access private international capital markets.

We invested heavily in infrastructure – modernizing highways, seaports and airports – and restructuring the financial sector, laying foundations for the greatest period of investment since the 1960s in tourism, mining, and information and communication technology.

The *Economist* (27 March 1993, 47) noted: "Patterson draws support not only from the poor, but also from the rapidly expanding class of entrepreneurs and small investors who, in a booming stock market, have done well from his Government's version of popular capitalism." I was somewhat amused by the reference to me in the magazine as "a reticent man in a loud-mouthed country". What I really wanted to be was a respected leader who would successfully lead my country into the new millennium, well equipped to take advantage of all it had to offer. I was determined to ensure optimal national participation in policymaking and to take the heat out of the system by a non-confrontational style of leadership. The *Economist* called it a "consultative brand" of politics, in contrast to the rough-and-tumble style of past Jamaican leadership.

In the foreword of our party manifesto for the 1997 elections, *For a Better Quality of Life in the New Millennium*, we painted a picture of the Jamaica I desired: "a society with positive values and attitudes, which is gentler, kinder, well informed, productive and equipped to earn its way in the global marketplace". The party emphasized the need for a consensual approach to nation-building and promised that the PNP would create a caring society; a proud and disciplined society; a fair and safe society; a productive society; and, above all, a quality society.

Seized with the importance of having and articulating a clear vision, the party published an agenda paper, the fourth in a series, entitled "Twenty-First Century Mission", in 2000.

The drafting committee, chaired by the vice president, Peter Phillips, was instructed to help our movement chart the course for its timeless objectives of empowerment and social justice in the face of the epochal changes taking place in global alignments and the world economy. I wrote in the foreword:

> With each passing day, we remain convinced that political modernization and total national development require the focus of our collective intelligence, translated into positive action, so as to realize the intrinsic worth of every Jamaican, at home or abroad.
>
> The dawn of the new millennium imposes a historical obligation on the P.N.P., a Party of destiny, to undertake a critical analysis of the prevailing environment – domestic and external; to evaluate existing policies, programmes and political approaches. This is essential in a world where change is the only constant. . . .
>
> Ours is a history from which we can draw inspiration, derive courage and fortitude to face the future.
>
> But it is clear that as we go forward, we must remain true to our historic role as the social conscience of the nation and the defender of the rights of citizens.
>
> We must re-commit ourselves to relentlessly pursue the cause of greater social equity and seek to create more opportunities for the upliftment of our people.

MICHAEL MANLEY'S DEATH

The morning after Boxing Day in 1996, I visited Michael at home, and despite his valiant attempt to be his usual buoyant self, it was clear that his health had suffered a sharp decline.

There was not a single word on politics; our conversation was largely about sports and the ongoing West Indies cricket tour of Australia, in great detail.

His wife Glynne relayed to me the advice of the medical team that arranged visits by representative groups would impose an undue strain on Michael and impede his recovery. I was asked to relay his personal love and sincere gratitude to all his fellow warriors and well-wishers, who were disappointed, but understood that their quiet thought and prayer would be the best way of conveying their love and support at this difficult time for the family.

I was awakened by a telephone call in the early morning of 6 March 1997 and drove myself to Wishaw Drive before the undertaker had arrived. By eight o'clock in the morning I had convened a meeting to put in place all the arrangements for a national period of mourning and appointed the membership of the group, under my immediate supervision, to plan a state funeral.

The huge crowd outside and the vast congregation inside the Holy Trinity Cathedral on North Street, Kingston, erupted in deafening applause when Fidel Castro arrived to join the impressive list of foreign dignitaries. No security threat could prevent him walking to the National Heroes Park for the interment. I closed the remembrance to my comrade, my brother and my friend with the solemn pledge: "The flame you have entrusted to us will never be allowed to flicker, nor to die."

Michael's daughter Rachel sent me the following after his funeral:

March 19th 97

My dear P.J.,

My Bible with its precious greeting from you now resides beside my bed. I am grateful for it, and for the faithful friendship that it represents.

You have been the kindest, the most thoughtful friend to myself and the family. Below all of my own efforts to survive the recent emotions engendered during the last six months . . . the vivid horror of Daddy's terrible illness, the poignant and redemptive personal exchanges . . . the simple humanity of his death and the awful subsequent sense of loss that I almost seemed to have felt before he actually went . . . below all this I have, all along, been aware of the unspoken safety net of your concern and affection. It has meant a lot to me.

I won't even try to list the multitude of kindnesses. At an official level, I know there is no way in heaven or earth we could have survived this marathon without the generosity of you and the Cabinet. Because of your unquestioning support we were able to do, I believe, for Daddy, everything that could have been done. And when nothing more could be done to contain the situation, we were able to afford the absolute best of nursing care to make him comfortable. Because of this, he was to continue to contribute through his work, and even to enjoy a good game of bridge almost to the end.

At a personal level, I almost feel to cry when I think of the time and effort and love you put into his send-off. It has reflected a huge generosity of spirit in you. But you demonstrated your loyalty and friendship to him long before that in the long periods when you held his work together through his many earlier illnesses. I often felt sad that yourself and my father were not personally closer, but have come to realize that there seems to be some stern quality of aloneness that afflicts natural leaders . . . maybe it is the instinct for independent thought. I saw it in NW and in MM, and I suspect it may likewise be in you. . . .

And so I want to thank you for all this; and for sending him off on his final journey with style, with due honour paid, and with the distinction he deserved.

In friendship and with love,

Rachel

CHAPTER 22
THE NEW PARADIGM

DURING THE ELECTION CAMPAIGN THE ELECTORATE WAS INVITED, on the strength of our record and vision, to vote PNP again. I called the elections for 18 December 1997 and the process was monitored by an international team of peacekeeper-observers, including former US president Jimmy Carter and former US general Colin Powell, who is of Jamaican descent, and who in 1989 was appointed the first black chairman of the Joint Chiefs of Staff.

The Electoral Advisory Committee had proposed that such an observer group should be invited. A strict interpretation of the committee's powers under the law indicated that that was not within its remit. Initially, like most of the cabinet, I was not in favour. On reflection, I relented, and worked hard to persuade the entire cabinet to give its approval, as I did not wish to set the precedent of failing to endorse a unanimous recommendation of the Electoral Advisory Committee. Those members of cabinet who eventually succumbed to my persuasive insistence agreed in hindsight that we had taken the correct decision.

When the ballots were counted, the party had secured an unprecedented third term in office, winning fifty of the sixty seats. Jamaicans had once again made a strong, unequivocal statement. They had decided to continue to put their faith in the stability and prudence they were seeing in the country's leadership as well as the performance of the government.

❧

No one under forty will remember those days in the 1970s when the cost of petrol was governed by price controls. Up to the 1980s, cabinet would ponder long and hard over every submission for a price increase, especially for diesel oil used by the trucks which took vendors and goods to market. The price of kerosene for lighting and cooking was often subsidized to discourage those customers from using charcoal, which threatened the country's forests and tree cover.

In January 1999, before settling the budget for the financial year 1999–2000, I had convened a three-day national roundtable where we discussed its financial contours. Among the measures agreed by the government, the opposition, the trade unions, the private sector, the church and non-governmental organizations was a road maintenance fund to be financed by a special tax on fuel.

As soon as finance minister Omar Davies announced the tax increase on gasoline during his budget presentation in April 1999, Edward Seaga, sitting in his place on the front bench, drew his fingers across his throat. The members of the opposition rushed outside and no one had to warn me that there was big trouble ahead.

Supporters of the opposition spent the weekend gathering and spreading rubble, oil drums, tyres, tree trunks and rocks for the total lockdown of the country by Monday morning. Roadblocks were mounted throughout the length and breadth of the island. Children were prevented from going to school, workers to their jobs, the sick to hospitals, and tourists from coming in or going out of the island.

I got to my office at Jamaica House early that Monday morning and pulled in as many people from the government and party as I could find.

The security forces got to work and comrades (PNP supporters) did their best to clear the roads in those communities we dominated. By Tuesday, a soldier had been shot on Mountain View Avenue in Kingston and another victim had died in Trelawny. On that day also, students marched from the University of the West Indies down to the Office of the Prime Minister. The police had barricaded the section of Hope Road from the gate of King's House (the governor general's residence) to Jamaica House so they could not get through to the gate of the Office of the Prime Minister. But I considered it important to meet with them and deputed Delano Franklyn and Heather Robinson to get a delegation of the marchers to meet with me.

During this difficult period I was aware that despite the mental anguish, my leadership required a calm demeanour and a cool head. So we immediately set about to craft a new approach.

I appointed a committee to make recommendations. Should we roll back the price? Were we going to roll it back 100 per cent or halfway? What items in the estimates of expenditure should be removed to compensate for the consequent loss of revenue? The person to head this committee could not be partisan, and had to command national respect. Peter Moses, then president of the

Private Sector Organization of Jamaica, was appointed chairman and independent senator Trevor Munroe was appointed deputy chair. The student leader of the delegation from the University of the West Indies, "Mac the Knife" Harvey, was made a member of the committee.

By the Wednesday afternoon it was clear that the nation was beginning to pull back and by the weekend the country had returned to normality. The committee's findings were published in the Moses Report, which the cabinet accepted. The results were presented by the finance minister Omar Davies when the budget debate continued.

This was a period in which the state was severely challenged. Issues, proposals, questions had been raised right, left and centre. No political party hitherto had recovered from such a crisis to win a subsequent election. The crisis threw up a number of political lessons which could not be ignored – how it had arisen and eventually ended. This shaped the tone and content of my presentation to Parliament on 4 May 1999:

> What are the lessons to be learnt from the demonstrations a fortnight ago?
>
> Firstly, that the old order – the closed, distant and authoritarian systems of governance – is being forced to give way to a structure which is inclusive, responsive and accountable to the new, proud, informed, assertive Jamaican citizen of the twenty-first century. This new Jamaican is the product of the profound changes that have taken place globally and at home, shaped and moulded by these forces: technological, social, political and economic.
>
> The process of change which began in the 1970s and continued during this decade must be accelerated. We are no longer a plantation society. We have become an open society, constantly exposed to a world culture. We enjoy the freedom of religion, education, travel, association, the press. This modern Jamaican knows what is happening in the world – culture, lifestyles, political events; disasters, natural and manmade. The rapid reforms – liberalization, deregulation – that the country has undertaken since the mid-1980s to integrate the Jamaican economy into the world economy have facilitated the transformation process at the individual level.
>
> The new Jamaican perceives that the constitutional and institutional arrangements now constitute the major obstacle to his or her future growth and development. The structures of governance now in place represent the old order. In essence, the foundation of society, the people, has been transformed at a much more rapid rate than the institutional and structural features of the society.
>
> The new, more informed Jamaican is demanding more than ever to be involved in a meaningful way in shaping his or her destiny. The younger

generation is also finding the existing structures unresponsive and, in some instances, irrelevant.

This crisis is national in character, because it affects not only the institutions of the state, but the private sector and civil society as well.

The old non-inclusive, often undemocratic methods of sharing and managing power that have evolved in post-independence Jamaica can be found across the entire spectrum of the society. We find them in political parties, Parliament, the cabinet, church organizations, the bureaucracy, organs of the state, private-sector firms, community groups.

We must change our approach to governance, or we will become part of the problem to be swept aside by the emerging new social order. This new social order requires participation where there is greater information-sharing and communication – in a clear, honest way, on the process of policy formulation and decision-making.

The government, by its own actions, is facilitating the change towards this new type of governance through constitutional changes, public-sector reform, freedom of information policy, roundtable discussions, willingness to listen and take advice from independent sources outside of government, parliamentary committees and duty-free importation of information technology. The changes that are occurring in our world and in our country are powerful and fundamental. They are here to stay.

This means, therefore, that our institutions, political systems and bureaucracy, must either change quickly, or disintegrate and be swept away. That is the main lesson of the recent demonstrations. The gas-price increase was but the trigger.

I accept that we must not simply diagnose the symptoms. I assure the nation that we are determined to address the cause. It has been a timely wake-up call. There can be no return to business as usual.

I realized that if Jamaica were to survive, grow and develop, it would have to find a way to engage all sectors and all Jamaicans regardless of politics, class, ethnic roots, creed, occupation or gender. Convinced of the value and effectiveness of a consensual approach to governance, I insisted that my entire team be committed to openness and consultations with all sections of the society on issues of national importance.

The goal of ending political tribalism and building one Jamaica could only be achieved through genuine political dialogue. For me, political inclusiveness would have to be a large part of the solution to tribalism. Government, private sector and civil society would need to work as partners to achieve the necessary trust and harmony, and this would in turn require the government to become more transparent and accountable. Every Jamaican should be able to feel a sense of belonging in his or her own homeland, proudly claiming this Jamaica as theirs.

I was a firm believer in effective communication of the government's intentions and achievements, the contextualizing of policies and programmes so that the public could understand what their government was doing and why and be able to express their views accordingly.

I was reminded of a conversation with Sir Egerton Richardson years before on the need for effective communication in which he said words to this effect: "For any leader to be successful, he or she must have a clear strategy to communicate his or her programmes and policies to citizens. The communication strategy must be systematic and targeted. It cannot be formulated without the leader having a lucid understanding of who he or she is talking with and what are their most urgent needs."

From the outset, I realized that my administration should design a strategic approach to connecting with Jamaican citizens. Through the Live and Direct programme and face-to-face communication, along with the groups of the PNP, we had to fashion a way to communicate the most complex issues to ordinary Jamaicans. The collapse of the financial sector in the mid-1990s was a hard economic blow. It had to be packaged and presented to the citizens in a manner they could understand. They had to be convinced that the policies of the administration were aimed at enhancing their social and economic freedom. Whether it was liberalizing the telecommunication sector to provide over two million Jamaicans with services; modernizing the road and transport system; rescuing the financial sector to protect approximately a million small depositors or to provide social security assistance to over two hundred thousand poor Jamaicans through the Programme for Advancement through Health and Education, citizens had to be convinced that the regime was sparing no effort to enhance and protect their interests.

Undoubtedly, this contributed to three consecutive victories for us. This would not have been possible without an effective communication strategy. But the Jamaican electorate is much too savvy for it to have succeeded without the requisite performance.

My administration had paid careful attention to expanding the mass media. The sole television station was privatized and two other television stations, as well as cable stations, were eventually added. Over time, the mass media expanded to include new radio stations, newspapers and the rapid growth of cable television.

People were more informed than ever before, but they also had more channels through which to air their dissatisfaction and frustration with their political representatives. They did so through the myriad radio call-in programmes, much to the chagrin of those representatives. This was important, however painful, to help facilitate political dialogue.

I believed that the time had come to initiate a national dialogue, beginning with coming together and agreeing on the broad outline of a vision and governance structure for a new Jamaica. The areas of focus would be the role of government; reform of the economy, the constitution and the public sector; and the role of civil society.

Jamaica, having ended its borrowing relationship with the IMF in 1995, was now ready to embark on a staff-monitored programme with that institution. This was a significant step, given the intense debate in the party two decades before and the trauma which engulfed the entire country as each quarterly test approached. The end of IMF borrowing was a monumental achievement and an historic landmark.

CHAPTER 23
FINANCE AND ECONOMY

BY 1998, I WAS CONVINCED OF THE FURTHER need to restate that the world was not waiting on us to catch up and we had to force reforms to survive and compete successfully. I noted that the forces of globalization were driving us to compete on the basis of price, quality and top-class service – not sentiment or history; and we needed to understand that the world owed us nothing.

In my budget speech of 2001, I assessed what we had accomplished over the decade, not to signal victory, but to show how far we had come and also the need for even greater effort. I pointed to the fact that ten years before, the Jamaican economy was heavily regulated, with price controls, import controls, exchange controls, heavy government ownership and a weak infrastructure. It was an economy with no foreign-exchange reserves and one which was unprepared to face global competition. We therefore set out to change all that.

Despite the great odds against us, we succeeded in sweeping away many of the major regulatory and bureaucratic logjams. Looking back, one enjoys a sense of satisfaction at the range of reform that we initiated or completed to support the new market-driven economy, including institutions such as the Financial Services Commission, Office of Utilities Regulation, Anti-Dumping Commission, Jamaica Fair Trading Commission, Consumer Protection Commission and Jamaica Deposit Insurance.

These reforms unleashed their own special set of forces and required new regulations. A particular example was the reform of the banking and financial industry, along with the removal of exchange control in 1991.

The international financial institutions insisted on greater competition between financial institutions and additional banking licences being granted to new players. The government was committed to broadening Jamaican ownership in the sector and, as a result, a number of Jamaican entrepreneurs and investors entered it before tight regulations and the oversight capacity of the

Bank of Jamaica were fully in place. The financial sector therefore expanded to the point where it dominated other sectors, rather than facilitating the financing of these sectors. In a sense, it appeared, at one point, to be crowding out the development of other sectors. This was particularly so for sectors that were not in external trade or which fell within the micro, small and medium sectors.

At the outset, the Bank of Jamaica's oversight and regulation capacity were inadequate. So, too, were the institutions for regulating and supervising the insurance and security industries. Until the crisis emerged, there was little understanding of the full extent of the inadequacy of the government's overall capacity to police the links between the banking, securities and insurance institutions. Only when forensic auditors were introduced, in an attempt to unravel some of the transactions, did the extent to which these linkages had been abused become evident.

The finance sector saw steady growth as a percentage of overall GDP from 1990 to 2002. In 1990 it accounted for 4.9 per cent of overall GDP. This rose to 8.2 per cent by 2002. By comparison, manufacturing saw its share falling from 17.8 per cent to 13.8 per cent over the same period. The agriculture sector share stagnated at 6 per cent between 1990 and 2002. Before the 1990s, these sectors had been highly protected by tariffs and quantitative restrictions. Now they were also faced with a difficult domestic environment: high costs, low productivity, poor infrastructure, high energy and security costs, small and stagnant domestic markets and limited access to capital, which at times was costly. The productive sectors were in the main operating with relatively obsolete technologies and needed large capital investment.

Manufacturing and agriculture were severely affected by globalization and the liberalization process. The old model of protection from foreign competition would have to be replaced by sustained initiatives to reduce production costs, adopt new technologies to produce new and better products and break into new markets.

It took some time for players within these vital sectors to accept the imperative of reform. This was a prerequisite to embarking on adjustment and reform, and allowed rapid growth in the years ahead.

⚜

My first three years as prime minister saw us grappling with major macro-economic challenges. At the time, the slow global recovery and the effects of a lopsided world economy, not geared to accommodating the needs of small, open, highly indebted and vulnerable economies like Jamaica's, presented a challenge. In taking stock of the economy, we decided to chart an internally driven course that would result in a more prosperous economic future and a better quality of life for the Jamaican people.

Despite claims to the contrary by the outgoing administration, the economic situation in 1989 was unstable. Servicing foreign debt accounted for the greater portion of our export earnings. The exchange rate was propped up by an auction system with considerable arrears. Net foreign reserves in 1989 stood at minus US$530.2 million. We were in the deep red. The current account was unsustainable.

High inflation encouraged the overvaluation of real estate, which often served to guarantee bank loans. Labour was increasingly demanding higher wages, without any increase in productivity. The public and the business community clamoured for inflation to be controlled and stability imposed on the foreign-exchange market. The manipulation of interest rates became the main tool available to the government to control inflation, impose stability in the foreign-exchange market and stem potential capital flight.

The inadequate monitoring of critical risk areas such as liquidity and foreign-exchange risks in a volatile market resulted in several large financial institutions experiencing severe liquidity and solvency crises. Our regulatory institutions were inadequately equipped and further handicapped by the separation of reporting accountability for banks, insurance, pensions and security groups. Once it started, the contagion spread rapidly – when major corporate entities such as Life of Jamaica and the National Commercial Bank were also revealed as malignant, urgent remedies had to be administered to prevent a disastrous end for the entire country.

That situation was further compounded by the lack of tight management, and intercompany interconnectedness, which resulted in complex conglomerate structures and overlapping ownership of multiple layers of financial institutions (banks, merchant banks, building societies, insurance companies) as well as other, non-financial businesses (tourism, real estate, farms and so on).

The earliest manifestation of the impending storm came from two financial institutions which were experiencing liquidity problems. Soon after the Financial Institutions Service was established as a remedy, it was discovered that the problem was much more severe and widespread than initially perceived. A task force comprising members of the public sector and advisors from Ernst and Young and Peat Marwick, both from the United Kingdom, did an assessment to determine its magnitude and extent. We discovered the life savings of thousands of ordinary Jamaicans were tied up in these institutions – as savings, insurance policies or pensions were under severe threat.

The principals of these institutions and the authorities both wanted to minimize the potential panic which could arise if government authorities were perceived to be assessing individual institutions.

The task force, including international expertise, recommended government intervention by way of a special-purpose vehicle. And so the Financial Sector Adjustment Company was set up in January 1997 to rescue the sector and provide a solid foundation going forward. Its mission was to "build for Jamaica a financial sector that is stable, sound, strong and well regulated". Its purpose was, essentially, to facilitate an orderly intervention in distressed financial institutions, preserve the deposits and life insurance policies and pensions and restore confidence in the financial sector. It was anticipated that the company would have a lifespan of seven to nine years and that its mandate would be executed in three phases: intervention, rehabilitation and divestment.

During his budget presentation in April 1998, Finance Minister Omar Davies gave an authoritative exposition of the cause of the problems which acknowledged the "impact of a prolonged high interest rate regime on a number of non-performing loans". He pointed out several areas of poor management practices and decisions by the private sector and individuals which were unethical and in breach of fiduciary responsibility.

There was no room for argument; of the many severe challenges my administration had to confront, none compared with that of averting a total financial meltdown. No other cabinet since independence has been obliged to take a more painful and far-reaching series of decisions.

Long before ours, there had been financial crises around the world. We witnessed them in Asia during the mid-1990s, in Japan towards the end of the 1980s and Chile earlier in that decade.

The annals must record that the same multilateral financial institutions which had advocated the granting of new banking licences, most of which went to a group that dubbed themselves the "Indigenous Banks", sought to persuade the government not to intervene. They urged us to accept the failure in the banking system as a risk outcome of the operations of a market economy. Their advice was to put receivers in the failed institutions who would eventually pay the creditors and depositors a percentage of their investment, calculated on the value of the assets eventually recovered.

But the foreign auditors discovered that several of their activities could not be excused as "management missteps", and reconstructed some of the more egregious transactions which had taken place. Had we accepted the advice of those institutions, Jamaica would not have yet recovered from the cataclysmic effects of eroding confidence at every level, and especially so among the diaspora and those who still believe savings are safest under your mattress.

There was a stark contrast, too, between the performance of several of the indigenous institutions as against those of the foreign-controlled entities. It is noteworthy that during this same period the local subsidiaries of the Bank of Nova Scotia, Canadian Imperial Bank of Commerce and Citibank encountered no difficulties in prospering within the same macroeconomic space. There were local institutions, such as the Jamaica National Building Society, the Victoria Mutual Building Society and indigenous credit unions, that maintained sound lending policies and suffered no adverse consequences. The main reason for their continuing success obviously lay in their operating within strict guidelines and avoiding questionable loans.

The economic consequences, had we failed to take decisive action, would have been disastrous. Allowing a meltdown would have resulted in an economic and financial earthquake, triggering severe losses in business, life savings and pensions. Overseas remittances would disappear. The social implosion would have been catastrophic.

In February 1998, I convened a special conference of the PNP to address a range of political and national issues. The agenda included a presentation and discussion on the economy and financial sector.

From my earliest days of political activism, I learned there were times when it was more important to listen than to speak. Over the many years, I knew the names of those delegates who came every year, always insisting on their right to speak. There were also some delegates who never missed a conference but did not take the floor. One such was a farmer from Daniel Town in Trelawny: Eric Thompson, a tall, slim, jet-black man with bulging eyes and a slight stammer. Whenever I wanted to test the pulse of northern Trelawny, he was the man to find, and he had never proven wrong. We had a special one-to-one relationship. It was surprising to see him move to the microphone that Sunday morning at the National Arena for the first time. What was he going to say, I wondered.

He said it loud and clear.

> Comrade Leader, you know me for thirty years now as an honest and peaceful man. You know I work hard in the boiling sun and you always see me in the Falmouth Square when I tek me little money to the bank. It does not matter which bank, because none of them could be there unless you and the government allow dem.

> Comrade Leader, hear me good. Any time I come down and ask for my money and dem can't give me all of it one time, I am going back to Daniel Town, sharpen my cutlass on both sides and when I return blood shall flow like a river down the Martha Brae.

As he returned to his seat, there was first a deafening silence and then a sudden eruption of shattering applause which nearly brought the arena down. It was chilling. It brought forcibly home to me that the ordinary man and woman had a stake in this crisis and our deliberations, one way or another, would have a direct impact on them.

The following Friday, when I saw him in Falmouth, Comrade Thompson was as warm, friendly and pleasant as ever. He uttered not one word about his speech at the conference and our conversation was about what we had to do to regain political ground in the constituency of North Trelawny.

Cabinet deliberated long and hard about the costs of full compensation for all depositors and policyholders. In accordance with the position of Jacques Bussieres, governor of the Central Bank, there was initial support by a number of ministers for the partial repayment of deposits above a certain level. Eventually, the entire cabinet was persuaded to take the decision of paying the depositors and policyholders in full so as to restore confidence in our financial system. But there was no way we could protect depositors and policyholders in full and at the same time write off the accumulation of interest payments on all outstanding loans.

It is the sad reality of political life that those entities who made the early call for help and received it have so far failed to utter one positive word for the action taken to protect the interests of their policyholders and depositors. It is not the financial institutions that have been pilloried for imprudent management practices but the administration instead.

Without access to external finance, the Government of Jamaica took the momentous decision to do so from our own resources. We opened the door to renegotiate the quantum and terms for outstanding debt obligations, particularly for the productive sector, but the country could not afford to allow debtors to renege on all their obligations.

The government moved decisively to strengthen the oversight scope and capacity of the Bank of Jamaica and to create the Jamaica Deposit Insurance Corporation and the Financial Services Commission. Because of the significant advances we made in our regulatory systems, by the creation of new institutions to protect depositors and boosting the capacity to supervise the operations of local financial institutions, Jamaica has been able, so far, to withstand the turbulence in the international financial marketplace. In subsequent years, we have witnessed financial crises in the United Kingdom and the United States.

All objective analyses of the impact of globalization on the Jamaican economy during the 1990s, following the spectacular effort at reforms and restructuring to allow greater competitiveness and integration, would have to conclude that the level of investment and innovation was not sufficient to drive sustainable growth.

Particularly disappointing was that for the four years 1996–99, GDP contracted in aggregate by 5.3 per cent. The period coincided with the severe financial-sector crisis, which cost about 40 per cent of GDP to resolve, severely disrupted the flow of credit to existing and new businesses, and was a major contributor to the weak domestic economic performance. Commercial bank loans to the private sector contracted sharply between 1996 and 2000, moving from J$50 billion in 1998 to J$33 billion in 2000.

The financial crisis exacerbated the public debt. Having to absorb the full costs of the crisis helped to move the debt-to-GDP ratio from just about 80 per cent in 1996 to close to 150 per cent by 2000. This high level of debt was a constant drag on economic growth. To satisfy our creditors, resources had to be shifted away from critical areas of desperate need such as health, education and security. In a real sense, therefore, the impact of the financial crisis of the 1990s will be felt for at least a generation.

The slowdown in economic activities had a negative impact on government revenues. The government found itself having to borrow fairly heavily from the domestic market, which had the effect of pushing up domestic interest rates. At the same time, interest rates were also being used to stabilize the exchange rate in order to achieve stability and preserve our limited foreign reserves.

The period 1992–2002 undoubtedly presented the toughest economic challenges. It was also the time of some of our greatest triumphs and achievements. Managing the transition from a closed, highly regulated and protected economy to one that was open, deregulated and integrated into the world economy was nothing short of a quiet revolution. For us to have achieved this without the society tearing itself apart, despite the pain and dislocation, was a miracle. It was an accomplishment in which the people of Jamaica can take pride.

Such a historic achievement and the process involved taught lessons of great and sobering importance. The first was how incredibly difficult and complex is the process of creating modern institutions to drive a market economy is. This was especially difficult because the natural and historical philosophical inclination of the party was towards a more state-oriented model of development. It was my clear understanding that the historical mission of any party forming the government in the 1990s was to do exactly what we set out to accomplish. Its dynamic and drawn-out nature took its toll on the population, and after about a decade the nation suffered from "adjustment fatigue".

The second important lesson was that integrating Jamaica into the global economy created winners and losers. At the onset, the extent of the change and its impact on certain groups were not fully appreciated. The winners were likely to come from groups, companies, sectors and individuals that were equipped to make a quick transition from the old plantation-oriented economy to become connected to and trade with the global economy.

Those who, owing largely to demographics, education levels, access to technology, scope and scale of operation, were unable to connect and trade competitively with the global economy were severely and negatively affected. One of the painful and early realizations was that the Jamaican state had limited capacity to help the many players who lost out.

We did, however, institute an extensive social safety net to help the most vulnerable. Despite the constraints on the state, our poverty eradication programme was implemented alongside the economic reforms. Programmes and projects like Lift Up Jamaica, Jamaica Social Investment Fund, Drugs for the Elderly and the National Health Fund not only helped to reduce poverty, but also facilitated the relative social peace necessary to pursue reform.

During this period the state could not fail to help the most vulnerable and marginalized, in order to be consistent with our fundamental philosophy of empowerment and people-centred development.

The reform programme needed a credible and well-communicated set of economic strategies, along with viable short-, medium- and long-term projects that gave hope to the population. The entire package needed a high degree of national consensus and partnership. This was especially important given that changes would be the subject of political contest and had to be pursued in accordance with the verdict of our people, as in any thriving democracy.

The financial crisis had severely affected our GDP. Other contributing factors were the high number of weather-related disasters, the effects of crime and violence and low total factor productivity. The data for the period, however, present a paradox which has not been fully explained or understood. From 1990 to 2008, Jamaica enjoyed one of the highest rates of gross capital formation as a percentage of GDP. The World Bank's development indicators placed Jamaica at twentieth out of 177 countries ranked between 2000 and 2008. This rate of investment was the same as that of the fast-growing East Asia region between 1960 and 2008 (World Bank 2011). In fact, during the rapid growth in Jamaica between 1960 and 1969, the World Bank report shows that the average annual rate of investment was just slightly less, at 27.7 per cent of GDP.

A major contributory factor was the significant growth in foreign direct investment. One of the unspoken successes of the liberalization of the economy during the 1990s was the restoration of confidence of foreign investors. Between 1995 and 2005, Jamaica was able to attract some US$4.7 billion in foreign direct investment. The average annual figure was US$430 million, or 4.7 per cent of GDP. Much of this investment went to build out and modernize the country's infrastructure in ports, airports, Highway 2000, telecommunications and the tourism sector. These were solid foundations for future growth.

CHAPTER 24

A MODERN PUBLIC SECTOR AND GOVERNANCE

THE 1990S MARKED THE CLOSE OF A CENTURY and a millennium; the decade heralded the Information or Digital Age, which revolutionized the way people interacted with business and how governments operated the world over. This phenomenon was as radical as the Industrial Age which marked the beginning of the modern era and a new social and economic regime.

The ease with which people from all walks of life could access information created a knowledgeable population with far greater expectations of having a say in the governance of their countries. Here in Jamaica, the new, proud, informed, assertive citizen of the twenty-first century would not for much longer accommodate the old, closed, distant and authoritarian model of governance, but would demand a structure that was inclusive, transparent, responsive and accountable.

The increasing impact of globalization demanded more sophisticated systems of public administration. Information technology, with its effects on the communication, storage and retrieval of information, required a trained cadre of workers.

The role of government was to enable sustainable development and ensure the effective and efficient delivery of services. From the outset, I realized that it could not be business as usual as far as the public sector was concerned. I was determined to bring about a more efficient and productive public service, which would improve the quality of governance. From early on, I made it clear that it was the duty and responsibility of the government to openly identify our problems, initiate possible solutions, and then consult with every sector to achieve consensus before deciding on final solutions. I therefore launched a public dialogue on the role of the state in the modern world. The government, private sector, trade unions and civil society met at a convention in Ocho Rios.

To improve the quality of governance, public-sector modernization had to improve what the World Bank defines as "the manner in which power is exercised in the management of a country's social and economic resources for development".[1] We had already anticipated the broader definition by Philippe Faucher, which came out of an Ottawa governance conference in May 2001: "the capacity of the government to effectively manage its resources and implement sound policies; and the respect of citizens and the State for the institutions that govern economic and social relations among them".[2]

We focused on six aspects of public-sector organization: policy formulation, organizational structures, systems, human resources, technology along with the legal framework, and strategies to ensure continuous improvement in performance.

CABINET OFFICE

Among the first reforms was a modern Cabinet Office. In 1991 two distinguished retired British civil servants, Sir Kenneth Stowe and Geoffrey Morgan, were commissioned to look at the reform of the public sector. One of their central recommendations was putting the Cabinet Office under the direct control of the prime minister, along the lines of those of the older Commonwealth countries like the United Kingdom, Australia, Canada and New Zealand. The Cabinet Office, under the direction of the cabinet secretary, would coordinate and direct the management of the affairs of state.

Hitherto, the Office of Cabinet Secretary, under the Jamaica constitution, had been largely confined to the routine confidential functions of preparing the agenda, compiling minutes and transmitting cabinet decisions to the relevant departments. Under the new dispensation the cabinet secretary would be the head of the civil service. He or she would report directly to the prime minister and have major responsibility for corporate planning for the government and for monitoring and implementing policy.

Before leaving government, Michael Manley had appointed a committee, led by Rex Nettleford, to make recommendations for a government structure

---

1. World Bank, *Governance and Development* (Washington, DC: International Bank for Reconstruction and Development/World Bank, 1992), 1.

2. Carlton E. Davis, "A Practitioner's Perspective on Governance" (paper presented at the World Bank Public Sector Day Conference, Washington, DC, 26 April 2004), 1.

that was more functional, efficient and responsive to the needs of the Jamaican people. The committee reiterated the need for a restructured Cabinet Office as recommended by Messrs Stowe and Morgan.

In July 1993, Carlton Davis was appointed cabinet secretary. His experience, stature and intellect made him the best person for the job. The reorganization of the office introduced heightened responsibilities, including the critical review of submissions before they were presented to cabinet. It was also responsible for providing accurate records of the proceedings of the cabinet, Council of Ministers' Meetings and the legislative committee to accelerate the implementation of decisions, the management of policy formulation, corporate planning and monitoring policy implementation. Of extreme importance was directing and managing the Public Sector Modernization Programme.

We saw the benefits immediately. The upgrade of the Cabinet Office improved the quality of cabinet submissions, aided by written guidelines. Cabinet committees were more effective, and were revamped to give careful consideration to many matters before they were submitted to cabinet, resulting in better monitoring and evaluation of cabinet decisions.

The *Consultation Code of Practice for the Public Sector* document, launched in January 2005, allowed greater involvement by stakeholders, such as the private sector, non-governmental organizations and trade unions, in policy matters.

CITIZENS' CHARTER

For those services which only the state could provide, we had to create special safeguards and incentives to ensure service of the quality that competition would otherwise engender.

In my first budget speech, on 17 June 1992, I initiated the process of improved service delivery, pointing out, among other things, that there would have to be more courtesy and promptness in delivering service, and the time spent waiting in lines had to be reduced and documents processed more speedily. These would be some of the criteria used to determine whether service in the public sector had improved.

The fundamental principle of the Citizens' Charter was that the taxpayer was a customer, who was entitled to courteous and efficient service from government agencies. It was about putting the taxpayer, citizen and customer in the driver's seat and emphasizing the importance of putting the people's needs first. The idea was to set out demanding realistic standards of service that the public should expect. It should also recapture within the civil service the sense of duty and obligation which is the essence of good customer service. It was my dream that whenever Jamaicans used public-service offices, whether health facilities, police stations, post offices, tax offices or public transport, they would be shown honour, respect and courtesy.

In 1994 we launched the Citizens' Charter Programme, with eight pilot agencies being asked to prepare charters which relocated the customer from the periphery to the centre of their businesses. The programme was a success: those agencies understood far better the relationship between themselves and the customer, and that the agency's *raison d'être* was to fulfil the needs of the customer. The National Housing Trust was among the first to launch a charter and gained greater respect through its outstanding customer service.

Ten years later, some twenty-five public-sector organizations had issued charters, and all ministries and major departments were required to implement customer-service improvement programmes. Features they shared were the establishment of one-stop windows, help desks, responsiveness to customer complaints, the introduction of e-government and redesigning application forms to make them more customer-friendly. By then, also, there was a Standards and Monitoring Unit in the Cabinet Office to promote and monitor customer-service improvement across the public sector.

The Citizens' Charter Programme was envisaged as an integral component of the larger Values and Attitudes Campaign, according to the maxim: "Do unto others what you would have them do unto you."

EXECUTIVE AGENCIES

The idea of executive agencies emerged from a cabinet retreat in July 1993. The ministerial roundtable on the emerging role of the state was sponsored by the Canadian International Development Agency and was attended by ministers and representatives from the private sector and non-governmental agencies.

The basis of the executive agencies was the government's vision of the new public sector, which allowed for efficiently delegating authority and disaggregating public bureaucracies in the managerial agencies. Statutory corporations and companies had been created to make the government more competitive with the private sector in attracting the most competent professionals and to achieve greater flexibility and responsiveness to customer needs as well as greater efficiencies, but had not always achieved those results.

We initiated the Public Sector Modernization Programme in 1994 with the broad objective of creating an effective, efficient and accountable public sector to provide high-quality service to taxpayers.

We mandated a number of government bodies to begin immediately, seriously and systematically improving the services they offered to the public. This represented a radical departure from public-service norms. These new agencies were given full responsibility and accountability for their finances, human resources and performance, in accordance with fixed standards. That required, in some instances, a major change in personnel to ensure that employees were suited to their tasks. "Shape up or ship out," they were told. The agency heads were selected by open competition and appointed on contract through a rigorous and demanding process. Performance would be consistently reviewed and renewal based on merit and performance.

The transformation was not a seamless one and was opposed by some groups accustomed to the traditional approach of the colonial civil service. We also had to address the workers' fears of dismissal. Consequently, we made every effort to sensitize and educate both those directly affected and the public at large to ensure they clearly understood that there was no hidden agenda.

We started cautiously, with four agencies: the Registrar General's Department and Island Record Office, the Management Institute for National Development, the Administrator General's Department and the Office of the Registrar of Companies.

When we felt confident that the executive-agency strategy was a viable one, the concept was spread to embrace four additional agencies – the National Land Agency, the Public Works Department, which morphed into the National Works Agency, the Jamaica Information Service and the National Environment and Planning Agency.

Naturally, this initiative had teething pains, but the gains became obvious within a few years. By 2001, the first four agencies showed increased timeliness in presenting reports, more effective and greater use of information technology, and improved customer service, demonstrated through adjusting opening hours to facilitate the customer. By virtue of greater efficiency, customer service was improved, and the increased fees flowing from more satisfied customers resulted in the initial investment being recovered within three years.

Other public-sector modernization initiatives included developing the financial-management and human-resources information systems, pensions, secondary education, tax administration and local-government reform programmes; we reviewed the public-service regulations and staff orders;

strengthened corporate planning as well as the audit system; decentralized the health delivery system; and modernized key ministries and organizations such as the Ministry of Transport and Works, the Jamaica Promotions Corporation and Customs.

A financial-management improvement project included, as its principal component, overhauling the public sector's computer technology. This was intended to lead to more efficiency in the statutory reporting required by the Ministry of Finance and other ministries. It included an integrated financial-management information system which provided more timely and accurate reporting on expenditure to improve government's treasury-management functions. Introduced on a phased basis, the project significantly strengthened planning and budgeting.

One of the most difficult tasks of any government is revenue collection. A programme was designed to broaden the tax base, encourage compliance, minimize tax evasion and generally make tax administration more effective. We explored reform strategies that would contribute to macroeconomic stability, through government's ability to garner additional resources to finance budgetary needs, reduce dependence on foreign borrowing and eventually enable us to reduce tax rates. This would be achieved by making revenue-collecting agencies and departments more efficient, to enable them to combat tax evasion.

The Tax Administration Reform Project, instituted in 1994, embraced all tax agencies – the Inland Revenue, Income Tax, General Consumption Tax, Stamp Duty and Transfer Tax and Land Valuation departments; the Revenue Board; the Tax Policy Unit in the Ministry of Finance; Fiscal Services Limited; and the Revenue Protection Division. It included simplifying the system; establishing a tax registration number; a computer administration system; and an improved legislative framework.

The tax registration number system introduced in April 1996 entailed assigning a unique number to all taxpayers which would be needed to do business with any government entity. By 2001, more than a million numbers had been assigned.

The tax reforms required modern information technology, trained personnel and a more streamlined system of administration. Income tax, general consumption tax, and the stamp duty and transfer tax departments were restructured into an assessment department to monitor taxpayer activities, audit returns, investigate fraud and prosecute tax evaders. The relevant laws were reviewed and the Revenue Administration Act enacted in 1998.

An important plank of the Public Sector Modernization Programme was the strategic and improved management of people. The intention was to develop human resources to create organizations that would be able to achieve their goals. Policies governing employees had to be aligned in a way that supported organizational performance goals. Strategies for improving the human-resource pool included targeted recruitment, and improving and developing the skills of those already in the service. Our intention was to restore the public sector to a competitive position and make it a preferred choice of employment for highly qualified candidates.

In seeking to make reform a permanent feature of governance, we established within the Cabinet Office the Public Sector Reform Unit, to create the vision and strategy for reform as well as to drive the agenda for promoting a strong and professionally managed public sector, capable of enabling national goals.

The unit immediately began preparing a ten-year framework to coordinate and integrate the reform programme to achieve sustainable development and the related aims of establishing a quality society; poverty reduction; increased accountability in both public and private sectors to reduce corruption; reduced national debt; and increased physical, economic and social security for all.

※

We set out to build a quality society – one in which there was economic growth and job creation, with human-resource development as the primary focus, suitable housing for most citizens, high standards of health care and reliable public transport with every family enjoying the basic necessities of life and, most important, justice for all.

In order to achieve this, we needed to inspire the population not only to unite behind all these goals but also to participate actively in achieving them. Similarly, the government was responsible for creating the legislative and policy framework that facilitated participation and protected the right and freedom to do so. While I was justifiably proud of the numerous policies, mechanisms, institutions and legislation implemented during my tenure, entrenching the rule of law, building participatory government, transparency, accountability and protecting the rights and freedoms of the people required the utmost vigilance.

The PNP was founded on the principles of social cohesion, individual responsibility, integrity in public life and the commitment to foster a nationalist spirit. In an era of technology and the cry of citizens for a new governing order, we set out to build a participatory democracy that would see more meaningful involvement through dialogue. To develop that framework and build a more inclusive society, in 2005 the cabinet promulgated a consultation code of practice for the public sector. The code stipulated new rules of engagement between the government, the technocrats and the Jamaican people.

The code laid down how stakeholders would be enabled to participate in consultation on proposals that were presented in a clear, concise form made widely accessible, and how their feedback would result in the best practices for developing projects and proposals. While the code was never binding in law, it was accepted as compulsory for all government ministries and agencies. It has served as a tool to enable all Jamaicans to enjoy a quality of life that is just, inclusive and for which our authorities are accountable.

Here I can highlight only a few initiatives my administration put into building a nation based firmly on the highest democratic ideals and principles. Key institutions we set up to protect and safeguard the rights of citizens included the Office of the Public Defender, the Corruption Prevention Commission, the political ombudsman, the Police Public Complaints Authority, the Electoral Commission and the Office of the Children's Advocate. We introduced legislation to protect the rights of our children and to ensure our citizens access to information; and measures to foster integrity and prudence among government representatives, to improve the local-government process and to expand and protect the rights and freedoms of citizens.

We worked assiduously to encourage the people to become more involved in decisions that would affect their lives, and we soon saw a change at the community level, where citizens began to demand this involvement. I noted with satisfaction that local authorities started to take the lead in forming development committees to coordinate planning, implementation and monitoring at the parish level. These committees touched on central government, local government, the private sector and civil society, and were a forum for moving the process along.

Notable initiatives that had an impact on community development included the Jamaica Social Investment Fund, created in 1996 as a part of the national poverty alleviation strategy. Another was the Lift Up Jamaica Programme, established in 1999, which provided J$2.5 billion in funding over two years to employ young people between eighteen and thirty. The projects had to be community-based. There was also the Parochial Revenue Fund, funded by two-thirds of all motor-vehicle licences, to be spent by local authorities on road maintenance.

Taken all together, these programmes represented a considerable investment. Local-government bodies and civil society were responsible for ensuring that money was judiciously spent on projects of long-lasting benefit to the community.

In an attempt to further encourage participatory governance, the Community Alliance for Education provided services at the community level. There were similar organizations in health, sports, heritage and cultural development, among others. These organizations worked through the parish and community development councils.

FIGHT AGAINST CORRUPTION

An important initiative in this regard was the Corruption Prevention Commission, an integral tool in safeguarding national integrity. It embraced several people and institutions, including Parliament, the Public Accounts Committee, auditor general, public defender, National Contracts Commission, the judiciary, the Office of Professional Responsibility in the Jamaica Constabulary Force and, importantly, the media, to name but a few. The establishment of the commission, and the companion Corruption Prevention Act (2000), in which resides its legal personality, speaks to Jamaica's democracy and my government's commitment to participatory democratic governance.

There were extensive consultations with people from all walks of life. For me, this building of consensus was not a matter of chance or expediency; it was a matter of principle, and fundamental to my vision.

Several other initiatives were introduced to fight against corruption and white-collar crime. Measures were put in place to address corruption within the Jamaica Constabulary Force, as its integrity was central to the effectiveness of the system.

The people and the media, naturally, also have serious roles to play in this regard. In a very real way, it is the media, with their control of information, and the vigilance they apply to investigation, which determine the issues to which the public responds. My administration understood that the role of the media was not to be taken lightly, and reaffirmed the rights of freedom of speech and the freedom of the press. For their credibility to be maintained, the voice of the media has to be unfettered and loud in exposing corruption in the private sector and in civil society.

Central to good governance are the principles of transparency and accountability. Nowhere is this more important than in granting contracts and spending public funds. In 2000, we established the National Contracts Commission to administer government contracts. The Access to Information Act of 2002 encouraged transparency in this regard.

I am particularly proud of our work to protect the nation's children. My administration enacted the Child Care and Protection Act (2004) and established the Office of the Children's Advocate, to enforce and protect the rights and interests of children. We also paved the way for the Office of the Children's Registry, used to record children who have been maltreated, the nature of the maltreatment, and its outcome, and to route reports to service partners for action. Many children are at the mercy of parents and guardians who themselves were the victims of abuse and who continue the cycle of cruelty exercised against our children in the name of discipline. New institutions sought to educate the public about what constituted abuse and the community's responsibility to protect them. The state would no longer condone the hands-off attitude that many people adopted, as they mistakenly thought adults had ultimate control and power over their children.

On the other hand, the state was also required to understand its responsibilities towards the children who ended up in its care. Even today the situation is not ideal, but there is a far greater awareness of the rights of the child.

The restructuring of the Children's Services Division in the Ministry of Health to create a more responsive and capable entity began with new, higher standards for children's homes and places of safety.

Patience is a necessary virtue in nation-building, as the wheels of development turn exceedingly slow. It was in July 1999 that I first proposed amending the constitution to include an expanded Charter of Rights. The proposals were discussed in several sittings. I was sure an agreement would be reached in 2002, and confidently referred to its conclusion in my budget presentation that year. However, it would be another nine years before it was finalized. But, again, the foundation had been laid for the consistent pursuit of the rights and freedoms to which our people are entitled.

Jamaica has been commended on the importance, thoroughness and relevance of Vision 2030, a bipartisan national development plan started during my incumbency. It would set out a vision to create a country recognized in the Americas as prosperous, democratic and one which afforded every citizen the opportunity to develop his or her full potential.

The plan was expected to include existing policies and sector plans and to comply with any international agreements and commitments. The framework was established to ensure that the process would embrace as wide a cross-section of Jamaicans as possible. The Planning Institute of Jamaica was given responsibility for this gargantuan project. It began with a visioning exercise and several seminars to decide on a sustainable framework for development. Task forces looked at plans for various sectors and, most important, there were ongoing national consultations to share information and allow engagement and participation.

The Vision 2030, which was later adopted, is encapsulated in the slogan: "Jamaica: the place of choice to live, work, do business and raise families." It is my wish that the fulfilment of its lofty goals by the leaders and citizens of Jamaica will promote a just and equitable society.

CHAPTER 25
THE NATIONAL INDUSTRIAL POLICY AND THE DEVELOPMENT AGENDA

WHEN THE PNP ASSUMED OFFICE IN 1989, THE Ministry of Development, Planning and Production was created under my leadership and given the task of transforming the economy.

Governance was fragmented and we needed policy coordination. The ministry had oversight of all the entities key to the development agenda – physical infrastructure, planning, environment, science and technology and development. The National Planning Council, chaired by me, and with Cezley Sampson as chief technical advisor, was created to put the necessary institutional systems and processes in place, with labour, the private sector and civil society on board. The Economic Planning Council was to bring together all the ministries, departments and agencies involved in pursuing programmes for economic development. Both councils proved invaluable in mustering broad-based support for our programmes.

Our strategy for economic growth involved creating a business and economic environment conducive to generating investment and employment. We identified major infrastructure projects for investment, economic growth and job creation. The more modern our infrastructure, the greater the prospects for growth, and so we immediately looked at rehabilitating and developing the island's infrastructure – roads, sea and airports, water and sewerage and public transport.

Owing to the accelerated decline of the sugar and banana industries in St James, Trelawny, St Mary and Portland, we had to expand economic activities to replace them. Tourism was identified to quickly stimulate job creation and accelerate growth. Our review indicated the need for a multifaceted approach focused on specific projects such as major road network improvement from Negril to

Port Antonio, major water and sewerage projects along the corridor, upgrading and privatizing the Sangster International Airport, building a sporting complex in Falmouth and expanding the cruise-ship port in Ocho Rios, as well as the Ken Wright Marina in Port Antonio.

Between the mid-1990s and the mid-2000s we designed, financed and completed the upgrading of the North Coast Development Road from Negril to Port Antonio. In addition, special incentives were put in place for lands along the north coast for tourism, commercial and residential development. These strategies have been critical to transforming the tourism industry over the last twenty years. Spanish investors came quietly to look at our infrastructure and decided to invest in Jamaica, as they were impressed by what they had seen.

The decision to formulate the National Industrial Policy was partly fuelled by an internal debate about the need to accelerate economic growth and the role of the state vis-à-vis that of the private sector. It was agreed that given the deeply rooted and systemic problems we faced, reform efforts would have to proceed coherently. Definite policies and implementation procedures would have to be devised, based on long-term strategic planning.

The foreword to the National Industrial Policy of 1996 pointed to "far-reaching changes in the international environment" and the consequent need for "radical adjustments to our economy". I wrote: "Important and pressing problems still remain to be tackled. We continue to experience persistently high rates of inflation, depreciation of the value of the currency, deficit in the balance of payments, unemployment of significant numbers of the work force and continuing inequality in the distribution of income. The Government's budget continues to carry a heavy burden of debt service payment."

While these issues of macroeconomic stability were of great importance, we did not have the luxury of waiting for the magical "stable state" before we set out to achieve investment, productivity and growth to raise living standards. The reforms themselves made the business classes and other stakeholders uncertain as they prudently waited to see the impact of the changes before committing investment capital. This had the effect of slowing the rate of growth and job creation when they were most needed.

It was acknowledged that transforming the Jamaican economy and society had to be a joint effort involving government, private-sector and non-state actors such as trade unions and civil-society groups. This was vital to winning trust and buy-in. It was equally clear that the government would have to take the lead role, given the interrelated nature of the economy and the problems involved.

Political change would have to proceed hand-in-hand with economic and social change.

Likewise, it was equally important to recognize that the private sector would have to be the main engine of growth.

The National Industrial Policy was therefore a strategic approach to growth and development. The policy framework was goal-oriented, with specific time-phasing, and definite priorities and policy measures to be adopted in each phase.

The resulting strategic plan had four essential interrelated components – macroeconomic, social and environmental policy and industrial strategy – all of which were considered mutually reinforcing and supportive.

The policy required a special mechanism to oversee and guide the process and so the Development Council, which I chaired, was set up as a cabinet committee. It was designed to be a partnership of stakeholders to ensure that key economic and development decisions would guarantee that the stabilization policies for the macro-economy would be integrated with policies that promoted growth and diversification of production. Professor Donald Harris was recruited as special advisor to assist in the overall design.

Social partnership, the first phase, involved government, the private sector and labour to ensure social stability and maintain focus on reducing poverty. We paid close attention to improving the welfare of the mass of the population through a significant number of social intervention initiatives to tackle the twin problems of poverty and underdevelopment.

We emphasized protecting the environment as we sought to expand the infrastructure and industrial base critical for the general welfare of the population and the continued expansion of the tourism sector. We also regarded the fragile ecosystem of the country as a gift of nature that should be protected and preserved for future generations.

INFRASTRUCTURE

By 1996, it was obvious that the government would have to be the catalyst to raise the living standards of our population. After prolonged internal debates, a clear strategy was agreed that would see the state continuing to emphasize investment in infrastructure to drive growth and create employment.

Infrastructure, however, was not an end in itself but a crucial vehicle for inducing other private-sector investments. Endorsing infrastructure as the main driver of our investment strategy was in keeping with our understanding of the role of government in development. Instead of seeking to "pick winners" in terms of firms and factories or even industries, our focus was on sectors and support programmes that would benefit all players in the economy. Our deliberations led to the view that adequate infrastructure is a *sine qua non* for any economy to achieve sustained economic growth and, more importantly, to gain competitiveness in a globalized environment.

On the clear understanding of the importance of infrastructure projects, particularly highways, cabinet authorized a series of major millennium projects in 2000 which we believed had the potential to be game-changers in transforming the Jamaican economy. The strategy had to have a medium- to long-term focus. Our analysis determined that the efforts of the local private sector would have to be supplemented by injections of significant foreign direct investment.

Even with the government's limited financial resources, infrastructure was given high priority and a renewed emphasis in terms of rehabilitation, maintenance and expansion. We began a major road rehabilitation programme. The primary roads benefiting were those radiating from major population centres with social and commercial infrastructure. By 1996, some 326 kilometres had been rehabilitated and design work had begun on a bypass for Old Harbour to improve traffic flow.

Early in our planning, we recognized that a complete overhaul of the infrastructure in the main tourism belt – the north coast – was vital for reinvigorating tourism. Consequently, we planned to reconstruct the 270 kilometres of road from Negril to Port Antonio under the Northern Coastal Highway Development Project. The first phase was the Negril to Montego Bay corridor. The second was the Montego Bay leg, and the final one, financed by Stabex funds from the European Union, ran from Ocho Rios to Port Antonio

We paid special attention to mitigating any negative impact the work might have on the environment, incorporating measures to control erosion, sedimentation, construction noise and dust as well as preserving the ecology, important archaeological sites and historical monuments. In addition, we took care to prevent any major disruption of commercial activities or the dislocation of people travelling between these areas.

As the new millennium approached, we felt it was important to do something befitting the magnitude of the landmark of a new century, and identified a menu of projects intended to put Jamaica on the growth path needed to create job opportunities. The centrepiece of that initiative was Highway 2000, a 230-kilometre, multi-lane toll expressway, linking Kingston and Montego Bay on one corridor, and Ocho Rios and Old Harbour on the other. Kingsley Thomas, president of the Development Bank of Jamaica, was its relentless driver.

The need for such a project had been recognized decades before, and plans had already started. The construction of this highway was a part of our mission to raise living standards by creating a platform for a dynamic economy which would generate long-term growth and job creation. It was to be the first modern, controlled-access, multi-lane highway, with related arterial roads, and the single largest investment project in our country's history, as well as the single largest project of its kind in the entire English-speaking Caribbean.

A public-private partnership, the Highway 2000 Project was structured to maximize operational efficiency and minimize cost. This was an effective means of increasing public infrastructure capacity by mobilizing financial and other resources from the private sector. It was designed as a build-finance-operate and transfer project under which the private-sector partner would find the necessary financing to construct and run the highway for thirty-five years, after which it would be turned over to the government.

On 21 November 2001, Finance Minister Omar Davies signed the contract with Bouygues of France. The National Road Operating and Constructing Company and the Government of Jamaica, operating through a company called the Trans-Jamaican Highway Company Limited, would provide oversight.

The benefits of Highway 2000 have already proved significant. Even as some have complained and pushed back against the toll, others have welcomed the many advantages of the highway, which today provides safe and speedy links with Kingston. It was the model for the North-South Highway, which has contributed to increasing numbers of the urban population moving to suburban and rural areas, particularly Old Harbour, Ocho Rios and St Ann's Bay.

It was anticipated that Highway 2000 would be the catalyst for the revitalization and expansion of Portmore, Spanish Town, Old Harbour and May Pen. The overall objective was to transform communities along the corridor into vibrant social and economic spaces. In April 2015, it was renamed the P.J. Patterson Highway.

TOURISM

During my administration we also invested significantly in upgrading our seaports and airports in the effort to make our facilities world-class and competitive. Through the Port Authority of Jamaica the government carried out continuous and systematic upgrading. In 1998, the authority undertook a study to identify the medium- and long-term land requirements for the Port of Kingston.

Hunts Bay and Fort Augusta were identified as the most appropriate areas for development, which required relocating the causeway and reclaiming adjacent land, all of which was done.

My administration recognized the importance of planning for the future and maximizing our investments. Jamaica possesses one of the world's largest natural harbours and developing the Port of Kingston was highly strategic, involving consistent investment to ensure that we kept pace with the rapid changes in shipping which saw continuous growth in both commercial and leisure vessels. It was imperative that our ports could accommodate such mega-vessels.

The fierce competition among the major global shipping companies for the thirty-year concession to run the Kingston Container Terminal, won by the French-owned CMA CGM consortium, demonstrated the viability and continuing potential of the port. While our location is indeed a major strategic advantage, there would not have been much interest if the infrastructure had not been in place to support further, timely expansion. The plans which had been laid down from the turn of the century, and our consistent programme of expansion, were among the factors which positioned Jamaica to attract the US$510 million deal with the consortium to privatize the terminal in 2015.

Our efforts were not isolated to the Port of Kingston. Significant work was also undertaken in Port Antonio, Montego Bay and Ocho Rios, the latter two to allow mega-cruise liners access.

In terms of air transport, we saw the potential of the Donald Sangster International Airport in Montego Bay as the gateway to Europe, Latin America and the rest of the Caribbean as early as 1990. It would reduce the hassle of intra-regional travel and let us become a regional conference, business and financial centre. Despite initial resistance from the opposition, the privatization and subsequent expansion of the airport triggered the most far-reaching expansion of the tourism industry and growth in tourism-related air traffic.

Infrastructural developments were important planks in our overall strategy to revitalize tourism with a view to making Jamaica the destination of choice in the Caribbean. By 2006, tourism was the island's leading economic sector. Our success had resulted in the three million mark for tourist arrivals being achieved and foreign-exchange earnings reaching US$1.9 billion and climbing.

The growth of the sector rested squarely on the strategies embedded in the Tourism Master Plan which we had commissioned and was completed during the watch of Portia Simpson-Miller as minister.

As early as 1990, as minister of development, I initiated a study of the south-west coast, which was acknowledged as the main area for ecotourism. It ensured that the environment would be fully taken into account in all ongoing plans for Manchester, St Elizabeth and Westmoreland. Even as we wished to attract investment through building hotels, the infrastructure from Negril to Ocho Rios was inadequate. It was therefore imperative to upgrade and expand the sewerage and water infrastructure as well as the road network.

Additionally, the gateways to the island, by air and sea, had been modernized and vastly improved to accommodate the increased flow of visitors.

As a result of aggressive promotion through Pat Francis at the Jamaica Promotions Corporation, the sector benefited from foreign direct investment, primarily from Spanish hotel chains. The local private sector supported the drive and entered into various joint-venture arrangements to invest in high-end properties such as the Ritz Carlton, Hotel Riu, Iberostar, Bahia Principe, Fiesta, Couples Negril, Hedonism III and Beaches Whitehouse. The combination of luxury condominiums, hotels and villas added some twelve thousand rooms, an almost 50 per cent increase in the room stock.

The growth in the sector, which was faster than that of the region as a whole, was supported by prioritizing environmental sustainability as, after all, our country's extraordinary beauty and diversity in landscape are important in attracting visitors. Our focus on further diversifying through ecotourism would also depend on preserving our flora and fauna. Through ecotourism, too, we would ensure expansion and help spread economic benefits across a wider network of communities.

The UDC, which I inherited as minister of development in 1989, was gasping for life support. Vin Lawrence was made executive chairman and the UDC had to be re-evaluated and refocused. In earlier times, it had done a good job of acquiring and holding lands and properties considered strategic to development. Among them were properties along the shoreline zoned for hotel construction. These we developed through joint ventures and partnerships with local and overseas investors.

When I first assumed responsibility for the UDC in 1975, the incumbent chairman was Moses Matalon, a pioneer in large-scale property development. Along with Gloria Knight as general manager, he had headed all the major urban development since its inception in 1968, under the watchful eyes of Edward Seaga. Matalon's influence spread well beyond the shores of Jamaica. He had been involved in major dredging activities in St Lucia, and John Compton, the first prime minister of that island, recounted on many occasions how much of the land expansion near Castries was attributable to Matalon's drive.

Moses Matalon always had his ear to the ground for a good deal. I remember he was a chain-smoker who never finished a cigarette. When I enquired about this strange habit, he quipped, "At all times my mouth must be free to speak whenever a good bargain appears." One excellent bargain he negotiated for the UDC was the Rose Hall lands in Montego Bay. I was chairing a conference in Montego Bay on 14 September 1976 when Moses sent a message asking to speak with me. I told him we would speak after the meeting adjourned, but he was insistent that I take his call because it was extremely urgent.

When I came to the phone, he could not conceal his excitement. "Minister, Chase Manhattan Bank, Jamaica, has made a proposal to sell the UDC all of the shares of Rose Hall (Holiday Inn) and the collateral 3,000 acres of mortgaged land for US$9.5 million. We must take it now, and I want your ministerial authority to proceed." The land was owned by RCL Corporation, of which John Rollins was the founder and major shareholder. He failed to make the required payments to the bank, resulting in the offer to the UDC. This I accepted immediately, and after cabinet approval, the deal was closed on 18 November 1976.

Rollins took Chase Manhattan Bank to court in Delaware, but did not get a favourable verdict. Nor did the proceedings in the Jamaican courts – all the way to the Privy Council – grant the relief or award the damages he sought.

Rollins, the former lieutenant governor of Delaware, with his considerable political clout in Washington, used every opportunity before Congress, the US-based Overseas Private Investment Corporation and the State Department to claim his property had been expropriated, and in so doing tarnished Jamaica's name.

On our return to office in 1989, the cabinet was persuaded that every effort should be made to negotiate a settlement which would confirm beyond a doubt that Jamaica was an attractive location for investment, and simultaneously open the door for significant expansion along the Rose Hall corridor, which an amicable resolution would allow to proceed without delay.

Another vital consideration influenced the cabinet. The acreage we had legitimately acquired would indeed become the key to the expansion of Montego Bay. But the adjacent lands at Success Pen, Lilliput and Barrett Town still belonged to Rollins, and on those 700 acres lived hundreds of families who had built substantial houses. There could be no solution to this squatting without acquiring the titles from Rollins. The government's team was led by Vincent Lawrence of the UDC and Ken Rattray, solicitor general, two of Jamaica's most sophisticated negotiators.

Although the lands to be transferred between the government and Rollins were priced by two of the country's leading valuators, the deal was denounced by the opposition as a "sell-out". I was pilloried and condemned by Edward Seaga and Bruce Golding for putting to bed a dispute in which our legal rights were impeccable but which nevertheless harmed our image in the investment marketplace.

But this resolution, in a single stroke, triggered a flood of investment to expand tourism and converted potential squatter slums to orderly suburban developments in the Rose Hall corridor. Land which had been idle for decades became the location for the explosion of resort developments such as Cinnamon Hill and other Spanish investments which Rose Hall has enjoyed since then. In Lilliput, Success and Barrett Town there are now settled communities, with improved infrastructure, housing estates, schools and spaces for private commerce.

We obtained funding to build the Montego Bay Convention Centre, also in the Rose Hall corridor, during one of my prime-ministerial visits to Beijing in 2005. This state-of-the-art multipurpose facility is now fast realizing its potential as a venue for tourist-related conferences, consumer shows, and indoor sporting and entertainment events for both local and international audiences. It has already met its objective of making Jamaica the foremost convention destination in the Caribbean.

After 1989, the UDC also undertook several projects. Here, again, I had to counter resistance from the JLP leader to leasing lands to the Spanish hotel chain Riu for a 380-room property at Bloody Bay in Negril. The infrastructure was extended to include a sewer line which made additional lands available for hotels and resort villas; improvements to the Rutland Point Craft Market and the Negril Town Centre; and a beach attraction at Booby Bay.

Other north coast ventures included the Green Grotto Caves, which the UDC acquired and refurbished to develop a world-renowned nature park/reserve, offering diversity and variation on sand, sea and sun. And the refurbishment of the Dunn's River Falls, also managed by the UDC, has kept it a premier attraction.

The UDC also completed the South Coast Sustainable Development Master Plan, which identified potential development opportunities to ensure sustainability. The Sandals Whitehouse Hotel, a joint venture with Gorstew Limited, which opened up the south coast for major tourism development, is now regarded as a gem within that chain, notwithstanding the legal controversy which surrounded its construction.

The projects the UDC undertook were critical to creating the infrastructure for national development. They also included refurbishing major towns, including Montego Bay city centre, restoring historic buildings in Spanish Town and Port Royal, and squatter regularization and upgrading, most notably in Lilliput and Barnett Estates in Montego Bay and its environs, as well as areas of Ocho Rios.

In downtown Kingston the UDC considered access and residential facilities critical to the city's redevelopment and focused on building the coast road and affordable housing such as Manley Meadows. This facelift was encouraged by a tax incentive for property owners and developers to improve their holdings. As part of this upgrading the UDC directly managed the tidying-up of the market district and its environs as well as upgrading the Kingston Public Hospital.

Development in the Kingston metropolitan region was being hindered by the lack of appropriate sewage treatment and disposal, which had become the main contributor to pollution in the city and the Kingston Harbour, which had been abandoned as an important centre for recreational activities. Major sewerage and treatment systems, the Soapberry Wastewater Treatment Facilities, were built and the obsolete treatment plants in western Kingston, which had become nothing more than collection points for dumping raw sewage into the harbour, were closed. Curtailing the degradation of the harbour and its environs was monumental, and recreational activities, including cruise shipping, are once again viable options.

Lift Up Jamaica was specially designed to undertake small infrastructure projects in parish capitals and neighbouring towns, with a focus on providing employment, enhancing the appearance of these towns and contributing to an improved quality of life.

Not all the plans came to fruition. Most notable was the vision for Port Royal/ Spanish Town and downtown Kingston to become an exciting and authentic cultural heritage destination and cruise-ship port of call.

AGRICULTURE

In receiving the Agricola Medal in 2001 from the United Nations Food and Agriculture Organization for our efforts in the area of food security, I accepted that my individual award was very much the result of the hard work of a range of organizations and the farmers of Jamaica who have been the lifeline of the island's economy for centuries.

The abiding commitment of the PNP administration to food security can be traced back to the 1970s, even before the term gained global recognition. Our social and economic reform platform of that era included an ambitious land reform programme on which to pursue self-sufficiency in food production and thereby achieve individual and national self-reliance.

By the time I became prime minister, it was clear that the global agricultural architecture was undergoing revolutionary change. The preferential trade arrangements enjoyed by the Caribbean were under threat from the new international administrative organizations, led by the WTO, which now governed global trade. Despite vigorous lobbying by joint government and private-sector interests in the international arena, it was evident that the conditions of trade were moving unequivocally towards open competition.

Even as we reluctantly accepted the new situation, we tried to persuade the WTO that vulnerable economies such as ours would require understanding and support to prepare ourselves for the new regime by phasing out uncompetitive production and diversifying into new areas in and out of agriculture.

I took the opportunity in my address "Free Trade, Technology and Agri-Food" at the fifth Montreal Conference on Globalized Economies in June 1999 to share our perspective:

> Like any other area in the world, the Caribbean should prepare for the day when it will have to compete on an equal basis with other countries. But, to get to that situation, it requires understanding and support both in terms of transitional arrangements for phasing out uncompetitive production and diversifying into new areas inside and outside of agriculture.
>
> The provision of capital and technical assistance is required to take advantage of diversification opportunities as well as to achieve greater efficiency throughout the economy. If the WTO does not provide sufficient space for such arrangements, it will injure our prospect for development.
>
> Let us in the new millennium attempt a new start by putting in place arrangements that can give a chance to every country, having regard to the particulars of its situation, to move ahead.
>
> The WTO should provide support for orderly advance, not be a shackle to small developing countries in their effort to make progress.

On the domestic front we recognized the need to use technology as the catalyst for driving our agricultural production. The efforts of the Ministry of Agriculture, the National Commission on Science and Technology, the Scientific Research Council, and the Biotechnology Centre and other departments of the University of the West Indies and the College of Agriculture, Science and Education worked relentlessly to create a massive reservoir of scientific information and technological applications required to develop and modernize our agricultural sector and to position it on a sustainable growth path.

We recognized that one of the critical paths to stability and self-sustaining growth was the development of rural Jamaica, with the central plank being technology-enhanced agriculture. We approached this type of development on all fronts, including the poultry industry, goat rearing, resuscitating our dairy industry, developing the beef industry, retooling the sugar industry to improve efficiency and capacity, and tree-crop and domestic food-production projects.

In conjunction with enhancing agricultural production, we focused on implementing strategies, policies and programmes to achieve increased levels of export in both traditional and non-traditional commodities by developing a more efficient and coordinated regulatory framework, providing support through extension services, improved agro-processing, and empowering small farmers to share in the added value of their produce by facilitating business development, including focused business training and developing social capital among groups of farmers.

The Caribbean is among those small island economies that are most vulnerable to the vagaries of nature, and our small farmers are certainly among those who suffer most from the devastation caused by hurricanes and flood rains. Cognizant of the vital role played by the farmers in the overall development and growth of the nation, we focused on the development of the small producers, we worked with agencies such as the Development Bank of Jamaica and the Jamaica Agricultural Society on initiatives to ensure the viability of the sector. Among those initiatives we implemented were marketing assistance for small farmers to get their produce into the market and loans, through the Development Bank of Jamaica, to offset the costs of irrigation wherever needed. Several programmes led by the Ministry of Agriculture saw the revitalization of derelict farms, in particular cocoa farms; the Orchard Development Programme received special funding from the Development Bank of Jamaica; the coffee industry also benefited from funding of some J$22 million; and in 2003 we relaunched a campaign that had its roots in the 1970s – the Eat Jamaica Campaign, which continues to have relevance and support today.

Praedial larceny has been the scourge of the agricultural sector for decades and increased significantly in the 1990s to become a major threat to the ability of many farmers, small and large, to sustain operations and resulted in costing the sector millions each year. To tackle the issue we recommended the amendment of the Praedial Larceny Act in 2000 and the Agricultural Produce Act in 2005. The latter included new provisions, such as a compulsory receipt-book system to be used by farmers, and the fines for breaches under the act were increased.

As we worked to protect and develop our agricultural sector, we were grateful for the assistance provided by international partners such as the UN's Food and Agriculture Organization. Their important and impressive role in the development of the sector, with particular focus on small farmers and rural development, has been outstanding. Its contribution through the dissemination of scientific and technological knowledge has helped to increase productivity, eliminate diseases and raise the standards of rural life.

INFORMATION AND COMMUNICATIONS TECHNOLOGY

The transformation of the information and communications technology sector was largely triggered by the liberalization of the telecommunications sector, precipitated by the agreement between the government and Cable and Wireless in 1999 and the subsequent Telecommunications Act in 2000. The heavy lifting was all done during my time at the Ministry of Development, Production and Planning. Cable and Wireless resisted strongly. It used every weapon in its armoury, which included a prepayment made to alleviate the acute shortage of foreign exchange. We were insistent on removing its monopoly, which paved the way for Phillip Paulwell, as the new minister of science and technology, to launch the telecommunications auction – which attracted investments of over US$92 million. Some was allocated to finance special projects in the sector. This resulted in the entry of two mobile operators – Digicel and Oceanic Digital Jamaica.

In no time, Digicel, chaired by Denis O'Brien, made its presence felt in every aspect of national development. As soon as he landed in Jamaica as its first general manager, Seamus Lynch recruited a team including people like Harry Smith, and Digicel began to spread its wings throughout Jamaica and beyond.

By 2006, our information and communications technology sector was quite advanced. The administration had invested some US$700 million in infrastructure, including over US$100 million in submarine fibre-optic links, ranking Jamaica among the top five countries in the Western Hemisphere. Jamaica was also the leading business-outsourcing destination in the Caribbean in areas such as finance, business processing, accounting and so on.

This was made possible by a carefully planned development strategy which had its genesis in the early 1990s. We recognized that embracing information technology was an absolute necessity in order to be an active player in the twenty-first-century global information society.

We understood the need to adopt a first-world attitude to technology. The challenge was how to manage the transition in policy and investment. One thing was clear: the government and the private sector would have to collaborate to understand the country's information and communication needs and to create a road map to the information superhighway. We would have to design a support network for fast-growing high-technology businesses which offered guidance on and access to appropriate finance, training and market development. Another important factor was to find ways to help the population at large overcome barriers and build confidence in using new technologies.

We welcomed the challenge. We were looking to set the stage for e-governance, that is, the delivery of government services online – paying pensions and taxes, sharing information online, reducing paperwork and improving service. This was important, as modern technology could help government reduce costs and improve service delivery. We were well aware that development was contingent on creating a modern policy and regulatory framework, in compliance with international requirements.

WATER IS LIFE

In May 2011, the Inter-Action Council convened our meeting in Quebec City with policymakers and technical experts to discuss one subject – water. We were presented with an abundance of well-researched papers which reminded us of its linkages with the economy, standards of living, urbanization, migration, border conflicts and security. From my brief contribution, the seminar participants learned that the mission statement of Jamaica's National Water Commission was simple and short – "Water is life." To my utter amazement and delight, it became the opening line of the communiqué.

Xaymaca is the land of wood and water. Jamaica has been abundantly blessed with springs, streams and valleys. And yet there were areas where water was in short supply. In 1990, only 61 per cent of households had piped water. Since I grew up in rural Jamaica, the village tanks, the district standpipes, the memory of children carrying pails of water on their heads, the donkeys with pans in their hampers, were unforgettable parts of my experience.

In forming the new cabinet after the 1993 electoral victory, I handpicked Karl Blythe as minister of water. As expected, the critics questioned the need for a portfolio with only one subject. That sole assignment reflected the urgency and priority I attached to water as a critical resource.

I was not alone. A few years later, President Nelson Mandela shared with our prime-ministerial caucus, at the CARICOM Conference of Heads in St Lucia, his own awakening, on a visit to his ancestral village, to the vital importance of water. I permitted myself a smile of vindication as he confessed how this led him also to establish a Ministry of Water in the first post-apartheid government of South Africa.

Karl Blythe took to the ministry like a duck to water, so to speak. In a short time, he assembled quality staff eager to drive the agenda and provide safe drinking water for the entire population.

We recognized that the costs of an efficient and comprehensive water system would be high and it was therefore necessary to take a long-term approach. But we had to restore water tanks, extend domestic water schemes, provide water and create programmes to truck water to remote areas during periods of drought.

By 1996, I was able to report to the people of Jamaica, in my budget presentation, on major infrastructural developments that were under way. These included the Ocho Rios, Port Maria, Montego Bay (Great River) and Savanna-la-Mar (Roaring River) water supply systems, which would collectively benefit some 197,000 people through an investment of J$320 million.

Extensive upgrading of the sewerage systems along the north coast was part and parcel of ensuring that efficient infrastructure capable of supporting a growing tourism industry was in place. The Ocho Rios and Negril projects were already under way and the Montego Bay project had begun. The total investment in state-of-the-art developments was J$1.3 billion, benefiting more than 230,000 people.

In addition to these projects, in this period the National Water Commission was restructured to make it more efficient and viable, and capable of negotiating the delicate balance between its financial obligations and social imperatives. A new board was mandated to establish a framework to make the organization financially viable. The result was a turnaround from a net loss of J$1.044 billion in the fiscal year 1994–95 to an unaudited profit of J$23 million in 1995–96. To permit this performance, the government took over the liabilities of the commission, amounting to J$4 billion, representing for the most part a J$868 million debt to the government and a J$644 million debt to the Jamaica Public Service Company. Service delivery was enhanced through a new Revenue Recovery Department, which regularized a number of illegal connections and recovered over J$12 million.

A moment of intense pride was the launch of the Great River Water Supply project, in March 2003, which represented a significant partnership with the private sector. The bulk of the financing came from local sources, through the National Commercial Bank and the Pan Caribbean Financial Services. It was the culmination of the government consciously, deliberately and systematically engaging the private sector in development. We calculated that US$2.2 billion would be required to put in place all the water supply, sewerage and irrigation systems necessary for universal access, and we were prepared to enter other such partnerships.

Two years later, I had the pleasure of breaking ground for the Martha Brae Water Treatment plant, another milestone in providing first-world infrastructure for the citizens of Jamaica. Areas of the north coast had long outgrown the existing water supply, and the Martha Brae project would provide massive improvement in capability, reliability and quality. This was the third major part of the larger Northern Coastal Water Supply Improvement Project. The refurbishment of the plant was completed with an investment of some US$40 million, and increased the water supply from two to three million gallons per day.

The framework was as important as the actual infrastructural improvements. We passed legislation which established institutions to create an environment that would facilitate growth. In 1995, the Water Resources Act ensured a legal framework for a system to provide adequate potable water and sewerage. The following year, we created the Water Resources Authority, an independent body responsible for managing and allocating water resources, so that problems of access would not deter private investment.

A new licensing regime was put in place for all service providers, public or private. In essence, all these government initiatives gave the private sector a legitimate and real role in the water sector, with appropriate regulatory controls to ensure high-quality service and fair tariffs.

In 1995, the Office of Utilities Regulation was established to set rates independently so private investors could be guaranteed a fair return on their investment, while protecting consumers from any inefficiencies in the delivery of utilities.

Over the period of my leadership we consistently and continually upgraded the island's water supply, increased access and improved the quality of water. The scope, intensity and pace of water expansion was unprecedented and unparalleled. For the first time, all schools had a reliable source of clean, safe drinking water. In 2006, 85 per cent of Jamaican families had access to potable water, and 75 per cent had piped water in their houses.

ENERGY

Energy is a piston in every engine of economic growth and vital to social development. The devastating effects of the sharp increases in OPEC pricing during the 1970s, given my ministerial responsibilities, are indelibly etched in my mind.

Energy, security, economic growth and sustainable development are inextricably linked with the survival of Jamaica. Over 90 per cent of Jamaica's energy needs are imported. A close analysis of our export earnings for 2003 revealed that over two-thirds was then spent on importing petroleum, used primarily in generating electricity and in the transport, mining and manufacturing sectors.

This heavy dependence on imported energy, with volatile oil prices, has had a crippling effect on financial planning in the Jamaican economy. We moved to improve energy efficiency and utilize renewable energy, which offer great potential for reducing the negative effects of the ever-increasing rates of energy consumption associated with economic growth.

There was a dire need to establish new management systems to reduce usage and costs and to increase efficiency by producing more from the same input. Whether it was renewable energy – wind, solar, hydropower, geothermal, or biomass – we sought to lift public awareness. We believed a committed public would more readily cooperate in using energy more efficiently.

In 1989, the energy situation could best be described as chaotic. Supplies to the customer were unreliable and caused much frustration, with the Jamaica Public Service Company undertaking almost daily load-shedding. This seriously affected national production as well as citizens' quality of life, and therefore had to be tackled immediately. Our preliminary analysis showed that the generating capacity needed to be upgraded and expanded. This was a costly exercise and ways would have to be found to finance this. One approach was to introduce independent power producers – Jamaica Private Power Limited and Jamaica Energy Partners – to generate and provide electricity to the Jamaica Public Service grid. One of these, Jamaica Private Power Limited, is still operating.

Later, there were discussions in cabinet on breaking the Jamaica Public Service into three distinct areas: generation, transmission and distribution, each operating independently. The decision was taken by cabinet to privatize the company and in 1996–97 we made our first attempt, based on this model. The bids we received, however, were not considered to be in the best interest of the country and the exercise was aborted. We decided to retain the company as a single entity and put in place a robust regulatory agency to replace the existing licensing authority. Thus it became the first entity regulated by the new Office of Utilities Regulation. In 2000, the Jamaica Public Service Company was privatized, with the government retaining 20 per cent of the shares. This arrangement has worked well, and as of 2007 more than 90 per cent of the country had ready access to electricity.

Post-privatization, the emphasis shifted to reducing the cost of electricity to the end user. A number of initiatives were undertaken, including sourcing less expensive fossil fuel, introducing renewables, most notably the wind farm at Wigton, and expanding the use of solar technology. The imperatives of energy security and efficiency make these considerations central to the pursuit of our regional and global relationships.

For a number of years, Jamaica had had the opportunity to import petroleum and petroleum products on favourable terms from Mexico under the San José Accord and from Venezuela under the Caracas Agreement. Under those agreements, both countries provided a significant volume of crude oil per day to Jamaica, which was then processed at our refinery. The PetroCaribe Agreement opened a new chapter in South-South cooperation.

In the 1970s, Eric Williams, Forbes Burnham and Michael Manley had discussed how best to combine the oil resources of Trinidad and Tobago with bauxite mineral deposits from Guyana and Jamaica to build an aluminium smelter. With the advent of the CARICOM Single Market and Economy (CSME), Trinidad and Tobago's prime minister, Patrick Manning, and I decided to boost our ability to compete effectively within and beyond Caribbean borders, as the time had come to increase the pace of economic integration. To that end, we signed an agreement in Port of Spain on 2 November 2004 for the supply of liquefied natural gas to Jamaica. We established a joint development team to refine the project's economic parameters. We envisaged a supply of approximately 1.1 million tons of liquefied natural gas per annum for a period of twenty years, at prices to be agreed.

Prime Minister Manning fully appreciated that such an agreement would have an additional bonus for Trinidad and Tobago, as it would stimulate the Jamaican economy and increase trade with his country's second largest market. In the confidence of those assurances, I presided over a number of strategic meetings before my departure from office so that the appropriate plans were in place.

CHAPTER 26

EDUCATION: THE PLATFORM FOR HUMAN DEVELOPMENT

IN THE CUT AND THRUST OF POLITICAL LIFE, the exchanges are between those who regard themselves as adversaries but ought to recognize they are really colleagues striving to secure the common good after fiery, abusive and even bitter arguments.

My many years of political involvement had exposed me somewhat to taking in my stride criticism which was at times personal, unfounded and even vitriolic. But a clip on the television news one night incited in me an extraordinary fit of anger and repulsion. During an intense battle between the teachers and the government for a bigger wage package, the president of the Jamaica Teachers' Association, Sherlock Allen, savagely attacked me and the government for our negotiating stance – fair enough – but went on to assert – "The cabinet is hostile to you, the teachers, because they have a vested interest to keep our people in ignorance." I virtually exploded. It was good that I was alone, and even better that the teachers' president was out of fighting range.

I felt mortally wounded, for there was never any doubt in my own mind that whatever goals I had achieved in life were due to my seizing educational opportunities. I have never forgotten how many of my bright classmates at Somerton were denied spaces in our secondary-school system because of severe financial constraints. I fully understood what advantage I gained from winning one of the few scholarships in the island. The most important factor in my own development was the commitment of both my parents to ensuring I had a proper educational foundation and that I would also be guided by the enlightened values on which they set great store. My progress through the stages of my personal growth in learning, awareness and academic discipline guaranteed that my political agenda would reflect a strong and sustained determination to facilitate human development, in its broadest sense, for the good of the Jamaican society.

I was clear that education was the platform on which Jamaica's future needed to be built, one that embraced an enlightened and inclusive approach to engaging all human resources in the cause of national advancement. I knew education and training were important elements of the investment which had to be made in building human and social capital in Caribbean nations.

The pressures on state resources were real, driven in part by the new financial strictures and also by the heightened expectations that the people of Jamaica have whenever a PNP government holds office. This was in a decade which had begun with the liberalization of the banking sector, substantially at the urging of our international funding partners, with consequences which challenged the traditional approach to managing our economy. At the same time, we recognized that education and the social services needed to be addressed urgently if social stability was to be preserved and the climate for investment and growth sustained.

In my first budget presentation, I made a point of establishing that "the level of economic development in any country is inevitably related to that country's investment in human-resource development".

Five years later, addressing Parliament and the nation, I was using stronger language: "I used the word 'crusade'. That is the mode in which we are . . . What I am seeking to accomplish when I speak of a quantum leap or the new five-year education thrust is the stimulation of a new awareness of the high place that education, training and human-resource development must occupy in the national scheme of things."

When we ordered an in-depth analysis of the school system, we found a number of sobering issues. Research in the 1980s had revealed that while the free education policy for high schools introduced by Michael Manley in 1973 had not been officially reversed, schools were being underfunded and were resorting to different devices to remain functional. These included employing the least qualified and therefore lower-paid teachers, and imposing a range of supplementary fees.

High school principals admitted they could not estimate what it would cost to deliver the programmes they offered or would like to offer at the quality level they wished. There were space, equipment and operational deficits throughout the system. At the beginning of the school year each September, there was chaos as schools opened in a less-than-ready state. At the primary level, in particular, children would turn up only to find they could not be accommodated. We had to find a way at least to have the basic requirements in place to give students a realistic chance of a meaningful education.

Between 1990 and 1991, the minister of education, Carlyle Dunkley, and the minister of state in education, Burchell Whiteman, held discussions with a range of experts and stakeholders. By the time of the 1994 budget, the cabinet had accepted the need to introduce a cost-sharing regime at the secondary level as a contribution to a base for quality education. It was acknowledged that the "cost-sharing model" would create some hardships, but it was my clear position that no child should be denied access because of an inability to pay the fees required under this new model. Once the need was genuine, parents could access funds. Of course, this required changes in how the schools operated. Those who were unsympathetic had to be closely monitored to ensure that the programme was not subverted.

Some years after the introduction of fees, we were able to formalize the distribution of the subsidy using the Programme for Advancement through Health and Education by ensuring that all beneficiaries qualified for relief from paying fees. We involved parents, students, school boards, academicians, the private sector, unions and the church in a national outreach, to ensure each child had a place and could attend school.

My fundamental concern extended to the quality of education. For me, education, formal and non-formal, has to be effective in shaping values, attitudes, behaviours and skills to build a socially cohesive society. Education may not be a panacea for our socio-economic ills, but it must provide the key to cultural awareness and help bring about sustained improvements in the quality of life for all.

Education has to be the key driver of social and economic transformation. The new age of technology has shifted the nexus of competition to knowledge and information. Jamaica, like the rest of the region, had to adopt the principles of knowledge creation and lifelong learning in order to remain viable and relevant in the global marketplace. Education, scientific literacy and technological innovation are precursors to a knowledge society. The ideal is a broad education base that emphasizes the trainability of workers up to secondary level, with specialization at the tertiary level.

In February 2004, I appointed the fourteen-member Task Force on Educational Reform to prepare and present an action plan consistent with a vision for creating a world-class education system to generate the human capital and produce the skills necessary for Jamaican citizens to compete in the global economy. Both Edward Seaga and I were determined to reach a national consensus on the future of education devoid of partisan politics. Education should never be a political football.

In 2002, we undertook to freeze secondary-school fees and ultimately abolished cost-sharing by 2005–6. By the time Parliament came to reflect on that decision in 2005, the Financing Successor Committee to the Task Force on Education Reform, chaired by Eric Crawford, viewed cost-sharing as "a part of the package of educational reform in the transformation exercise".

I shared in my budget presentation of 2005 the recommendation of the task force that the "cost-sharing scheme be retained and secondary schools allowed to continue to charge fees. Such fees should be limited to a set percentage of the economic cost of educating each child." The fees remained frozen at the 2002–3 level and the book rental charge was absorbed by the portion of the fees paid by the government.

The availability of funds on a timely basis was critical to sustaining the transformation. There were some long-term decisions to be taken which would require further consideration. The creation of additional housing stock, primarily through the NHT, had led to significant population shifts and changes in settlement patterns, and had a bearing on the location of schools and the availability of school places.

The NHT recognizes its social responsibility for the creation of homes and communities rather than dwellings in housing schemes. Hence the board decided to make a one-off contribution of J$5 billion towards the transformation. This required amendment of the NHT Act.

The parliamentary resolution put quality primary and secondary education at the top of the agenda. We were determined to reverse the decline in the consistency of the quality of education across the island; ensure the proficiency of school leavers; and to equip them adequately to assimilate into the workplace and the wider society.

The task force, chaired by Rae Davis, former president of the University of Technology, undertook the most fundamental examination of our education system in the post-independence era. Its recommendations were designed to transform the entire system within approximately ten to fifteen years.

Among the key recommendations were: the modernization of the Ministry of Education to become a policy ministry; upgrading curriculum teaching and learning support systems with particular focus on literacy and numeracy; exposing school boards and principals to new concepts of governance, with emphasis on leadership and administration; and building community participation and ownership of schools to influence positive behavioural changes and stimulate a higher level of involvement.

That vision was reached through a consultative process involving a steering team appointed by the minister of education, Maxine Henry-Wilson. A shared national vision for education emphasized the tremendous value of full stakeholder participation, equitable and accessible education for all, and accountability, transparency and performance at all levels to produce a disciplined and ethical Jamaican citizen who is culturally aware. The elements of this vision informed the review and provided the contextual framework to understand where the country was and where we should go within the shortest possible time.

The cabinet accepted that the education sector should receive the largest percentage of the disposable national budget, but it was never as much as we would have liked. In debates on the size of our external debt, I was obliged to point out that huge portions of our repayment and servicing it involved meeting obligations for capital and related projects directly linked to building schools, as well as development loans for tertiary education and teacher training.

Not all of our youngsters will profit to the same extent from what is essentially an academic programme, but our schools must be equipped with the facilities and the teachers to guarantee optimal personal achievement for each student. There can be no hard dividing line between the academic and technological on the one hand and the practical and vocational on the other. Now more than ever, our schools must be genuine places of learning where the emphasis is on the learner. Education is not only about acquiring skills and knowledge. It is about integrating both with the development of a sense of self and a sense of belonging. It was my hope that the transformation programme would lead us to that point.

Even before this, we were showing signs of improvement and growth. In terms of funding the sector, we made significant progress in real terms over the decade and a half. From as early as 1993, there was a year-on-year increase in the budgetary allocation of 4 per cent, bringing the share to 13 per cent. By 2001, that had risen to 17.5 per cent, well ahead of our commitment to a minimum of 15 per cent. In terms of expenditure on education as a percentage of the country's GDP, we were ahead of most of the Latin American and Caribbean region, not excluding some of the more advanced economies. The World Bank reported that Jamaica's public spending on education in constant dollar terms had increased by 68.2 per cent between 1987 and 1997 and had grown to 6.3 per cent of GDP in 1996–97. Five years later, the 1987 level of spending had tripled, standing at US$422 million.

Did we receive value for money? There are some indicators from which I draw encouragement. The *World Bank Statistical Report* for 2004 gives a gross enrolment ratio of the eligible quintile for tertiary education in Jamaica as moving from 6.5 per cent in 1991 to 19.5 per cent in 2004. This represents a significant advance. Even so, some analyses which examine the enrolment of the eighteen-to-thirty-five age cohort, the traditionally accepted measurement, would put the 2004 figure higher. Suffice it to say that by any measure we have come a long way – but not nearly far enough for me. In my 1996 budget speech, I voiced my concerns on what was then reported as 22 per cent enrolment in tertiary institutions: "This is the group which provides the professional, managerial and technical leadership of the country. To fulfil the needs of the National Industrial Policy, we require an enrolment of 120,000. So we need to increase tertiary enrolment by five times."

The fact is, however, that Jamaica was by then and remains today well ahead of the target set by CARICOM: a 15 per cent tertiary education enrolment rate by the year 2015. It is also the case that the paradigm shift for the sector has been accepted, as we continue to expand the range of tertiary-level offerings and to embrace new technologies for delivery, while preserving the structures for ensuring quality and relevance. Of course, vertical integration of the system was always central to my thinking about education and training and the relevance of both to productivity, economic growth and social inclusion.

By 1999, I had to remind the public and the managers of the education system that teachers' training colleges were facing the prospect of accepting an average of only one student out of every seven qualified applicants. Community colleges and sixth forms were in a similar situation. In the previous five years, the number of students gaining the Certificate of Secondary Education set by the Caribbean Examinations Council had doubled. More significantly, in that period, the number obtaining what, for qualification purposes, were regarded as passing grades had almost tripled, from approximately thirty-seven hundred to over ten thousand. Some investments were certainly showing returns, but it was important that the momentum should be preserved as we approached the new millennium.

I chose to take as broad a view of our human-development strategy as I could. Through the Ministry of Education, the formal system pursued its mandate. By the end of the 1990s, there were major changes from early childhood through to the tertiary level. A degree programme in early childhood education had been started as a joint venture between the University of the West Indies and the Shortwood Teachers' College. A programme to place a minimum of one trained teacher, paid by the ministry, in each of the nearly two thousand basic (community) schools had been set in train.

The 2004 Task Force on Education was mandated by parliamentary resolution to report how to fix early childhood education and ensure that all our children received a solid start. We have seen the Early Childhood Commission make great strides in raising standards and output. This has led to improved quality among the students entering the primary sector, with the emphasis on early detection and intervention before grade 4. Some improvements are already evident, but there is still far to go.

Physical improvements to basic schools and the construction of new ones had allowed for greater access and some quality improvements. Pilot schools had been selected to test the value of using more technology-supported learning programmes at that level. At my insistence, a programme was funded for providing enriched nutrition, targeted at the most vulnerable children.

Work was started on what was to become the Child Development Agency by consolidating the administration of day-care supervision and early childhood education management within the Ministry of Education.

At the primary level, we increased investment in school maintenance, separate and apart from building new schools and refurbishing others. Grants to primary schools and the book stock for libraries were increased, and computer-assisted learning was beginning to take root.

The government recognized the importance of supporting teachers to master new technologies and improve their ability to facilitate their students' learning alongside their own personal competencies. In partnership with the Human Employment and Resource Training Trust, the Ministry of Education supported the Jamaica Teachers' Association's establishment of an onsite training facility and provided a revolving loan fund to help teachers acquire their own computers.

The teachers, for their part, accepted the need for retraining to achieve optimum returns from the new curricula at primary and secondary levels introduced during the decade. While there is no doubt that the monitoring and management of teacher performance left much to be desired, much was done to improve their skills and sense of well-being. Not only did they receive the largest salary increases – in real terms – for a generation, but they were also exposed to new skills and approaches to teaching and learning which would serve them well.

The feud between the Jamaica Teachers' Association president and me had a happy ending. During the bitter dispute, a comparative salary review of teachers' salaries was put in train. No matter how hard I tried, the association had refused to accept that this was a separate exercise which would have to await the outcome of reclassification. However, they were all smiling when I presented the report at the Jamaica Conference Centre. I could not fail to remind them of the harsh things which had been said. The past president sent me a note, "True, Prime

Minister, harsh things were said, indeed. Some of your people even called me a Labourite (smile)." And so we buried the hatchet.

Our teachers' ambition to do well for themselves, their students and their families has always been a feature of the profession. I believe that the policies of my administration helped to sharpen this ambition. We are not a society which places arbitrary limits on individual choice or individual aspiration and therefore, when the prospect beckoned of migrating to other countries and higher-paying jobs, with the prospect of further education, a few hundred took advantage of the opportunity. Many returned to Jamaica better for the experience, often more appreciative of our country as a result of having served elsewhere, and the teaching service both survived and benefited.

One of the outcomes of the transformation programme, through the National Teaching Council, was a programme to ensure that all teachers had at least an undergraduate degree. This approach to certification and qualification was often discussed in the 1990s, although it was left for a later administration to convert the vision to reality.

The primary curriculum was revised and a student assessment structure created to give our students the best chance of learning what was required at their age and developmental stage. Teachers were again critical to this approach, because it required them to pay close attention to assessing each child and to tailor the learning process to meet the child's particular needs. While there was no uniformity of compliance, it remains my hope that as performance management improves, worthy edifices will be built on the foundations laid then.

In 1999, I said that we were closing the century with "a change in the rites of passage from primary to secondary education. The predictive Common Entrance Examination was replaced by a test which emphasizes that achievement is available to all and continues the process of improving performance on the basis of ongoing assessment."

Despite the outcry from anxious parents, and the continuing reality that not all our secondary institutions were as yet appealing to many members of the society, I remained convinced that the change was the correct one. A child must be taught, or, more correctly, facilitated to learn both skills and content appropriate to his or her age. It is on that basis that the next level of that child's education must be continued. It is up to us, in government, in the teaching profession and in the society to create the environment which makes the ongoing development of the young person possible, effective and fulfilling. I do not wish any child in my country to feel less appreciated, valued, supported or fulfilled than I did when I entered Calabar High School or when I left it six years later.

And what of tertiary access? In 1992, there was one recognized university in Jamaica. That was the University of the West Indies, with an enrolment under ten thousand. A number of offshore universities were operating here, usually in partnership with a local tertiary-level education or industrial management training institution.

In 1995, the University of Technology was established, with full protection of academic standards and professional integrity. Its antecedents were proud ones. The College of Arts, Science and Technology had been producing highly competent, skilled and educated people for both the private and public sectors for decades. Since 1986, it had been doing so under a special charter which allowed it to grant degrees in a limited range of disciplines. Between 1959 and 1986, it had operated under the College of Arts, Science and Technology Scheme, validated formally by Parliament in 1964. For one year before that, it was known as the Jamaica Institute of Technology. On 1 September 1995, it was formally accorded university status and became the University of Technology, Jamaica. The act which made permanent provisions for its establishment was approved by Parliament on 8 June 1999 and signed into law by Governor General Sir Howard Cooke on 29 June.

It was my pleasure to deliver the main address at its ceremonial opening. It represented for me an important step towards enlarging the critical mass of skilled graduates needed for development. It was also a celebration of home-grown talent and academic and institutional leadership.

Four years later, in 1999, another tertiary institution became a national university with the requisite international reach and reputation. Led then by Herbert Thompson, Northern Caribbean University grew out of the West Indies College, a Seventh-Day Adventist institution on the outskirts of Mandeville, which enjoyed a reputation for scholarship, effective teaching and the moral underpinnings of its institutional practice.

Like the University of Technology, it had a long history. It had started as a secondary-level facility, teaching students up to grade 12. In 1936, it became a training college, operating first as a junior college, then achieved senior college status in the late 1950s, and was renamed West Indies College in 1959. Since then, baccalaureate programmes in some twenty other disciplines have been added.

In 1999, the Jamaican government granted the college university status and it was renamed Northern Caribbean University. Serving central Jamaica, with campuses in the east, north and west, it was certainly a welcome addition.

The University Council of Jamaica, established in 1987, provides the quality assurance required for national and international acceptance of our tertiary-level graduates. What might seem like an explosion of degree-granting institutions will best support the national development goals for our country.

Under the rules of the WTO, education services – certainly at the tertiary level – were included in those open to international competition. While we could not close our borders to either well-meaning or predatory invasion by foreign universities, we were obliged to protect our capacity for self-development by strengthening our own tertiary and higher-education institutions. Indeed, our goal was to make them attractive to foreign students, fully appreciating the value of earning foreign exchange as well as demonstrating the competence of our local academic and professional staff.

I was delighted by a later decision to grant university college status to The Mico Teachers' College, an institution that many describe as Jamaica's first university, Mico having produced so many outstanding men and women in its 170-year history. Many Jamaicans and other Caribbean nationals, notably from the Bahamas, Turks and Caicos and Cayman Islands, owe a debt of gratitude to Mico for their education, either directly or through its graduates.

At the other end of the spectrum, I found it both personally rewarding and socially important to initiate the Possibility Programme. In partnership with the church, the YMCA and the private sector, this programme catered to the needs of young boys on the streets of Kingston who were caught between eking out a living by wiping windscreens and living on the margins of the criminal underworld. Within the first year, eighty-two young people were supported by social workers and given training and employment to set them on a new path.

Jamaica has no short-term prospects of full employment, given the national and global realities of the times. I was painfully aware that the social stability of the country and our prospects for sustained economic development were vulnerable to the threats posed not only by high unemployment but also by high youth unemployment. We would, for a long time, be unable to provide the kind of social safety net which more-developed countries were able to offer to their citizens. It was necessary therefore to marry training opportunities to the emerging technologies as far as possible and find creative ways of equipping more of our young people for gainful employment.

The National Youth Service was restored as part of the development spectrum. A related initiative was a programme for tertiary students created under the two banners of the Youth Service and the Values and Attitudes initiative. The Jamaica Values and Attitudes Programme for Tertiary Level Students came into being to help finance students' college and university fees and at the same time provide community service in areas of national need. Credits were given for the hours they served and the work they did, allowing the government to give a subsidy to offset the students' fees. Participating students were required to complete two hundred hours of service annually. Of course, an important objective was to reinforce the concept of service and to improve the young people's ability to work with others cooperatively and efficiently. The fields of work included not only schools, hospitals, hospices and homework centres but also beautification and construction projects. For many of the students, dealing with adult authority outside the high school setting would have been a new experience. Now they had to accept the role of employees, responsible for outputs which directly affected the well-being of other people.

All these initiatives were designed to support a broader programme which I believed was of central importance to Jamaica's social and economic development. Unless people are liberated by access to education and experience – the real power to change their existence for the better – a debilitating and incapacitating sense of injustice will always limit their ability to be fully involved in the development of their society. That link between efficiency at the workplace, productivity and a sense of responsibility for self and others has always been at the centre of my thinking about the human-development component of our national effort.

☙

I was privileged to chair the 1997 CARICOM summit, which focused substantially on education and the human-development aspect of the community's preparation for life in the twenty-first century. With the participation of regional ministers of education, heads of government adopted a statement on the "Ideal Caribbean Person" with which I fully identified and was privileged to endorse and promote:

> The Ideal Caribbean Person should be someone who among other things:
> - is imbued with a respect for human life, since it is the foundation on which all the other desired values must rest; is emotionally secure, with a high level of self-confidence and self-esteem;
> - sees ethnic, religious and other diversity as a source of potential strength and richness; is aware of the importance of living in harmony with the environment; has a strong appreciation of family and kinship values, community cohesion, and moral issues, including responsibility for and

accountability to self and community; has an informed respect for the cultural heritage; demonstrates multiple literacies and independent and critical thinking, questions the beliefs and practices of past and present and brings this to bear on the innovative application of science and technology to problem-solving; demonstrates a positive work ethic; values and displays the creative imagination in its various manifestations and nurtures its development in the economic and entrepreneurial spheres in all other areas of life.

Such a person would be equipped to be in the truest sense a productive citizen of country, region and the world, because he or she "has developed the capacity to create and take advantage of opportunities to control, improve, maintain and promote physical, mental, social and spiritual well-being and to contribute to the health and welfare of the community and country and nourishes in him/herself and in others the fullest development of each person's potential without gender stereotyping and embraces differences and similarities between females and males as a source of mutual strength".[1]

I retain the hope that we will realize the potential that this country and this region still hold to become a place of peace as well as a focal point of social, cultural and economic power within this hemisphere and in the larger global community.

Formal education has generally been identified as the principal means by which the holistic development of the person is achieved. The 1997 declaration clearly implied that. But optimal facilitation of that holistic development has to depend on and be supported by a broader framework of empowerment, deliberately and carefully constructed. In Jamaica's case, I identified three particular elements of that framework.

The first was telecommunications. In the 1990s the information and communications technology revolution was taking the world by storm. There were doubts about where it would lead, its sustainability, its affordability for small economies and whether investing in it was the best use of our resources. The records will show that in the formulation of the National Industrial Policy we took the bold step of identifying information technology as one of the critical clusters which offered opportunities for industrial growth and comparative advantage.

Jamaica worked with prominent telecommunications companies to instal a

---

1. CARICOM Secretariat, *CARICOM*, 146.

modern system of fixed lines and broadband across the island. It is true to say that cell-phone coverage is almost complete, with most families having a fair degree of access. We take it for granted, in the twenty-first century, that mobile telephones are the most effective vehicle for personal communication and that the associated technologies enhance the efficiency of doing business at all levels. But it should not be forgotten that what we enjoy today is the direct result of a deliberate strategy to empower people at all levels of the society. I recall one parliamentarian, in a sectoral debate of 1997, illustrating graphically the difference to the lives and the profits of the farmers in the hills of Clarendon, who no longer had to make two trips to the hotels on the north coast to sell their produce, but relied on a much improved telephone system.

In the education sector, the evolution of the application of information technology was also a major cause for satisfaction. The process might not have been linear or rapid, as the schools moved from setting up computer laboratories to the more systemic and strategic use of computers. The managers of institutions improved their administrative and management. Educators were able to make increasingly good use of programmes, whether purchased from abroad, created by local experts, or judiciously selected from Internet sources, to improve methods and quality of learning as well as the broadening the students' knowledge base. What happened in schools also affected the larger community as parents, out-of-school youth, and teachers themselves increased their own opportunities to make the technology work for them and enrich their personal lives.

A knowledge society was being created in real terms. I am reminded of the familiar observation of the eighteenth-century English scholar Samuel Johnson: "Knowledge is of two kinds. We know a subject ourselves, or we know where we can find information on it." Both kinds were becoming more accessible to our people, and the effect of this development is unlikely ever to be reversed.

The second element of the framework complements the first. Media policy in the last years of the twentieth century and the first years of the twenty-first was aimed both at increasing the involvement of local entrepreneurs and established enterprises in diversifying the industry, and providing a greater spread of information sources. Of course, newspapers have always responded to market needs and opportunities, and, while operating under the laws of Jamaica, have not come under any form of regulatory control. With centuries-old traditions of a free press behind us, we cherish their right to be free and to provide the extremely valuable service which a democratic society requires.

Radio and television, however, are constrained by the availability of spectrum, which governments or their agents control the world over. Those media are also the ones with the greatest reach and immediacy of impact.

Jamaica Broadcasting Corporation radio had been created by Norman Manley as a national broadcast entity in 1959. By 1963 Jamaica Broadcasting Corporation television was established as our only television station. There is no doubt that the corporation had served our people well over the years. It fulfilled its mandate to let Jamaicans see and hear themselves. Despite the high costs of producing and transmitting locally created programmes, especially on television, it showcased local talent and whetted our appetites for Jamaican cultural products of high quality. The late Wycliffe Bennett played a seminal role in that development, and his legacy lives on today. But the corporation suffered from two major disabilities. The first was a chronic shortage of funding. The second was political manipulation of its content under different administrations. Despite our best efforts to preserve its national rather than governmental profile, it became necessary on the grounds of both economic necessity and sound information policy to divest it.

So it was that Television Jamaica came into being and the RJR Communications Group developed into a conglomerate. But, very importantly, the space was opened for other players, and the principles of openness and of competition in the market were honoured. Now, of course, there are many other local channels on Jamaican television screens.

With the advent of satellite transmission, governments had to meet the need for new policies and regulations and deal with international conventions governing cross-border transmissions. In the 1990s we recognized the entrepreneurial initiative of small and medium-sized operators who responded to the need to offer subscriber television services – commonly called "cable" – to a demanding public. We also had to take into account the potential of radio to supply a greater variety of news, entertainment and other services to the listening public.

The fledgling subscriber television industry had to be managed sensitively. We were always mindful of the need to comply with copyright and intellectual property requirements and also aware that some operators were tempted to cut costs by not paying their bills to overseas suppliers. The Broadcasting Commission worked assiduously to manage the licensing and regulatory processes in a fair and transparent way, and to educate the public about its own responsibilities as well.

In the case of radio, the growth was exponential. The administration of the 1980s had privatized the three regional Jamaica Broadcasting Corporation radio stations, paving the way for the further expansion of sound broadcasting. We took the process to another level in the next decade and a half, with the result that there are now twenty-seven radio stations in the country, with fewer than six having only limited-area reception.

The opening of the media landscape clearly did more for Jamaica than providing a greater choice of entertainment. It gave us more sources, more opportunity for news which was not only international or national but community-focused, and it provided a voice for the people as much as it gave them choice. The talk-radio component of local broadcasting has allowed a two-way expression of views and sharing of information which has played a major part in widening the national information and opinion base. Talk-show hosts, listeners from every social stratum, political leaders, providers of goods and services, students have an opportunity to learn from people in every corner of the country and can benefit from what is said by some who would otherwise have been unheard.

This aspect of the media policy has certainly changed the nature of communication and flattened the information pyramid. No longer can a dominant voice speak without challenge to the broad mass of the population. No longer can it be fairly claimed that "the little person" has no voice. And certainly the Jamaican people, who have always known more about the world than the world knows about them, can not only strengthen their appreciation of what is right and what is not quite right within their own country, but can share it with all who wish to listen.

The third and final plank in the platform of human development through opportunity for education and personal growth was providing people with access to government information.

At a meeting at the Carter Center in Atlanta, President Jimmy Carter offered technical support for framing our policy on access to information, legislation and implementation. This was a relatively new departure for governance as it obtained in most countries throughout the world, and certainly in developing countries. I was quite aware that our traditions, inherited from the pre-independence period, led us more in the direction of secrecy than of openness. Quite apart from the new trends in modern western democracies, it was also my belief that we needed to build more trust between government and people in the Jamaica of today.

This initiative was not popular with everyone in government. Both the political directorate and public officers had misgivings. The latter had concerns about the amount of time they would have to spend combing files and following paper trails to answer questions from the media and the general public. The introduction of the regime was accompanied by measures to improve record-keeping in government ministries and agencies. Officials were also concerned about the loss of their anonymity in respect of advice they might have given to ministers. In my experience, a minister is better off getting the frankest and most challenging opinions and indeed facts from his technical officers and working through them systematically than being improperly advised and then having to face the consequences.

Ministers understood the value of transparency, but had a concern that the items that remained protected under the act might be too limited, and that political mischief could be made by the public exposure of some facts without an appreciation of context.

The Access to Information Act has made it possible for any Jamaican to hold his or her government accountable. This is an important part of building trust, of giving people a sense of ownership and responsibility in relation to the government, and of creating a greater sense of justice and equity in the society as a whole.

One of the notable features of the programme, during the early implementation, was the forums in tertiary institutions to sensitize teachers and other potential leaders to their opportunities and indeed obligations under the act. In a sense, formal education and the broader set of initiatives to empower our people within a human-development framework were coming together.

Politicians and economists are among the groups most likely to fall prey to the imperatives of demonstrating short- and medium-term benefits and also responding to market forces. By upbringing, political philosophy and by direct experience, I have tried to avoid taking extreme positions driven by these imperatives.

We have come a long way. We should never downplay the role of political action in bringing us to the level of development which we enjoy today. We need to appreciate the continuum initiated at the time of universal adult suffrage in 1944, of which it is our duty to be a part, as each succeeding administration responds to the people's needs. We perhaps forget, for example, that despite legislation in the 1970s which removed the status of "illegitimate child" from our vocabulary, it was by virtue of a constitutional amendment in 1993 that a Jamaican mother was empowered to claim the same rights as a Jamaican father in determining her child's nationality, if the other parent is from a different country.

SCIENCE AND TECHNOLOGY

Even before the days of full self-government, Jamaica had established the Scientific Research Council. Thanks largely to the foresight of Norman Manley, Jamaica was one of the first countries in the developing world to formulate the laws and policy framework – in the first national science and technology policy, established in 1960 – that would make better use of science to harness its natural resources and spur better use of research for national development.

The council spun off a variety of science and technology institutions, but there was little agreement on how to strike a harmonious relationship between these institutions and the Scientific Research Council and among themselves. This led to empire-building and self-centredness, which stifled the cooperative essence of several scientific enterprises.

Previous attempts by successive administrations to upgrade the 1960 law and fashion a science and technology policy were resisted and openly ridiculed as politicizing science by a few members of the scientific community. The principles adopted by the 1979 science and technology World Vienna Conference, convened by the United Nations, left little doubt that a new science and technology policy was long overdue. It was an imperative in the age of technology.

Arnoldo Ventura, the first science and technology advisor, was charged with leading the evolution of a more cohesive and reactive domestic research and development framework. Gerald Lalor, whose devotion to and acumen for science is renowned, was mandated to collaborate with his colleagues and stakeholders to draft a modern and comprehensive policy, which I supported and ushered through the process for its acceptance in 1990. It was tabled in Parliament and received unanimous approval after the debate I led.

Among the main recommendations of the policy was the creation of a National Commission on Science and Technology (NCST). The NCST was imbued with two important features. The first was that it should be chaired by the prime minister and include the ministers whose responsibilities had an impact on science and technology policies and projects. Secondly, it would not be confined to government, but be an amalgam of the private sector, academia, civil society and labour. Its funding and support should reflect this. The NCST was seen as the focal point to coordinate and energize Jamaica's science and technology efforts. It allowed for the organization of a modern national science and technology information and decision-making system, with the NCST as its hub.

The remit of the council included promoting a research culture, something which a developing country in a competitive global environment needs to foster.

It is necessary in social policy planning as much as it is the lifeblood of pro-gressive industrial and commercial enterprises. In any event, I saw the NCST and the Scientific Research Council having a direct impact on the society. The former was more focused on demystifying science and helping people to appre-ciate the service which science and technology can provide for them if properly respected and applied. The latter was charged to encourage the kind of innova-tion and entrepreneurship which would move science and technology from the laboratories and experimental environments into mainstream production of goods and services and the creation of new employment.

It was then, and still is, important for our people to recognize the value of science in their lives. Whether we want to focus on the scientific method – involving curiosity, hypothesis, testing, and the clinical analysis which scientists generally apply to matter and to theories – or we choose to improve our ability to understand the natural environment in which we exist, there is a compelling case for including science and technology in the mainstream of our personal, social and national development.

This new infrastructural arrangement was not much different from what existed in the more S& T-advanced states and was welcomed by the international science and technology fraternity as a major step in Jamaica's upliftment. Many developing countries requested details of the new arrangements and copied aspects of them. Jamaica was asked to provide policy assistance to developing countries in the Caribbean as well as other regions by those who appreciated the scheme.

In 1996, I launched the National Industrial Policy. That was the first year that we outlined fiscal measures and fiscal policy without being under debt obligations to the International Monetary Fund. The policy was predicated on a technologically sound and innovative human and institutional infrastructure. The NCST was tasked with strengthening our capacity in that area and building synergies between the public and private sectors.

At the time, I pointed out that in light of these demands and rapid contem-porary global changes, the building of the island's human-resources capability would have to be centred on scientific and technological education, training and general orientation, in full acknowledgement of the fact that science is the primary mover of global competition, trade and communication.

To organize and initiate sustainable support for the NCST, a National Science and Technology Foundation was established with initial trust-fund dona-tions from the private sector. Further to this, the government contributed J$100 million to seed a technology investment fund to help support technology-led projects that were not attractive to commercial banks but had significant socio-economic promise.

A popular NCST entity was the Research and Development Committee, which, through collaborative action, spurred a decided increase in research and development and science and technology integration by creating joint projects, hitherto hampered by inadequate collaboration and cooperation.

One of the most successful outcomes of this arrangement was a joint project between the private sector and the Jamaican government to extract and market flavours and essences from the island's rich fruits, vegetables and spices. This led to the formation of the Jamaica Flavours and Essences Company Limited, at Bull Savannah, which has begun to reduce the imports of these commodities and diversify the use of agricultural products.

The idea of marketing quality was conceived as an answer to the problems of dumped produce from the United States, which was depriving farmers in south St Elizabeth of their livelihoods. It was not designed to compete in the primary mass-production market, but rather to capture and sell the richness of Jamaican fruit, vegetables, flowers and spices.

A major international contribution to the national effort was the establishment of a Centre of Excellence at the University of the West Indies to probe the geomineral features of the island and thereby demonstrate the practical use of science at its best. This centre, formerly led by Gerald Lalor, has done much to illuminate factors that can influence health, agriculture and mining. My association with the Group of 15 (G15) countries opened the doors for financial assistance from the Commission for Sustainable Development in the South and the Jamaican government.

Scientists and technologists often work not for money but to discover new knowledge, and we introduced the recognition of these efforts: as part of the Millennium Celebrations we instituted a National Science and Technology Medal, now presented biennially as the Prime Minister's NCST Award.

The NCST's website is popular, and students from various parts of the world continue to seek advice, especially on the use of science and technology for eradicating poverty. Jamaica also made significant international contributions to the debates on such topics as information communication technology in agriculture and food security, the safety and efficacy of biotechnologies, how the Internet can better accommodate the interests of individuals in a safer and more reliable fashion, and the need for security against bioweapons.

Jamaica's contributions to international and regional science and technology endeavours were officially recognized when it was selected to represent the

Caribbean at the UN Educational, Scientific and Cultural Organization's World Conference on Science in 1999.

More than ever, the world needs science and technology. A timely way out of the massive global economic recession and development reversals depends on harnessing science and technology for innovations. The old ways and means are no longer sufficient. The dire consequences of food insecurity and hunger, of environmental degradation and climate change, as well as rising energy costs, have begun to be felt in all corners of the earth. Jamaica is in a good position to use its knowledge base to weather such storms, and it is up to the present and future generations to build on this legacy. Jamaica has much to teach itself and the rest of the small islands on the planet on the use of science and technology to preserve their environments and chart a sustainable way through the excesses that have plunged the earth down an unrealistic development path.

CHAPTER 27

HEALTH: A NATION'S PRIMARY WEALTH

"THE HEALTH OF THE NATION IS THE WEALTH OF A NATION" expresses an adage which no one can dispute, but its full implication is not always reflected in the allocation of resources by many nation states. Jamaica accepted the resolutions and initiatives of the United Nations, which regard health as a fundamental human right of every citizen and not a privilege to be enjoyed by a few. That pushed us to provide the highest standard of health care and thereby actively seek to reduce the social and economic inequities which result in inadequate health conditions for those at the bottom end of the economic ladder.

The Report of the World Health Organization (WHO) on Macroeconomics and Health, published in December 2001, concluded that better health is not only an important goal in its own right, but a major catalyst for economic development and poverty reduction. From the outset, the administration made a commitment to improving and maintaining the health and longevity of the population, especially the poor, by ensuring equity, access and continuous improvement in the quality of care, despite limited financial resources.

Under Easton Douglas as minister of health, we had negotiated, by 1992, an IDB loan which helped to significantly expand our physical facilities and improve our technical capacity at major hospitals in Kingston, Mandeville, May Pen and St Ann's Bay. We sought to strike a balance between the Ministry of Health's being central to promoting access to cost-effective promotional, preventative, curative and rehabilitative services on the one hand, and achieving the objectives of the wider concept of health, to achieve the productive, social, spiritual well-being of the population.

The 1990s saw major transformations of many of our economic and social institutions, and health care reform was high on our agenda. The focus was on six primary areas: preventing and reducing illness; timely, efficient and effective treatment of illness; improved organization, management and financing of health services; client-centred service; creating a learning and developmental organization through research and collaboration; and the safety, health and development of children at risk.

Towards meeting these objectives, a number of initiatives required my direct oversight. The projects were funded with the assistance of the IDB, the Pan American Health Organization and the Overseas Development Agency and were designed to bring about reform and improve the financial sustainability, equity, efficiency and quality of health care services.

In 1997, the National Health Services Act gave legal status to the regional health authorities, which were set up to manage the delivery of health care – primary, secondary and tertiary – in the four regions: southeast, southern, northeast and western Jamaica. They were semi-autonomous units of the Ministry of Health, each with its own board and management teams, and run through service-level agreements with the ministry, with the aim of providing standardized service.

Organizational structures for all four regional health authorities were developed, staff hired and offices opened to bring management of the health facilities closer to the people they served directly. The objective was to ensure access to and the availability of services; quality health care; and improved efficiency. However, decentralization was not without its problems. They all inherited challenges from previous years which had to be tackled, while at the same time providing the services demanded by the public.

Approximately 80 per cent of the health budget at the time went towards salaries, and the balance to operational expenses. This of course put tremendous pressure on the institutions to provide the equipment and drugs needed for patient care. Introducing user fees was one of the most difficult decisions to make, because it required patients in public hospitals to contribute towards their medical care. Fee collection, therefore, played a vital role in providing medical supplies and services. Special efforts were made to ensure that patients were not turned away from any public hospital because they were unable to pay. Where they had difficulty, patients were asked to make arrangements to pay. Where it was impossible, such patients were exempted by assessment officers in each public facility.

As a result of commendable progress in the health sector we were pleased that by World Health Organization indicators, Jamaica's population enjoyed a standard of health equal to many industrialized countries in life expectancy, maternal mortality, infant mortality and immunization rates.

There was a marked improvement in the maternal mortality rate. Under the UN Millennium Development Goals, the target for maternal mortality was a reduction of 75 per cent for all countries by 2015. To meet this goal, Jamaica had to reduce its maternal mortality to 27 per 100,000. The Reproductive Health Strategic Plan, developed under my watch, outlined a gradual reduction. During the early 1990s there was a reduction in the major causes of death among mothers – hypertensive disease/eclampsia, haemorrhage and sepsis. However, the indirect causes of such deaths increased during that same period, owing largely to HIV/AIDS, violence, and chronic conditions such as obesity and cardiac disease.

Of significance during the period was a decline in teenage fertility from 112 per 1,000 to about 70 per 1,000. Despite this decrease, I left office with deep concern that the level of teenage pregnancy in Jamaica was still far too high.

HIV/AIDS posed a most serious threat to health in Jamaica, as it did elsewhere. Instructions were given to pursue an aggressive programme of intervention to prevent it spreading, through educating the populace, and facilitating treatment and access to care for people living with HIV/AIDS.

The negative effects of HIV/AIDS on productivity and savings were a real threat to development. Many skilled adults died from AIDS, adding to the economic impact of lost income and productivity. Naturally, the macroeconomics of AIDS mirrored what the disease did at individual and family levels, draining resources from education and welfare and resulting in a decline in income, consumption and savings.

The HIV/AIDS issue was not merely a health problem but a development one as well, and had to be treated as such. Consequently, the government developed a comprehensive plan incorporating all sectors – the private sector, the church, community groups, various ministries of government and governmental organizations – to confront this scourge.

We also entered into a loan agreement with the World Bank to finance the national strategic plan on HIV/AIDS. In 2002, the government, through the Ministry of Health, signed a memorandum of agreement with Jamaica AIDS Support, which carried out interventions with groups vulnerable to HIV/AIDS as well as delivering care and support services for people living with HIV/AIDS.

Chronic disease has adversely affected our productivity and national health costs. According to internationally recognized classifications, non-communicable diseases account for 60 per cent of our total disease burden. Of this population, 62 per cent will die prematurely, that is, not attain their life expectancy; 58 per cent will incur a disability.

Under our Health Care Reform Programme a comprehensive health policy was formulated which included some form of national health financing so as to provide a more sustainable and equitable strategy.

The most revolutionary development in the sector was the National Health Fund, introduced during the stewardship of Minister John Junor. At its launch on 28 November 2003, I pointed out that the underlying rationale for the fund stemmed from the desire to provide access, efficiency and equity for our citizens. We were determined to reduce the burden on the health care system and assist citizens who faced serious difficulties in meeting their health care costs.

The National Health Fund was designed and established to provide supplemental financing for care for individuals, as well as improving the delivery of health care. Individual benefits included provisions for all those who suffer from fifteen identified illnesses, regardless of age or gender. The Jamaica Drugs for the Elderly Programme, for those sixty and over, covers any of ten chronic illnesses. The drugs are free to beneficiaries, but they may have to pay the pharmacy a fee for the prescription. To this day, whenever I enter a pharmacy, there are always many people filling their prescriptions who say thanks, as this has meant so much to them.

The National Health Fund also provides institutional benefits through grants to public- and private-sector entities for health promotion and illness prevention, as well as public-sector projects to improve infrastructure.

By 2006, ninety-two project requests had been approved for government organizations, and twenty-eight for non-governmental organizations, for a total commitment of J$4.1 billion. Projects were funded for acquiring equipment and vehicles, improving infrastructure and facilities, public health, including healthy lifestyle promotion, immunization, environmental health, training and research.

The National Health Fund brought a novel approach that took into account the financial and economic resources of the country in a practical and effective manner. It was a good beginning. It was certified by the International Organization for Standardization as having a world-class quality management system that delivers service of the highest standard to its customers.

I also used the opportunity to congratulate the pioneers of the Jamaica Drugs for the Elderly Programme, who had done such a good job in educating the public and in registering so many of the targeted beneficiaries.

The National Health Fund moved our health care services up another level, by helping people of all ages with the cost of medication for the fourteen most prevalent chronic diseases in our population. The National Health Fund was also charged with educating the population on lifestyle changes to reduce the incidence of these diseases.

The increase in life expectancy marked a demographic transition and increased the numbers of the population over sixty years old. In 2003, some 267,000 people – that is, about 10 per cent of the population – fell into that age bracket. By 2025, the projections showed an increase of some 471,000, or between 14 and 15 per cent of the population. The challenge for our policy-makers was to devise measures that ensured adequate provision for that sector.

We were able to introduce a new health plan for National Insurance Scheme pensioners to access a range of benefits such as hospitalization, diagnostics, surgical services, prescription, dental, optical and doctor's visits. The funds were easily identified because of the excellent management and fine performance of the National Insurance Fund. It proved one of the most appreciated innovations for the population over sixty, who were no longer regarded as a liability but as a resource to be harnessed for the national good.

These decisions, which were taken during my time as prime minister, led to Jamaica being able to achieve and maintain excellent health standards when compared to both developed and developing countries. The 2004 Pan American Health Organization report on basic health indicators showed Jamaica's life expectancy at birth as 76.1 years. This compared favourably with the United States, which was 77.4; Barbados, 77.5; Canada, 77; and Trinidad and Tobago, 71.1.

Despite these achievements, however, there are still challenges to be overcome. These include physical facilities in need of repair; service delivery, which has been affected by population growth; and demographic shifts.

CHAPTER 28

LAND, HOUSING AND THE ENVIRONMENT

THE JAMAICA HANDBOOK OF 1926 LISTS MY FATHER, Henry Patterson, as "the owner of a 25-acre farm at Mt. Pleasant, Hanover, on which he grew bananas and reared cattle, and where he built his house, 'May Park'". As late as 1930, there were only 31,038 Jamaicans with holdings between 5 and 49 acres. He seemed to be a man of enterprise and ambition, for when the Sanftlebens put up the entire property for sale, Henry Patterson, using his house as part of the security, obtained a loan from the Hanover Building Society to make the downpayment.

As fate would have it, successive storms in the first two years of his prospective ownership wiped him out. In 1931 the Hanover Building Society put up the family house, as well as the property, for sale. He managed to retain his house on the 25-acre property. My father's house was just across the road from one of the land settlements in the district of Santoy which have formed the backbone of the country's food-crop and small-livestock industries.

As I visited with him the parcels of land he had acquired at Logwood and Cave Valley, it could not escape my attention, even as a child, how precious, motivational and empowering was the ownership of land. My maternal grandmother, Eliza James, after her husband's death, had bought plots at Kingsvale and Riverside in Hanover.

But it was my granduncle, Daniel Carter-Henry, who really made me fully understand why the tenure of land in Jamaica has been such a burning issue from the days of conquest and slavery. For those descendants of the enslaved who were intent on establishing their independence and self-worth, land was even more valuable than money in the bank. It established the permanence of their space and place in the New World.

As we picked pimento berries during the summer holidays in the hills

261

of Springfield, St James, "Teacher Dan", a true Miconian, retired principal of Mount Peto School and senior deacon of the Springfield Baptist Church, expounded on the sordid past and the bitter and perennial struggles for land tenure. The British slave owner was the original and biggest capturer of lands in our history. The plantocracy seized land and established estates which extended as far as the eye could see.

During slavery, the enslaved workers, in addition to their labours on the plantations, grew ground provisions and other food items on hillside lands, which were unsuitable for estate cultivation, to feed themselves and the planters. The British colonial governor at the time, the Earl of Sligo, made a ruling that these hillside lands, "inherited" by the slaves for generations, would, following the principles of English common law, become their property at emancipation. The white planters protested, and the Colonial Office recalled Sligo to Britain. So, on the eve of emancipation, the people lost access to land which had been in their family for generations.

My granduncle, Teacher Dan, explained that the Colonial Office, in January 1836, in order to maintain a labour supply for planters in Jamaica, ordered that it should be made harder for the people to obtain access to and buy lands, and the price of such lands fixed out of the reach of those with limited capital. This meant that for former slaves and their descendants to own land became next to impossible, unless it was granted by employers. The Baptists created history when they launched a programme to buy parcels of land for independent, free villages for the people.

My experience as a lawyer served to deepen my understanding of the real impact of land ownership and its emotional effect on the majority of our people, who have endured a history of marginalization and exclusion. What was the situation when I was admitted to the Bar in 1963? In the resident magistrates' courts, there was an overload of cases relating to boundaries and trespass. Conveyance, ownership and inheritance matters and land development proved challenging because of the different types of rights and ownership, including prescriptive rights, adverse possession and "family lands", a customary, non-legal form of ownership. In fact, many of the larger and more ostentatious houses on "family lands" and even on squatter land are really "family houses", owned by several members of a family, many of whom might be living in a different part of the island or even overseas. Illegal possession and the squatting and capturing of land further compound the issue.

The PNP has always placed land reform and empowerment of the people at the top of its agenda. It began with Norman Manley at Rhymesbury and All-sides and continued with the Land Lease Programme under Michael Manley. To redress these traditional inequities and to advance the reform agenda, I made an early decision to develop a comprehensive national land policy, as "a blueprint to protect an asset so vital to every aspect of our growth and development". I told Parliament in July 1996, "Land, next only to our people, is clearly our most precious resource. We cannot abuse it or exploit it for ourselves. It is a heritage which we hold in solemn trust for all succeeding generations."

As early as 1991, the government had recognized that collecting, maintaining, analysing and managing complete, comprehensive and accurate data were fundamental to preparing, developing and implementing a land policy, as well as for planning and decision-making. Consequently, the Land Information Council of Jamaica was established by cabinet that year, as well as the Spatial Data Management Unit as its secretariat. Directed by Jacqueline DaCosta, the council has been at the forefront of increasing knowledge and awareness of cutting-edge spatial technologies. In association with ESRI, the largest software producer in the world, it launched the Geographical Information System in Schools Education Programme. ESRI's contribution was a grant of US$1 million in software and training material.

Over 750 data sets now exist in Jamaica. The Land Information Council, over the years, encouraged and fostered this growth, and provided guidance to its members, who helped formulate policies, mapping, data, metadata and other standards. A cadre of world-class geographical information system professionals and a growing local spatial-sciences sector now exist.

The National Land Policy was tabled in April 1996. I fervently believed that land was a major resource and an important means of production and must be made more accessible to provide secure shelter, to let the landless become productive citizens and improve their standard of living. Only by empowering our people in this manner would true emancipation be achieved.

The policy would be the vehicle through which we could best manage the country's natural resources and promote sustainable, productive and equitable development. It would bring about comprehensive and integrated development in rural and urban areas alike. The aim was to complement socio-economic development plans and programmes, and to remove inefficient and outdated bureaucratic obstacles.

The National Land Policy had to address matters of human settlements, rural and agricultural planning, manufacturing and industrial development, infrastructure, roads, drainage, water resources, utilities, youth and culture, education, health, community development, social amenities, beaches, coastal zones and watersheds. Virtually every ministry, department and agency had to be involved. This work had to be led by the Cabinet Office, and I chaired the inter-ministerial subcommittee myself.

Given my strong belief that national policies are best formulated by forming partnerships and using participatory approaches, I ordered that the land policy and integrated development plans should include full participation by the public and private sectors as well as civil society. We therefore established guidelines and procedures for participatory approaches for planning and other major activities arising from the policy.

The policy sought to emphasize and enhance the land information system through improving and strengthening the national geographic information system. That would include a comprehensive and integrated digital database to provide information on every parcel of land.

Land policy in an island that is highly vulnerable to hurricanes and flooding had to include a disaster-management component as well as guidelines for the sustainable development of our environment, one of our greatest economic assets. Consequently, the plan covered the protection and conservation of sensitive areas and scarce resources and as well as forestry and land use.

Embedded in the policy was the protection of the rights of women and youth. The government, in deciding to make land available to low-income families, instructed that equal consideration be given to women, especially heads of households. Special allocations were to be made available to young people interested in agriculture.

I announced that government lands to be divested should be priced at market value, but there would be discounted rates or varying rates by income bands, extended repayment periods and lower deposits. This allowed us to make better use of our limited financial, human and technical resources.

The policy resulted in decisions that stood a greater chance of being implemented because all stakeholders were involved. This made it easier to carry out various projects of national importance, such as building new schools, refurbishing hospitals, clinics and other health facilities and support programmes, major housing settlements and infrastructure, including Highway 2000 and the North Coast Highway.

Even before the completion of the land policy, in the budget presentation of 18 May 1994, I had launched Operation PRIDE. The Programme for Resettlement and Integrated Development Enterprise (PRIDE) was our attempt to redress the social strains and pressures the poor experienced over the previous decades; address the inequity which left the majority of Jamaicans landless; and curb the indiscriminate capturing of government and privately owned land by providing an alternative.

Operation PRIDE included an agricultural programme on emancipation lands and was intended for people involved in small businesses and light industrial and manufacturing activities that required community economic centres.

This was not the first attempt at divestment; there had been a number of land distribution programmes over the years under previous administrations. In addition, the NHT has made home ownership a reasonable possibility for thousands of people since its inception in 1976. But there were still a large number of Jamaicans who could not benefit from any of the formal solutions in place, and these were the people we targeted.

The role of the government in Operation PRIDE was as a facilitator, to help low-income communities to incrementally develop affordable and environmentally sound shelter solutions. The beneficiaries working with government and other groups, such as non-governmental organizations, community-based organizations, church groups and provident societies, were expected to ensure that legal and environmentally safe communities were developed. The communities and groups to benefit, with professional guidance, were to become more involved in planning, implementing and managing the development of their communities. Many had been using their initiative and resources, sometimes illegally, to help themselves to shelter and economic opportunities. My aim was to continue to implement this non-partisan programme in a properly planned and timely manner. I viewed it as an integral part of my government's social agenda.

It turned out that the high quality of the infrastructure of a number of these projects resulted in huge overruns. The award of several contracts was not watertight and would require levels of subsidy which the government and the buyers could not afford.

The Erwin Angus Report pointed to a number of management errors. A well-researched legal opinion from Ken Rattray did not support the contention that Karl Blythe had exceeded his authority, taking into account his position as a corporation sole, and exonerated him from any charge of ministerial abuse.

The programme in that form was unsustainable and had to be discontinued. But I still believed that a programme which utilizes the skills and resources of our people can create viable and genuine integrated communities capable of sustainable and environmentally safe development. We need to find the right model and put in place effective management and technical competence to create shelter solutions which can generate employment opportunities and viable communities, reduce crime and violence, encourage social harmony and family unity, and instil in the beneficiaries the values and attitudes which the society needs for survival and prosperity.

The National Land Policy showed that government was the largest landowner, with some 22 per cent of real estate in Jamaica. Analysis of its inventory showed that the government owned approximately forty-five thousand parcels, held by over twenty entities. Many were forest reserves, protected areas, coastal zones and wetlands. There were, however, many parcels that were underutilized and not properly managed.

The policy recognized the critical nature of land tenure patterns in Jamaica and the related social and economic implications, and stated government's decision to accelerate its divestment. Consistent with the privatization policy, it was intended to alleviate, as far as possible, the problems associated with landlessness, while motivating the nation to realize higher productivity. The major areas of focus were to provide land for low-income earners and government employees, and upgrading and regularizing squatter settlement. In 1996, the cabinet approved recommendations for divesting government-owned lands in a fair and transparent manner.

Historically, land tenure has been a vexing and frustrating issue. Conveyance, ownership, inheritance and development proved challenging because of the many different types of ownership. More legal research had to be done to ensure solutions would cover all the owners and varied forms of ownership which exist in many parts of the world. The scope of the problem was highlighted when prospective NHT beneficiaries were unable to access loans because they did not have the proper documentation.

Efficient titling of land was therefore an obvious goal and we undertook to simplify and, in some instances, eliminate various aspects of registration, transfer and related areas. This was critical, since more than half of the estimated parcels of land in Jamaica did not have registered titles, which affected the ability of homeowners, farmers and businesspeople to get mortgages and related financing.

It also influenced the levels of property taxes collected for reinvestment in communities. Fifty per cent of those interviewed during the cadastral mapping and tenure regularization programme and who owned land were not on the tax roll. Many expressed the view that since their names were not on the roll, they were under no obligation to pay taxes. People with insecure tenure also felt long-term development of land was risky; hence many erected houses and planted cash crops that were not of a long-term nature.

Regularizing tenure has always been costly. Transfer tax on death amounted to 15 per cent of improved value, while *inter vivos* transfers attracted stamp duties and transfer taxes of 13 per cent. The minimum total cost of bringing the smallest parcel of land under the Registration of Titles Act (where there was no complexity) was approximately J$49,000. When subdivision was necessary, the costs multiplied. The government enacted legislation to simplify land registration and transfer while reducing these costs.

HOUSING

Shelter has been and still is of immense importance, especially so for those from lower socio-economic backgrounds. The PNP had always seen it as a fundamental need and has been committed to helping Jamaicans fulfil one of their greatest desires: a home of their own. The NHT, established to provide housing for low-income workers, over the years became the most important housing finance institution as it widened its net to accommodate middle-income workers, who also had major difficulty in getting mortgages. We have repeatedly had to defend it against a variety of bilateral, multilateral and multinational financial institutions that wished to close this important national organization.

The NHT created a mix of benefits to meet various needs. There were NHT schemes in every parish; there were serviced lots and starter houses, as well as mortgages so people could either build on their own land or buy on the open market. The latter could be accessed directly from the NHT or in partnership with institutions such as building societies and banks.

When the PNP administration resumed leadership in 1989, there had been a decline in the momentum, as the focus had been on providing liquidity to meet IMF financial targets for the public sector, rather than construction. If we were to fulfil our original mission of providing shelter for NHT subscribers, we had to increase the construction of units at a subsidized cost.

The NHT worked closely with both public- and private-sector partners – the Ministry of Construction (Housing), UDC, National Housing Corporation and West Indies Home Contractors – to form a network of housing schemes incorporating every single parish. Between 1990 and 2006 some thirty-five NHT schemes offered a mix of solutions, including serviced lots, studios, and one- and two-bedroom units.

When I became leader, Portmore was being developed, and grew to be the second largest town in the country. More housing solutions were put in place in Portmore and Greater Portmore alone than during the entire Seaga administration.

Over the years, through the UDC and private-sector companies, the dormitory town became a more viable urban area with a town centre, schools, social amenities, malls and restaurants. It has the largest number of civil servants, teachers, police, and other professionals who commute daily to work.

The Ministry of Housing, the NHT and the private sector also entered joint-venture arrangements to build houses in urban centres such as May Pen, Spanish Town and Montego Bay. Housing was needed right across Jamaica and many people in informal settlements and the large numbers who make up the informal sector were encouraged to join the NHT. In 1992 the development of serviced lots on lands owned by the Ministry of Housing was aimed at providing land and infrastructure for those with median incomes to build their own homes on an incremental basis.

Partnerships were also sought to access funding to build affordable housing. There were long-standing partnerships with organizations such as the Jamaica Teachers' Association and the Sugar Industry Housing Limited, but we also encouraged corporations such as JAMALCO (Alcoa Minerals of Jamaica), Life of Jamaica and Jamaica Mutual Life Assurance Society to partner with the NHT to finance housing for their employees.

In order to ensure a large number of rural townships acquired physical infrastructure, social amenities, and socio-economic action, the UDC had been charged to start the Comprehensive Rural Township Programme in support of existing and new housing solutions. In an effort to halve the number of people living below the poverty level, said to be 29.2 per cent in 1993, the Integrated Community Development Programme was also started. This required a multifaceted approach including several government entities, which would respond to the communities that answered the call to participate in solving their needs and problems. The Planning Institute was charged with determining and ranking the communities by priority, utilizing Jamaica's poverty map and geographic targeting.

These critical and multifaceted approaches were deliberate on my part and my government's. We strongly believed that tackling the problems of the society by providing housing or land without dealing with related physical and social issues would not achieve our aims. Improving our communities would also require financial support to match the sweat equity of community members. Because of the need for grant funding, we approached the World Bank to help set up the Jamaica Social Investment Fund.

In fiscal year 1993 we planned an assault on the problem of land capturing by providing ten thousand new housing solutions. These were mixed solutions, and included provisions for workers who could not afford a completed home, and an effort to stem squatting, especially in unsuitable, environmentally unsafe and disaster-prone areas. In 1994, I announced the launch of Operation PRIDE. Planning started in eight pilot areas and by 1995, work had begun at Riverton City in Kingston.

As we were cognizant of the plans for the tourist belt, it was necessary to address the housing needs of the increasing numbers of workers in the industry, and we paid special attention to housing in the western end of the island.

We entered into an arrangement with Food for the Poor to undertake a "poor starter home programme" to provide some two thousand homes with the basic or minimum acceptable standards of infrastructure, for J$200 million. Phase 1 consisted of seven sites and approximately one thousand units. The founder of Food for the Poor told us Jamaica was the only country in Latin America and the Caribbean that had offered land at no cost for starter homes for the poor and indigent. To enable as many people as possible who qualified to benefit, my government committed to a policy of access to land for as many projects as necessary to provide shelter for the people. Those targeted could not obtain secure tenure under any other programme. Consequently, a safety net was put in place to meet these special needs.

Another programme to improve some urban centres was relocating families from squatter sites to other areas. Railway Lane/Barracks Road in St James, with three hundred families, saw people relocated to Providence. The Seville squatter community in St Ann, with three hundred families, was on land of extremely high archaeological and cultural value. They were relocated to Belair in St Ann.

The government provided the land, and the NHT provided the financing for infrastructure and building basic housing units. To ensure they were built at minimal cost, the NHT acquired the necessary equipment for members of the Jamaica Defence Force to lay down the infrastructure. Individuals repaid mortgage loans from the NHT. To underscore a sense of responsibility, those eligible had to register as NHT contributors.

The island's sugar workers also benefited, under the Sugar Workers Housing Programme, the product of a memorandum of understanding between the sugar estates and the NHT. It involved plans for the some five thousand houses, over a five-year period, on land provided by eight sugar estates.

Even while we could be justifiably proud of our success in providing housing for a great many low-income workers, I was uncomfortable with the increasing squalor in our inner cities over the past few decades. A part of the answer was creating healthy, sustainable communities through an urban renewal pro-gramme, with the goal of ensuring residents' ownership of the process from the inception. We aimed to transform inner-city areas into attractive, sustain-able neighbourhoods through a combination of new housing and refurbish-ing existing housing stock. The challenge was balancing adequate space with affordability.

We targeted inner-city communities in Kingston, St Andrew, St Catherine and Westmoreland, where we built low-cost units with four-storey walk-up blocks of forty-eight homes, each containing three bedrooms, with a minimum living area of 650 square feet, and two-bedroom units for smaller families. The environment and setting of these units were important, as various studies had pointed to the need for adequate open spaces for recreation and relaxation in high-density communities. So each block included green areas and safe play-grounds. We adapted a low-cost housing solution to meet local conditions and codes.

From the outset, we incorporated residents' views on managing their com-munities. Management and maintenance systems were instituted to ensure sustainability. Training and resocialization to prepare residents to accept their responsibilities and inculcating habits to ensure harmonious living were an essential component of the programme. Tivoli Gardens, Denham Town, Lizard Town, Majesty Gardens, Tavares Gardens, Wilton Gardens, Federal Gardens and Tavares Pen, Little King Street in Denham Town and Trench Town were among the communities that benefited.

THE ENVIRONMENT

The human condition is largely dependent on the state of our natural environ-ment: for the Caribbean, it is a rich physical heritage and considerable biologi-cal endowment. It is also the source of our propensity for natural disasters and vulnerability to climate change, deforestation and marine pollution.

During the 1980s, the international community and financial institutions became increasingly aware of the effects of the degradation of the global envi-ronment and the need to take serious action if we were to save the planet for future generations.

As part of my portfolio in the shadow cabinet, I had recruited a fine team, who were not only experts in this field, but also prepared to serve in a new admin-istration. The Environmental Management Division of the Ministry of Development, Planning and Production was ready to roll, with Sam Lawrence as my co-pilot and Ted Aldridge as lead engineer. The division had overall responsibility for policies, strategies and programmes to guide the protection, conservation and sustainable use of the island's natural resources.

The first international conference I attended as prime minister was the UN Rio Summit on Environment and Development, in Brazil in May 1992, which was convened to increase conservation and protect the environment in order to promote sustainable development.

I presented a bill to Parliament, enacted in 1991, to create a new regime for the institutional and management framework of our environment.

The Environment Foundation of Jamaica, incorporated in 1993 after a debt-for-nature swap agreement between the governments of Jamaica and the United States, promotes and supports the conservation of natural resources and the environment. By 2005, the foundation had disbursed J$100.1 million to assist in capacity development, natural-resources management and sustainable livelihoods to foster the well-being of children, child survival and environmental awareness.

In keeping with the government's thrust for a better coordinated and integrated approach, in 2001 we merged the Natural Resources Conservation Authority, Town Planning Department and the Land Development and Utilization Commission into the National Environmental and Planning Agency.

With the approach of the new millennium, it seemed timely to promote a qualitative change in how we treat and protect the environment. We had witnessed the effects of climate change, pollution, soil erosion and how poverty, unplanned settlements, deforestation and reckless excavation had damaged our environment and threatened our livelihood.

On 28 July 1999, we launched a project which would emphasize the inclusion of environmental bodies in all corporate and public-sector plans. In partnership with the Canadian International Development Agency and the UN Development Programme, we strengthened the corporate planning process and maximized the outcome of investments and public spending to promote sustainable development and foster behavioural change.

Effective enforcement, compliance and monitoring of environmental laws are critical to protecting the environment. In 1996, the Environmental Warden Services were particularly successful with regard to illegal sand mining, eforestation and non-conforming uses of buildings.

In 2002, the Island Special Constabulary Force was reorganized as the principal vehicle for municipal policing and its mandate broadened to include enforcing environment and planning laws. In 2003, a series of seminars sensitized the Judiciary and those concerned with investigating and prosecuting environmental offences, for an integrated approach to enforcing environmental laws.

Our geography, as a small island, has made Jamaica subject to several natural hazards. Numerous infrastructure and social programmes have had to be cancelled over the years and funds diverted to disaster-recovery efforts after hurricanes, tropical storms, landslips, flooding, tidal waves and drought.

In many instances these disasters have been made worse by man's actions, such as illegal sand mining in coastal areas and rivers, and building on river and gully banks too near the coast and in places prone to flooding or landslips. The indiscriminate felling of trees, inadequate disposal of sewage and solid, hazardous, medical and ship-generated waste have had disastrous consequences.

Between 1995 and 2010, Jamaica experienced a significant increase in the frequency and intensity of weather-related events. We were the victims of floods, tropical depressions, tropical storms, hurricanes and droughts. Between 2001 and 2010, Jamaica had been affected by ten natural disasters, resulting in costs estimated at approximately J$111.81 billion. There were adverse environmental effects, social dislocation, economic losses and damage. Hurricane Ivan, in 2004, resulted in damage totalling J$35 billion; Hurricane Dean, in 2007, left J$23 billion in damage. The magnitude of the damage and loss averaged 2 per cent of GDP per annum in the first decade of the new millennium. Hurricane Ivan in 2004, Hurricanes Emily and Dennis in 2005, Dean in 2007 and Tropical Storm Gustav in 2008 severely affected the economy and society.

The Planning Institute of Jamaica's Socio-Economic and Environmental Disaster Impact Assessment Study of 2012 revealed that the severe losses and damage to capital assets and infrastructure contributed directly to the low rate of GDP growth during the decade ending in 2005.

We began a number of programmes and projects for hazard mitigation and better management of natural resources. These included greater support to the National Integrated Watershed Management Council, established by cabinet in 2000 to organize and coordinate activities in the country's watersheds more effectively. This joint government, private-sector, non-governmental organization approach included working with international donor and lending institutions on several successful initiatives.

We started preparing a national drainage policy and plan with priority drainage projects, to be coordinated by the Ministry of Transport and Works and the National Works Agency, in conjunction with other relevant agencies. These included a programme for river training, with special emphasis on those rivers known to cause severe flooding and where sand mining was taking place.

The adaptation of the International Building Code that was prepared by the Jamaica Institute of Engineers, the promulgation of the National Building Act and the preparation of simple plans which people from the lower socio-economic groups could use to build their homes on an incremental basis were intended to improve our building stock and the safety of our people.

Regional Vulnerability

The Caribbean is renowned for its natural beauty, but is also vulnerable to a range of natural disasters. For instance, Montserrat's volcano destroyed the island, after four hundred years of dormancy, with an eruption which covered two-thirds of its land mass. On 25 September 1997, as chairman of CARICOM, I appealed to the General Assembly of the United Nations to adopt tangible measures to help in the rebuilding and sustainable development of the island.

At a meeting in Guadeloupe, as President Chirac welcomed us to this overseas department of France on 10 March 2000, I reminded the France/CARIFORUM summit that when natural disasters come, they do not discriminate between one island and another. There has been cooperation between the Caribbean and France at times of natural disasters, but this needs to be more systematic, extending to prevention and post-disaster construction.

In the negotiations for the Free Trade Area of the Americas, we were pushing disaster preparedness and post-disaster reconstruction. The plenary session of the Twenty-Fourth Meeting of the Miami Conference of the Caribbean Latin America Action in Europe was told in December 2000, at our Miami gathering, that the scale of destruction caused by the hurricane season was beyond the capacity of any single country to restore. The combination and devastating sequence of Hurricanes George and Mitch in Antigua, St Kitts, Dominica and Haiti were grim reminders of the formidable forces of nature which Andrew, Hugo, Gilbert, Louis and Marilyn had unleashed in the previous decade.

In considering the relevance of CARICOM to the daily lives of our people, the role of the Caribbean Disaster Emergency Response Agency in providing vital services when our people are most vulnerable is often forgotten.

At the twentieth meeting of the CARICOM Conference of Heads, Prime Minister George Price of Belize, after the catastrophe unleashed on Central America by Hurricane Mitch in 1998, spoke convincingly, saying Belize had found the agency's services essential to overall development and planning. We heeded his plea to give it more importance and support by extending the scope and strengthening our collective capacity by creating the Caribbean Disaster Emergency Response Agency, which has been able to mobilize our response to the effects of global warming and the spate of natural disasters which has plagued us since then.

CHAPTER 29
SOCIAL TRANSFORMATION: THE POVERTY STRATEGY

DEEPLY EMBEDDED IN OUR HISTORY OF SLAVERY AND colonialism was the provision of labour at the lowest possible cost. Rex Nettleford so often reminded us that the only period of full employment throughout the Caribbean occurred during the days of the plantation system, when every enslaved person was engaged without cost. From then on, poverty has been endemic to Caribbean society.

The phenomenon of poverty is neither new nor peculiar to Jamaica, and is one to which every administration in Jamaica since the advent of universal adult suffrage has devoted much of its intellectual and material resources to resolving.

In the 1970s, the much-maligned Impact Work Programme was designed to reduce chronic unemployment and create the sparks of a work ethic rather than a welfare handout. That programme was no longer affordable nor practicable going into the 1990s. Similarly, the Food Stamp and Solidarity Programmes of the 1980s, though well intentioned, proved inadequate and not sustainable.

While acknowledging the genuine efforts of all my predecessors, I felt that someone from my social background had a special mission to combat poverty and underdevelopment. Reducing poverty was, therefore, front and centre of the administration I led for fourteen years. We recognized from the outset that welfare programmes by themselves could mitigate the hardships, but never remove the scourge of poverty. Education had to become the primary tool of national development.

In the 1992 budget, the Social and Economic Support Programme and the Micro Investment Development Agency received additional funding to broaden the base of ownership, increase productive capacity and help the micro-enterprise sector grow more quickly.

In my first budget presentation as prime minister, I accepted that during the transition to a market-driven economy there would be those who would suffer dislocation and would need to be protected. Consequently, the Food Stamp Programme was expanded and a window opened to provide for children who were most vulnerable to malnutrition.

The deep economic and social reforms undertaken as part of the modernization effort were vital for integrating Jamaica into the global economy. The Structural Adjustment Programme of the 1980s was an essential component of this effort and imperative for national survival.

The overall adjustment process was, however, painful for the large and marginalized sections of the population that had only known social and economic underdevelopment from the post-slavery and colonial era. It was also difficult for firms and industries that were not prepared for international competition. This was particularly the case for industries that survived under "colonial preferences". By the mid-2000s, sugar and banana were in serious decline owing to a myriad of structural and market-related problems, including the loss of preferences in the British and European markets. The decline of these industries, starting in the 1980s, had a distinctly rural bias and called for special attention. It was within these sectors that large numbers of the working poor were to be found. It was evident from the 1980s that the reforms would have a severe impact on the poorest, and policy measures would have to be put in place to provide some protection.

By the 1990s, more than 70 per cent of those identified as poor lived in the rural areas, with agriculture being their main source of employment. The data also showed that women comprised over 60 per cent of the rural adult population. As a product of rural Jamaica from humble beginnings, I truly understood the need to deal not just with poverty, but particularly rural poverty. This understanding, to a large extent, explained my government's strong support for agriculture, and small farmers in particular.

The year 1996 was a watershed one for the country in terms of having to grapple with the major shocks of the financial crisis and reforms in general. For me, it also entailed the first budget presentation after the country ended our borrowing relationship with the IMF after nearly two decades of a rather tempestuous affair.

In that budget speech I stated that "my administration naturally carries into office the heightened expectations of the overwhelming majority of the Jamaican people, who see in us not only themselves, but also their hope for a just reward for their labour and efforts – a reward that is their due". This was at the core of my mission.

In my address to the Millennium Summit of the United Nations on 7 September 2000, I reiterated my deeply held belief that "poverty remains the single greatest challenge facing mankind". For me, this was not just a global issue but a moral one, and to this day it remains so.

In our bid to achieve substantial economic growth as a weapon to combat poverty and fuel social development, my administration set out to build the social partnership as an essential framework. In launching these discussions at the Jamaica Conference Centre on 14 February 1996, I indicated:

> The era of IMF borrowings is now behind us. We must ensure that we never pass that way again.
>
> Jamaica has implemented strong measures during the last decade to adjust our economy, in order to meet the demands of a competitive world market. We have performed extremely well. We have moved from a deficit of 17 per cent of Gross Domestic Product in 1980 to a cash surplus balance. From being among the world's highest deficits, we are now joining the world's highest fiscal surpluses.
>
> We have moved the fiscal accounts to a cash surplus balance, defined as revenue plus grants, less capital expenditure, less all the debt amortization and debt principal.
>
> For 1994/95, the targeted surplus was J$2.1 billion, representing three per cent of government revenue and about 2 per cent of GDP. For 1995/96, it will be 3 per cent of GDP – among the world's highest fiscal surpluses.
>
> Our net international reserves are at an all-time high, having moved from minus US$803 million to US$460 million, enough to provide for thirteen weeks' total imports, including those for the bauxite sector.
>
> The exchange rate remained stable for some eighteen months, but experienced temporary instability, largely because the anticipation that the dollar would eventually fall became a self-fulfilling prophecy.

Our fiscal and monetary policies reflected a focus on fighting inflation, conscious of its destructive consequences for vulnerable groups such as the aged and the poor. While the tripartite agreement between government, the private sector and the trade unions was not signed then, most of its salient features were followed and helped to create an environment of partnership in which the social agenda could be pursued.

POVERTY PROGRAMMES

At the UN World Summit for Social Development in Copenhagen in 1995, Jamaica gave an ambitious commitment to reduce poverty by 50 per cent over the ensuing three years. This commitment was embodied in the government's overall poverty eradication strategy, finalized after widespread public consultation led by the Planning Institute of Jamaica. The National Poverty Eradication Programme, based in Jamaica House under my watch, provided overall guidance and coordination. It proved a huge challenge to coordinate over sixty poverty-reduction measures across the country.

We emphasized three primary areas: geographic targeting of the most deprived communities and focusing efforts through integrated community development to address poverty there; population groups, mainly youth and families with children, to benefit from intensified social support services; and safety nets expanded through improved welfare assistance for the needy, including the new poor, to promote self-reliance.

A vital feature was linking programmes to institutions to ensure ownership of implementation, as well as mandatory collaboration between agencies involved in related activities to eliminate duplication and optimize resource allocation. This was crucial, as we needed to implement the poverty strategy within the context of the ongoing reform of the economy and the public sector to achieve greater efficiency.

Among the critical agencies in this integrated fight were the Social Development Commission, which had primary responsibility for community development; the Office of the Prime Minister, which was responsible for monitoring the programme and acting as the secretariat for the Partnership Board, which advised the government on poverty and social development policies, with membership from government, the private sector and international donor/lending institutions; the UDC, which managed programmes such as Lift Up Jamaica to assist with infrastructure projects and training in various areas; the Social and Economic Support Programme, developed to provide funding for short-term assistance to non-governmental organizations and communities, and as a critical element of the social safety net by providing matching grants to agencies to fund viable small and micro-businesses; and the Jamaica Social Investment Fund, established in 1995 to fund demand-driven projects to deliver services and infrastructure to the poorest communities across Jamaica.

Under executive director Scarlette Gillings, this fund was developed into one of the most successful of its type globally. I am especially proud of the fund and how it performed, certainly during its first decade. It operated truly on a non-partisan basis and gained the support of all the political parties, international funding agencies and non-governmental organizations.

The first board and management of the Jamaica Social Investment Fund set a fine example of the kind of institutional arrangement and capacity-building that embodied my desire for a more integrated and cohesive society. Their mandate was to "operate as a rule-based institution that was non-partisan, free of corruption and inefficiency". As an indication of my deep desire for the organization to set a new pathway, they were advised that "if the only project that met the objective criteria for funding during the year came from a constituency of the opposition party, then let that be the only project that is funded". Indeed, the first project was in the West Kingston constituency of the leader of the opposition, Edward Seaga.

※

The years 1995 and 1996 saw some ten poverty-reduction strategies being implemented after research and policy development.[1]

In 1995, with the poverty rate at 27.5 per cent, the government implemented Skill 2000; the Secondary School Fee Assistance Programme; Operation PRIDE; the Integrated Community Development Programme; and the Special Training and Employment Programmes. These focused on skills training, education, formal housing and community development.

While the 1995 programmes were important in demonstrating the government's commitment to tackling poverty, we were convinced that much more had to be done. In 1996, therefore, another raft of poverty initiatives, targeted to cover the elderly, or the poorest communities for infrastructure development and community-based economic activities, was rolled out. They were the Jamaica Drugs for the Elderly Programme, Bauxite Community Development Programme, Strategy to Rehabilitate Inner-City Communities through Viable Enterprises; Jamaica Social Investment Fund; and the National Poverty Eradication Programme.

The difficulty associated with coordinating over sixty poverty-reduction measures across the country and the impact of the broader reform of the economy stretched the government to its limits from both policy and administrative per-

---

1. Wesley Hughes, "A Historical Perspective on Poverty", in *The Transforming Landscape of Jamaica* (Kingston: Communications Unit, Office of the Prime Minister, 2006).

spectives. At the end of the decade, it was obvious that the overall social welfare system needed serious modernization which would require additional funding.

My administration commissioned a social safety net assessment and review in 2000 to cover six areas: institutional and administrative framework; life-cycle needs of the poor; people with disabilities; homelessness; drug abuse; and people living with HIV/AIDS.[2]

The Programme for Advancement through Health and Education in 2003 was the most significant outcome of the Social Safety Net Reform Programme. It allowed a highly targeted cash-transfer programme for the poorest households to incentivize schooling and health care. It was well targeted and encompassing, while encouraging beneficiaries to become self-sufficient.

The years from 1995 to 2003 saw the greatest period of reform of the social welfare and poverty-reduction system in the post-independence period. Apart from having a coherent and rational social welfare system, there were two major outcomes we emphasized – a significant reduction in the administrative cost of the programmes, and also in the rate of poverty. By consolidating three programmes – Outdoor Poor Relief, the Food Stamp Programme and the Old Age/ Incapacity Allowances – we realized significant savings on delivering benefits to the poor.

The rate of poverty was reduced from 35 per cent in 1992 to 15 per cent in 1998, and to below 20 per cent by 2000. This was significant, especially in the context of slow growth in the economy. Indeed, there has been much debate about the reasons for such an accomplishment. There is no doubt that the various poverty programmes played a significant role. Wesley Hughes, director general of the Planning Institute of Jamaica, highlighted some key economic factors that contributed to the reduction in poverty from 1990 to 2003: the sharp reduction in inflation, which fell from 80 per cent to 8 per cent; the sharp increase in the flow of remittances into Jamaica; growth in real wages; and the growth in the informal sector of the economy, which coincided with imports of inexpensive consumer goods from China. These factors, along with the impressive array of poverty-reduction projects, were important in improving social welfare and were critical to the overall reform programme's staying on course.

In June 1972, the minister of commerce, Wills Ogilvy Isaacs, had dispatched a private-sector team led by Carlton Alexander, then chairman and chief executive officer of GraceKennedy Limited, to explore new sources of cheaper goods in China, Russia and the Far East. Included in the team were Lester Woolery, chief

---

2. Ibid., 18.

pharmacist, and Lloyd Barnett from our embassy in Washington. Their visit had a surprising outcome. Michael Manley, Dudley Thompson and I, as minister of trade, were in favour of recognizing the People's Republic of China, but were preparing the ground before seeking cabinet approval. We were delighted that morning in cabinet when none other than my old colleague, the veteran minister of commerce of the 1970s, Wills Isaacs, proposed that in view of the trade mission's report, it was time for the Taiwan embassy to disappear and for us to establish full diplomatic relations with the People's Republic of China. Cabinet took the decision there and then, with the formal submission to be confirmed the following Monday.

China has never ceased to welcome our bold decision, at a time when permanent members of the UN Security Council had not yet sanctioned the change of seat from Taiwan in the council. We have reaped rich dividends. Our informal traders and Chinese nationals have now established an enormous trade cycle.

This was a difficult period of reform, and, at times, painful. We could not afford to lose public support and could never abandon policies geared towards protecting the poor and vulnerable. The fact that the institutional, legislative and policy framework, given the polarized political environment of the era, continues to survive decades later speaks to both the soundness of these interventions and, importantly, the democratic consensus we were able to reach.

No one is claiming that poverty in Jamaica was eradicated. The tough domestic and global conditions of the period and turbulence in the finance sector, with which we had to cope entirely from our own resources, adversely affected our rate of growth. But we made marked progress and we showed dedication, passion and commitment to this historic task. The legacy of the fight against poverty remained in place, and future leaders were able to build on it. For some time yet, the scourge of poverty will remain a struggle which we must continue to address.

During the 1990s, the social dislocation caused by structural adjustment had to be addressed in a context of weak economic growth and high debt-payment demand. Resources for social expenditure while carrying out the normal functions of government were, to put it mildly, limited. The government therefore had to make hard choices.

The urgency of the tasks to be undertaken under the social agenda was set out in my 1996 budget speech: "Fourteen years of structural adjustment, beginning in 1981, relegated social services and the entire process of social development to the back burner. Throughout the length and breadth of Jamaica, every institution for community development and for youth training was closed down. The consequent social dislocation, upsurge in antisocial behaviour and the increase in crime among adolescents and young adults are all directly related to this virtual shutdown of social programmes."

Fundamentally, the social agenda sought to achieve greater social integration and cohesiveness, which had been a major weakness of post-slavery Jamaican society. It was designed to marry the role of the state to that of the voluntarism of the wider citizenry. This was to ensure social capital was built and harnessed for national development. The overall agenda formed the foundation for the entire social programme.

My view of development and the role of government in social policy was captured in the evolution of this agenda throughout the 1990s. To prevent the entire reform project from blowing up required the most skilful, calm and nuanced political management. The problems the country faced at the time significantly influenced my own approach to governance and leadership.

CHAPTER 30

OUR CARIBBEAN VILLAGE IN THE GLOBAL SPACE

AS A STUDENT OF THE HISTORY, GEOGRAPHY AND POLITICS of the Caribbean, I had learned how the differences of style and clash of personalities had contributed to the demise of the West Indies Federation.

In a previous generation, our leaders – Grantley Adams, Norman Manley, Eric Williams – were all fine scholars from Oxbridge. Whatever differences existed among them over the best direction for the region could have been resolved but for the clash of personalities and their deliberate refusal to communicate properly among themselves at critical moments.

Errol Barrow, Forbes Burnham and Michael Manley belonged to that generation who, after World War II, forged a close friendship and effective working alliance during their student days in London. They were in the core of that second wave of militancy which would disperse throughout the African continent and the Caribbean to eradicate colonialism and its mental legacy.

Mine was the first generation to enter the University College of the West Indies, Mona, which then had only three faculties – medicine, arts and natural sciences. Many of us had to further or complete our professional training in the United Kingdom and were influenced by both our regional and metropolitan sojourns.

The West Indies Student Centre at Collingham Gardens in London was a beehive of political activism, with Tom Adams, Stuart Hall, Billy Hibbert, Hugh and Richard Small, Gerry Watt, Fitzroy Bryan, Jackie Farrell and my own wife, Shirley Field-Ridley.

I benefited immensely from a personal relationship with all three waves. First, Norman Manley, Eric Williams and Robert Bradshaw, masters of the craft of nationalist politics, but with a keen sense of our Caribbean destiny.

In later years, Errol Barrow, a veteran of the Royal Air Force, would pilot a Cessna to pick me up in Dominica and have me laughing loudly but praying quietly all the way to a safe landing in Bridgetown as we barely climbed above the coconut trees and bumped from one air pocket to another.

Forbes Burnham, a passionate regionalist, wily and shrewd in the political craft, spared no effort to share the special delights of Guyana with me as one of the chosen few.

As Jamaica's sixth prime minister, I was ready to draw on the previous years of collaboration with Lynden Pindling, James Mitchell, John Compton and George Price to help guide the regional vessel through narrow channels into safe harbour. I knew that a deliberate strategy was essential to identify and deal effectively with the personalities, idiosyncrasies and circumstances of colleagues who could change with the swing of the electoral pendulum in our constitutional democracies.

There were in most national delegations technocrats well known to me from our days at Mona. Regional prime ministers Patrick Manning, Ralph Gonsalves, Owen Arthur and Kenny Anthony would often indulge with me in anecdotes about hall rivalry until we realized it was causing some jealousy among those who never went there.

As a new Caribbean leader, Prime Minister Denzil Douglas of St Kitts and Nevis is on record in these terms:

> When I first came to this setting back in 1995, I was quite apprehensive because I knew that I had defeated, to get here, a longstanding friend of P.J. In fact on many occasions I heard that the Rt Hon Dr Kennedy Simmonds was a Chancellorite and was in fact at university with P.J. I felt apprehensive that I may not have been well received. It has been the opposite.
>
> In fact, I must say that over the years I have had personally to rely on his personal guidance. We have had some tense moments at home and some difficult situations dealing with external powers and on many occasions my cabinet has asked me personally to try to have a private sitting with Prime Minister Patterson so that he can guide us as to the best decision to take on some critical matters.[1]

I insisted, when occupying the CARICOM chair, that the opposition in each

---

1. Communications Unit, Office of the Prime Minister, *P.J. Patterson: In the Eyes of the World* [collection of tributes on his retirement] (Kingston: Office of the Prime Minister, 2006), 24.

member state was kept in the loop to further the participatory process. On my initiative, we held the first meeting which included the leaders of the opposition at Sandals La Toc in St Lucia. I wanted to avoid any CARICOM issue becoming unduly contentious within domestic politics and to ensure continuity whenever our electorates effect a change.

I grasped the importance of opening and keeping open private channels of communication with my counterparts and of finding ways to gather contending parties to the table in the search for acceptable solutions. Finding a moment for leisure, and a shared passion for cricket and calypso music, are useful stimulants in promoting friendship.

I attended my first meeting of the conference of heads of government as prime minister in Port of Spain, Trinidad, at the end of June 1992. It was the same venue where, twenty years earlier, I was part of the ministerial meeting preceding the conference of heads which decided to transform the CARIFTA into CARICOM.

In my address to the opening session I posited the region as facing the great danger of being ignored by a world that was completely indifferent to its fate. This was a new reality consequent on the break-up of the Soviet Union and the end of the Cold War, the movement towards competitive globalization, the coming into being of the European Single Market and the imminent North American Free Trade Area (NAFTA). The collapse of the bipolar world configuration had reduced our strategic importance and we were in danger of being marginalized.

As political leaders we had to answer two fundamental questions. First, whether we had the will to implement the unfinished agenda of the Treaty of Chaguaramas and the logical consequences of that agenda. Second, whether we had the vision to lead the community into a new and more dynamic relationship with our neighbours in and around the Caribbean Sea.

The Grand Anse Declaration three years earlier had set 1992 as the date to receive the reports that were to begin the transformation to the CSME.

Before the conference was the pathbreaking report *Time for Action*, by the formidable West Indies Commission, led by Shridath Ramphal.[2] The report gave guidance on both issues. The unfinished agenda essentially involved the movement beyond cooperation on the market side to include our production and sectoral policies. *Time for Action* proposed an independent commission to secure

---

2. West Indian Commission, *Time for Action: Report of the West Indian Commission* (Kingston: University of the West Indies Press, 1994).

the implementation of conference decisions. It was apparent this would become a thorny issue relating to questions of sovereignty and affordability.

The conference was not ready to pronounce on the range of salient issues in the commission's report. Some of the recommendations were substantive and required detailed study, which some member states wanted time to complete. We therefore agreed to convene in a special session from 28 to 30 October 1992, again in Port of Spain. Twelve of the thirteen member states were represented at the level of head of state or government and the other by the long-standing deputy prime minister of Antigua, Lester Bird.

It was clear that member states, having studied the report, had accepted the need to strengthen the institutions of implementation with urgency and had the desire that by the end of the decade of the 1990s, the West Indies would be a more closely integrated community of sovereign states. The logic begged acceptance of the central recommendation, namely the CARICOM Commission. Patrick Manning, Lester Bird and I strongly supported and urged a CARICOM Commission with the power to accelerate and enforce the implementation of decisions. Many of the delegations which had argued against the recommendations now openly raised the cost of financing and were clearly not ready to cede that level of influence.

The positions were deeply held and threatened to disrupt the movement. To avert such a possibility, I proposed what was to my mind a holding measure: a bureau of the conference. It would comprise the hierarchy – the outgoing chairman, the incumbent chairman and the incoming chairman – together with the secretary general, in his capacity as chief executive officer. Its functions would include updating the consensus of the member states on issues determined by the conference and facilitating the implementation of community decisions, at both the regional and national levels.

The proposal was accepted and it was decided to implement it as of 1 January 1993. This would allow the membership, with the obvious exception of the secretary general, to rotate on the same six-monthly basis as the chairmanship of the conference. The bureau has remained the instrument of choice, even though it has never served as a robust "whip" for implementing decisions of the community.

The special session approved several other seminal recommendations in the commission's report. These included

- Promoting an Association of Caribbean States as the framework for a new and more dynamic relationship with our neighbours in and around the Caribbean

Sea. We negotiated and signed an agreement establishing the association in Cartagena, Colombia, in July 1994, with twenty-five countries and three observer states.

- A Caribbean Community Council of Ministers was constituted which would become the second highest organ of the community. This council was specifically charged at the national level with responsibility for CARICOM affairs. In the case of Jamaica, I assigned this responsibility to the minister of foreign affairs, and that practice continued after my tenure.
- The development of a CARICOM charter of civil society.
- A commitment to the early signing and ratification of the agreement to establish the Assembly of Caribbean Community Parliamentarians. This was to comprise national delegations selected from the government and opposition benches of the Parliament.

While these major recommendations of the West Indian Commission were accepted, the prevailing view is that the heads of government rejected the report, because its salient recommendation – a commission with power to implement decisions of the conference – was not and has not been accepted. The conference returned to that issue in 1997 at Montego Bay and again in 2003 at the thirtieth-anniversary conference of CARICOM.

REVISED TREATY OF CHAGUARAMAS

At our fourteenth conference in Nassau, Bahamas, I was pleased to announce Jamaica's completion of the study assigned for the Caribbean Investment Fund to introduce additional capital and increase investment in the region.

To accommodate the ambitions of a single market and economy, a substantial revision of the 1973 Chaguaramas Treaty was required. Kenny Anthony, former legal counsel in the CARICOM Secretariat, on becoming prime minister of St Lucia, was the obvious choice to superintend this area. Charmaine Constantine, permanent secretary in the Office of the Prime Minister, Barbara Gunter, deputy financial secretary, and Hyacinth Lindsay, chief parliamentary counsel, were members of a formidable Jamaican team which dealt with all discussions and drafts that needed ministerial clearance.

Our reaffirmation of the Grand Anse Declaration to advance towards a single market economy would entail removing restrictions on goods, harnessing resources and promoting entrepreneurship at the regional level to give greater scope and stimulus to our development in the context of liberalization.

The task was undertaken in two stages, for expediency. The first was to develop and adopt nine protocols, each addressing a specific issue, and the over-all governance and administrative arrangements. These were implemented as they were agreed alongside the original treaty framework.

The second was to reconcile and bring those nine protocols into a single treaty which would replace the original. Rights enjoyed under the original treaty could be affected. Negotiating the revised treaty took much longer than originally anticipated, as there were important issues and vested interests to be reconciled and agreed. The negotiations were testy and, at times, explosive. Jamaica was deeply involved in the search for provisions acceptable to all. With persuasion and encouragement we always managed to find a formula.

At the intersessional meeting of heads in Barbados in February 1997, we signed Protocol One of the amended treaty. A highlight of our Montego Bay conference in June was the signing of Protocol Two, on the free movement of the factors of production, procurement of services and movement of capital.

To facilitate the free movement of goods and all necessary services, it became necessary to establish recognizable and acceptable standards. Consequently, CARICOM members established the CARICOM Regional Organisation for Standards and Quality, which was responsible for establishing regional standards for the manufacture and trade of goods for all member states.

A most important agreement was on creating regional accreditation bodies, equipped to assess qualifications for equivalency to facilitate the free movement of people. To this end, the member states concluded the Agreement on Accreditation for Education in Medical and other Health Professions. An authority was established for accrediting health care personnel throughout the region. In addition to the formal structures, there were times when CARICOM needed informal or ad hoc arrangements to defuse frictions between or within member states that could threaten the community's cohesion.

Along with the free trade in goods, the Revised Treaty provides a framework for free trade in services, to facilitate trade and investment in the services sectors of member states. In light of the span and complexity of the services sector, expediency dictated a phased approach. The first step was to abolish the require-ment for work permits for a limited range of skilled individuals. It was achieved through an agreed CARICOM policy, the Free Movement of Skilled Persons Act, implemented in advance of the original Protocol Two of the Revised Treaty of Chaguaramas. We had to remove, by virtue of Protocol Two, all restrictions on the movement of managerial, technical and supervisory staff required for business, commercial, industrial and professional enterprises. Eight categories of nationals were made eligible for free movement throughout the CSME without the need for work permits: university graduates, media workers, artistes, musicians, sportspersons, managers, technical and supervisory staff attached to a company and self-employed people/service providers. Their spouses and immediate dependent family members were also exempt. The freedom to live and work throughout the CSME is signified by a certificate of recognition of CARICOM skills qualification which replaced work permits.

At the July 2006 conference, it was agreed to allow the free movement of two other categories, tertiary-trained teachers and nurses. Informal commercial importers, artisans, domestic workers and hospitality workers would be added as soon as there was agreement on their certification.

The free movement of labour is also being facilitated by measures to harmonize social services such as health and education and allow the transfer of social security benefits.

In November 1992, Jamaica was a member of the Rio Group which met in Argentina. Its purpose was to coordinate our responses to external events, to monitor political events within our region and to begin to seek ways of forging economic links to cope with the challenges we all face.

At our fourteenth meeting of CARICOM heads, I was invited to speak at the opening ceremony as a newly re-elected leader, by dint of our earlier success in the general elections. Among the issues I addressed was the rapid transformation in the international economic landscape, with the emergence of new centres of power and new partnerships. No longer did we enjoy special arrangements which gave us a foothold in the markets of Europe and North America. The emergence of NAFTA and the erosion of preferential arrangements within Lomé, particularly for sugar, bananas and rum, posed new challenges.

As we met in July 1993, we were faced with impending negotiations in the Uruguay Round, the prospective Free Trade Area of the Americas and Europe as a single market that had to operate within a yet-to-be-determined WTO framework.

The region had seen the beneficial results of the Lomé Convention when we combined our limited financial resources and our admirable technical skills to negotiate as a group. After a masterful analysis by Sir Alister McIntyre, the conference resolved to establish a prime-ministerial committee on external economic negotiations and, on the nomination of our elder statesman, Prime

Minister Sir John Compton of St Lucia, "condemned" me for my "past sins" to assume the chair. We were to build on this model in later years, when individual heads were assigned coordinating responsibilities for specific areas and so developed a CARICOM cabinet of presidents and prime ministers.

Our first task was the preparation and evolution of a broad overall strategy for complex and simultaneous negotiations, and an appropriate institutional arrangement. We recognized from the outset that even as a group we were small in size, and new alliances had to be forged outside our historical and traditional associations.

In building such alliances and leveraging precedents, the asymmetrical trade and economic cooperation agreement CARICOM negotiated with Venezuela under President Carlos Andres Pérez in 1991 provided the framework for the CARICOM/Colombia Agreement on Trade, Economic and Technical Cooperation, signed in 1994. These agreements signalled CARICOM's willingness to grant reciprocity in trade, provided that such reciprocity bore an acceptable relationship to the relative economic strength of CARICOM and the negotiating partner.

The formation of the Association of Caribbean States (ACS) in 1994, with one of its principal pillars being trade, would not only increase intra-ACS trade, but provide a greater capacity to negotiate trade arrangements in the hemisphere. We quickly realized that selecting partners and the timing of negotiations for trade agreements were no longer within CARICOM's exclusive control. In order to cope with the extent and speed of external changes, mobilizing our negotiating teams with the backing of technical expertise in vast areas of critical fields was an urgent priority.

Mexico's joining NAFTA in 1994, and the convening of the First Summit of the Americas by President Clinton in December of that same year, with the decision to start negotiations for a Free Trade Area of the Americas, created a seismic shift towards the use of the ACS as a unit for negotiating trade in the Americas. The impact of the Free Trade Area of the Americas required that we move urgently to counteract the erosion of our market and investments share.

Elsewhere in the hemisphere, the Common Market of the South, MERCOSUR, was fast establishing its own influence and defining its linkages in international trading centres. The Andean Pact and the Central American Integration System were also deepening their integration efforts. Bilateral or trilateral free-trade agreements among countries of the Americas were either in place or were being negotiated. All this was taking place in NAFTA by 2005.

The regional negotiating machinery was designed as a unique part of a collaborative mechanism based in Barbados. It was structured to work closely with the secretariat as the body most sensitive to the policy directions of the region. We needed a flexible arrangement which could be expanded to supplement the capacities of the permanent national and regional bureaucracies in keeping with the negotiating load.

The budget for the negotiating arrangements included not only the cost of the personnel and facilities, but the logistical arrangements for negotiations which took place literally around the globe. The time and costs of travel imposed a heavy burden on every regional activity. The member states naturally had to bear a considerable share of the costs, but we also mobilized support from external agencies such as the Commonwealth Secretariat, the European Union and the IDB.

In the light of the region's financial constraints, we were forced to secure financial grants from a number of external agencies, while being able to operate independently from such sponsors.

While my subcommittee had permanent membership owing to the interwoven issues and interests, it was open, so that every country had the right to attend whenever it chose during our deliberations. While governments shape the rules of international trade, we also sought to include the private sector, labour and civil society. For these reasons we endeavoured to meet a day or so in advance of the conference, and there were occasions when the heads ordered us to meet to consider a range of issues.

As we gathered on 6 September 1996 for our sixth meeting, in Kingston, the impact of NAFTA meant we needed to move urgently to counteract the erosion of our market and investment share. We had to examine our trade relations with third parties in the hemisphere on issues related to the Caribbean Basin Initiative, the European Union banana regime, the expiration of the Lomé IV Convention and the decisions of the WTO.

The Santiago Summit of the Americas took place in April 1998, when the heads reaffirmed their determination to realize the Free Trade Area of the Americas by 2005. At the same time, we had to mobilize on interests which ranged from traditional areas of production to new fields such as intellectual property, telecommunications and tertiary education.

By then, none other than Sir Shridath Ramphal had been persuaded to serve as our chief negotiator and undertake an overall plan, from a management perspective, for how the region could best tackle all the negotiations in which it was involved. We were also fortunate in securing Sir Alister McIntyre, who had by then retired as vice chancellor of the University of the West Indies, to coordinate the vast numbers of technical studies we required.

The regional negotiating machinery reported through the prime-ministerial committee to the conference of heads. Managing a process which required a common negotiating stance, with different spheres of jurisdiction and competing interests, was no easy task. There had to be agreement on the broad strategy for each set of negotiations and a system of fine-tuning as each unfolded.

From time to time, I served as the referee in the fight for turf. With help from my colleagues I had to manage the relationships between the regional negotiating machinery and the ministers and ministerial councils responsible for foreign trade and foreign affairs and even subjects pertaining to industry, between the regional negotiating machinery and the CARICOM Secretariat. We appointed a minister with responsibility for each theatre of negotiation. K.D. Knight of Jamaica was responsible for the Free Trade Area of the Americas; Clement Rohee of Guyana for the WTO; Billie Miller of Barbados for the European Union; and Ken Valley of Trinidad and Tobago for bilateral negotiations.

Our negotiations were done through CARIFORUM (including the Dominican Republic) in respect of the post-Lomé Convention, as part of the ACP; and CARICOM, in close association with the Central American Common Market, as well as other hemispheric groupings.

In formulating our own position, we held national consultations, involving ministers of our respective governments, the private sector, the labour movement and other elements of civil society.

As chairman of the prime-ministerial subcommittee, I drew to the attention of leaders of the European Union and heads of state and government of the ACP our main concerns on the draft proposals of the European Commission. These were the overconcentration on political issues, which the European Union proposed to address almost exclusively in the first phase of the negotiations for 1998–2000, deferring the trade and economic aspects of the new arrangement for 2000–2005, and the European Union's unilateral approach in setting its own selective political criteria on which to judge ACP states in making its decisions on future ACP/European Union trade and economic cooperation. These criteria focused on the ACP countries' treatment of issues relating to human rights, democracy and the rule of law and good governance.

We remained of the view that any new cooperation agreement should support regional arrangements and not dismantle existing structures for cooperation between the ACP and the European Union.

≋

I found myself intervening in another regional dispute on behalf of CARICOM when the results of the Guyana elections in December 1997 triggered a dispute between the two main political parties which threatened its democracy and an eruption of bitter ethnic conflict. CARICOM accepted its obligation to help find a solution to restore peace and maintain the rule of law. Both President Janet Jagan and former president Desmond Hoyte agreed to seek my mediation, in view of the confidence the People's Progressive Party and People's National Congress shared that my stance would be balanced.

After three days of rough exchanges, intractable positions gave way to a genuine search for a mutual agreement. This paved the way for an outline agreement subsequently formalized as the Herdmanston Accord, in which the political contenders agreed to accept the findings of the first stage of the audit as binding, but could not be prevented from exercising their right to pursue a number of election petitions filed in the courts by both parties; and it was agreed that the proposal for constitutional reform should be implemented in accordance with the regional timetable and the requisite legislation passed promptly.

The community invited both Janet Jagan and Desmond Hoyte to our 1998 meeting in Castries for dialogue with us which settled the St Lucia Statement, ending street protests in Guyana and allowing the return of democratic governance. This required enabling legislation to allow opposition members to take their seats in the National Assembly rather than forfeit them; a parliamentary management committee to ensure better organizing and functioning of their parliament; and dialogue which would entail meetings between the two main political leaders.

As a follow-up, CARICOM decided to appoint a high-level official acceptable to both leaders and whose function would be developed in conjunction with them. CARICOM had thus secured peaceful resolution of differences and disputes within our region by our own efforts, making external intervention unnecessary.

Another instance where I found myself assuming the role of peacemaker in the region was when vast resources of oil were discovered offshore, and our conference was involved in negotiating bitter boundary dispute between Guyana and Suriname at our Canouan Summit in July 2000. The community deployed me to seek a way forward. I convened a special meeting at Half Moon Hotel in Rose Hall, Montego Bay, and with the aid of our own experts on the law of the sea, we crafted an agreement acceptable to both delegations.

But the Suriname delegation was hesitant to sign, as national elections were pending, and feared it could become a partisan political issue in the campaign.

President Bharrat Jagdeo of Guyana summed up my efforts thus:

> I personally will long remember and be grateful for the efforts he exerted to reconcile Guyana and Suriname to undertake an urgent search for an amicable solution to the boundary problems which separated the two countries. Even now, I recall the many hours we spent in Canouan, St Vincent and the Grenadines, under "P.J.'s" watchful eye, trying to find agreement on several crucial issues. The search continued on to Jamaica, in both Kingston and Montego Bay, where Prime Minister Patterson, always the ready facilitator, pushed the parties toward a solution. Unfortunately, despite his intervention a final settlement proved elusive. However, even though the talks were unsuccessful, there was general recognition that the conciliatory efforts of our host have been most helpful.[3]

And President Ronaldo Venetiaan of Suriname: "When I learnt that P.J. Patterson was the one to be the facilitator, I felt confident and at ease. The two countries were not able to solve the problem then, but what you have done cooled down the situation and brought us back to the conference table."[4]

❚❚

At the twenty-fourth conference of heads in July 2003, CARICOM celebrated its thirtieth anniversary. As I prepared once again to assume the chair – for the last time – it seemed appropriate to present some perspectives from the vantage point of the sole Caribbean Free Trade Association minister involved in negotiating the Treaty of Chaguaramas who still held public office.

As chair, I submitted a document to the conference entitled "CARICOM beyond Thirty: Charting New Directions". To prepare it I constituted an expert group which recommended that "the community's institutional machinery be further strengthened by the establishment of a CARICOM Commission in the near future in order to introduce a meaningful executive function at the regional level and strengthen implementation in the community". I urged our association of states, exercising sovereignty individually and collectively for the betterment of our people, to build a truly loving community that would enlarge our common space to unleash entrepreneurial energies and, as Norman Manley once said, "a community that provides a wider field for individual ambition".

---

3. Communications Office, *P.J. Patterson*, 19.

4. Ibid.

Although several heads were still not ready for this major leap, they were prepared to take some step. This was recorded in the Rose Hall Declaration on Regional Governance and Integrated Development, in which we agreed in principle to "the establishment of a CARICOM Commission or other executive mechanism, whose purpose will be to facilitate the deepening of regional integration in areas of responsibility specified . . ." The specified areas "relate to the CARICOM Single Market and Economy and such other areas of the integration process as the conference may from time to time determine". The commission was to be accountable to the heads of government.

Ralph Gonsalves, prime minister of St Vincent and the Grenadines, was tasked with chairing the prime-ministerial group, in which I served with Owen Arthur of Barbados and Patrick Manning of Trinidad and Tobago.

We worked hard to produce our report to a meeting of heads in Suriname, but at the end of my tenure, it was still a work in progress to convert principle into action. This has stultified the growth and sapped the strength of our regional machinery.

> Nowhere else on the planet is there a region where encounters between people of different cultures have been as challenged to make sense of human existence in modern times as in the Caribbean, where such encounters between Africa, Europe, and Asia and they, in turn, with the indigenous Native Americans (Caribs, Arawaks, Tainos) have resulted in dynamic interplay to produce a new and unique people shaping what many of us describe as a Caribbean civilization.
>
> It is to that civilization that a reformed CARICOM must pay far more attention if that sense of self and society embedded in a strong regional consciousness is to be fostered. For it is such regionalism, rooted in psychic and intellectual commitment, that will sustain the institutions that are vital but by themselves will mean nothing without the passionate commitment by those who must lead, manage, operate and constantly evaluate them.[5]

Fourteen years after the Grand Anse Declaration, leaders remained convinced that a clear and coherent response to the turbulence of globalization impelled us to regard the CSME as our major focus. This would allow us to harmonize our productive capacity and export activities alongside a common international

5. P.J. Patterson, "CARICOM beyond Thirty: Charting New Directions". Presentation at the Twenty-Fourth Meeting of the CARICOM Heads of Government. Montego Bay, Jamaica, 2003.

economic policy. Greater productive capacity, increased competitiveness and more targeted global market penetration would be given greater emphasis.

Within another two years, when Jamaica was afforded the singular privilege of hosting my final CARICOM ceremony, the Mona campus was chosen as the most fitting location for such a historic occasion. On 30 January 2006, the persistence and ingenuity of those who have never wavered in the quest to achieve sustained economic development was justly rewarded. If the common market was perceived in 1973 as a romantic or idealistic notion, the CSME had now become an absolute imperative.

It was clear that any analysis of the benefits to individual states, based purely on balance-of-trade statistics, would be inherently superficial, as it failed to calculate the gains to be made from a pooling of our collective resources, and more so in an era when traditional preferences for primary commodities had disappeared. Knowledge and creative skills would determine our chances of success in a global marketplace, where providing unique and quality service holds the key to our survival.

The CSME plays two fundamental roles in CARICOM's interface with the external environment. It determines the policy foundation which must guide CARICOM's external trade policy with third parties, and therefore establishes the limits of CARICOM's ambit in our external trade negotiations.

It also provides a framework in which CARICOM countries, and by extension, CARICOM firms, can enhance their global competitiveness in order to capitalize on market-access opportunities secured through external negotiations.

I left the stage with a closing exhortation to my colleagues at the CSME signing ceremony:

> I implore you never to abandon that passionate commitment to the full advancement of the region which has allowed us to fulfil this part of the dream today.
>
> The challenges abound, but with unity of purpose and direction, the region will conquer whatever mountains we encounter on the journey so that all people of the Caribbean can realize their full economic and social potential.
>
> The people we serve will judge us on the basis of the actions we have taken to enhance their lives and that of future generations.
>
> Let us therefore together advance, with courage and determination.

CHAPTER 31
THE WIDER CARIBBEAN
IN OUR HEMISPHERE

I BELONG TO THAT GROUP OF FOREIGN-POLICY LEADERS who subscribe to the strategy of concentric diplomacy, which envisages widening circles of cooperation that extend to the wider Caribbean, the Latin American region, the hemisphere and, ultimately, the global system, embracing the United Nations and its agencies, the Non-Aligned Movement, the G77 and China, the Commonwealth and the ACP.

Whatever our historic experience – Spanish, Dutch, French or English – the reality of the countries of the Caribbean Basin is that of small nations struggling to survive in a competitive global economy, but determined to make our mark and preserve our identity in the age of technological revolution.

We believe that since Columbus lost his way on his voyage to India and arrived in the Caribbean instead five centuries ago, the history of our region has been too reflective of the legacy of European domination and fragmentation. As we entered the new millennium, we were determined to close centuries of separateness and to end a chapter of being fractured by the struggles of colonial conquest and the barriers of language. No longer should the relationships among nations of the Caribbean be dictated or unduly influenced by the interests of metropolitan powers.

The case for widening and deepening intra-regional relationships was the more compelling to meet the challenges of globalization, the expansion of the European Union, and the advent of fifteen republics when the Soviet Union was dismantled. It was rooted in the pragmatic appreciation of our own self-interest and the imperatives of coping with the world around us.

The ACS was the fruit of the visionary *Time for Action* report by the West Indian Commission. It pinpointed the rationale for extending CARICOM beyond the anglophone states and demonstrated how "to transform geographical proximity into economic networking" and other forms of practical cooperation. The report properly emphasized the value of an ACS in helping to resolve age-old border disputes affecting Guyana and Belize, in trade negotiations with the metropolitan powers and cooperation in transport, tourism and the environment. It made sense for countries with a similar history, tradition and geographical location to work closely together in order to handle radical changes in the international marketplace.

Within months of my taking office, the foreign trade ministers of CARICOM and the Central American Common Market countries held an historic meeting in response to the need for wider and deeper association despite our different linguistic, cultural and colonial experiences.

After the formal signing of the ACS Treaty, we met in 1994 to launch the ACS in Port of Spain, to work together on what Simón Bolívar saw over a hundred years ago, when he shared his vision of the Americas coming together to chart our own destiny, enabling us to assert our rightful place in the community of nations.

We accepted that the politics of "left" or "right" should not prevent us from collaborating in trade, tourism and transport to accelerate regional development. Cuba had to be an integral and active part of the process.

We declared the Caribbean Sea our patrimony and the unifying factor among all Caribbean countries. As that included the French Overseas Departments, France became an active observer in the ACS and supported our proposal to have the international community recognize the Caribbean Sea as a special area in the context of sustainable development.

HAITI

Separated by a small channel of water in the Caribbean Sea, Jamaica and Hispaniola were home to the three rival colonial powers which dominated Caribbean history – Britain, France and Spain.

Interchange between the enslaved people of Haiti, ruled by the French, and Jamaica, ruled by the British, began soon after the first Africans, many originating in the same areas of West Africa, were separated on their arrival in the Caribbean. A key mover in the fight of the enslaved Haitians for independence, something that startled the entire world, was Dutty Boukman, a Jamaican. The Boukman Rebellion in August 1791 is credited by several historical sources as the true beginning of the revolution in Haiti.

Haiti, or Saint-Domingue as it was named by its French colonizers, was undoubtedly the jewel in the French crown in the mid-sixteenth century and up to the time of the revolution. Its exports of sugar, coffee, indigo and cotton represented at least 35 per cent of France's foreign trade. Slave traders and plantation owners, most of whom lived in France, amassed great fortunes on the backs of over four hundred thousand enslaved Africans in Saint-Domingue, the largest enslaved population in the Caribbean. Like other Caribbean populations, that of Saint-Domingue was divided into a rigid caste system that privileged only the whites. The free coloureds were the first to protest French domination, with a call for equal rights. The denial of their request led to civil war. It was this situation which encouraged Boukman and other enslaved rebels to initiate their bid for freedom, which resulted in the greatest revolt against slavery. Boukman lost his life in the battle, but his death strengthened the resolve of his followers, who included the great military strategist Toussaint L'Ouverture, whose brilliant leadership is legendary. His eventual kidnapping and confinement in a French prison in 1803 did not diminish the magnitude of his successes.

Neville Dawes, my tutor in English literature at Calabar, ensured that every scholar understood the triumph of the human spirit and the significance of the victory achieved by L'Ouverture as we analysed the poetry of William Wordsworth his elegy "To Toussaint L'Ouverture".

> Though fallen thyself, never to rise again,
> Live, and take comfort. Thou hast left behind
> Powers that will work for thee; air, earth, and skies;
> There's not a breathing of the common wind
> That will forget thee; thou hast great allies;
> Thy friends are exultations, agonies,
> And love, and man's unconquerable mind.

History professor Elsa Goveia made sure every student knew of the other great revolutionary leaders Jean-Jacques Dessalines and Henri Christophe. In 1804, Dessalines declared independence from France and became the country's first president. France agreed to recognize Haiti's independence in 1825, after President Jean-Pierre Boyer agreed to pay reparation to the tune of 150 million francs, a debt the country carried until 1922. Through many years Haiti paid a heavy price for having defeated the Napoleonic army. The French have never forgotten or forgiven. The colonial powers, threatened by Haiti's successful revolt, feared that other colonies, particularly Cuba and Jamaica, might be emboldened to follow its example. As a result Haiti was isolated from world affairs and received US diplomatic recognition only in 1862.

But the success of the Haitian Revolution inspired those who sought to be free of the colonial yoke and people of colour everywhere in the world. As students, my contemporaries and I were influenced by C.L.R. James's *Black Jacobins,* which described the struggles and successes of the leaders of the Haitian Revolution.

In succeeding years a number of Jamaicans went to Haiti, some to work on the sugar plantations and some in administrative positions. One of them was O.T. Fairclough, who can truly be credited as the original source who motivated N.W. Manley to found the PNP in 1938.

Internally, Haiti suffered from severe class divisions. The country has never enjoyed any lengthy period of political stability. And in the second half of the twentieth century it suffered the Duvaliers' dictatorship, which lasted over three decades. After Jean-Claude Duvalier was overthrown in 1986, Haiti was ruled by a series of provisional governments. The first elections, in December 1990, resulted in the emergence of Jean-Bertrand Aristide. We in Jamaica expressed support for the new government and invited president-elect Aristide to visit Jamaica.

Aristide was overthrown in a military coup nine months after assuming power and had to take refuge in the United States while already there on a visit to the United Nations. CARICOM and Jamaica condemned the overthrow strongly and Jamaica was instrumental in galvanizing an appropriate response through the Organization of American States. Aristide was reinstated in October 1994 by the Bill Clinton administration after a mission to Haiti by former president Jimmy Carter, retired general Colin Powell and Senator Sam Nunn of Georgia, then chairman of the Senate Armed Services Committee.

The US support was prompted by the lobbying of the influential congressional Black Caucus on Aristide's behalf, as well as by the critical refugee problem that the fleeing Haitians created in the United States. Thousands of Haitians, in an effort to escape the tyranny and poverty in Haiti, were prepared to risk their lives to get there. The majority travelled in small boats totally unsuited for such a journey, which resulted in hundreds of people drowning at sea. The exodus began immediately after the military took control of the government. By December 1991, over eighty refugees had arrived in Jamaica.

The flight escalated in ensuing years and created a major problem in the United States, where, unlike Cubans, who were treated as political refugees and quickly processed and assigned green cards, the Haitians were put in detention centres. By 1993 there were thousands of refugees in the United States, with those detained in the Krone Centre protesting their treatment by going on a hunger strike.

President Clinton sought support from Jamaica and the Bahamas for having ships stationed in our waters as processing centres for Haitians intercepted by US Coast Guard vessels. Haitians who were granted refugee status were shipped to Guantánamo Bay and then sent on to the United States. The rest would be sent back to Haiti.

While Jamaica deplored the fact that there was not one US policy that dictated the same treatment for Haitian and Cuban refugees landing in the country, we could not stand by and let people drown. At least the ships prevented the loss of more Haitian lives.

Aristide's tenure did not last long after his reinstatement in 1994. By December 1995 he had agreed to step aside, in keeping with the Haitian constitution, and to support his political ally René Préval. When President Préval came to office, as the chairman of CARICOM I convinced my colleagues that we owed it to Haiti and its people to end their years of isolation. In Central America and the Caribbean there were alliances of Spanish-speaking and English-speaking countries, but Haiti stood alone. To that end I made an official visit to Haiti to spur its interest in joining CARICOM. I flew to Port-au-Prince to invite President Préval to our summit in Montego Bay in July 1997, when he expressed the strong desire to join CARICOM. While there were formalities with which Haiti would have to comply, he left with the clear assurance that Haiti would be accepted.

During this period there was electoral turbulence in Haiti. First of all, it had never had an efficient electoral process, and secondly, the conduct and results of the elections were disputed and there was no effective legal machinery for dispute resolution. CARICOM asked Sir John Compton to visit Haiti in an effort to resolve the situation. We were also engaged with the Organization of American States.

Although Préval was president, the effective political power resided with Aristide as the head of Fanmi Lavalas, the party to which Préval also belonged. When Préval's term ended, Aristide was eligible to run, and did so successfully, with an overwhelming majority. Contentious issues remained regarding the methodology used to calculate the votes in several senatorial races, but Aristide was accepted as the clear winner as president. Despite this, political tensions increased, with Aristide on one side and a combination of other forces aligned against him. It reached a point where conflagration seemed imminent.

The bicentennial of its independence in 2004 was naturally a cause for major celebrations in Haiti, for all people who stood for liberty and for people of colour everywhere. President Thabo Mbeki, chairman of the African Union, journeyed from South Africa, and activities had been planned for the entire year to commemorate the anniversary. But trouble loomed.

The spark that ignited the political furore was the 5 December attack by pro-Aristide activists on some hundred members of the university community who were calling for Aristide to step down. The clash, which left at least five people injured, was the climax of intensifying violence and insecurity. The incident was viewed as a watershed: the situation was increasingly turning against Aristide, and focused international attention on the crisis.

I wrote to President Aristide at the end of December 2003 congratulating the country on its bicentennial celebration, while also conveying CARICOM's concerns over the growing instability and our intention to contribute to a solution to the political unrest which would be acceptable to all the contending parties.

Between 5 and 7 January, Jamaica participated in a CARICOM fact-finding mission. The delegation, led by Prime Minister Perry Christie of the Bahamas, included Jamaica's minister of foreign affairs, K.D. Knight, and minister of state, Delano Franklyn. They held talks separately with representatives of the government, leaders of the opposition and major stakeholders, including the religious, business and international communities. We did this in order to assess the factors leading to the upsurge of violence and to make recommendations for possible compromise within the parameters of the Haitian constitution and democratic governance. They were also charged with inviting President Aristide to meet with a core group of CARICOM prime ministers in Jamaica at the end of January.

While CARICOM would itself have become engaged in dealing with the problems in Haiti, we were also exhorted to do so through a conversation between US president George W. Bush and Trinidad and Tobago's Prime Minister Manning at the end of 2003. When he had a special meeting of the Summit of the Americas in Monterrey on 12–13 January 2004, at which Aristide was present, President Bush expressed pleasure and satisfaction that the Caribbean was seeking to resolve this problem. CARICOM heads used the opportunity to speak to Aristide, who expressed his support for the CARICOM initiatives and assured us that he would cooperate fully with CARICOM and the Haitian opposition to protect the interests of his people.

As chairman of CARICOM I convened a meeting to discuss the situation in Nassau, Bahamas on 20–21 January. It included representatives of the Haitian opposition and observers from the United States, Canada and the Organization of American States. Our position included the endorsement of full democracy in Haiti; acceptance of Aristide's voluntary resignation before the end of his term; and the desire that all changes would be made in accordance with the country's constitution. We made it emphatically clear that we would not accept a coup in any form. We asked the opposition to consider, among other things, a broad-based advisory committee, the opposition and government cooperating in choosing a prime minister, the immediate release of prisoners who had been arbitrarily detained and the disarming of gangs. We promised that CARICOM would hold President Aristide accountable for carrying out his side of the bargain.

Aristide came to Jamaica, and I hosted a meeting on 31 January which was also attended by our international partners, including representatives from the European Union. He accepted the principles and elements of the CARICOM plan and made it clear that he would not seek an additional term and that his wife would not run so as to make him a surrogate president. He even promised to cut his term short.

André Apaid, the leader of the broad-based civic Group of 184, had been invited to the Kingston meeting, but did not attend. Consequently, to ensure that all parties were aware of our thinking, a CARICOM team went to Haiti on 3 February to meet with him, but our efforts to persuade him to agree to the action plan were unsuccessful.

Several other CARICOM missions visited Haiti in an attempt to resolve the rapidly deteriorating situation. As I was then chairman, Jamaica took the lead position. The Bahamas was also integrally involved – through Prime Minister Christie and his foreign minister, Fred Mitchell – because of its proximity to Haiti as so many Haitians lived there and because of the boat exodus countless numbers ended up drowning in Bahamian waters. The Bahamas had also opened an embassy in Haiti, the only Caribbean embassy there at the time. Prime Minister Kenny Anthony of St Lucia was responsible for governance within CARICOM and so was also involved.

The meetings with the contending parties recognized the influence of the United States, which was not only kept fully abreast but was actively involved. When the Nassau proposal was fine-tuned to create the CARICOM Prior Action Plan, which was to have been implemented within four to six weeks, I instructed the CARICOM foreign ministers to present it to the US secretary of state, Colin Powell.

A meeting was scheduled for 13 February 2004. The CARICOM delegation included foreign ministers K.D. Knight of Jamaica and Fred Mitchell of the Bahamas, as well as Ambassador Sonia Johnny of St Lucia and the assistant secretary general of CARICOM, Ambassador Colin Granderson. They met with the secretary general of the Organization of American States, César Gaviria; the Canadian minister of foreign affairs, Bill Graham; the US secretary of state, Colin Powell; and representatives of France and the European Union. The CARICOM plan enjoyed the full support of the meeting, and Colin Powell not only fully endorsed it but recognized it as the only feasible plan. He promised that the United States, as a member of the UN Security Council, would ensure that it was accepted as the only way forward. Both the United States and Canada committed themselves to providing resources to strengthen the policy advisory capacity of the Organization of American States' special mission in Haiti and to help it to better monitor the implementation of the CARICOM plan.

But at that time American troops were stretched in Afghanistan and in Iraq, and the Americans were looking for help. The French offered – and that, to my mind, was when everything changed. Because the French never forgot their grudge against Haiti, they saw it as an opportunity to pay back Haiti for its audacity in successfully challenging French dominance two centuries earlier. Aristide, in his second term, had declared that it was the French who owed Haiti reparations, and demanded that they repay the 150 million francs. The moment the French entered, the whole picture changed and the resolution taken to the Security Council, which should have had easy passage, could not be passed.

Meanwhile, the situation on the ground was worsening, and Aristide had problems countering mercenaries in the country. Up to then he had had a private US protection team. That disappeared, and his arsenal was now bare. He appealed to South Africa for assistance with arms, and President Mbeki responded. This message was transmitted through me as the chairman of CAR-ICOM. I deliberately made it known to the United States that this assistance was being sought, and was being provided.

A delegation was sent to Haiti on 21 February in a last-ditch attempt to broker a peaceful solution to the worsening crisis. The plan was rejected by the opposition. On 25 February the UN secretary general appointed Reginald Dumas, retired Trinidad and Tobago ambassador, special advisor. On 26 February the UN Security Council met at my request, on behalf of CARICOM, to discuss the need for urgent action to stabilize the situation. We called on the council to approve the dispatch of a multinational force to Haiti, to which CARICOM would contribute troops. The council took no action, but made a statement that international security presence would be contingent on a political settlement.

Over the weekend of 28 February 2004, I sensed that things had reached a crisis, cut short my attendance at a G15 meeting in Caracas, and came home. I briefed UN Secretary General Annan on the situation.

The flight from South Africa bearing the arms for Haiti landed in Jamaica that day and awaited instructions on proceeding to Haiti. I called President Aristide to tell him, and he was quite happy to hear it.

Around six o'clock in the morning on 29 February, I was awakened by K.D. Knight, who said Colin Powell had called to tell him that the Americans had taken Aristide out of Port-au-Prince, at his request, for his own safety. They were still unsure what his final destination would be. I was flabbergasted, as when I spoke to Aristide the previous night, far from indicating any such intention, he had in fact expressed relief that he would be getting support through the arrival of arms and equipment from South Africa. I told Minister Knight to tell our counterparts throughout the Caribbean what had taken place.

There was uncertainty as to where the plane carrying Aristide was. We later learned that it had landed briefly in the Dominican Republic, then in Antigua. I immediately contacted Prime Minister Lester Bird, and when he made checks he was told a plane had landed and refuelled. The manifest showed: "Cargo, no passengers aboard." By that time it had refuelled and flown across the Atlantic, heading for the Central African Republic. Again, the hand of France was obvious in selecting the destination.

I was incensed. I issued a strong statement of protest, in which I was joined by CARICOM colleagues. In response, US Ambassador Roger Noriega, assistant secretary for Western Hemisphere Affairs and one of the principal architects of US Haitian policy, made a statement seeking to justify Aristide's removal and denouncing our position.

I convened a special meeting of CARICOM, attended by several prime ministers, during which we spoke with President Aristide. He told us that he had been removed from Haiti by force: they had swooped down on the palace and swept up everybody, including a goddaughter of his and her father who were visiting at the time. They flew them all the way across the Atlantic to the Central African Republic and eventually took them back to our hemisphere.

The UN Security Council met that same Sunday evening, agreed with what had been done. It installed a UN stabilization mission to go into Haiti, and installed Boniface Alexandre, chief justice of the Supreme Court, as interim president, and later Gérard Latortue, foreign minister in the short-lived Leslie Manigat presidency.

There was no disguising our shock and alarm at the sequence of events and the role played by the United States. We had been meticulous in keeping the United States informed of all our actions and intentions at every step of the way, and we were outraged that it should remove a democratically elected leader in this way. Had we not stood firm and expressed our dissatisfaction we would have put all leaders in the region in an equally vulnerable position. My statement to the press was unequivocal in expressing my disgust at Aristide's ouster: I described it as a dangerous precedent for democratic societies in the region and called for a UN investigation into his removal.

Aristide had left this side of the Atlantic without seeing his wife and his children, who had been in Miami at the time of his forced departure. He quickly got in touch with me, saying he wanted to come back to the Caribbean and be reunited with his family. I could only imagine the agony of being torn from his home and family and from the country that he had fought so long to protect. I agreed, but that upset the Americans greatly. South Africa had agreed that it would eventually give him asylum.

Aristide assured me that he had agreed to come to Jamaica to see his family and would not use it as a launch pad to return to Haiti, nor use his proximity to stir up trouble there. I took him at his word and agreed. The plan was that he would stay for thirty days.

In a last-ditch attempt to stop me from hosting Aristide, the Americans told me that they had received a special intelligence report that he would be unsafe here because a Haitian family was plotting to assassinate him in Jamaica in reprisal for something they claimed had happened to their family. I thanked them for sharing this information and said we would ensure his full protection. And so we did.

The Americans put a lot of pressure on us. I received a call from National Security Adviser Condoleezza Rice, who said she was calling on behalf of the president, with whom she had just concluded a meeting. She said they were holding Jamaica entirely responsible for anything that might happen in Haiti, and that if one strand of the hair of any American marine was singed, or hurt befell any American sent there, she would hold me and Jamaica responsible for that too. I responded that we had taken a decision and would not be intimidated by the threat.

Colin Powell called me on Friday morning (5 March) at Vale Royal, and repeated his earlier statement to K.D. Knight that Aristide, through the US ambassador in Port-au-Prince, had requested his removal for his own safety. I told him that was inconsistent with my own conversation with Aristide. He asked me if I was accusing him of lying. I told him that I was not accusing him of inventing the story, as that was no doubt what he had been told. Look at what happened in respect of Iraq regarding the weapons of mass destruction.

I had never been more furious in all my years in public office. I said to him, "First you encouraged us to mediate the situation. Secondly, you then approved the plan we designed." What hurt most of all and what I could not possibly condone, was the reference to President Aristide as cargo. When we remember that our ancestors were forcibly brought across the Atlantic as cargo, now to take one of us across the Atlantic and refer to us as cargo was unforgivable. I would resist and denounce any description or treatment of a human being as cargo.

I was even more incensed when he alleged that Aristide had been removed because he was involved in drug trafficking, and asked why this information had not been previously shared with us. I enquired whether Powell had failed to do so for fear of breaching confidence or because he thought I, too, was involved in drug trafficking – and lost my cool completely as he attempted in vain to mollify my rage.

We called in the Jamaica Defence Force and put them in charge of President Aristide's security. Before we sent him to Lydford in St Ann, where he was to stay, we had to inform the community that he would be coming, and they readily accepted him. Special staffing arrangements were put in place for him.

Sharon Hay-Webster went as my representative to the Central African Republic, accompanied by US Congresswoman Maxine Waters and supporting staff from the Black Caucus, to collect him, taking with her my letter to the president asking for his release. The Central African Republic was reluctant to release him at first, but eventually acquiesced, and Aristide was reunited with his family, who stayed with him for the duration of his time in Jamaica. The children attended school in Lydford and were well accepted by the community. I saw them all together as a family when they were leaving Jamaica to go to South Africa. I flew them from Moneague to Jamaica House, and when I saw the children and how they reacted at being reunited with their father, I would have done the same thing again and again.

The members of the US Black Caucus were appreciative and supportive. Maxine Waters, Charles Randle, Barbara Lee and Jesse Jackson were in constant contact with me while he was here. Maxine Waters visited him while he was in Jamaica.

As it turned out, Aristide stayed longer than thirty days, and that presented some problems. He could not go to South Africa as scheduled, because of upcoming general elections there; obviously that would not have been an appropriate time to bring him in. His extended stay naturally increased the pressure on us. Consideration was given to taking him elsewhere until he could go to South Africa. Among the places that said they were prepared to consider it were Mexico and Brazil, but they eventually declined. Nigeria offered to do so, but this was about the time when it was preparing to accommodate Charles Taylor, and the Black Caucus was concerned at the possibility of any taint by association, so Aristide did not want to go there, though when I spoke to President Obasanjo, his response was: "You asked and we will take him." Around two o'clock on Thursday morning, my telephone rang and I was told the presidential plane was on the runway, about to depart from Nigeria for Jamaica. We were in the nick of time to stop it taking off, as we had decided to keep Aristide until South Africa was ready for him.

By then Thabo Mbeki had demitted the chairmanship of the African Union and President Joaquim Chissano of Mozambique had assumed the position. President Mbeki said that the invitation for South Africa to accommodate Aristide should come from the current head of the African Union. Once President Aristide received the invitation, all the arrangements were finalized and it was time for him to go. Minister of State Delano Franklyn escorted Aristide to South Africa to ensure his safe arrival and relocation.

Ironically, at that time I was the leader of CARICOM by default. My term of office had come to an end on 31 December 2003 and the prime minister of Antigua was to take over the chairmanship on 1 January in the rotation. However, an election was taking place in Antigua, so I was asked to hold on as chairman, and agreed. When Antigua finally took over, after the worst of the crisis had passed, Prime Minister Baldwin Spencer said, "Thank God P.J. was in the chair!" The Black Caucus of the US Congress gave me the Charles Diggs Award in recognition of my role.

CUBA

With the end of the Cold War, there was rapprochement between the United States and Russia. All states in the hemisphere, except the United States, had accorded Cuba diplomatic recognition and begun to carve out their special areas of common interest.

Jamaica vehemently denounced the Helms-Burton Act of 1996, which toughened the US trade and economic embargo which punished investors from third countries who did business with Cuba. It was a clear violation of international law, as it sought to establish a legislative and judicial decision of territoriality. We regarded it as a severe trespass on our sovereignty and a grave impediment to ventures into Cuba by enterprising Jamaican hoteliers.

Within CARICOM, all traces of resistance to a healthy working relationship with Cuba had disappeared. No longer was it a source of partisan division in any Caribbean territory, nor did any suspicion remain of Cuban interference in internal democratic contests. That this became so was thanks to the sustained and tremendous support which Cuba has extended to every Caribbean state in training, health and response to natural disasters, which deserves the loudest applause. No matter their political stripe, every CARICOM head came to reject the moral illegitimacy of the US embargo and to support the full reintegration of Cuba into the political and economic life of the Caribbean.

At the first meeting of the ACS in Port of Spain, Fidel Castro and I met in his suite at the Hilton Hotel for nearly two hours. We had known each other well for over twenty years. While we knew the chemistry between Michael Manley and himself would always remain unique, we had our own affinity, which we maintained to the end.

Two weeks after that meeting and with Fidel's approval, I raised directly in a one-to-one White House discussion the lifting of the embargo. President Clinton responded, "It's immoral, isn't it? I intend to remove it during my second term. We may differ in our political views, but I have the highest respect for Fidel Castro, who is a man of his word." He cited Cuba's strong backing of the war on the trade in illicit drugs.

Several months before the 1996 presidential elections, planes from Florida were shot down over Cuban airspace – and so was the Clinton promise.

The only issue on which Fidel and I did not see eye to eye was the timing of my retirement. At the ceremony in Montego Bay to mark the first anniversary of PetroCaribe, he cursed me rotten rich when I told him of my intention to retire and write history, retorting: "Why are you going now, when we are making history?"

When he realized I would not be moved, he did not conceal his regrets, and wrote:

> I think that Patterson is one of the most brilliant men of this epoch. I have known him for many years. It is with regret that he has already taken the decision to devote himself to other activities. I feel for him a great admiration, a big fondness. He has always been a brilliant speaker, a unifier, a representative of the best of the peoples of the Caribbean.
>
> Our people will remember him and will keep on remembering him while he lives and always as one of the best friends of Cuba and the Revolution. He is one of the fairest and most inspiring men that the Caribbean has had.[1]

---

1. Communications Office, *P.J. Patterson*, 15.

It did not take Fidel's death for history to absolve him as an indomitable warrior in the fight for liberation and the struggle for an equitable world order which manifests our kindred humanity.

VENEZUELA

Jamaica's bond with Venezuela was irrevocably established just under two centuries ago, when Simón Bolívar, "The Liberator" of the Spanish Americas, spent a year in Jamaica in self-imposed exile after Spanish forces overcame his attempt to declare Venezuela independent from Spain.

Bolívar's sojourn in Jamaica turned out to be a most eventful one, thanks to his famous "Jamaica Letter" outlining his thoughts on republican government and Latin American unity, and an attempt on his life. These events ensured that his time in Jamaica would forever be a significant chapter in the story of the relations between the two countries.

Jamaica has since celebrated its link with Venezuela and continued to recognize Bolívar's role through the Bolivarian Society, the establishment of a Venezuelan embassy in Jamaica and the Venezuelan Institute, which for many decades has promoted cultural understanding between the two countries.

An important element of the strategy of building the regional economic process was promoting Latin American and Caribbean cooperation. In 1974 Jamaica received trade missions from India, Venezuela, Italy, China and Puerto Rico, among others. This outreach would pay huge dividends in due course, particularly in the case of Venezuela, with which Jamaica has shared warm and fraternal relations for many decades. Since our independence we have been in the vanguard of strategies to redress the North-South divide. This has been evidenced by the several efforts by Venezuela to assist Jamaica, among other Caribbean countries, to cope with the pressures of access to the energy we need.

When the international oil market was experiencing its second shock, we began negotiations with Venezuela and Mexico to design the San José Accord and cushion the heavy oil import burden. Under the agreement, Mexico and Venezuela, under concessionary financial terms, provided up to 29,000 barrels of crude oil per day to Jamaica. An important aspect of this agreement was that it allowed Jamaica to retain funds from its oil payments to invest in various projects, including housing. These funds had not been used for several years and the West Indies Home Contractors Limited took the initiative to negotiate with the three governments (Jamaica, Venezuela and Mexico) for use of the funds to provide interim and mortgage financing for the Greater Portmore Housing Development. The agreement was signed on 31 July 1990 at the official opening of the eleventh CARICOM summit, held at the Jamaica Conference Centre in Kingston. The Greater Portmore project today provides homes for thousands of Jamaicans.

The strong relationship between Carlos Andres Pérez and Michael Manley continued after I took office. The San José Accord, with strong support from Venezuela, was used to undertake several other major projects which have been of significant benefit to the country. These include: refurbishing the National Stadium and the National Arena; expanding the National Gallery; a multimedia centre at the Edna Manley School of Visual and Performing Arts; upgrading the swimming pool, tennis and basketball courts at the G.C. Foster College of Physical Education and Sport and the Montego Bay Sports Complex; the Montego Bay Civic Centre, which houses a museum of the history of the people of St James and an art gallery to exhibit works from western Jamaica; rehabilitating the Port Maria Court House and expanding it to house a civic and cultural centre for the town; improving the facilities at Frome in Westmoreland to include a club house and fencing the football field; and extending a line of credit to the Jamaica Mortgage Bank to finance affordable housing throughout the country.

Hugo Chávez

It was El Comandante who, during an official visit I made to Cuba, first drew my attention to the prospect and significance of Hugo Chávez winning the 1998 presidential election campaign in Venezuela. *"Es hombre militar, pero muy progresista. Creo que Chávez puede hacer una diferencia enorme en nuestra lucha para justicia en el mundo"* ("He is a military man, but very progressive. I believe Chávez will make a tremendous difference in our fight for justice in the world"), Fidel told me. Immediately after his installation, we had the honour of receiving President Chavez of Venezuela on 10 February 1999 in Montego Bay at the Ninth Summit of the G15, on his first trip abroad.

In his opening presentation, Chávez pledged "to advance the Bolivarian agenda, which promotes the pace and scope of integration between the nations in the Caribbean space, and to embrace initiatives which would redress the inequalities between developing countries of the South and the industrialized nations of the North".

It was not long before he demonstrated the total commitment of the Bolivarian Republic of Venezuela to alleviate the plight of energy-deficient countries in our region. When the San José Accord expired, Chávez immediately put in place the Caracas Accord, which provided tremendous assistance. There were early misgivings within CARICOM that Guyana would be excluded owing to their age-old border disputes. On my arrival in Caracas, I persuaded Chávez to include Guyana among the recipients. For some time thereafter the tensions created by the border disputes were reduced.

In October 2000, the agreement to supply oil to the tune of eighty thousand bolivares to ten Central American and Caribbean states, including Jamaica, complemented the San José Accord. It was dubbed the Caracas Energy Agreement and established preferential price levels and percentages for financing long-term, low-interest loans to the various countries based on the quantity of oil they purchased. Loans ranged from 10 to 25 per cent of the payment for the oil, depending on the prices paid. There was a one-year grace period, with payments extending over fifteen years at an interest rate of 2 per cent.

Jamaica was able to access some 7.4 million barrels of oil annually at a cost of US$15–US$30 per barrel and pay 80 per cent of the cost upfront. The remaining 20 per cent was converted into a soft fifteen-year loan.

When heads of state and government gathered in New York for a special convocation of the United Nations to mark the new millennium, Hugo Chávez invited Fidel Castro and me to a meeting in his suite at the Manhattan Hotel. At a time of high and volatile oil prices and insecure supplies, Chávez sought our views on how best to forge an energy cooperation agreement, which would enhance energy security, advance regional economic integration and foster socio-economic development for our people.

Having reaffirmed the sovereign right of all nations to control and manage their natural resources, we had a fruitful exchange, based on our experiences of futile efforts between oil producers and consuming countries within the developing world two decades before. The triumvirate shared a common resolve to create new frontiers for trade, energy cooperation, and human-resource development.

Both Fidel and Hugo insisted on my active engagement in the conceptual design, given my previous involvement in the Paris Conference on International Economic Cooperation and Jamaica's membership in the G15.

We recognized it would take considerable time for the seeds to germinate and decided to remain in close and continuing contact before and during the intensive work we mandated our ministers of energy to undertake.

We wanted to deepen and strengthen the economic and social bonds between those countries willing to subscribe to and enhance energy security, promote capacity-building and accelerate the agenda for development throughout our region.

In 2003, the Government of Venezuela presented the concept to the member states of the Latin American Energy Organization in Quito, Ecuador. In July 2004, the concept was shared at a meeting in Caracas with the energy ministers of the Caribbean, who embraced it as a viable way to "secure access to energy at just and reasonable prices within the framework of Latin American and Caribbean energy integration".

On 29 June 2005, the Government of Venezuela and fourteen Caribbean states signed the PetroCaribe Energy Cooperation Agreement. The environment of Puerto La Cruz in Venezuela was exquisite for a memorable ceremony. Before signing, we had to clear a final hurdle which would enable the region's two energy-rich countries – Trinidad and Tobago and Venezuela – to assist the energy-deficient countries of the wider region in complementary mechanisms.

At one point, the gulf appeared too wide to cross. My intervention reflected how far we had come and proposed some steps which would enable us to end on a triumphant note. The PetroCaribe Energy Agreement opened a new era of collaboration to uplift and advance the economic and social conditions of people within our territorial borders. Chávez was emphatic that it should encompass those who have been historically oppressed and downtrodden: "*Nunca olvide los pobres*" ("Never forget the poor"), he insisted.

We left Puerto La Cruz with the confidence that the unique structure and the spectacular advantages which the new regime provided would reduce the crippling effect of financial stringency and allow the appropriate allocation of scarce resources in all energy-deficient countries. This would allow us to expand our social programmes, build physical infrastructure and promote education, housing and health.

A month later, on 24 August, Jamaica signed our bilateral agreement with Venezuela. Under that arrangement Jamaica had access to twenty-one thousand barrels of crude oil per day. This was not at a concessionary price, as within the framework of the OPEC Venezuela was not permitted to sell below the world market price. However, we did not have to pay the cost in full and the balance was converted into a concessionary loan at 1 per cent over twenty-five years.

The agreement included a grace period of up to two years for capital repayment, as well as an annual interest rate of 2 per cent on the applicable volumes, when the price of oil is less than US$40 per barrel. When the price exceeds

US$40, the interest is reduced to 1 per cent and the repayment period is extended from fifteen to twenty-three years, plus a two-year grace period for a total of twenty-five years. A more generous agreement could not have been made.

Loans were made available to fund social and economic development programmes and to improve our physical infrastructure. The immediate substantial benefits included:

- Averting a severe reduction in our foreign-exchange reserves, thus easing the pressure for currency devaluation, which would trigger inflation
- Accumulating loan funds at concessionary rates which could not have been secured from the international lending agencies without conditionalities.
- Enabling us to repay portions of the loan by way of goods and services, including commodities such as sugar, bananas, the traditional markets for which had suffered from adverse rulings by the WTO, and opening a new chapter for the expansion of regional trade and economic partnership in an era when developing countries were striving to meet UN Millennium Development Goals. The partnership also facilitated the exploration of areas for increased cooperation, such as energy generation, conservation programmes, maritime and air transport, tourism marketing, disaster preparedness and mitigation, and environmental protection.

I was honoured that Jamaica had the privilege of hosting the second Petro-Caribe Summit on 6 September 2005, which coincided with the 190th anniversary of the writing of Simón Bolívar's famous Jamaica Letter. His vision was to put to use all the resources for public prosperity to improve, educate and perfect the New World. I was co-chairman of the conference with Hugo Chávez as nations from the wider Caribbean gathered in a spirit of unity and collaboration to achieve the prosperity and development that he had envisaged so long before.

It was a week after Hurricane Katrina had devastated Louisiana, and the price of oil spiked to US$70 a barrel. It was a timely reminder of our common vulnerability to natural disasters.

"In this volatile environment, security of supplies and stability in the price of this vital commodity are issues of great concern, especially for small non-producing states such as ours in the Caribbean," I reminded colleagues in my opening statement.

The meeting marked another milestone in the efforts to forge a unified approach to social and economic development in CARICOM, and served to strengthen our ties with Venezuela, Cuba and the Dominican Republic.

Important developments coming out of the summit included the ministerial council's decision that the executive secretariat would undertake initiatives in relation to strategic study for the characterization of energy in the Central American and Caribbean region, and advancing renewable energy technology in the region, a study based on a proposal presented jointly by Dominica and Jamaica. The heads also accepted the urgent need to examine the feasibility of greater cooperation in aviation, natural disaster and the fight against HIV/AIDS.

Objectives of PetroCaribe for the coordination of public policies in energy-related matters included decisions to minimize the risk associated with security of energy supply, and defend the sovereign right to administer the rate of development of non-renewable natural resources; make proper use of energy resources to close the gap among member countries within the framework of regional integration; and create mechanisms to guarantee that resources generated by energy-bill savings under PetroCaribe are used for social and economic development, promotion and employment and to increase production and services, public health, educational, cultural and sports activities. The initiative came, appropriately, at a time when the oil market was extremely volatile and prices continued to escalate, putting our already fragile economies under severe social and financial pressure.

We welcomed the wide range of benefits received through the PetroCaribe Agreement. It has made a substantial contribution towards the fight against poverty, unemployment, illiteracy and lack of medical services in member countries and was instrumental in stimulating economic growth and addressing the social inequities that had bedevilled us for centuries.

Hugo Chávez was, unarguably, a friend of Jamaica and a champion for the region. His death in March 2013 was mourned by those who understood the overwhelming generosity of a man who was willing to promote regional development by using the resources of his own country. His indelible contribution to regional solidarity and economic progress will forever have a positive impact on every aspect of our daily lives.

THE UNITED STATES

Shortly after his inauguration, President Bill Clinton, in August 1993, invited to the White House the president of Guyana and the prime ministers of Barbados, Trinidad and Tobago, Jamaica and the Bahamas.

President Cheddi Jagan and prime ministers Sandiford, Manning, Ingraham and I decided that we had an obligation to represent the interests of all

CARICOM states, and allocated among ourselves the responsibilities to speak on security, development, environment, hemispheric partnerships, trade and investment.

In initiating the exchange on trade and investment, I began with the issue of most immediate concern – bananas – as the major US-led multinational corporations had begun to encourage Latin American governments to join them in challenging the arrangements that allowed bananas from the ACP to enter the European Union, in accordance with our Lomé protocol. I told him bananas to the Caribbean were like motor vehicles to Detroit.

The following day a member of his team told me the president had chastised them for not having prepared him fully for his discussions with the CARICOM team. We had presented a convincing case and were satisfied with his assurances to address our concerns.

President Clinton erupted in uncontrollable laughter at the press conference, when, as the fourth head to make opening remarks, I said, "Good wine needs no bush." I had to tell him it was not an original or political remark, but taken from the sign good vintners would place outside their taverns in rural English villages many centuries ago, when the quality of the wine they served needed no advertisement.

Our next direct encounter with President Clinton was in December 1994, when he invited all leaders in the Americas, except Cuba, to Miami for the first Summit of the Americas.

The challenge to the European banana-import regime had by then become total war. Our intelligence was that the United States was preparing to challenge the EU regime at the Disputes Settlement Body in the WTO. The Caribbean states made it known that they were not prepared to participate in the summit while the United States was threatening the continued viability of the main industry of several of our member states.

President Clinton dispatched the US secretary of state, Warren Christopher, to meet with our ministers. The secretary of state accepted the justice of our case and assured us that the United States would not act in the matter. President Clinton accepted the outcome of our negotiations with his secretary of state – but within two weeks of the summit, the United States proceeded against the EU banana-import regime in the WTO.

The Caribbean and African banana-exporting countries supplied a mere 7 per cent of the world banana market, all to Europe, while the Latin American banana-exporting countries supplied the other 93 per cent, mainly to Europe, the United States and Canada. The United States, which did not export a single finger of banana, was leading a full-scale war to take that small slice of the market from the Caribbean.

We met next with President Clinton on 10 May 1997 in Barbados. Fourteen Caribbean leaders – twelve CARICOM heads, the president of Haiti (an observer in CARICOM) and the president of the Dominican Republic. Barbados's prime minister, Owen Arthur, was our host, but I continued as chairman of CARICOM, since Montserrat could not take its turn, as a non-sovereign member state.

The United States, which had some of the most aggressive states in the Union providing tax and other benefits to individuals and corporations to hold money in their jurisdictions, had joined Europe, with similar jurisdictions, to seek to put Caribbean jurisdictions out of business, using the full might of the Organisation for Economic Cooperation and Development.

There were issues such as security and law enforcement, the narcotics trade and the environment, where the interest of the Caribbean and the United States converged. But even in those cases the United States was using its overwhelming power to force the costs of response disproportionately onto the Caribbean.

Caribbean states are among the states in the world most threatened by climate change. The Global Conference on Small Island Developing States had been held in that very conference centre three years earlier, in 1994. The United States, the main emitter of greenhouse gases, had taken no steps to reduce its impact.

As I feared, the Barbados Declaration of Principles and Plan of Action which we adopted proved yet to be another pious statement of intent, and yielded little actual result.

At the Third Summit of the Americas, President George W. Bush met the group of Caribbean heads in Quebec. The Americans said to us, "We will be giving special attention to the Caribbean as our fourth border. We intend to go well beyond the farm worker programme to provide for those areas of shortage in our workforce where recruitment of your people can result in a brain drain."

We readily agreed to design a joint programme for human-resource development, concentrating on education and health, to provide adequate numbers of nurses, teachers and specialist technicians. We were excited at the prospect of a partnership which would significantly expand the resources of money, trainers and physical space to meet the expanded demand in a knowledge-based economy, and began work on a partnership framework agreement.

But that initiative went missing in the desert sands of Iraq.

CHAPTER 32
THE JAMAICAN DIASPORA

FOR OUR CARIBBEAN PEOPLE, MIGRATION HAS BECOME A cult, transcending class, age, gender, colour or professional category. It is as though within the region there is an irresistible urge to migrate to the metropolis, or, in the case of the Rastafari, to the ancestral homeland, Africa.

During the early years, when migration laws were not as severe as they are today, many Jamaicans decided to make their homes in the countries where they worked. Their movements were not haphazard but influenced by the prospect of jobs, adequate remuneration, acceptable working conditions and personal security. While yearning to fulfil their hopes for a better life through gainful employment and honing their skills, in the main, Jamaican migrants preserve and promote their cultural identity, and often maintain a nostalgic desire to return home eventually. Jamaica's early political development was largely due to returning residents and members of the diaspora. With a broadened perspective, informed and sharpened by his travels in Central America, the United Kingdom and the United States, Marcus Garvey returned to Jamaica in 1927 and spent several years raising the awareness of the ordinary Jamaican through his teachings.

Jamaicans are perhaps the most adventurous and numerous of Caribbean migrants, establishing communities in several Central American countries as well as the metropoles of New York, London and Toronto. We are scattered across the world, and it is often said that there is no country in which one could not find a Jamaican. I recall that on the evening I arrived in Seoul, Korea, on a ministerial visit, I had a warm welcome by telephone from an evangelist with a distinctly Jamaican accent.

My first experience with the diaspora dates back to my first day at Calabar, in 1948, when I met Simon Clarke, Carlos Malcolm and John Stratman, who would all become lifelong friends and colleagues. They had come to Calabar from Panama, where their parents had migrated. At that time it was customary for those

Caribbean people who could afford it to send their children back to their islands to school. Jamaica's large-scale migration eventually became a cause for concern. The exodus of skilled workers, technicians, doctors, lawyers, and managers in essential services resulted in a serious brain drain. During the 1970s and early 1980s about 15 per cent of the population had migrated. In the early 1990s the government began offering incentives to people with technical, business and managerial skills to return to Jamaica for short periods to help with managerial and technical skills-training.

❧

The continued flow of remittances to Jamaica, whether by way of investment or support of individual families, constituted a highly valued economic asset. We should also recognize the part played by remittances in kind, or the "barrel phenomenon": numerous migrant dependents have come to rely on the goods sent home regularly, as they do on the actual cash remittances. This contribution has constituted a highly valued economic resource. Migrant remittances comprise a significant part of the implicit social safety net.

Within a few years of taking on the leadership of the country I recognized that one of our most important national assets was those Jamaicans in the diaspora, and their cooperation in national development in a more direct way was crucial.

As early as 1992, the report of the West India Commission noted that it was important for us to engage with the diaspora in a more methodical way. By the following year, January 1993, I tabled a ministry paper authorizing a returning residents' facilitation unit in the Ministry of Foreign Affairs. In 1998 we further developed our relationship with the diaspora through the Jamaican Overseas Department. Its objectives were, on the one hand, to encourage continuing assistance from our overseas communities, and, on the other, to ensure that their interests were protected and advanced.

It soon became clear that while it was a step in the right direction, the department was unable to effectively manage the task. So we set up a separate division in the Ministry of Foreign Affairs to deal with diaspora affairs. The estimated size of the diaspora, at 2.6 million, combined with the economic impact of remittances, justified this move. Finally, in 2002, after our mandate had been renewed by the Jamaican electorate, we assigned a minister of state, Delano Franklyn, to advance the relationship between Jamaica and her diaspora communities across the globe.

In the years between the creation of the Jamaican Overseas Department and the new assignment in the ministry in 2002, we organized a series of dialogues with diaspora communities in the United States, Canada and the United Kingdom. These meetings represented the first coming together of Jamaican officials and the diasporic communities. In October 2003 a symposium was planned at the Mona School of Business at the University of the West Indies which provided a strategic direction for cooperation. One of the decisions coming out of this was to stage biennial conferences at which representatives of the different branches of the diaspora could have an input in policy decisions and strategies for the nation's development.

The first conference was held in June 2004 and subsequent ones in 2006 and 2008. They represented a giant leap in terms of our relationship and an invaluable practical and workable process that enabled us to utilize our diverse skills, energies and collective experience for the economic, social and spiritual betterment of all our citizens, both here at home and throughout the diaspora. Also significant was the focus on improving consular services.

I am heartened by the growing consciousness of more and more Jamaicans who live overseas, however temporary their stay, that they are a valuable asset and can contribute to nation-building in various ways. Diaspora communities constitute a formidable force for advancing Caribbean interests in their host countries. Today's political environment in the host countries requires the assertion of one's unique identity in order to find one's legitimate place and fulfil one's economic, social and spiritual potential. Any assertion of rights redounds not only to the benefit of members of the diaspora but to the benefit of Jamaica. Migrant communities should not feel that they are doing a disservice to their host societies if they defend our interests in the political systems of those countries.

More and more we are seeing instances where local political concerns have an impact on national policy through representation. I therefore urge members of the diaspora to get actively involved in local politics as voters, organizers, petitioners, and so on. The formalization of the relationship between Jamaica and our diaspora can only continue to have a positive effect on the development of Jamaica through more organized support.

I had arrived in England, albeit as a university student, about a decade after the *Windrush* had brought hundreds of West Indians, the grandchildren and great-grandchildren of slaves, to rebuild postwar England. They rebuilt the physical infrastructure – roads, rails, houses; manned the social services – schools, hospitals and transport; and even cleaned the streets and delivered the mail. They were welcomed. They were essential and vital to recovery and development.

As a student of history, the irony was not lost on me.

It was with that reality and the reality of the earlier contribution of West Indian wealth to the industrialization and original development of Great Britain deeply etched in my psyche that I listened to British prime minister David Cameron address the joint houses of the Parliament of Jamaica on 30 September 2015.

The UK prime minister sought to trivialize and diminish the three hundred years of British enslavement of Africans and exploitation of territories, including the West Indies; the psychological impact on the enslaved and their descendants; and their positive contribution to past and present British economy and society.

No longer shackled by the protocol of being a member of Parliament, I was constrained to bring the affront and the misuse of privilege directly to Prime Minister Cameron's attention. I wrote him a six-page open letter (see chapter 38, this volume).

David Cameron is a direct beneficiary of slavery and the exploitation of West Indians. His position is not, however, unique. Unfazed by the outrage at Prime Minister Cameron's action, the coalition government of Theresa May launched an offensive against *Windrush* migrants and their descendants who had not officially become British citizens or kept documentation of their arrival in the United Kingdom. Citizens have been denied access to services, incarcerated and deported.

Members of the diaspora in the United Kingdom and governments and citizens in the region have confronted the UK government on these repugnant actions. Caribbean governments and people must be ever-vigilant to protect the rights and interests of our diaspora.

CHAPTER 33
THE DECADE OF INTERNATIONAL ENGAGEMENT

ASKED ON THE EVE OF OUR INDEPENDENCE ABOUT the foreign policy the nation would pursue, Prime Minister Sir Alexander Bustamante was blunt in his response: "We are with the West." Within a year of becoming a member, Jamaica proposed the designation of 1968 as the International Year for Human Rights to celebrate the twentieth anniversary of the UN Declaration. By 1967, Jamaica's proposal of an international conference to assess the fulfilment of human rights had been accepted by the UN General Assembly. This led to the Proclamation of Teheran in May 1968.

Notwithstanding Sir Alexander's declaration, Jamaica's elite squad of diplomats at the Ministry of Foreign Affairs positioned Jamaica within the Group of 77, established in 1964, and in 1969 with the Non-Aligned Movement, as a foundation member and powerful advocate.

Jamaica's participation in the international arena since independence points to several trends and tendencies reflecting the interplay between efforts aimed at overcoming the constraints imposed by its historical relationships, its geographical location and its size, and an activist role designed to increase the options available to itself and other countries in a similar position.

The outcome of this interplay of forces suggests that Jamaica's contribution was significant, that its role was predominantly one of leadership and that its involvement was based on a conception of a world order in which small developing countries could find a place to assert their sovereignty. Jamaica contributed to the creation of an international system based on the concept of the sovereign equality of states. In pursuing these goals, Jamaica perforce had to develop partnerships and coalitions at the regional, hemispheric and global levels, identify the bases of those coalitions and partnerships and manage them to expand the operating space for itself and its partners.

There is a consensus that Jamaica has been well served by political and diplomatic staff who were equipped to identify opportunities in the international arena and to place Jamaica on the leading edge of the prevailing trends.

By defining itself as part of a region – that is, CARICOM – and using CARICOM as a vehicle to intervene in hemispheric issues, such as relationships with Cuba, Haiti and Latin America as a whole, and its specialized agencies in Brussels, Geneva and London and at the bilateral level in the United States, the United Kingdom and Canada, Jamaica acquired the reputation of a country pursuing a foreign policy on the basis of principles that included equality, fair trade and economic rules and structures that would enable it and similar countries to continue to function effectively as sovereign states.

In addition to its political leadership, the country's reputation benefited enormously from the outstanding roles played by its representatives at the UN headquarters in New York and its specialized agencies in Brussels, Washington, and London. Herbie Walker, Don Mills, Sir Egerton Richardson, Keith Johnson, Carmen Parris, Frank Francis, Lucille Mair, Anthony Hill and Douglas Saunders had the ability to articulate definitively the positions of the Third World and, in particular, the interests of small developing countries.

When Jamaica was first elected to the UN Security Council, it had on the first day to serve as president, and the main issue on the agenda was the perplexing problems in Cambodia. Don Mills and our delegation were thoroughly prepared. Furthermore, Jamaica chaired the Economic and Social Council of the United Nations and played a leading role in all the conferences sponsored by that body. Within the broader North-South context, which included groups like the Non-Aligned Movement and the Group of 77 and China, Jamaica's role has been prominent, and on several occasions it was elected to eminent positions. Its leadership on decolonization, the anti-apartheid movement in South Africa and negotiations on trade and development between Europe and the ACP has also been universally acknowledged.

Jamaica used its position to articulate, with considerable success, the case for small developing countries and the need for special and differential arrangements in the new globalized trading system. Our role in formulating ideas and creating coalitions that have shaped the structure, content, orientation and broad outcomes of the new globalized community is undisputed.

The stances we adopted on regional and global issues during the 1970s, 1990s and early twenty-first century were keenly followed and often emulated by other developing countries, particularly within the UN system, the Non-Aligned

Movement and the Group of 77. Jamaica chaired the G77 twice during that time, including a period of reshaping relationships as the international community grappled with difficult geopolitical and economic issues, including the effects of globalization.

Anecdotes from the 1970s often recall occasions when Jamaica's delegations at the United Nations and other international forums were consulted by other representatives who sought their views so they, in turn, could advise their respective capitals in their decision-making. During the 1970s we were prepared to pay the price for our resolve to espouse and advocate positions of principle on the international stage. We were fully engaged in the struggle against apartheid, colonialism and violation of human rights. Jamaica led the fight for economic justice and equity and a new international economic order. We led the struggle against the inequities of the international financial institutions which ravaged the economies of developing countries. We rejected attempts to be used as a pawn by competing geopolitical blocs during the Cold War and after its end.

While recognizing the limitations of our size and natural economic resources, we sought to maximize the intellectual power with which we were endowed. Whenever there was a controversial resolution before the UN General Assembly, US Ambassador Andrew Young would insist that the best way of testing the pulse of the developing Third World countries would be through early contact and consultations with the Jamaican delegation.

Many Jamaicans have served, and continue to serve, in high positions in regional and international organizations, bodies and agencies, thanks, in large part, to the respect our country has built up. G. Arthur Brown was appointed deputy head of the UN Development Programme, Pat Durrant UN ombudsman, and Angela King assistant secretary general of the United Nations.

Among our many accomplishments was the choice of Jamaica as the site for the International Seabed Authority. Ken Rattray was rapporteur general during the conference on the law of the sea. His skill and dedication helped the participating states to go "boldly where no one had gone before". From the earliest days Jamaica was first inserted in the text as the headquarters by Dudley Thompson. It was kept so during my tenure as foreign minister and thereafter by Hugh Shearer. Jamaica maintained continuity of national policy and made a relentless effort to ensure that the International Seabed Authority would ultimately call Jamaica home.

I was in Amsterdam, attending a conference of the United Nations, when I watched on television the collapse of the Berlin Wall, brick by brick. This led to the reunification of Germany and a stronger Europe. It was done without a single shot being fired and achieved through the irresistible will of the people, bolstered by the flow of information technology, to tear down the wall that blocked freedom.

The disintegration of the Soviet Union resulted in a single hegemony and the emergence of a sole superpower. The end of the Cold War meant that there was no longer a contest for unswerving allegiance to one of two contending powers, but the need for a counterbalance to the sway of a single dominion.

The process of decolonization had advanced with the independence of Mozambique and Zimbabwe, but the abhorrent regime of apartheid in South Africa still cast its evil shadow over Namibia.

The decade of the late 1980s to 1990s witnessed more profound changes in the global environment than any other time in recent history. It was a period when power blocs were dismantled and disintegrating trade barriers rapidly removed. These resulted in a much more competitive world environment in which small countries, such as Jamaica, had to increase their struggles for survival.

With the end of the Cold War, no longer were there alternative economic options for most countries of the developing world. The market economy became the only model acceptable to the World Bank, the IMF and the European Union.

The Common Fund, introduced by the UN Trade and Development Council, with our own Herbie Walker in Geneva as a leading spokesman, was no longer on the table. The goal of 0.7 per cent of GDP to be shared by developed nations with the developing countries by way of overseas development assistance had not been attained, nor did several of the Group B countries consider it feasible or worthwhile.

Mention of the New International Economic Order had disappeared from the global dialogue without a trace. The old international architecture, archaic and inequitable, was propped up, even when the cracks and strains were evident.

During the 1980s many new issues had emerged as a part of the dynamics of globalization, and changes in international relationships threatened our pivotal role in the dialogue. We had to play catch-up in the 1990s in order to return to leadership on issues of grave concern to the Third World. It was imperative for us to become a more active participant in multilateral decision-making bodies once again. In our most recent tenure on the UN Security Council, shrewd commentators marvelled at how a country with such a small delegation could have been so effective in the council's deliberations during 2000–2001. This was a period when the political climate became increasingly unstable owing to the spread of armed conflict, nuclear proliferation and alarming global terrorism.

Ambassador Curtis Ward was appointed to strengthen the Permanent Representative Office team in New York, ably led by the sagacious ambassador Patricia Durrant. This was a rather challenging period for the Security Council, as it was involved in many critical issues of peace and security, including the scourge of ethnic cleansing.

The catastrophic acts of terrorism on 9/11 marked a defining moment in human history. We were members of the Security Council at that time, and chairman when the most far-reaching decisions were made in the fight against terrorism. Jamaica's dominance among non-permanent members on the Security Council on these issues established new precedents and created new dynamics for the council vis-à-vis permanent and non-permanent members.

During Jamaica's membership of the Security Council, our principled and steadfast, sometimes uncompromising, defence of justice, gender equity, human rights, the right to self-determination, and the end to impunity for crimes against humanity emboldened other non-permanent members to stand up.

When we entered the new millennium, the global poverty gap, measured as the ratio of the average income of the richest country in the world to that of the poorest, had widened over the preceding century from nine to one to the frightening level of sixty to one. Yet resistance to any meaningful reform of the global financial institutions continued. In spite of continued statements to the contrary, those institutions continued to impose economic policies detrimental to the human and social development of the developing world.

On 30 September 1992, I addressed the forty-seventh session of the UN General Assembly for the first time as prime minister of Jamaica: "It was twelve years ago, in 1980, that as foreign minister of my country I last addressed this august assembly. It was a time of great optimism. There was ongoing dialogue between North and South. We seemed to share a common understanding of the requirements for international cooperation and development."

I pinpointed the fundamental changes in the global political landscape with the end of the Cold War and called upon the United Nations "to take decisive action based on the merits of each issue, rather than in response to fixed ideological positions, buttressed by the use of the veto power".

While the world was experiencing revolutionary alteration, "the fundamental and unchanging reality was the widening of the gap between the rich industrialized countries of the North and the poor developing countries in the South".

Barely had the 1980s begun when the dialogue abruptly ended. The international economic environment became even more unfavourable. The developing countries of the South were left to grapple with enormous external debt. The decade was spent undertaking major structural reform, and the painful adjustment weighed heavily on the poor and vulnerable. Only now are we beginning to see prospects for growth and development as a result of these reforms. It is important that a favourable international economic environment is created to complete the process.

THE COMMONWEALTH

With the strong endorsement of both Sir Alexander Bustamante and Norman Manley, Jamaica's membership in the Commonwealth was axiomatic. The only possible reservation disappeared when, in 1961, Prime Minister Hendrik Verwoerd withdrew South Africa's application to remain, after a number of African heads of state had expressed strong misgivings.

I attended my first meeting of Commonwealth Heads in Canada, in 1973, as that country's prime minister, Pierre Trudeau, had indicated a desire to include economic and trade relationships as dominant areas for that meeting. He persuaded Michael Manley to host the 1975 meeting in Jamaica, and I was charged with coordinating the logistics and arrangements.

The Kingston meeting was a turning point in the evolution of the Commonwealth. For the first time, representatives of the liberation movement in southern Africa were invited to speak directly with heads on their struggle for freedom. The hardships imposed on landlocked countries without access to the ports of South Africa – Zambia, Rhodesia and Malawi – were revealed. Mozambique was providing welcome help and the heads decided it would be good for the Commonwealth to provide that country with some aid, mainly by way of technical assistance in the first instance. And so began a relationship with Mozambique.

The debate on reducing the economic gap between the developed countries and the developing world, led by Harold Wilson and Forbes Burnham respectively, was intense, and resulted in two technical working groups which included Alister McIntyre and G. Arthur Brown. The two reports made a difference in the ongoing dialogue and served to influence the United Kingdom's approach and sensitivities in the European Common Market.

The issues tackled by those expert studies also informed the work of the United Nations, the World Bank and the General Agreement on Tariffs and Trade, precursor to the WTO. They included the North-South Dialogue; the shape of a new international economic order; commodity arrangements and the Common Fund for Commodities; industrialization; protectionism and market access; economic recession; debt problems; and financial institutions.

Of no less significance was the election of Sir Shridath Ramphal, at the Pegasus Hotel, as the new secretary general, by acclaim. His taking office resulted in a dramatic shift within the secretariat and, consequently, the entire Commonwealth family. No longer would the Commonwealth ignore issues of major global concern or regional import. In his view, it had to become engaged because it represented a unique combination of developed, middle-income, developing and small island states. It includes Christian countries, Muslim countries, Hindu countries. Its members are over 20 per cent of the Organisation of Islamic Cooperation; more than 25 per cent of the United Nations; over 25 per cent of the G20; nearly 40 per cent of the WTO; just under 40 per cent of the African Union; and 60 per cent of the South Asia Association for Regional Cooperation. It is multi-ethnic, and although we converse in English, it is also multilingual. It also has a striking proportion of small island states – small countries with small economies – and it also includes landlocked countries. These all relate to problems which have to be dealt with at the international level.

To the extent that the Commonwealth provides some bridge of understanding, it has a special role and purpose. It has been of great importance in terms of technical studies and technical assistance. This has aided our development in broad terms through the provision of experts by the Commonwealth Fund for Technical Co-operation.

One can successfully contend that of all the multilateral organizations to which the countries of CARICOM belong, none is as important to the advancement of our interests in the international community as the Commonwealth. It has had a determining impact in influencing multilateral organizations, such as the IMF and World Bank, on debt relief, and UN bodies on climate change. Its pioneering work on small and vulnerable economies has had an effect in the UN system. It has influenced discussions within the WTO in seeking flexibility in the treatment of small economies in the Doha Round of global trade negotiations.

There is a multitude of regional and other organizations of which Commonwealth countries are members and in which they can act to promote the concerns of its member states. Those organizations include the European Union, NAFTA, the African Union, the Association of Southeast Asian Nations and the Organisation for Economic Co-operation and Development, to name a few.

Additionally, if each of our CARICOM countries individually and all of them collectively were to attempt diplomacy in forty-two nations, we simply could not afford it. The Commonwealth provides us with that reach. The Commonwealth allows relatively inexpensive but nonetheless effective diplomacy. None of our countries could afford to have a presence and conduct productive diplomatic relations with nations as far away as Australia and New Zealand, India, Pakistan and Bangladesh, the islands of the Pacific, and even the Mediterranean and Africa.

The Commonwealth Heads of Government conferences allow the leaders of our twelve independent Commonwealth Caribbean countries to put forward our concerns, challenges and problems to forty-two other heads of government from every continent in an intimate and personal way. The same is true for the many Commonwealth ministerial meetings on finance, law, health, education and climate change. When the Commonwealth is able to find common ground, it offers a rational voice in global affairs, representing as it does, one-third of the world's people of every race and religion.

My first Commonwealth meeting as prime minister was in Cyprus in 1993. After years of continuing effort by the United Nations and the Commonwealth, the country remained divided. It was my first encounter with John Major, and as we worked together in a group tasked with presenting the Limassol Statement on Multilateral Trade, we quickly developed a warm and collegiate relationship (including but not confined to cricket), which served us well.

The emphasis in my statement to the opening session of the conference in Scotland on 21 October 1997 was the importance of knowledge to economic growth and development in the wake of rapid technological changes. The Commonwealth was urged to collect a pool of knowledge to work for one common goal, with particular regard for the special needs of the poor. So as to place our youth at the forefront of human development, the Commonwealth was invited to broaden its existing programme for youth leadership and development. In commending the Association of Commonwealth Universities and the Commonwealth Foundation, I proposed that a special human-resources initiative should be built around these institutions to embrace the interrelated areas of education, training and research.

Before the meeting in Edinburgh, Idi Amin announced he would not attend unless the Queen ordered a special squadron to escort him. That attempt at comic relief did not affect the joy and delight with which we greeted, at long last, Nelson Mandela – the man himself, who led that fight for freedom and human dignity where those who had sought to protect abhorrent racism in the defence of kith and kin had been vanquished by a spirit of steel.

In Edinburgh, considerable attention was devoted to small, middle-income, heavily indebted countries, a large portion of whose debt was due to international financial institutions opposed to rescheduling. The Commonwealth includes small island states constrained by low economic resources and the effects of climate change. In this area, the Commonwealth had acquired technical expertise and political acumen. Prime Minister Owen Arthur of Barbados was mandated to lead the mobilization of support and resources essential for the survival of small states.

There are times when what happens outside meetings of heads is no less valuable and important than what happens inside. Informal exchanges in the corridors serve, at times, to develop personal working relationships which frequently make all the difference in both bilateral and sometimes multilateral affairs.

To this date, the Commonwealth has neither a charter nor a single document which sets out rules and regulations. It is a family of sovereign nations which shares common values and has over the years evolved clear principles which stipulate its purpose and conduct.

Within the British Empire, the first colonial conference was convened for Queen Victoria's golden jubilee in 1887. For a time, regular meetings were held between the independent nations, and set out the equality of status among the autonomous states which owed common allegiance to the British crown.

At the 1971 Commonwealth Heads of Government meeting in Singapore, the declaration of principles enshrined support for peace, liberty and cooperation while condemning racial and colonial domination and gross inequalities of wealth.

At the Harare meeting of 1991, chaired by President Robert Mugabe, the fundamental political values were extended to include democracy and democratic process, the rule of law and the independence of the judiciary, fundamental human rights, good governance and equality of opportunity. After this Harare Declaration of 1991, the Commonwealth Heads of Government accepted that violations of these principles would attract sanctions ranging from statements of disapproval to suspension.

When Prime Minister Ian Smith of Rhodesia had unilaterally declared independence in 1965, Jamaica was vociferous in its condemnation. The search for a unified approach to liberate what became Zimbabwe began at the 1975 Commonwealth meeting in Kingston. It was at the 1979 Commonwealth Heads of Government Conference in Lusaka that President Kenneth Kaunda of Zambia secured consensus on action which culminated in a series of meetings at Lancaster House involving the United Kingdom, the Zimbabwe African National

Union, the party opposed to white-minority rule, and a group of Commonwealth countries which included Jamaica.

The British insisted that there should be compensation for their kith and kin who had seized the land. The only difference between this and slavery was that it was the capture of land and not human beings. The issue of the ownership of land proved most difficult, for the freedom fighters would have struggled in vain if the white settlers were to remain owners in perpetuity of the properties they had stolen. Jamaica helped to broker and witness the final breakthrough.

Lord Carrington claimed that the amount for adequate compensation was beyond what the Treasury could afford. Michael Manley and Secretary General Ramphal suggested that he call the Americans, and so he telephoned Cyrus Vance, the US secretary of state. They agreed between them that funding would be provided by the United Kingdom and the United States for compensation for the land that would have to be acquired from the white settlers in Rhodesia, now Zimbabwe.

Lord Carrington and Secretary Vance did not simply promise substantial funds, which was the clincher to resolve the October crisis over land. Before Zimbabwe's independence, in March 1980, Prime Minister Thatcher wrote to President Carter asking him to put up more money, because Britain intended to do so too. President Carter responded positively. His defeat in November 1980 and the election of Ronald Reagan changed all that.

The quid pro quo when the delegations left Lancaster House was the clear understanding that there would be no change in the constitution of Zimbabwe for a period that would permit the funding provided by the United Kingdom and the United States to coincide with the compensation and acquisition of property from the white settlers.

The government of Margaret Thatcher and the Reagan administration reneged on their commitment. Zanu-PF had not fought and sacrificed lives to perpetuate the capture by white settlers of land from their ancestors. Only then did Robert Mugabe begin to remove the constitutional restraints: once the United Kingdom and the United States reneged on that commitment, and without any source of funding, Mugabe proceeded to take back the land which had been stolen. Most of the subsequent developments in Zimbabwe can only be understood against this background.

After the Harare Declaration, heads decided in 1995 to form the Commonwealth Ministerial Action Group, comprising foreign ministers from eight countries, to monitor implementation and report to the conference of heads wherever breaches occurred. The membership rotated after every conference. Zimbabwe was a member for several terms and during one period, its foreign minister served as chair. The group's report on Zimbabwe to the Abuja Conference in 2003 listed grave deficiencies in the electoral system, the conduct of elections, the functions and roles of the judiciary and the freedom of the press.

On the opening day, the conference set up a committee consisting of the heads of Australia, Canada, India, Jamaica, Mozambique and South Africa to examine the issue of Zimbabwe and make recommendations on the way forward. I was elected chair. In accordance with Commonwealth tradition, I worked long and hard to obtain a consensus rather than a majority position. The debate within the committee was intense. Prime Minister John Howard of Australia was a hardliner, who wanted Zimbabwe expelled. Jean Chrétien of Canada, also a member of that group, was a moderating influence. The two Southern African Development Community members, represented by the sober and experienced Thabo Mbeki and Joaquim Chissano, worked hard to avoid the most punitive sanction of expulsion.

We were bound to consider this matter in accordance with the Harare Declaration, which defined criteria for membership. The report from the ministerial action group which came to us had pointed out Zimbabwe's deficiencies in critical areas. Sympathetic as we were to the disappointment, the upset and the understandable grief at the failure to implement the Lancaster House understandings which had driven Mugabe to the position we had to examine, we could not but conclude that Zimbabwe should be given the opportunity to conform with those principles and standards set by the Harare Declaration.

In our recommendations, we set out a well thought-out procedure for assisting Zimbabwe, led by Mbeki and Chissano, who would play a critical role. President Obasanjo of Nigeria, as chairman, had actually identified emissaries who were ready to work with Zimbabwe on the national reconciliation which would assist its early return to the Commonwealth should it be asked to leave. Our recommendations were endorsed by the Commonwealth Heads of Government and the door left open for Zimbabwe's return to full Commonwealth membership, once sufficient progress had been made on the contentious issues. The conference reaffirmed the importance of separating and consolidating democracy, ensuring peace and harmony, and promoting development and growth.

President Obasanjo, Mbeki and I made a telephone call to President Mugabe. I knew that Zimbabwe was on its way out when Robert Mugabe, who had always referred to me as "My brother", said instead, "Prime Minister Patterson". He told us that within minutes, he would issue a presidential statement. By the time the three of us returned to the conference room, the release from Harare had announced Zimbabwe's exit from the Commonwealth.

The skilful balance of our recommendations and the astute guidance of President Obasanjo in the chair facilitated our smooth passage of the Commonwealth Heads of Government statement on the night of 7 December 2003. The mood was entirely different when we gathered on the morning of 8 December. In all my Commonwealth meetings, never had I seen such turmoil and turbulence. What was the cause?

Those of us who were exhausted by the arduous assignment had gone to bed before the television coverage of Tony Blair's departure. He had gone straight to the airport after our meeting at Aso Rock, and on boarding the flight to London, held up the "V for victory" sign. Heads, particularly those from the Southern African Development Community, were outraged at what went beyond cockiness to the border of triumphant contempt. That display of arrogance in a few hours rekindled all the horrors of empire and racism. Many delegations were in open rebellion and demanded that the decision on Zimbabwe should be rescinded. By then, Zimbabwe had already quit; and we could not afford to abandon the fundamental values of the Commonwealth.

In comparison to this situation, all we had done seemed like a stroll in the park. It is no exaggeration to say the unity of the group and indeed the existence of the Commonwealth itself were in mortal peril. Several hurriedly arranged side meetings were needed before calm could be restored. Even then, when all else had failed, my final appeal helped to win the day. If we were to dismantle the Commonwealth, it should be by deliberate action and not merely a knee-jerk reaction to impudent behaviour. Moreover, it would have been an abuse of the fine hospitality we had received and the expert leadership of our host chairman, President Obasanjo.

THE NON-ALIGNED MOVEMENT AND THE G15

When President Suharto convened the first summit of the Non-Aligned Movement in Bandung, Tito of Yugoslavia and Nasser of Egypt envisaged the movement to be a third global force which would fight against imperialism and racism in order to secure universal peace and freedom. As the world stood in 1955, in a confrontation between East and West, there was good reason to fear that the build-up of nuclear weaponry and the intensity of the arms race threatened a holocaust which would spread far beyond the borders of the superpowers to destroy us all. Not surprisingly, therefore the movement focused on disarmament, the liberation struggle and the power of an equal voice within the international system.

My first address as prime minister to a forum on foreign policy took place on 17 May 1992, forty-six years after Winston Churchill had spoken of the Cold War and the Iron Curtain for the first time. In the field of security, the threat of a nuclear holocaust had receded on a global scale, but nuclear proliferation continued. The disappearance of the bipolar world to which we had all grown accustomed, and with it the East-West confrontation, gave hope for a more prominent role for the United Nations in a new world order. The disappearance of a bipolar axis also required a change in the focus of the Non-Aligned Movement to meet the new challenges of economic independence.

The Non-Aligned Movement had increasingly come to recognize the need to put more emphasis on economic issues and promote greater cooperation among its membership. That led to the constitution, at the 1989 summit in Belgrade, of the G15, to find solutions and pursue collective international action, given the similarity of our common experiences.

In November 1992, among the leaders at our G15 summit was the president of Brazil. I had no hesitation in writing to ask Itamar Franco, as a tangible expression of South-South cultural cooperation, for a top Brazilian coach to prepare the Jamaican football team for the road to the World Cup France in 1998. The letter-bearer, Captain Burrell, boasted that he was given an official escort with outriders and all, as he left the airport for the palace to deliver my letter. René Simões was appointed and fate made him my next-door neighbour at my private home. His coaching led to Jamaica's Reggae Boyz qualifying for the World Cup.

At the thirteenth summit of the movement in Kuala Lumpur, Malaysia, in 2003, my statement was on "Restructuring and Rebranding Non-Alignment: Rethinking the Basis and Modalities for Cooperation among Developing Countries". The conference, under the superb guidance of Prime Minister Mahathir Bin Mohammad, accepted that to avoid all nations becoming subject to a single dominion, the Non-Aligned Movement offered the only counterforce for reason, balance and objectivity.

Jamaica's contribution to the internal dialogue, over many years, earned us membership of the G15 and permitted us to host the ninth summit in Montego Bay, in February 1999. It was also fate which determined that within a few days of being sworn in as president of Venezuela, Hugo Chávez's first visit abroad was to the Montego Bay Summit at the Half Moon Hotel. We forged then a special friendship and fraternal trust which never waned.

At Montego Bay, the implementation of initiatives in science and technology was essential to accelerate our progress in communication and information technology. The International Centre for Environmental and Nuclear Sciences, headed by Gerald Lalor, had, a few months before, begun work on the Mona campus of the University of the West Indies. It epitomized the vast potential for developing countries to share information, experience and expertise in science and technology.

At the twelfth summit of the group in Caracas, 27–28 February 2004, energy was the dominant topic, owing to a looming energy crisis in oil-deficient developing countries.

Within the African continent, the New Partnership for Africa's Development had formed an African Energy Commission and had allied with the Latin American Energy Organization to lay the foundation for new energy cooperation between the two regions. The Caracas Declaration on energy and development and the emergence of PetroCaribe stand as the best testimony as to how South-South cooperation can fuel economic growth and sustainable development.

My final words in Caracas were taken from Simón Bolívar: "We have already seen the light, and it is not our desire to be thrust back into darkness."

CHAPTER 34

GLOBAL GOVERNANCE AND THE NEW ARCHITECTURAL FRAMEWORK

AT THE THIRD SUMMIT OF THE AMERICAS IN Quebec, Canada, in 2001, the topic was democracy and globalization. My contribution to that discussion was: "You can't be talking about democracy and not apply it to the global village in which we are all supposed to live. That means, among other things, a voice through meaningful participation by all those who lead, but also democratic accountability."

That intervention, at a lunch for heads only, prompted President George W. Bush of the United States to ask Prime Minister Lester Bird of Antigua and Barbuda, "Who is he? Where did he get all that knowledge from?" Bird's reply, "He was Jamaica's foreign minister in the 1970s."

The WTO is decidedly not democratic. It is not only socially discontented people who have on various occasions protested at meetings of the WTO, World Bank, IMF and Summits of the Americas. There are those who seek global development which does not run in a manner consistent with the pursuit of peace and global stability.

While we have moved from the G8, which used to dominate decisions of the World Bank and the IMF, to the G20, a large number of countries have no voice at the table. If we are not persistent in pointing out the dangers, most of the developing world will remain excluded and voiceless.

The issue of small developing economies participating in the governance of the multilateral system goes beyond the ambit of economic institutions such as the IMF, the World Bank and the WTO to encompass governance in other multilateral institutions, including the United Nations. Global governance systems reflect the power relations in world affairs. The UN Security Council reflects the constellation of power at the end of World War II and the award of veto power to the five victorious nations. There are vast difficulties in international society that ought to be taken into full account if the United Nations is to adapt to the realities of today.

The developed countries have held a stranglehold on decision-making in the IMF and World Bank on the ground that this gives confidence to creditors and investors and reassures those countries contributing the most resources. The voting arrangements lack transparency and disenfranchise the developing countries that constitute the majority of members; represent the vast majority of the world's population; and are the major borrowers from these institutions.

I expressed these sentiments in my address to the sixtieth UN General Assembly in September 2005:

Mr President,

Our ministers agreed in Monterrey one year ago that it was necessary to reform and make the international economic system more coherent and supportive of the development policies of member states. We agreed that it was necessary to increase the voice and participation of developing countries in the international financial and trade institutions. Yet nothing has happened. We cannot allow the Bretton Woods institutions to remain forever impervious to our calls. To attain the agreed development objectives, there must be a renunciation of the ill-conceived policies imposed on a number of developing countries under structural adjustment programmes three decades ago.

Some firms in Jamaica have become multinational corporations, but most remain small, especially when compared to their global competitors. A merger movement would enlarge these firms and make them more viable and more likely joint-venture partners with foreign investors. This is critical when they have to compete in the world market and major export markets like the United States and Europe. Small size puts exporting firms at a severe disadvantage and therefore they need strategic alliances or mergers to provide a larger capital base, pool resources and expertise, and access the latest technology.

However, they have a persistent ambiguous attitude, tending to the defensive and giving rise to a preoccupation with challenges instead of a proactive stance towards the opportunities. This is difficult to understand, given the self-confidence of Jamaicans and their record of excellence in a range of products and services.

The IMF and World Bank have still not conceded that small developing economies constitute a specific genre of economy and have therefore not accepted the need for policies designed specifically for these economies. Jamaica's struggles with the IMF called attention to and had some effect in modifying the "one size fits all" approach and the need for social cushioning and stabilization.

The decision-making process in the WTO, while formally by consensus, is in reality dominated by a small number of developed countries. The power exerted by the developed countries overwhelms the formal decision-making rules, and their pre-eminence has been institutionalized in what is known as the "Green Room" process. Criticism of the current arrangements for decision-making in the WTO is widespread and is especially strident among the developing countries and the international community of non-governmental organizations. There has been no progress in addressing the obvious defects of the system.

Mr President, five years ago we adopted a declaration revealing our vision for the shaping of international society in the new millennium. The records show that the results have fallen far short of our expectations.

We have failed to meet the targets we set: poverty and infectious diseases remain rampant; tensions from war and terrorism are straining the fabric of international security; the proliferation of weapons of all kinds generates fear and threatens domestic peace.

The world has become more insecure. There is still too much instability and conflict. There is still too much hardship and suffering. Too many are being left behind in the march towards the Millennium Development Goals.

This summit must send a message of hope to millions who are still living in misery.

For this to happen, three things are paramount.

First, we must strengthen the global partnership. The principles are well established. Shared responsibility and mutual accountability constitute the basic foundation. But we must get the partnership to work and show concrete results. Commitments solemnly given must be implemented. An adequate and predictable flow of resources and their effective utilization is the essence of the partnership between donors and recipients, based on the discharge of mutual obligations and accountability. It should be carried out without burdensome policy conditionalities and with institutional safeguards for good governance.

Second, this process should be complemented by action to eliminate inequities in the global system through positive adjustments in global economic policies which will give developing countries a better chance to benefit from access to markets, capital flows and more favourable terms in the transfer of technology.

Third, reform in global economic governance can no longer be postponed. Reform should not just be confined to this organization but should be undertaken in all institutions within the system, particularly those involved in economic policymaking. The basic prescription for progress is equity, inclusiveness, accountability and democratic participation. The Bretton Woods institutions, whose decisions have such a profound impact on our lives, should be among the first candidates for reform. It is long overdue.

The summit document placed before us sets out a framework. It falls short of what we sought to provide for a more substantive development agenda, but it will have to serve as a starting point and demands early implementation.

Mr President, there is no doubt that a reform of the UN institutions is necessary but it is important that what we decide on is carefully designed to remedy the real deficiencies and strengthen multilateralism.

The result should not be to entrench the world power structure for the United Nations to become its instrument. The system must work for all of us: the Security Council should be reformed in its structure and procedures to become more representative and to inspire greater confidence in its decisions. ECOSOC [the UN Economic and Social Council] should be strengthened and empowered to participate in global economic policymaking and enabled to provide effective coordination and to promote coherence. Reform should bring an end to the excessive politicization and adversarial approaches which have discredited the operations of the Human Rights Commission.

There is an urgent need to create a cohesive and effective strategic alliance among small developing economies. Such a caucus should operate in all the international fora and institutions in which these states have vital interests. In the WTO, there is an informal, poorly organized group of countries that regard themselves as "small economies". There needs to be an established caucus of small developing economies, which meets on a regular basis and pursues the existing work programme on small economies.

※

The effects of external economic events and the importance in international economic relations can hardly be exaggerated for small developing economies such as Jamaica.

We are acutely vulnerable, owing to a high degree of openness and the high degree of concentration on a few export products, particularly some primary products and services whose prices and demand are subject to sharp fluctuations in world markets.

In Jamaica, there is a high ratio of trade to GDP, as external transactions are large in relation to total economic activity. The heavy reliance on external trade reflects the narrow range of resources and the inability to support certain types of production, given the small scale of the national market. In extreme cases, industrial export, often a primary product or tourism, can account for nearly all our exports. There is significant direct relationship between export concentration and export instability. The effect of export-market concentration on sugar and bananas and then bauxite and tourism can be detrimental to economic development if the export marketing is controlled or dominated by a single group or a few multinational corporations, as was the case with bananas and bauxite in the 1960s.

Our fragile ecologies are exposed to natural disasters and our susceptibility to environmental damage is a result. Natural disasters have been a recurring factor in the volatility of economic growth in Jamaica. The damage from Hurricane Gilbert in 1988 amounted to about 33 per cent of GDP. The numerous hurricanes, floods and droughts since then have made all the difference in our levels of growth.

Larger economies are better able to counter real shocks, as they are more diversified in structure and exports. Small size has implications for economic growth, vulnerability and the capacity to adjust to external economic change. The undiversified economic structure of small economies translates into an adjustment process that is more difficult and of necessity slower than for larger economies.

Stabilization policy must be designed specifically for small, developing countries such as Jamaica, taking cognizance of the structure of markets and the nature of their operations. The uncompetitive nature of these markets, particularly where monopolies and oligopolies exist, makes resource utilization and allocation more problematic than in large, developed economies. These types of market situations are characterized by rigidities which make the adjustment process more time-consuming. They diminish the efficacy of conventional policy measures such as open-market operations and recalibration of economy-wide prices such as the exchange rate. The nature of small markets also restricts the ability of private-sector entities and the government to mobilize additional resources, both within these economies and from external sources.

Although bauxite and tourism have replaced sugar and bananas, the acute vulnerability of the economy requires an ongoing process rather than a once-and-for-all adjustment.

After a meeting of trade ministers in Buenos Aires to negotiate the terms of a trade agreement, which never materialized, I pointed out in my budget presentation to Parliament on 6 April 2001, "the negative effects of trade liberalization on our domestic production where producers are not yet in a position to compete with imports. This includes agriculture and manufacturers as well as services. We have to ensure that the companies, firms and operators involved can secure the necessary inputs to bring them up to competitive levels during an agreed period of time." Anthony Hylton, our minister of foreign trade, was instructed to convey this message to our private sector and every ministerial forum in which Jamaica was represented

Globalization is a multidimensional process, which is happening at a rapid rate and in profound ways affecting all aspects of national and global activities and interactions. Barriers to the international flow of goods, services, capital, money and information are being increasingly eroded or eliminated.

There is an inexorable increase in the extent and intensity of international competition. Coping with exposure to more international competition has posed severe challenges to all countries, but more so to developing countries. As the world economy becomes more integrated, competition in global markets has intensified among firms and countries.

❧

It has often been asked whether there is an international rule of law. The international legal order, unlike the domestic, is fragmented in that there is no single, unitary, sovereign power. The United Nations exercises important global functions, by virtue of its charter.

The decisions made by the UN General Assembly, while they have no legal force, formulate policies and set standards that are at least a source of moral suasion.

It is the UN Security Council, charged with maintaining international peace and security, which takes binding decisions and orders enforceable sanctions. It is the Security Council alone which has the power and competence to take decisions which have the effect and force of international law. But the council is constituted in a fashion that causes impotence when the situation demands decisive action but the permanent members have conflicting interests.

Treaties and customs constitute the main source of international law. There is also customary international law, which binds all states equally, though states may agree to derogate from it and views will differ as to what constitutes a rule of customary international law. Treaties, customary international law and *jus cogens* constitute important prescriptive norms in international law. They serve as deontological forces for building a culture whereby individuals, states and international organizations conform to standards.

Together, they make the compelling case that there is an international rule of law to which all states should conform. We know in practice this is not so, as the powerful ignore or circumvent them, while the weak and poor cannot escape any infringement.

The International Criminal Court was established by the Treaty of Rome in 1998. A vociferous voice for its creation, and one hugely influential in prescribing the powers and procedures for the court, has gone further than simply refusing to sign. The Bush administration demanded that signatories to the International Criminal Court must expressly consent to the exemption of US citizens from prosecution and trial before the court, or suffer the withdrawal of aid support for defence and security programmes. The late Robin Cook, foreign secretary of the United Kingdom, more renowned for his bluntness than his diplomatic choice of words, said with characteristic candour, "If I may say so, this is not a court set up to bring to book prime ministers of the United Kingdom or presidents of the USA."

What is clearly implied is that the International Criminal Court and similar tribunals exempt the leaders of powerful states, no matter the illegality of their acts, while those who belong to the "lesser breeds" would be subject to punishment – that group which Sir William Blackstone described as those belonging to an "infidel country" who were not entitled to the birthright of the common law. Those brought before the International Criminal Court or the special tribunals have originated from the nations of Europe, Africa and the Balkan states, where ethnic cleansing erupted.

While small and powerful states do not in fact receive equal treatment in the application of international law, we in the Caribbean who lack military power are nevertheless compelled to continue the search for that ideal in which the international system will uphold right over might and law over force. As an immediate step in that direction, Jamaica strongly urged completing the work of the International Law Commission in developing and codifying international rules to advance the rule of law at the global level.

THE GROUP OF 77

Ever since its birth in 1964, the Group of 77 has been the main voice for the countries of Africa, Asia, Latin America and the Caribbean on the global stage relating to economic, trade and social issues. Every developing country, on attaining independence, has entered its open doors. China chose to be a part of this group, once it took its rightful place in the United Nations. Throughout its tumultuous existence, the Group of 77 and China have been at the forefront in championing the cause of the developing world and the struggle for an equitable economic order for all mankind. This makes it the more surprising that the first summit of the Group of 77 and China was not convened until it attained the age of thirty-six. Our incomparable host was none other than Fidel Castro, as Nigeria chaired a historic gathering of heads and high-level plenipotentiaries from 133 member countries in June 2000. The Havana summit marked a turning point in the history and efforts of the South as we resolved to achieve a fairer share in decision-making as well as global governance in order to reap the fruits of human production and trade. Heads took a decision to transform the South Commission into a working G77 Coordinating Commission, to be headed by an executive coordinator. That commission would ensure that decisions made at each summit were executed and also do the research necessary for the further advancement of the objectives of the South.

Our delegation bemoaned the move by the G7 to appropriate global economic power and relegate the South to the role of spectator to globalization and liberalization. I urged: "Here in Havana, and in every corridor of power, let the collective voice of the G77 be heard and respected on the fundamental issues of debt, the terms of trade and the reform of the international financial architecture."

I was chosen to join presidents Olusegun Obasanjo of Nigeria, Thabo Mbeki of South Africa, Bouteflika of Algeria and Prime Minister Mahathir of Malaysia as the leaders of the South responsible for overseeing the creation and monitoring of this commission.

We worked assiduously to prepare a report with a number of clear recommendations for a secretariat which would build on the framework which Julius Nyerere, the great icon of the developing world, had put in place for the South Commission in Geneva. It was shot down by the permanent representatives in New York who had been delegated by the heads at the meeting of the UN General Assembly. They saw it as an intrusion on their domain and a reduction of the power they had seized.

We deplored the negative effects of globalization on developing countries, and more so on small island state economies, and stressed the need for an urgent and radical response to the debt overhang of developing states. We called for an overhaul of the world financial architecture and the absolute necessity of a review and reform of the WTO.

As developing countries, we pledged to work more closely together to advance our common objectives of increased production, trade, technical cooperation, cultural interaction and a better quality of life for our people.

To survive in the global village of today, we recognized that developing countries must acquire and train their people to effectively utilize cutting-edge technology and scientific advancements. These must be applied to the production and trade processes if we are not to be left behind.

The summit agreed to adopt a health care delivery programme among G77 member states as one tangible example of South-South cooperation emanating from Havana. Cuba agreed to provide three thousand doctors for the programme, while other member states would join in due course to put the programme into action in the most needy countries of the South.

Jamaica's chairmanship of the Group of 77 and China in 2005 came in a year when several important international meetings had been organized, and Jamaica was expected to give sustained leadership to the Group of 77.

By more efficiently pooling our technical expertise, the capacity of developing countries was enhanced and equipped to carry out an international agenda, taking into account our primary social and economic interests.

From our position as chair of the group we identified the priority areas that we had established, and worked with our partner countries to implement studies and positions on increasing the flow of resources to developing countries; improving global governance; advancing the global development agenda; enhancing South-South cooperation; and improving disaster-relief management.

I chaired the second South summit, held in Doha, Qatar, in June 2005, as heads of state and government sought to advance the global agenda for development and to give impetus to the Doha Round of the WTO negotiations which had stalled. No one could question that the glaring inequities in the international regime had to be removed for trade to become an engine of growth. We all agreed in Doha that trade policies, rules and modalities should have a development focus.

During the summit, China, India and Qatar pledged donations to launch the South Fund for development and humanitarian assistance. Tragically, from Doha to Hong Kong there was no forward movement. The collapse has been dismal, and the international trading rules and systems remain heavily stacked against developing nations.

The G77 welcomed the gradual increase in overseas development assistance and the recovery of private foreign direct investment. Much of the increase after 2000 was the result of resources targeted for emergency assistance, debt relief and technical assistance. In 2004, they accounted for fifty cents of every aid dollar.

Since 1998, there had been annual net transfers from the developing countries, as a significant portion of the resources which had been mobilized were used to finance debt-servicing payments to the multilateral development banks and increase foreign-exchange resources in the developed countries.

CHAPTER 35
FIGHTING CRIME: A HERCULEAN TASK

THE CONTINUING HIGH LEVELS OF CRIME THROUGHOUT THE tenure of the JLP government in the 1980s led the PNP to offer to cooperate in a bipartisan committee to address the spectre of political violence. Talks started in July 1986 and continued into 1987 and 1988. This joint approach of the political parties resulted in a slight, temporary decrease in crime, but was unable to truly turn the tide. As elections approached, the impetus to make it last quickly disappeared.

The defeat of the scourge of crime has to be a major priority for any administration. Crime not only threatens the comfort, security and safety of citizens, but has an impact on all aspects of the economy. Without it, a visiting Caribbean head once told me, "Jamaica would have to turn back visitors or ration the rooms."

While successive administrations had reacted with a crisis-management approach to various upsurges of violent crime, it was manifest that intervention would have to be underpinned by companion measures dealing with the root causes of crime.

In 1993 alone we instituted two high-level initiatives in an attempt to curb the levels of crime sweeping the country. Operation Ardent, a joint operation by the security forces, was launched as a special task force to operate out of military camps across the island. The second was the Anti-Crime Investigation Detachment, a special police squad established in July, made up of police officers selected from various branches of the force, including the Flying Squad, Mobile Reserve and Operations base. Members would be fighting against hard-core criminals, and were expected to display courage, professionalism and integrity.

Both achieved some level of success and some criminals were caught, but it was clear that a more fundamental and sustainable approach had to be found.

After much discussion with K.D. Knight, minister of national security, cabinet determined to establish a national task force on crime. In November 1992, the task force was set up under the chairmanship of Justice Lesley Wolfe and the members were Harold Crooks, Elsa Leo-Rhynie, Elizabeth Phillips, Douglas Orane, Donald Rainford, Marjorie Stair and Clover Parker. The task force was mandated to consult with the public to find out their concerns and their suggestions. Meetings were held in every parish, and organizations and individuals invited to send in oral and written submissions. The colossal nature of the task required additional expertise, and renowned criminologist Hyacinth Ellis was employed as a researcher and resource person.

The terms of reference of the task force were far-reaching. The focus was on the people, in an attempt to bring about a change in social and economic conditions and offer some realistic hope for a better standard of living. It was expected to identify the main causes of crime and recommend measures for its reduction in the short term and gradual abatement in the long term. It was to recommend steps to modernize and increase the efficiency and professionalism of the security forces; redefine their mission statement and recommend amendments to the laws and regulations governing their operations; suggest ways of ensuring that the security forces were free from political influence and interference; and ensure accountability among members of the forces.

In addition, it was expected to submit proposals designed to foster harmonious relations between the security forces and the public, and community support for the security forces.

It was also expected to examine the penal system and propose improvements. A major task was to examine the legislative and judicial framework to markedly improve its efficiency. It should also recommend social and economic programmes, in keeping with the limitations of national resources, to discourage participation in crime, and suggest ways of enlisting public support for the fight against crime.

Perhaps most far-reaching of the recommendations were the measures to change those socio-economic conditions identified as being conducive to crime. Youth training and the problems of our inner cities were targeted for priority attention, as well as the resocialization of Jamaican people through family and educational and religious institutions and the media. Values should stress decency, discipline, respect for each other, respect for life, non-violent solutions to conflicts and disagreements, and fairness in dealings.

Another area of focus was the relations between the security forces and the community. Successful crime-fighting and crime prevention required close cooperation between the security forces and law-abiding citizens in individual communities. All sectors of society have an equal obligation in the fight against crime. Those in a position to set an example at the national and community level must exhibit the highest respect for the laws and for those with the duty to enforce them.

Perhaps the recommendation that attracted most attention from the public was what I described as the political dimension. My administration was committed to promoting and ensuring the integrity of the police force and its ability to carry out its duties without partisan considerations. We were committed to supporting any measures designed to ensure that promotions and transfers were made on the basis of merit and performance, as well as implementing strategies to improve the operations of the force immediately. The Jamaica Constabulary Force Law was amended to separate the functions of the minister and the commissioner into policy and operations respectively.

In 1999, the security forces employed the operation dubbed Intrepid, an intelligence-driven initiative to stem the flow of guns into the island and cripple the drug trade while bringing criminal elements to justice. To enhance the effectiveness of the police in intelligence-gathering and investigation techniques, they were given training and diverse vehicles – bicycles, boats, jet skis and motor vehicles.

Despite this consistent, unrelenting struggle, violence continued to be the preferred channel through which Jamaicans resolved their differences. As we moved towards the close of the twentieth century, crime and violence remained one of the greatest challenges facing our nation.

In recognition of the serious threat posed by organized criminal networks, the administration focused on systematically attacking the illegal drug trade and its links to the importation of guns and ammunition. This included tightening border controls, increasing interdiction efforts and targeting the proceeds of crime. We also launched a national campaign to recover guns from criminal hands, and intensified detection and conviction.

Despite the increase in crime squads, police cars, and improved weapons, the crisis we were facing remained obdurate. Up to that time, under my administration, some seven such initiatives had been implemented. There had been Operation Ardent (1993), the Anti-Crime Investigation Detachment (1993), Operation Crest (1995), Operation Justice (1995), Operation Dovetail (1997), the Organised Crime Unit and Operation Intrepid (1999).

What was needed was a new philosophy of policing, anchored in respect for the human rights of all citizens, to create a new respect for law and order.

In a national broadcast on 1 December 2002, I announced to the nation the new strategy we would pursue to curb the wave of violence. The security forces were authorized to move from a policy of containment to a more proactive mode of dismantling the paramilitary groups of organized gangs wreaking havoc in several communities. The military and police were instructed to maintain an active, vigilant presence where available intelligence revealed drug dealers and their well-armed thugs were fighting for turf and unleashing a reign of terror. There would be joint patrols to search for guns and roadblocks to intercept criminals on the move.

The overseas law-enforcement agencies of the United States, Britain and Canada pledged welcome material and technical assistance in respect of drugs.

To ensure a focused, multifaceted and integrated effort to a multi-agency approach, Alister Cooke was seconded from the Shipping Association of Jamaica to help coordinate efforts to address poverty, inner-city decay and social alienation.

For a while there was some respite – but as the pressures increased on the Colombian drug trade, the merchants of death intensified their violence along the route to the American market – hence the surge of murders in 2005.

Measures we introduced to fight crime included increased numbers of police in the field and expansion of fleets to improve mobility and response time, including high-speed marine vessels for the coastguard; legislation to enforce a greater control over access to air and seaports, amending the Money Laundering Act to allow the confiscation of proceeds of the trade, and legislation to allow the interception of communication; strengthening the Financial Crimes Unit; a major recruitment drive to attract qualified personnel to bring the security forces up to strength through the graduate entry programme; introducing electronic monitoring devices; and a broad-based social effort to reverse the pervasive culture of violence through the Peace Management Initiative.

Various researchers have propounded in their several findings and theories on the level of homicides in Jamaica and our Caribbean counterparts. The deadly conflicts in communities and families have been attributed to a number of reasons, among them

- a lessening of respect for authority and rapidly changing moral values;
- family dysfunction and the reduction in the number of positive role models in the communities generally and changes in the value system;
- the general effects of globalization, which bring increased contact with different lifestyles and different values and materialism, which contribute not only to violent crime but also to white-collar crime;

- urban drift, as a result of the lack of social and economic opportunities in rural areas;
- higher levels of unemployment among the urban population and increased inequality in distribution of income;
- an increase in gun- and narco-trafficking;
- an educational system that did not prepare its graduates for economic survival;
- structural deficiencies in the criminal justice system, especially those relating to the reduction of deterrents to criminal behaviour, inadequate resources which adversely affect a just and efficient trial process, an inhuman penal system which results in a high level of recidivism, the failure of past administrations to reform and equip the police force to carry out its duties effectively and the emergence and proliferation of "garrison" communities;
- the over-centralization of power and authority that leaves communities without the wherewithal to solve their own problems or to settle disputes;
- excesses in policing which have fractured the relationship with communities and caused some people to look elsewhere for protection;
- political tribalism, which bred a dependency syndrome in many citizens and divided communities along party lines; and
- protracted economic hardships which have denied many people the opportunity to earn a livelihood and enjoy any meaningful quality of life.

On the basis of the best professional analysis, we prepared the National Security Strategy, issued by the Ministry of Security in November 2005 as the blueprint for major security initiatives to follow. This document presented the government's overarching policies on national security matters through a process of strategic environmental analysis, describing the threats that worked against the full achievement of the country's security goals, determining Jamaica's security priorities in relation to the capabilities and policies required to counter those threats, and establishing the responsibilities, structures, and timelines for implementation. The strategy sought to enhance coordination and cooperation among the different ministries and national security agencies, as the new security environment blurred traditional boundaries.

While maintaining its sovereignty, Jamaica would continue to meet its international obligations and play its role in contributing to the security and development of its partners in the Caribbean, the Americas and the global international community. This included providing for substantial linkages with the evolving

CARICOM security initiatives endorsed by the heads of government in July 2005 – bilateral and multilateral arrangements. In collaboration with our partners, the aim was to eradicate transnational organized crime, illicit trafficking and international terrorism and move towards international peace and sustainable development.

To counter police abuse and protect the rights of our citizenry we emphasized training that included courses for recruits in human rights and human dignity. We introduced a chaplaincy programme and a station pastor programme to provide moral guidance and reinforce the new ethos of the force, to "serve, protect and reassure the citizens of Jamaica".

In conjunction with the International Investigative Training Assistance Programme we formulated and published guidelines based on UN principles of the use of force and firearms by law-enforcement personnel.

We also established the Bureau of Special Investigations to investigate all police shootings and the independent Police Public Complaints Authority to initiate and monitor investigations of complaints against the police. There were several improvements in the justice system that enhanced access to justice. We revolutionized the legal-aid regime to provide legal assistance to the poor; enacted the Bail Act; established a victim support unit which has catered to the needs of thousands (our facility was launched two years before the call by Amnesty International for similar bodies around the globe); increased the number of judges and magistrates and established night courts; expanded family courts as well as the jurisdictions of justices of the peace; set up a rehabilitation unit in the Correctional Services Department to ensure that people who entered the system left with a better attitude and acquired some skills training so that they could reenter society and the job market; built a new remand centre; and partnered with the UK Department for International Development to enlarge the Community Service Sentencing Programme, which received an excellent response. Also in association with the department, a programme was implemented to improve public confidence in the security forces, which included organizational restructuring, crime management, community policing and human-resource development.

Even though they no longer constantly preach it, successive administrations in the United States have practised the basic tenets of the Monroe Doctrine. In the 1970s, it was manifested by the hostility shown to our administration for daring to pursue international relationships and trade arrangements which did not always coincide with the American agenda and corporate interests. It was that logical sequence which triggered the Grenada invasion of 1983. With that crushing blow, the Caribbean could be offensively described by a deputy secretary of state as being part of "America's backyard". In recent times, there has been a reiteration of the Monroe hegemonic domination in the response of the United States to the apparent spread of Chinese trade and investment in Latin America and the Caribbean.

The Caribbean, undisputedly the fourth border of the United States, is no longer regarded as a strategic area of geopolitical significance, and seems only to be remembered when our fourteen votes make the difference. It remains, however, a zone of security concern, as such a large proportion of the illicit drugs destined for the US market is channelled through the Caribbean.

Jamaica, like all our nations in the Caribbean, has a vested interest in prohibiting the flow of illicit drugs across its borders. We are a sovereign country, which must protect the rights of our citizens, respect for our laws and institutions and resist the violation of our territorial spaces by illicit drug traffickers or unauthorized intruders.

The day after I left for an official visit to Canada, K.D. Knight, then minister of national security, called me in Toronto to alert me to a diplomatic note brought to him by US Embassy officials asking him to sign, over the weekend, the Shiprider Agreement to deter the movement of illegal drugs from South America to the United States through Jamaican territorial waters. There had been no prior discussions with our officials, and the minister was seeing it for the first time.

The Americans were deeply upset to hear our firm position: an agreement of such a far-reaching nature would require full bilateral discussions, a document reflecting our mutual rights and responsibilities, and the full approval of our cabinet.

During that weekend, we found out that two other Caribbean countries had already signed, and I asked for a special CARICOM meeting of heads in Barbados so that we could formulate a common regional stance. Dean Barrow, then foreign minister of Belize, made an outstanding contribution to our deliberations, as we were all adamant on negotiating a maritime drug enforcement agreement with the United States which reflected our national interests.

Jamaica is an archipelagic state by gift of nature, as recognized in the Independence Act and formally proclaimed in the Maritime Areas Bill. Within the archipelagic state – incorporating the main island, Pedro Cays, Morant Cays, South West Rock and other geographic features – the sovereign state of Jamaica has sole and total jurisdiction cover, which it will not share with any other nation. In respect of our maritime space and the airspace above, our exclusive criminal jurisdiction covers the internal waters, archipelagic waters and the territorial sea.

Extending beyond our twelve miles of territorial waters for another 188 nautical miles is an area of maritime space known as the Exclusive Economic Zone. Within that area the coastal state has sovereign jurisdiction over certain economic activities. Jamaica had made no claim to exclusive criminal jurisdiction within the area of the zone, but any search had to be conducted in accordance with international law. Jamaica's negotiating team was led by Kenneth Rattray, with a supporting cast with skills that made the Americans realize we would be no pushover.

While finding it difficult to accept that negotiations should proceed with the threat of US decertification hanging over our heads, we had to make sure all the necessary steps were taken to prevent a unilateral and unwarranted degrading of control which would have grave consequences for our economy and security. I had to convey through diplomatic channels that Jamaica's record in combating illicit trafficking in narcotics could stand up to any fair and reasonable scrutiny, but we were not prepared to breach our constitution nor to compromise the sovereignty of our nation.

The agreement which was eventually announced in the House on May 27 1997 reflected mutual respect and recognized the provisions of the Jamaican constitution. Also, it removed blanket immunity in respect of US personnel taking action against a suspected vessel. It enabled US and Jamaican law-enforcement teams to continue to work together in Jamaica's territorial waters to beat drug traffickers' attempts to move cocaine from South America to the United States through Jamaica and its waters. The agreement allowed them to cooperate in shipboarding, shipriding, and overflight.

The Shiprider Agreement continues to be an essential component of the fight against illicit drugs, because much of the trafficking of cocaine, heroin, ganja (marijuana) and other drugs takes place at sea. Essential to the success of any maritime drug interdiction campaign is cooperation among nations, because drug trafficking cuts across national borders and territorial waters and threatens the security of every country.

Jamaica was appreciative of its traditional and current relationship with the United States and the high levels of cooperation we have enjoyed in various fields. That relationship could only endure so long as it was based on the fundamental acceptance of mutual respect and sovereign equality.

A major concern for CARICOM states was the new forms of crime and violence that threatened the stability and the social and economic well-being of the region. While the problems varied from country to country, we recognized the need for collaborative approaches to the interrelated problems of crime, illicit drugs and terrorism. By virtue of our geographical location, we found ourselves in the position of being the main route used by drug dealers from the producing countries to their markets in North America and Europe.

The threats posed by drug trafficking presented serious challenges and risks, particularly for small states, which are confronted with overwhelming pressures on limited national resources. The Regional Task Force on Crime and Security provided CARICOM with policy directives and recommendations for dealing with the range of complex security concerns. These included the need for a developmental and multi-sectoral approach to crime-prevention initiatives.

The regional plan for a coordinated response incorporated ongoing work on the causes of crime, illicit drugs and their links to crime, the impact of Jamaican-born criminals deported home from the United States on the escalating rate of crime, trafficking in illicit arms and formulating a policy for getting guns off the street.

CHAPTER 36

CONSTITUTIONAL REFORM, JUSTICE AND THE LAW

FOLLOWING THE VERDICT IN THE FEDERATION REFERENDUM OF 1961, the Jamaican Parliament set up a bicameral committee of members of the Legislative Council and House of Representatives to settle the constitutional framework for an independent Jamaica. As we have previously observed, this became the subject of discussion in London between delegations from the PNP government and the JLP opposition on the one hand with the Colonial Office at Lancaster House on the other. The outcome was then the subject of extensive discussion in our parliamentary chambers, but the Constitution of Jamaica, which came into being on 6 August 1962, was by way of an Order in Council and still remains so.

It was the first of a new model, reflecting largely the legal genius of the luminary Norman Manley, but also the uncertainty as to whether he or Alexander Bustamante would become the first prime minister of our independent nation.

Accordingly, the office of leader of opposition was instituted in the constitution, with clearly defined roles and functions. Not only were certain appointments by the governor to be made by the prime minister after consultation with the leader of the opposition, but the composition of the Senate – thirteen government and eight opposition appointees – gave an effective veto before entrenched portions of the constitution could be altered, regardless of the size of membership in the House.

Proposed changes to those portions of the constitution which were deeply entrenched, even after obtaining a two-thirds majority vote in both chambers, would still have to be submitted to the electorate for approval in a referendum. When the planned measure had not secured the necessary two-thirds majority, changes to or removal of the deeply entrenched sections would require a two-thirds approval by voters. Simply put, no entrenched or deeply entrenched section of our constitution can be changed without the support of our two major political parties. Unless the political will exists on both sides, Jamaica will never be able to enact our constitution by our own sovereign act.

In 1977, Michael Manley set up, under his direct leadership, a working team, which included Paul Miller and Paul Robertson, to spearhead constitutional reform. Between the groups led by Hugh Shearer and myself to formalize the Electoral Advisory Committee, some progress was made during our discussions in 1978 on areas of constitutional reform which would include entrenching the Electoral Advisory Committee and local government, and amending section 18 of the constitution relating to property rights. Unfortunately, all of this became an early casualty in the savage internecine campaign of 1980.

Soon after his return to the cabinet on 31 March 1992, Carl Rattray, QC, was authorized to announce that on the recommendation of the Joint Select Committee on Constitutional and Electoral Reform, Parliament had decided to establish a constitutional commission to examine proposals from the general public and hold public discussions to permit inputs from those outside Parliament. The commission consisted of thirty-eight people, sixteen nominated by the political parties, and the remainder from the Bar, the Press Association, the University of the West Indies, trade unions, churches, the private sector, women's groups, teachers, farmers and youth.

In addressing the plenary ceremony at Headquarters House, Duke Street, Kingston, on 13 May 1992, I took note of the fact that while as far back as 1978 agreement had been reached on several amendments to the constitution, this was the first comprehensive constitutional exercise over which a sovereign Jamaica had complete control.

In its approach to the commission's task and the general framework of the documents, I suggested that our constitution should effectively address experiences and reflect the aspirations of the people, be the supreme law and those laws which are not consonant with the constitution should be repealed or altered. There had to be easy and direct access to the courts if any breach of constitutional rights occurred, and appropriate sanctions for those breaches, and I emphasized that all discriminatory actions, including those based on gender, had to be outlawed to create a climate which promoted greater participation in the democratic process in both the political and economic spheres. I noted also that the reformed constitution should seek to capture the popular will, symbolize national values and aspirations, and reflect the soul and spirit of the people. In addition, it had to characterize the mission of economic independence, the fostering of the entrepreneurial spirit and the regulation of equality of opportunity.

Among the conclusions of the final report of the commission, which Justice James Kerr chaired in 1993, were these salient two points: "The new constitution should be the product of the Jamaican people and rid our basic law of its present colonial form; and the monarchical form should be replaced by a republican form so as to enhance our sense of national identity and consciousness and to foster our self-esteem."

Once again, despite their full participation in the exercise and the public forums, no member of the opposition signed the report of 1993. They gave no reason for their refusal.

In my 1994 budget speech, I reiterated the intention to "Jamaicanize" our constitution by promulgating it as an act of our own which would provide for a head of state appointed by the Jamaican people through their representatives in Parliament and recast the existing chapter on fundamental rights and freedoms in the light of our experience to make it more readily understandable by the general public and be a more effective and efficient instrument for protecting the individual against the abuse of power.

It has always been my view that independence should entitle us to update our constitutional provisions as we refashion our own image as a people and how we collectively choose to be known. The focal point, based on public dialogue, must be the upliftment of our people through our political and economic systems. Contending and simplistic arguments about balance of power versus the concentration of power, as against the virtues of a "separation of powers", often obscure the need "to create the kind of confidence in and a definition of ourselves that make the fulfilment of our obligations and responsibilities as important as exercising our rights according to the law and the constitution and reject all systems which accept that political tribalism is axiomatic and thereby make it a self-fulfilling prophecy", as I said in my 1998 budget speech.

Parliament managed after arduous toil to reach consensus on a new and expanded Charter of Rights. We recast the existing chapter in the constitution on fundamental rights and freedoms to embrace new areas. By that act, we made that chapter more easily understood by the general public and made it a more effective and efficient instrument for protecting our people against the abuse of power. But this only became a reality when the PNP, in opposition, gave it the requisite parliamentary support in 2008.

This product of direct consultation resulted in a widening and substantial strengthening of the entitlements of all citizens

Norman Manley had declined a knighthood from Queen Elizabeth, but both he and Sir Alexander Bustamante were committed to retaining Her Majesty as the head of state. Their justification for maintaining the Westminster system instead of opting for some form of the presidential structure is recorded in our Hansard and worth the attention of scholars and the younger political generation alike.

The constitution of 1962 stipulated precisely the functions to be exercised by our first governor general, Sir Kenneth Blackburn, and our first native governor general, Sir Clifford Campbell. Since then, an increasing number of functions have been vested in the governor general. Most have related to appointments to numerous offices which have been created in the course of time, beginning with the Electoral Advisory Committee. In nearly all these cases, the appointment is made by the governor general after consultation with the prime minister and leader of the opposition. In 1995, when opposition leader Edward Seaga, proposed that the governor general be allowed to express his personal views in the throne speech, I was forced to insist that in accordance with the Westminster model, the throne speech would remain at the start of each parliamentary year and be crafted by the prime minister and the cabinet to reflect government policy.

In exploring constitutional reform during the 1978 conversations, the PNP was insistent on an executive president, chosen by the electorate. The JLP favoured a ceremonial head of state appointed by parliamentary procedure(s).

The Kerr Commission, by a majority decision, after extensive debate, recommended "that the formal head of state should not be an active politician and head of government". It proposed that the head of state should be appointed, on the nomination of the prime minister in consultation with the leader of the opposition, subject to confirmation by a two-thirds majority of the members of both houses of Parliament sitting in joint session.

This, it felt, "would invest the selection with an aura of democratic approval and the republican form would replace the monarchical "in a manner indicative of our national identity and consciousness of our self-esteem as a nation", as we prepared to enter our fortieth year of independence. In a statement in Parliament in April 2001, I implored that we should move forward to complete the structures of our independence: "The process towards our self-definition as a people must now be accelerated. The institution of our own indigenous president as head of state in the Republic of Jamaica must now be placed on the front burner of the public agenda."

In the search for a consensus on these new constitutional arrangements, I sought and obtained, at our annual party conference in 2001, the authorization to accept a ceremonial head. But soon after that, Bruce Golding returned to the JLP from the National Democratic Movement, and Edward Seaga told me at one of our regular meetings at Vale Royal that his party would now have to resolve the differences of views resulting from Golding's National Democratic Movement position, which advocated a presidential format akin to the US model.

In the 2001 budget presentation, I said: "I can think of hardly anyone required to take the oath of allegiance who does not feel a sense of discomfort at being obliged to swear allegiance to a foreign monarch, rather than the nation and Constitution of Jamaica. For us to swear allegiance to the state and people of Jamaica, only a simple majority vote of the members of both Houses of Parliament is required."

I was determined that by 2002, the prime minister would take an oath of office pledging to observe the laws and Constitution of Jamaica and allegiance to its people. So it was on 23 October 2002 at Emancipation Park, where I swore to "be faithful and bear true allegiance to Jamaica . . . uphold and defend the constitution and the laws of Jamaica . . . conscientiously and impartially discharge my responsibilities to the people of Jamaica".

The Office of the Public Defender was introduced in 1999. That institution forms a seminal plank of the constitutional arrangements the administration sought to put in place.

The Family Property (Rights of Spouses) Bill introduced new statutory rules governing the division of property between spouses when a union came to an end, whether recognized by legal marriage or otherwise.

The Incest (Punishment) Act was amended to widen the categories and scope of incestuous relationships, in order to further protect our vulnerable young people.

The Domestic Violence Act, passed in 1995, was updated. The act introduced additional remedies to counter domestic violence by granting speedier and more effective relief to victims. We had to deal with a gaping omission in the act – the visiting relationship. We sought to protect our women and children, who are the primary victims of domestic violence.

The court was empowered by the Inheritance (Provision for Family and Dependents) Act to make maintenance provisions from the estate of a deceased person for certain family members and dependents. In most cases, it is our women and our children who are left unprovided for, and the power conferred on the court may be used where, under a will or by the law of intestacy, no adequate provision is made for dependents. This law takes into account those who have enjoyed and shared a stable relationship out of wedlock for five years or more.

One of the commitments I made during my term was that I would not tolerate any form of corrupt practice in government. The Corruption Prevention Regulations made possible the launch of the Commission for the Prevention of Corruption. Under the regulations, public-sector workers earning over a certain amount are required to declare their assets every year.

All citizens can now bring to the attention of the commission any act of corruption encountered in the public and private sectors. There is no longer any justification to undertake smear or whispering campaigns, as the appropriate mechanism for dealing with corruption is in place.

A National Contracts Commission was established in 1999 to ensure that the award of contracts by ministries, departments and agencies of government was governed by systems that are transparent, fair and efficient, manifestly independent and free of improper influence.

The Contractor General's Office was strengthened to ensure that it could effectively discharge its new responsibilities, and legislative amendments made to ensure that the office could do so legally. The new system led to great improvement.

The devolution of authority from central to local government was designed to give greater power to people at the community level. We went about it in a measured way to ensure that local government became more efficient, effective and duly accountable. As a consequence, we amended some laws to allow fees to be made dedicated revenues for local government.

Amendments were also made to give local authorities the power to impose fees and greater flexibility in setting or adjusting those fees and removing bottlenecks. The Association of Local Government Authorities of Jamaica was empowered by the passing of the ALGAJ Act. Building by-laws for all parish councils were revised. New regulations gave them regulatory authority over several activities. We also worked towards entrenching local government in the constitution and the relevant acts were recently passed.

THE CARIBBEAN COURT OF JUSTICE

Norman Manley was a fine jurist who never contemplated that our judicial arm would rest forever in a final court in a foreign land, constituted and maintained by the United Kingdom and incapable of moulding a Caribbean jurisprudence.

As practising counsel, it was my privilege to be in attendance when the Organization of Commonwealth Caribbean Bar Associations, with Leacroft Robinson, QC, presiding, met in early 1970 and fired from Kingston the first salvo against our continued arrangements with the Judicial Committee of the Privy Council. It declared that final judicial determination in the United Kingdom was inconsistent with our sovereignty and an impediment to the evolution of our jurisprudence. It posed three questions. First, should not the Commonwealth West Indian countries, as independent nations, provide their own final Court of Appeal, staffed by West Indian judges? Second, have we not the people of character, learning and ability to be judges of such a court of final adjudication in our own legal affairs? Third, is it fair for the British government and British judges to continue giving us these gratuitous services if we are able to provide for ourselves?

It fell to Prime Minister Hugh Shearer and Attorney General Victor Grant, QC, to persuade CARICOM heads that the time had come for the Caribbean to cease appeals to the Privy Council.

In the years which followed, Caribbean heads and their ministers were so preoccupied with forging new economic and trading relations within the region as well as with the European metropoles that a Caribbean Court of Justice (CCJ) did not return to the regional agenda until the seventh conference of heads in Trinidad and Tobago. On the instructions of the heads, attorneys general met in Dominica to present proposals, which the heads approved unanimously at their eighth summit, to make the CCJ our final court.

With the coming into being of the CSME, it became necessary to provide for the settlement of disputes arising from the Treaty of Chaguaramas and its protocols. The 1998 conference of heads decided in St Lucia to establish the CCJ with an original and appellate jurisdiction. In its appellate jurisdiction, the CCJ applies the laws of the member states from which it is hearing appeals. In the exercise of its original jurisdiction, the CCJ performs the role of an international court, applying international law in interpreting and applying the revised Treaty of Chaguaramas. The court's appellate jurisdiction would be coterminous with that of the Judicial Committee of the Privy Council and would mirror the constitutional provisions of Section 110 of our Jamaican constitution.

In a prime-ministerial statement to our Parliament on 22 June 1999, based on my own knowledge of the background and the opinion of our former attorney general David Coore, QC, former solicitor general Kenneth Rattray, QC, and then solicitor general Michael Hylton, QC, I stated:

It is by virtue of Section 110 of the constitution that the right of appeal to Her Majesty in Council was created when we became independent. The section addresses both the right of appeal and the jurisdiction to be exercised by the Privy Council. That jurisdiction includes the hearing of "final decisions in any civil, criminal or other proceedings on questions as to the interpretation of this constitution and such other cases as may be prescribed by Parliament".

To amend the provisions concerning the right of appeal to the Privy Council, Section 110 requires no special procedure. It falls within the category addressed in Section 49(4)(b) of the constitution which only requires "the votes of a majority of all the members of each House of Parliament".

The framers of our constitution, in their wisdom, envisaged that appeals to the Privy Council should not assume a form or state of permanence. Certainly, they did not wish that amendments to that provision should follow any procedure other than that which applies to simple legislation. The Joint Select Committee on Constitutional and Electoral Reform, in its final report submitted to Parliament in May 1995, stated: "The present system of appeal to the Privy Council should continue, but subject to the introduction of a Caribbean Court of Appeal, if and when such a decision is taken."

In early 2001, CARICOM heads signed the agreement to establish the court. Kenny Anthony was responsible for superintending the steps required, including the legislation member states would need to pass before we could establish our own court of last resort.

By bringing the court to the people, the CCJ will enhance access to justice in terms of reducing distance and expense, and will have the challenge of establishing respect as a binding authority, while assuring public support for and confidence in its administration of justice.

As an appeal court, the CCJ is designed to give moral leadership to our societies. As an international court, the CCJ will ensure that the regional international movement develops in a structured, sustainable and rule-based manner.[1] More importantly, as the tribunal responsible for interpreting and applying the Revised Treaty of Chaguaramas establishing CARICOM, including the CSME, the CCJ will be the guarantor of the rights of nationals accorded by the revised treaty. Important rights in this context are the rights of skilled professionals to practise in any jurisdiction of the community and for artisans and other

---

1. To date, few CARICOM states have actually replaced the Privy Council with the CCJ as their final appellate court. Jamaica is not among them.

specified categories of skilled workers to work as independent contractors in any area of the community.

In terms of staffing, the Regional Judicial and Legal Services Commission is responsible for appointing judges and other court employees. The court is made up of a president and at least nine judges. The president, who chairs the commission, determines wages, salaries and conditions of work.

A trust fund has been set up to finance the court and is managed by a board of trustees, to insulate it from political interference. The agreement establishing the fund came into force with its signature by members at the twenty-fourth heads of government conference in Montego Bay.

The seat of the court is in Trinidad and Tobago, but as the circumstances warrant, the court may sit in the territory of any other contracting party.

In February 2005, the Privy Council ruled that our legislature had not followed "the procedure appropriate for amendment of an entrenched provision" affecting our superior courts. As prime minister I was bound by this decision. I had to accept it as valid because it emanated from a final court and we are obliged to obey the law. Its rulings are final, but that does not mean the Law Lords are infallible. From time to time, the Privy Council has changed its previous rulings. There are many of Her Majesty's counsel who have engaged in a jurisprudential analysis of the judgment and continue to question the intrinsic merit of the Privy Council rules.

There are portions of Lord Bingham's judgment which smack of imperial arrogance: "the independence of the Privy Council, which although enjoying no entrenched protection, is known to be immune from local Parliamentary or Executive pressure and whose members are all but irremovable".

The Privy Council accepted "that without doubt the CCJ Agreement represents a serious and conscientious endeavour to create a regional court of high quality and complete independence".

Why then did the court find it necessary to invoke the doctrine of "anticipatory wrongdoing" to give protection against governmental misbehaviour? When members of Her Majesty's cabinet err, they are subject to the jurisdiction of England's Supreme Court. The ruling implies a malicious propensity which will block or counter the erudition and the integrity of our judges.

᠅

I have always been proud to be a member of the noble Bar. Throughout my political life I remained a servant of the court, who, like all those who really deserve to be called counsel, must always strive to secure the justice which our people seek and yearn to establish a Caribbean civilization of our own creation.

The purity of the law does not permit any form of contamination. "Law maintains the highest standards of all the secular professions," asserted Oliver Wendell Holmes.

The nations of the Caribbean have all inherited the rich legacy of the common law. Our concepts of justice have emerged from principles forged in the cauldron of time and the unfolding of knowledge. The right to a fair hearing and trial by one's peers and the presumption of innocence remain the pillars on which our democracy has been built. At the same time the law satisfies the instinctive human test of what is just and fair as we seek to separate right from wrong.

We who live in emergent societies, alert to the need for social change and mobility, are daily concerned with the search for the solutions needed to achieve economic stability. For us the law must be viewed as an instrument for the development of our people and therefore must serve as a vehicle to reach our social and economic goals.

When we became a nation, we inherited good laws and bad laws. The genesis of some of these bad laws, particularly in the area of criminal justice, lay in the concepts of what was necessary for the ruling power to maintain control over the overwhelming numbers of the formerly enslaved population. The vagrancy laws made criminal anyone found wandering abroad without any visible means of sustenance. The basis of this "crime" lay in the need for plantation owners to keep the former slaves working on the plantations, and the propensity of the former slaves to flee the plantation. We fulfilled the promise I made to the banquet of the Jamaica Bar Association in July 1992 to repeal the Vagrancy Act. My administration endeavoured to provide all that it could within the ambit of severe competition for limited budgetary resources. Spurred by a passionate minister of justice, A.J. Nicholson, QC, there were improvements in the system to enhance access to justice and the speed and quality of justice.

The numbers of judges and magistrates were increased, the jurisdiction of the justices of the peace expanded and all resident magistrates' courts had attorneys as clerks. The Office of the Director of Public Prosecutions had its full complement of prosecutors. Night courts were established, family courts expanded and drug courts introduced to focus on treating and rehabilitating drug abusers.

As a result of bipartisan consensus, the Office of the Public Defender and the Victim Support Unit were established. We revolutionized the legal-aid regime to provide legal assistance to the poor, from arrest to appeal.

With the UN Children's Fund we started a project which required the Ministry of National Security and Justice, in conjunction with the Ministry of Health, to reform the entire juvenile justice system to make it consistent with international standards.

CHAPTER 37
CULTURAL HERITAGE AND SOCIAL RENEWAL

IN 1937, OUR FIRST NATIONAL HERO, MARCUS GARVEY, urged his audience in Menelik Hall, Nova Scotia, to emancipate themselves from the mental slavery that was the result of a long period of dehumanization and ugly violations of the human spirit.

Norman Manley's final address to the PNP annual conference, in 1968, summed up his achievements: "I say that the mission of my generation was to win self-government for Jamaica, to win political power which is the final power for the black masses of my country from which I spring."

By then, Hugh Shearer, a veteran of the labour movement, had become the third prime minister of Jamaica, albeit by the decision of his parliamentary colleagues rather than the choice of the people in a national election.

Over the forty years of independence, Jamaicans had become more comfortable and self-assured in dealing with race, colour and class. Jackie Ranston, in her book on the legal career of Norman Manley,[1] recounts the civil case for land trespass in the resident magistrates' courts of Manchester with an exchange between a black woman and her Chinese neighbour. The black woman says, "You have no right to our land here. Go back to your country." To which the Chinese shopkeeper replies, "If I don't, neither do you. Why you don't go back to Africa where you come from?" This banter reflects the undeniable reality of the inseparable links between slavery, emancipation, the colonial plantation system and the migration from India and China which followed.

I knew too well that the exchanges in London in 1962 on whether to establish 1 August as our Independence Day or to maintain Emancipation Day for prime

---

1. Jackie Ranston, *Lawyer Manley, vol. 1: First Time Up* (Kingston: University of the West Indies Press, 1999).

national observance went far beyond the concern about the loss of productive time.

In February 1996, I established a broad-based national committee, chaired by Rex Nettleford, to examine how our national symbols and observances could contribute to sustaining cultural unity and foster national values to renew the soul and uplift the spirit of our people and arrest social alienation.

I was ecstatic when the committee recommended the reinstatement of Emancipation Day on 1 August. In consultations held in four parishes, in written and oral submissions and press contributions, our people revealed their deepest feelings on issues they regard as part of their psychic inheritance, which could avert cultural chaos and release their creative potential.

In the minds of many of our young people there was confusion as to the actual date of our independence. With the passage of time, the observance of Independence Day had weakened considerably. I shared the view that designating 6 August, rather than the first Monday of the month, as the holiday, would help sharpen the focus and reawaken a consciousness of independence as an important national event.

We accepted the recommendation that Independence Day ought to be given its proper date – 6 August – so as to remove any doubt in the minds of our people about the timing and significance of that historic date.

President Jerry Rawlings of Ghana was our special guest at the 1996 ceremony in Spanish Town (where the Emancipation Declaration was read on 1 August, 1838, to commemorate that historic day which marked full freedom for our people). The restoration of Emancipation Day and its separation from Independence Day ignited within several other Caribbean nations the desire to commemorate the journey that had taken our ancestors from their home across the Middle Passage to cultivate sugar to enrich Britain, and laid the basis for industrial exploitation and much else on both sides of the globe.

In August 2002, I opened Emancipation Park as a site dedicated to the independence of spirit, the enduring commitment to freedom and the strength and resilience of our people whose forebears fought against the indecency of dehumanization and the denigration of the millions of involuntary labourers forced into bondage and treated as beasts of burden for over two centuries.

Both Rex and I, sitting at the feet of Philip Sherlock at Mona, realized the power of symbols in human behaviour. He taught us that the deep meanings of the collective life of a people are reflected in symbols and observances and themselves reflect the social and cultural movers of the times. In his draft preamble to the Jamaican constitution sent to the Kerr Commission in 1993, Sherlock suggested the guiding principles should recognize that Jamaica is: "predominantly a black nation, the majority of its people being of African origin, who claim a European heritage and whose way of life has been greatly enriched by the cultures of Jews, Arabs, Indians and Chinese".

From the time the design of our national flag was announced, Sir Philip had expressed his disquiet that the black in the Jamaican flag signified hardships. Many of our people regarded it as demeaning things African and perpetuating the use of the term "black" in negative and disagreeable terms – as in "Black Friday", "blackmail" and the *Oxford Dictionary* definitions of "black" as "deadly, sinister, wicked, hateful . . . threatening" and "implying disgrace".

I would not ignore the deep feelings of our people, the vast majority of whom are descendants of a people who continue to suffer disparagement for no other reason than for the way they look. Parliament accepted readily the recommendation in the report that the colour black should no longer signify hardships, but resilience and strength. The decisions of the commission marked another step on the road to self-discovery and "smadification" which we travelled in the 1970s. They were calculated to encourage patriotism and national pride, to empower the Jamaican people through a greater sense of self-worth and creative energy:

> The guiding beacons of economic development and social well-being cannot be achieved without a full grasp of what it means to be Jamaican, taking on board the entire heritage bequeathed us by our rich history of struggle and survival. Nor will it be achieved in the face of a lingering unease with the very notion of blackness and the cultural alienation among youths and adults alike. And we stand no chance of success, Mr. Speaker, if we who represent the people of this country in this honourable House fail to appreciate the creativity that resides in the society at all levels and certainly among those from the lower socioeconomic groups evident in our great achievements in the world of popular music, sports (especially track and field) and much more.

VALUES AND ATTITUDES

I was born at a time when the church, the school and the extended family were all seeking to rid our society of the brutality and oppression of the past and build instead respect for the dignity of the human condition. The virtues of tolerance, decency, honesty and respect were preached in rural and urban communities alike.

By the start of my own full term in 1993, the dangers to the national fabric were manifested by the increase in crime and violence, and the links between trafficking in guns, drugs and corruption. Our social environment was experiencing severe threats from the deterioration in moral standards, the materialism that seeks instant gratification and the breakdown of family structures. The influences of the church and the community were waning. That many of our people could no longer differentiate right from wrong was the most frightening concern of all.

There was a need to recalibrate, as the soundest policies for national development were bound to fail if the society continued to dehumanize itself. The only way out was for us to restore, as a nation, sound values and better attitudes.

This inspired the National Conference on Values and Attitudes. Sponsored jointly by the Government of Jamaica and the UN Educational, Scientific and Cultural Organization, it was the core of a national programme of social renewal. Speaking slots were deliberately assigned to debar a partisan divide and permit the broadest reflection of views. It was arranged to allow reasonable time for discourse before workshops that would embrace our political parties, the church, the private sector, the trades unions, the youth, women, non-governmental organizations and community representatives.

In opening the conference I stressed that to halt the indiscipline, incivility and violence in our daily discourse and relationships, the exercise had to begin with vigorous self-examination. Each person must resolve to "let it begin with me".

I sought to make it abundantly clear that the crusade was not a nostalgic yearning for a past which we could not recapture. It was, instead, an attempt to redress the inequity of the past. It deprecated a polarized society, in which the fight for scarce benefits and political spoils had made us appear perpetually at war.

That statement was deliberately distorted, by radio talk-show host Wilmot Perkins and other miscreants, to suggest I was endorsing that kind of political system. To the contrary, I was expressing my total repudiation of such a legacy, which would prevent us working together to realize a common goal.

I was on the verge of ascending the platform when a message came from the office of the opposition leader to convey his regrets at being unable to attend. It was worse than a submarine attack, because no effort had been spared in the preparation for the conference to ensure his participation. The following day, the JLP's chairman, Bruce Golding, issued a release attacking the programme as a partisan political ploy and distancing the JLP from it.

The entrenchment of political loyalties on both sides is so strong, the contests so fierce and the divisions so sharp that no national programme can fully succeed in the absence of support from both the JLP and PNP. After that tragic block to secure a united effort, the Values and Attitudes Campaign was never able to fire on all cylinders, no matter how hard we tried. I invited the church to take the lead and remove any semblance of political taint. While nearly every church minister supported the campaign, the Seventh-Day Adventist Church was the only denomination to do so openly.

In all succeeding years, there has not been a single day when, from the pulpit, in the media, or in some commentary, the call is not made for a restoration of the Values and Attitudes Campaign. It is simply not true, however, to say the campaign was abandoned or that we did not pursue the recommendations of its workshops.

Among them were the restoration of the National Youth Service, which was abolished in the 1980s and is now established by law; addressing the problems of informal and squatter settlements through shelter strategies for land owner-ship and schemes like Operation PRIDE; the creation of the Jamaican Urban Transport Corporation for population centres in Kingston, St Andrew, St Cath-erine and St James; and awakening religious bodies, civic groups and corporate interests to the realization that they too had a vested interest in promoting values and attitudes.

It spurred the Council of Voluntary Social Services to heighten its profile and triggered the launch of the Peace Management Initiative. Corporate groups com-bined their efforts to create the Peace and Love in Schools Foundation in 1994 and launch the Digicel-sponsored Respect Programme to help young people manage anger and reduce violence in schools. Our service clubs contributed immensely to several aspects of the campaign.

During the regional consultations which followed in Mandeville, Montego Bay, Ocho Rios and Port Antonio, I emphasized the obligations of the state to establish patterns of conduct and rules of behaviour, where necessary through appropriate laws and the capacity to enforce them.

For their part, the citizens highlighted their entitlement to receive efficient social services responsive to their needs and reflective of their most urgent pri-orities. These ideas helped in the design of the Jamaica Social Investment Fund to maximize the use of financial and technical resources for projects designed and owned by communities themselves.

Speaking at the regional consultation in Portland on 15 June 1994, I said:

In a very real way, our efforts at national development are going to be judged by the impact we make on national culture. The word culture I use here in the widest sense to imply all the means by which we as a people express ourselves.

Increasingly, for large numbers of our young people sports and popular music are seen as not only leisure-time activities but opportunities for bettering themselves economically and socially.

In both areas, taking into account our size and population, Jamaica's impact on the world has been nothing short of phenomenal.

As the last Olympics came to an end, Juliet Cuthbert and Winthrop Graham had joined Merlene Ottey at the very pinnacle of international athletic success.

Even years after his death, we are still being reminded that Bob Marley is the best known Jamaican of all times and Jimmy Cliff is not far behind.

It is in these two areas that the energies of our young people are being increasingly deployed. And so we must create the framework to allow for a disciplined and structured development which brings out the best in us.

All those references were made before Usain Bolt had earned global recognition as a track superstar.

The government was committed to a major initiative in the cultural sphere, beginning with empowering the Cultural Training Centre to broaden its range of training programmes. Specialists and large numbers of cultural agents were recruited to nurture and develop the vast talent in the visual and performing arts. The School of Art, Drama, Music and Dance started courses that took into account the special needs of performers and part-time artistes.

The Cultural Development Commission was directed to specialize in designing and staging competitions and bringing the work of our young artistes to the attention of the entire society.

This would nurture Jamaica's cultural riches and complement the thriving tourist industry, and in so doing expose every citizen of Jamaica and every visitor to the best of our cultural efforts.

In 1995, we repositioned the Social Development Commission as a primary institution through which the state would intervene in the community.

Poverty, which often led to a lack of cohesion at the community level, resulted from time to time in explosive situations, particularly in overcrowded and depressed communities. The commission, chaired by Garnet Roper, was to organize state intervention to prevent different state agencies acting without proper coordination. It had to prepare the community for the intervention and, further, make sure the community got value for money. The years 1995 to 2000 witnessed a marked surge by the Social Development Commission in moving community and social development forward. Commission officers became an important link between community development on the one hand and local-government reform on the other.

Portmore is the best example of an infrastructure in which these two processes merged. Many middle managers, civil servants and police went to live there. Out of this grew the desire for the population to have a direct say in the development of their community. We needed to find a mechanism to give them that say. The Social Development Commission developed committees to build a relationship between them and the local authority, which in turn fuelled the need and desire for autonomy. The community wanted to take ownership, and under the leadership of Mayor George Lee; Arnold Bertram, minister of local government, and his team; community activists; and a host of non-governmental organizations, Portmore became a municipality. That happened because of a responsive state and exemplified a mechanism suitable for transfer to other towns. The Social Development Commission anchored much of this activity.

Owing to a population bulge, there were some 250,000 young people who had left school but who were not working. An immediate obligation of the Social Development Commission was not just to reorganize the process of community development, but also urgently to develop mechanisms to mitigate this group's social dysfunctionality.

There were three programmes aimed at them: the Youth Empowerment Programme, the Special Employment Programme and the National Youth Service.

The Youth Empowerment Programme was intended to encourage small-scale entrepreneurship through training – this was basic skills training, below the Human Employment and Resource Training Trust threshold of community-based skills training. The Special Training Employment Programme targeted the sixteen-to-twenty-four age group. The National Youth Service was relaunched as a statutory body so that it could never again be scrapped by ministerial fiat. It was designed to tackle the problems of poverty and unattachment, and the hope was to increase the total numbers to close to ten thousand a year, but it has never gone beyond four thousand. The Summer Employment Programme was developed to spread its impact. It started with J$1 million and moved to J$50 million a year under my watch, when it employed six thousand young people. It had a precipitatory effect on attitudes.

We also began a programme to develop the values and attitudes of those young people who did not come into the National Youth Service, called Jamaica Values and Attitudes. It brought social development policy close to economic development, which ensured its success, because we found out what the market required, then found the required young people and gave them the necessary training. That increased the chances for recruits to move from a social intervention to sustained employment and career development.

MUSIC

In music, as in sports, Jamaica is a first-world nation. Much of our music was inspired by the teachings of Marcus Garvey. The Rastafarian movement has also been a dominant influence in the evolution and wealth of Jamaican music. Jamaicans, with their binding affection for the rhythms of Africa, saw the first signs of their music on the international stage through mento songs.

As it was the Jamaican Boukman who helped to instigate the Haitian Revolution, so did the Skatalites give birth and identity to our popular music. A band which lasted no more than eighteen months backed Delroy Wilson, Bob Marley and the Wailers, Phyllis Dillon, Stranger Cole, Toots and the Maytals, Justin Hines and Doreen Schaffer.

Ska engaged the imagination of the working poor and unemployed proletariat; it inspired the hope and aspiration that came with our independence and spawned the modern sounds of rock steady and reggae, authentic musical genres through which Jamaicans have expressed their freedom and identity.

As a nation, we had barely scratched the surface of its economic potential. But I was steadfast in the view that while we had to work assiduously to maximize the economic returns from our music, we should never lose sight of its value to the psychological well-being of our people at home and abroad. With a society in desperate need of healing, there is no greater balm in Gilead than that which our cultural remedies, and particularly our music, can provide.

Self-discovery involves paying attention to the history of music-making, giving greater prominence to innovators in the industry such as Derrick Morgan and Prince Buster, the impact of the music of resistance on our social, religious and political evolution, the breakthrough into international markets long before Bob Marley – all of which tell a story of perseverance, confidence, faith, energy and risk-taking.

If we could find ways of sharing with the widest possible audience the relevant research into the history of Jamaican music, be it in the folk genre and the legacy of Olive Lewin, the talent exposure made possible from the days of Vere Johns's *Opportunity Knocks* through to numerous contests to find rising stars, the technological creativity of a Coxsone Dodd, the expertise of Duke Reid in marketing our composers and performers – if we could expose the broader society to this history, our attitude to ourselves and our willingness and ability to succeed could be dramatically enhanced.

SPORTS DEVELOPMENT

Sport has been a critical component of nation-building. Athletes such as Herb McKenley, Arthur Wint, George Rhoden, Les Laing and Dennis Johnson were among those who, during the 1940s and 1950s, first put Jamaica on the international sporting stage. Batsman George Headley was an immortal in the world of cricket, and Lindy Delapenha played football at the highest level.

In later years, the likes of Lennox "Billy" Miller, Donald Quarrie, Merlene Ottey and Deon Hemmings and current world-beaters such as Veronica Campbell-Brown, Usain Bolt, Asafa Powell and Shelly-Ann Fraser-Pryce have led to Jamaica being classed as the sprint capital of the world.

Not to be outdone are Michael McCallum in boxing, David Weller in cycling, Michael Holding, Lawrence Rowe and Courtney Walsh in cricket, Alan Cole, Syd Bartlett and Bibi Gardner in football, and our current swimming champion, Alia Atkinson, along with our netball teams. They have all made Jamaica a force to be reckoned with in the international arena.

The primary objective of sports policies and projects was always to develop the talent of the Jamaican people and enhance community development.

It was with this in mind that the national stadium was built in 1962. Today, it remains the centrepiece of the country's sporting programme, although since then, several additional complexes have housed indoor and outdoor sports.

Among the most beneficial moves was building the G.C. Foster College of Physical Education and Sport, which was opened in 1980, with the assistance of the Cuban government. The college has produced coaches who have worked at every level across Jamaica to help our younger generation to realize their full potential. Training quality coaches has led to significant improvement in the skills and personal development of participants and resulted in far more vibrant sporting competitions at the primary, secondary, tertiary, community and national levels. Perhaps the epitome of the qualitative impact of these coaches is the deep reservoir of talent on display at the yearly Boys and Girls Track and Field Championship, popularly known as "Champs".

Jamaica, like most developing countries, has always had a challenge when it comes to finding the resources to advance the interest of sports, so the Sports Development Foundation was established in 1995. The foundation received government revenue under a licence granted, in the first instance, to the Jamaica Lottery Company, and thereafter to Supreme Ventures Limited. Agreed amounts paid by the lottery group would be listed as a tax, and this tax was paid to the Sports Development Foundation, and now to the Culture, Health, Arts, Sports and Education Fund (CHASE) created in 2002.

By this means funds are allocated annually to national sporting organizations and are also used towards building and refurbishing sports facilities across the country, as well as helping many athletes.

Funds from the Sports Development Foundation assisted greatly with financing Jamaica's "Road to France" when the country qualified for the football World Cup in 1998; hosting the Cricket World Cup in 2007; a number of international netball competitions we have hosted; and the annual Jamaica International Invitational Athletic Meet, which is now listed on the international track and field calendar.

Our conquests on the Road to France, more than any other single achievement in sports, renewed the confidence of our own people in their possibilities. The emergence of order, discipline and success in an activity previously known for unacceptable levels of antisocial behaviour, served to unite and carry the nation forward and upward.

In order to advance sports, I formed the National Sports Council, chaired by the prime minister and consisting of representatives from sports bodies and other sectors. It was to act as a coordinating and advisory body in developing a national consensus on sports and ensuring the coordination and proper monitoring of sports by the different arms of government. No matter where she went, the responsibility for sports remained with Portia Simpson-Miller.

The country's non-partisan approach to sports development has led to a considerable reduction in tension in a number of communities previously divided along partisan lines. One classic example is the role played by sports in Western Kingston and South St Andrew, in which Tivoli Gardens and Arnett Gardens are located. The existence of up-to-date sports complexes in both areas, where major competitions can be held, was critical in bringing the communities together, and by extension suppressing, if not eradicating, hostilities between them.

The performance of our athletes and players over the years, both nationally and internationally, has left Jamaica with a rich legacy. Numerous programmes, policies and projects have enhanced it. Our country must keep sports as a jewel in our crown.

P.J. Patterson, candidate for the presidency of the PNP and the position of prime minister of Jamaica, acknowledges the cheers of supporters at the official launch of his campaign at the PNP headquarters in Kingston, 17 March 1992. © The Gleaner Co. (Media) Ltd

Former prime minister Michael Manley embraces his successor, P.J Patterson, at his swearing-in ceremony at King's House, Jamaica, 30 March 1992. © The Gleaner Co. (Media) Ltd

Prime Minister Patterson (*centre front row*) with his cabinet at his swearing in ceremony, 30 March 1992. *Front row, left to right:* Carlyle Dunkley, Easton Douglas, Peter Phillips, Portia Simpson, Seymour Mullings, Paul Robertson, David Coore, Desmond Leaky; *second row, left to right:* Carl Rattray, Burchell Whiteman, O.D. Ramtallie, John Junor, K.D. Knight, Robert Pickersgill; *back row:* Hugh Small. (Jamaica Information Service)

Prime Minister Patterson (*right*) with (*from left*) former prime ministers Hugh Shearer and Michael Manley at the rededication of the statue of national hero Norman Manley, St William Grant Park, Kingston, 27 October 1994. © The Gleaner Co. (Media) Ltd

Prime Minister Patterson addressing the fifth regional consultation on the Values and Attitudes Campaign, Holiday Inn Hotel, Montego Bay, Jamaica, 29 June 1994. © The Gleaner Co. (Media) Ltd

Prime Minister Patterson celebrates his sixtieth birthday in 1995 with Prime Minister Patrick Manning of Trinidad and Tobago (*left*) and artist Barrington Watson (*right*). (Jamaica Information Service)

Governor General Sir Howard Cooke (*right*) and Prime Minister Patterson welcome the president of Ghana, Flight Lieutenant Jerry John Rawlings (*left*), on his visit to Jamaica in 1997. © The Gleaner Co. (Media) Ltd

CARICOM Heads of Government Conference at Rose Hall, Montego Bay, 1997. *Seated, from left:* Hubert Ingram, Lester Bird, P.J. Patterson, Edwin Carringson, Keith Mitchell, Denzil Douglas; *standing, from left:* Derek Taylor, Basdeo Panday, Manuel Esquivel, Ralph O'Neil, Edison James, Jules Wjendbosch, James Mitchell, Kenny Anthony, Hubert Hughes, Sam Hinds and Owen Arthur. (Patterson collection)

Prime Minister Patterson at the 1999 G15 conference in Jamaica. *From left:* President Robert Mugabe (Zimbabwe); Amr Moussa (Egypt); Prime Minister Mahathir Mohammed (Malaysia) and General Abdulsalami Aboubakar (Nigeria). (Patterson collection)

President Thabo Mbeki of South Africa greets Prime Minister Patterson at the 1999 Common-wealth Heads of Government Conference in Durban. (Patterson collection)

Prime Minister Patterson with Prime Minister Jean Chrétien of Canada, 2001.
(Patterson collection)

Prime Minister Patterson hosts HRH Queen Elizabeth II and Prince Phillip on their February 2002 visit to Jamaica. (Jamaica Information Service)

Triumphant Prime Minister Patterson escorted into party headquarters after the 2002 elections, his fourth victory. (Jamaica Information Service)

P.J. Patterson at his fourth swearing-in ceremony as prime minister in 2002. Officiating is Governor General Sir Howard Cooke. © The Gleaner Co. (Media) Ltd

Prime Minister Patterson is introduced to the Jamaican national football team, the Reggae Boyz, by captain Warren Barrett in 1997. © The Gleaner Co. (Media) Ltd

Prime Minister Patterson with farmers at the annual Denbigh Agricultural Show in 2003. (Jamaica Information Service)

Prime Minister Patterson with cultural icon Louise Bennett-Coverley (Miss Lou) in 2003. (Jamaica Information Service)

Prime Minister Patterson at the launch of the Bicentenary of the Abolition of Slavery. *At left:* Andrew Holness, Verene Shepherd; *second from right and far right*: Maxine Henry-Wilson, Rex Nettleford. (Jamaica Information Service)

Prime Minister Patterson greets children on his tour of schools on Read Across Jamaica Day 2005. (Jamaica Information Service)

Prime Minister Patterson interacting with children on his tour of schools on Read Across Jamaica Day 2005. (Jamaica Information Service)

Prime Minister Patterson opens Highway 2000 on 3 October 2003. (Patterson collection)

Prime Minister Patterson on the road with the Lift Up Jamaica programme. (Jamaica Information Service)

Prime Minister Patterson and musician Ernie Ranglin, March 2005. (Jamaican Information Service)

Prime Minister Patterson receives a CD from band members of Third World Stephen "Cat" Coore (*centre*) and Richard "Richie" Daley (*left*), August 2005. (Jamaica Information Service)

Prime Minister Patterson hosts a reception for staff and students of his alma mater, Calabar High School, May 2005. (Jamaica Information Service)

Prime Minister Patterson hosts a reception for the president of Ghana, John Kufuor, July 2005. (Jamaica Information Service)

Celebrating a historic bipartisan occasion as Tivoli prepares to play Arnett Gardens, for the first time, at Arnett Gardens Football Field. *From left:* former prime minister Edward Seaga; Arnett Gardens member of Parliament Omar Davies; Prime Minister Patterson; and the minister of sports, Portia Simpson-Miller. © Headley "Delmar" Samuels

Prime Minister Patterson with President Ricardo Lagos of Chile, July 2004. (Patterson collection)

Prime Minister Patterson rings the opening bell at the New York Stock Exchange, 3 June 2005. (Patterson collection)

Prime Minister Patterson, accompanied by Premier Wen Jiabao, inspecting the guards at Tiananmen Square, Beijing, as part of his visit to China in 2005. (Patterson collection)

Prime Minister Patterson celebrates his induction to chieftaincy with Lady Cherry and Sir Chief Gabriel Osawaru Igbinedion in Benin, Nigeria.

Prime Minister Patterson with President Hugo Chávez of Venezuela (*left*) and President Fidel Castro of Cuba (*right*), in Jamaica, June 2005, for the signing of the PetroCaribe Agreement. (Jamaica Information Service)

Prime Minister Patterson giving his farewell address in Parliament, March 2006. © The Gleaner Co. (Media) Ltd

CHAPTER 38

PARLIAMENT AND THE
SEARCH FOR CONSENSUS

THE PRESENT GENERATION IS HARDLY AWARE THAT ALEXANDER Bustamante was a member of the PNP when it was founded and that while he was incarcerated at the army base at Up Park Camp during the Second World War, it was PNP stalwarts like "Crab" Nethersole, Ken Sterling, Winston Grubb, Thossy Kelly, Osmond Dyer, Florizel Glasspole and the 4Hs – Richard Hart, Frank Hill, Ken Hill and Arthur Henry – who ran the Bustamante Industrial Trade Union. We should recall that between 1938 and 1943 we had one major political party, the PNP, and one major trade union, the Bustamante Industrial Trade Union, working for a common cause on behalf of the Jamaican people.

By the time of the first elections after universal adult suffrage, in 1944, the undisputed labour leader, Bustamante, had formed the JLP, and the PNP had the Trade Union Congress as its union arm. That was the genesis of our two political parties, which since then have dominated the political landscape and served as the foundation pillars of our democracy,

The assertion at my inaugural installation as prime minister, "A nation divided against itself cannot stand", was a recognition that there are times when we must strive to forge a unity of purpose for the national good, and hence my emphasis has always been on consensus-building. To those who equate that with weak leadership, I say simply: you could not be more mistaken.

Analysts may differ on the indicators and levels of national unity. But history will show we have never advanced as a people without a common front, whether in the fight against slavery or the fight for every adult to have the franchise.

As I accepted my own mandate from the people to pursue a historic journey, a memorable first for me and my kind, I observed at the swearing-in ceremony at King's House in December 1993:

In the aftermath of a sweeping electoral victory, one must take special care to avoid being intoxicated by the heady wine of success. Real power comes only from the Almighty; political power can stem only from the people. It will vanish like midnight sun if used to puff up personal glory. Power has true meaning and will only last when it is used for the people and to serve their real needs.

Democracy is a precious but extremely fragile plant. It must be properly bred and carefully nurtured and must be based always on popular consent. The will of the majority must prevail without the fear of tyranny to those who constitute a minority. In turn, the minority is entitled to maintain and seek to advance its views and positions, but in a way that does not impede the progress of the nation or engender social turmoil and conflict.

During the 1950s, political violence was largely manifested in the use of sticks and stones. In the 1960s, guns in factional conflicts became a new feature. In the wake of the 1980 escalation of political violence to fight ideological holy wars, some significant steps were taken before the elections of 1989 to pull back from the precipice. In 1988 the leaders of the two parties signed a peace agreement, which included a code of ethics to be honoured by their candidates and campaign teams. An ombudsman for political affairs was appointed to investigate complaints of breaches of the agreement. Any candidate found guilty would be withdrawn from the campaign.

In the report of the National Committee on Political Tribalism (23 July 1997), that tribalism was defined as "having to demonstrate unswerving support for a particular party or persons within the tribal area or suffer the consequences; the use of violence in political activities, the creation of political garrisons . . . nurtured and nourished as strategic initiatives to secure or retain political power; the development of the garrison within constituencies which have evolved from the same process of partisan scarce benefit distribution".

The creation of garrison communities was due to the state's developing large-scale housing schemes and the allocation of houses to supporters of the party in power. This led to the communities with homogenous political allegiances and the expulsion of anyone with divergent views. The report asserted that in 1993 there were eight "unambiguously" garrisoned constituencies. The practice of electoral manipulation – bogus voting, electoral rigging and homogenous voting – is said to be central to the garrison phenomenon.

For reasons best known to them and yet to be disclosed, the opposition refused to sign the final report. It is worthy of note, however, that they accepted several of the recommendations embodied in subsequent reforms of the electoral system and the powers conferred on the political ombudsman by a new code of conduct.

The PNP, in accepting the report, set up its own process for vetting candidates to eliminate people with questionable backgrounds and connections.

For its part, the government introduced a number of changes in allotting benefits and providing services to discourage garrisons and tribalism. Land-divestment committees were formed to encourage a fair and non-partisan system of land allocation. The NHT and other housing agencies were tasked with allocating houses so as to prevent selection based on party affiliation. "One man, one vote" was the only way to ensure that confidence in our democracy would be maintained and to erode the urge to build or maintain garrisons for political supremacy.

The Electoral Advisory Committee was established in 1979 to reduce the risk of politically inspired abuse by the party forming the government, since elections were managed by a government department. Reflection on earlier history, however, revealed that an advisory committee did not guarantee transparency and engender bipartisan or national trust and confidence in the electoral process.

It had become clear to me that we could not, as a young nation, continue the social and human haemorrhage resulting from political tribalism. The year 1980 remains a disturbing memory of how close we came to social disintegration. The number of deaths related to political conflicts became a permanent scar on our national records. If our democracy and our treasured reputation for tolerance and hospitality were not to be severely damaged, that had to change.

Between 1995 and 2005, we took steps to deal with that deficiency. Legislation was introduced to improve the system itself, including the registration of electors, the verification process and the timely generation of voters' lists.

The most fundamental change, however, was in the composition of the oversight body, which in 2006 was to become the Electoral Commission and which by then, chaired by Errol Miller, had established for itself and for Jamaica a reputation for excellence worthy of international emulation. It was structured so that nominated party representatives would always be in a minority and the selected members, people of eminence and high respect, in the majority.

That system has served us well and I have no doubt will continue to do so. The commission generates recommendations for ongoing modification of policies and practices. Its work and status have been enhanced by the convention that the proposals it makes to Parliament are generally accepted and approved without amendment.

In 2002, a fingerprint identification system was introduced to allow cross-matching of priority in some constituencies on election day. An authority was created under the umbrella of the Electoral Commission which was empowered to halt elections or order reruns where massive violations occurred.

I am obliged to point out, however, that while internal structural and systemic changes have been necessary and have proved their worth, it was also important to change the political culture on the ground. I have always been profoundly aware that democracy, political engagement and development – social and economic – are inextricably linked. The quality of political behaviour affects the extent to which the people trust the process and, consequently, accept their individual and collective responsibility, and their involvement in development – as citizens, workers and producers of goods and services. There was little virtue in inciting or encouraging a divisive and disabling tribalism which would weaken the social fabric or, worse, return us to the situation of 1980, when Jamaica was seen by some as being on the brink of civil war.

I made it a point to encourage effective political organization within the PNP and civility in public and private conduct in dealing with everyone, including the most aggressive and hostile political opponents. In the election campaigns of 1993, 1997 and 2002, there were situations in which the public offensiveness of some opponents reached a disturbing level. But, through it all, I held to my position, and ensured that my team members did likewise. It was not easy, but it was a non-negotiable element of shaping a Jamaica which put the nation first.

By the time of the elections of 2002 and 2007, we had supporters in green and orange mixing together, holding hands and making merry on nomination day. This represented a significant change in the political culture. It is possible for us to change behaviours. It is possible for us to show respect to those who hold views different from our own. It is possible for us to engage with the better angels of our nature.

But we have to take the steps to change the mindset of our people, particularly the young and the working population. The approach has to begin with, as I once said, looking at "the man in the mirror". I certainly did, and I have no regrets.

My own early experiences left me convinced that my concern with and promotion of wholesome values, coupled with education, with human development in its broadest sense, made possible whatever else I was able to accomplish in the political arena. Even the critics concede that these elements have made a most meaningful contribution to building the nation and shaping a stronger and more enlightened Jamaica.

Mine has always been an inclusive and consensual style of leadership. It has often been misconstrued as indecision, but rather it reflects a personal aversion to confrontation. Every leader possesses their own habits and idiosyncrasies. Good personal interrelationships, while helpful, are not all that count. There must be a mutual willingness to find common ground when it matters most and foster that civility and respect which can be transmitted through the ranks.

PARLIAMENT

My fascination with Parliament began when I was attending primary school in Somerton. I was an avid reader of any material available – the Bible, Hardy Boys novels, comic books, Louise Bennett poems, novels. Every page of the only daily newspaper, the *Gleaner*, was eagerly devoured, including the columns of *Hansard* which were published in full at each meeting of the legislature. From then one could discern whose presentations were masterly, and learn about the cut and thrust of exchanges and rulings of the Speaker in accordance with standing orders.

During my period of political apprenticeship between the University College of the West Indies and the London School of Economics, I was in frequent attendance at Headquarters House as Norman Manley and Alexander Bustamante, with their marked differences of style in presentation, engaged in exchanges which ranged from fiery and vitriolic to affectionate and humorous. Donald Sangster and Florizel Glasspole were the agile models of parliamentary strategy and control for students of the craft.

My short stint as leader of opposition business in the Senate from 1968 to 1970 exposed me to the adept skills of Neville Ashenheim, who, as the leader of government business, piloted through the upper chamber one complex bill after another.

When I entered the House of Representatives in 1970, our opposition second bench needed the aggression of Winston Jones, Sydney Pagon, Ernest Peart and Noel Silvera to counter the ministerial heavyweights of Wilton Hill, Herbie Eldemire, Edwin Allen and J.P. Gyles, who sought to score massive political points at every stage of parliamentary conduct.

Every historian of the Westminster tradition can cite examples of prime ministers and cabinet ministers who recognize the essential functions of their legislature, but yet regard it somewhat of an unavoidable nuisance and resent the tedium of having to indulge in what they regard as dull, uninformed or obstructionist contributions from the other side. I belong to that other group of people who are excited by the prospect of a vigorous debate, the thrust and parry in the exchange of contending ideas, the planning and execution of delicate parliamentary manoeuvres.

The courts and Parliament are distinct theatres but for both arenas thorough preparation is key. Whether it is the evidence for the court or the supporting material for parliamentary debate, the presenter must be in full command of the basic grounds, supporting grounds and relevant precedents to counter any agreement to the contrary in convincing fashion. Faced with parliamentary sharpshooters on the opposition bench, such as Edward Seaga, Bruce Golding, Audley Shaw and Karl Samuda, I insisted that my colleague ministers prepare themselves thoroughly for every bill or resolution before us, but there were always occasions when one had to pad up for keeping things on the right track.

Parliament is no Sunday school, but everyone on my side knew that I would not tolerate the kind of vitriolic abuse or loss of personal control which would bring Parliament into contempt. A short and timely adjournment of the House often served to cool tempers when things were getting too hot on the floor and a visit to the canteen downstairs could help to restore order.

I benefited from two distinct advantages: we enjoyed a comfortable majority which fell to a low of eight between 2002 and 2006 and gave us a cushion. While regularly insisting on good attendance, we were never in doubt of losing any crucial vote except when a two-thirds majority was stipulated by the constitution. We had to work harder in securing a quorum for meetings of standing committees and select committees which were created to deal with bills that required wider consultation with particular interest groups.

Another advantage was that I had not served in the legislature during our years in opposition (1980–89). There was therefore no position or statement from me in the Senate or House that I would have to retract or seek to distinguish. That allowed me the luxury of enunciating bold new policies and projects without the risk of being individually vulnerable to opposition attacks for inconsistency.

My professor of constitutional law at the London School of Economics, S.A. de Smith, had exposed those of his students who displayed an interest in the intricacies of an unwritten constitution to the details and nuances of Erskine May's *Parliamentary Practice*. I was delighted to rely on that tutoring when it became necessary to write an open letter on 8 October 2015 to the British prime minister, David Cameron, for his abuse of parliamentary privilege as he addressed a joint sitting of our legislature on 30 September 2015, and threw down the gauntlet on the reparation issue when our parliamentarians had no right of reply.

Dear Prime Minister Cameron,

We who belong to the Commonwealth Parliamentary Association and cherish the value of the Westminster tradition should seek continually to foster rather than diminish it.

Given the honour which you were afforded to address the Joint Sitting of Jamaica's Parliament on Tuesday, September 30, 2015, the traditional Parliamentary right of debate and reply could not be exercised by any of our Members who were in attendance. As I watched your presentation, knowing them on both sides of the aisle as I do, their good behaviour which you commended ought not to be interpreted as acquiescence in everything you said.

The gifts you presented in Gordon House were both welcome and timely. Only the shrewdest observers of Parliamentary custom would have noticed that the package you offered there discreetly omitted any mention of a £25 million contribution for the building of a prison.

That was understandable, as what exists constitutes no more than a Non-binding Memorandum of Understanding. You rightfully appreciated that its inclusion would have been premature as the framework Agreement has to be followed by further intensive negotiations and then the requisite legislation.

You wisely chose instead to add there the announcement of £30 million to make our hospitals more resilient to natural disasters. Given our vulnerability and the danger of climate change, this donation was highly appreciated.

Despite your recognition of not being "the only show in town", the words of strengthening the bonds of friendship and the down-payment you brought would have been well received throughout the entire Caribbean.

Prime Minister, the most noble intentions were jarred by those portions of your address which asserted that slavery was a long time ago, in the historical past and "as friends we can move on together to build for the future".

Your host, The Most Hon. Portia Simpson-Miller, in her gracious welcome referred to the difficult issue of reparation which should be discussed in "a spirit of mutual respect, openness and understanding as we seek to actively engage the U.K. on the matter".

You chose instead to throw down the gauntlet.

Mere acknowledgement of its horror will not suffice. It was and still is a most heinous crime against humanity – a stain which cannot be removed merely by the passage of time.

Those who perished in the Middle Passage and the fatal victims on the sugar plantations were the victims of *genocide*. This is a crime in accordance with International Law.

The attempt to trivialize and diminish the significance of 300 years of British enslavement of Africans and the trade in their bodies reflects the continued ethnic targeting of our ancestors and their progeny for discriminatory treatment in both the annals of history and in the present.

The 180 years of slavery in Jamaica remain fresh in living memory. There are people alive in Jamaica today whose great-grandparents were a part of the slavery system and the memory of slavery still lingers in these households and communities.

Those 180 years were followed by another 100 years of imposed racial apartheid in which these families were racially oppressed by British armies and colonial machinery. The scars of this oppression are still alive in the minds and hearts of millions of Jamaicans.

To speak of slavery as something from the Middle Ages is insufficient. For our communities its legacies are still present in their memory and emotions. To reject this living experience is to repudiate the very meaning and existence of these people's lives.

How can we simply forget it and move on to the future? If there is no explicit admission of guilt now, when will be the proper time?

You argue that Britain abolished the slave system and the credit for this resonates in the British Parliament today and shows British compassion and diplomacy.

Where is the prior confession that Britain fashioned, legalized, perpetuated and prospered from the slave trade?

Indeed, the facts speak to a different explanation. In Jamaica the enslaved led by Sam Sharpe tried to abolish slavery themselves three years before your Parliament acted. The British army destroyed these freedom fighters and executed their leaders.

This attempt to destroy the seed of freedom and justice in Jamaica continued for another hundred years. In 1865 the peasants sought to occupy Crown lands in order to survive widespread hunger. The British government sent in the army and massacred those people, executing Paul Bogle, George William Gordon and other leaders.

Furthermore, the British Act of Emancipation reflected that the enslaved people of Jamaica were not human but property. The 800,000 Africans in the Caribbean and elsewhere were valued at £47 million. The government agreed to compensate the slave owners £20 million, and passed an Emancipation Act in which the enslaved had to work free for another four to six years in order to work off the £27 million promised slave owners. It was they who paid for their eventual freedom.

The enslaved paid more than 50 per cent of the cost of their market value in compensation to slave owners. This is what your Emancipation Act did. The enslaved got nothing by way of compensation. The Act of Emancipation was self-serving and was designed to support British national commercial interests alone.

You have refused to apologize. Yet your Government has apologized to everyone else for horrid crimes. Are we not worthy of an apology or less deserving?

Mere acknowledgment of the crime is insufficient. The international community and international law call for formal apologies when crimes against humanity are committed. The UN has deemed slave trading and slavery as crimes against humanity. The refusal to apologize is a refusal to take responsibility for the crime. *In a law-abiding world this is not acceptable.*

Recently you urged your own nation to keep the memory of the Jewish experience alive in memorials and education curricula. We urge you to do the same for the black experience which remains before us all. It is precisely because we all want to move on that the reparatory justice movement is alive and growing. We all want to move on, but with justice and equality.

Contrary to your view, the Caribbean people will never emerge completely from the "long, dark shadow" of slavery until there is a full confession of guilt by those who committed this evil atrocity.

"The resilience and spirit of its people" is no ground to impair the solemnity of a privileged parliamentary occasion and allow the memory of our ancestors to be offended once again.

The Caribbean people have long been looking to the future. This is what we do in our development visions, but these legacies are like millstones around our necks. We look to reparatory justice as the beginning of shaping a new future. We invite Britain to engage in removing this blot on human civilization so that together we can create a new and secure future.

ONE LOVE.

Yours sincerely,
P. J. Patterson
Former Prime Minister,
Jamaica (1992–2006)

DEALING WITH THE OPPOSITION

In 1992, the pundits were predicting that Edward Seaga would chew me up at the polls. Our first one-to-one meeting at Vale Royal, one week after my installation, got off to a rocky start, but I knew it was crucial to promote mutual respect for our separate constitutional exercise by building an acceptable working relationship.

I had to be patient but steadfast in preparing the ground which would initiate a series of meetings between Seaga and the leading members of our teams. His eventual willingness to participate made it possible to address issues of national importance and matters which could spark political explosions in an atmosphere of calm discussion and a spirit of give and take to find the best solution. We were able to reach consensus on several areas where the constitution required consultation between the prime minister and leader of the opposition; to find a formula which ensured fair distribution of work; and to create party working groups in several areas needing reform or urgent action.

I bolstered the practice of inviting representatives of the opposition to be part of Jamaica's delegations on historic international occasions, for example the fiftieth anniversary of the United Nations, the inauguration of President Nelson Mandela in South Africa, or the 1998 World Cup in France.

After the ceremonial opening of Parliament and the throne speech, political representatives from both sides of the Senate and House were invited to a lunch at Vale Royal, where for a time we could greet each other as colleagues and avoid partisan rancour.

The PNP was founded on the principles of social cohesion, individual responsibility, integrity in public life and the commitment to foster a nationalist spirit. In an era of technology and the cry of citizens for a new governing order, we set out to build a participatory democracy that would see more meaningful involvement through dialogue. To develop that framework and build a more inclusive society, in 2005 the cabinet promulgated a consultation code of practice for the public sector. The code stipulated new rules of engagement between the government, the technocrats and the Jamaican people.

The code laid down how stakeholders would be enabled to participate in consultation on proposals that were presented in a clear, concise form made widely accessible, and how their feedback would result in the best practices for developing projects and proposals. While the code was never binding in law, it was accepted as compulsory for all government ministries and agencies. It has served as a tool to enable all Jamaicans to enjoy a quality of life that is just, inclusive and for which our authorities are accountable.

CHAPTER 39

FORGING MY PATH

BEFORE OUR VICTORY IN 1997, NO JAMAICAN POLITICAL party had ever won a third successive term in government. The pattern from 1944 to then had been two terms for the JLP, followed by the next two terms for the PNP. No party leader had ever taken the oath of office as premier or prime minister on three consecutive occasions.

Breaking those barriers in 1997 was no walk in the park, but as my administration approached the end of its preceding five-year term, I spoke with confidence as we prepared for the term ahead. In my budget presentation on 22 April 1997, I tried to resist the temptation of election giveaways and gimmickry because: "We have a record of performance on which we are proud to be judged."

Those critics who regard it as a sin or crime to win elections fail to realize or accept that no matter the propaganda, the electorate will not return a government that has failed to deliver. In every election campaign we were able to report on programmes that increased access to roads, potable water and electricity; a motor-vehicle policy that relieved daily frustration and indignation; a scheme to provide houses; and vast improvements that new technology provided to enhance communication and the flow of knowledge.

It is impossible to win without achievements, but it is possible to lose despite them. My early exposure in the field had instilled in me the conviction that a party that is not well organized can suffer a humiliating defeat despite worthwhile achievements. During periods in government, the needs of the party are often overlooked with grave consequences. If the party machinery does not get the proper and constant lubrication it needs, it will be unable to respond efficiently when elections are imminent. I sought to have policy positions settled in accordance with the traditions of vigorous internal debate and dissemination at the grassroots level.

I was resolute that the disunity of the party in 1980 should never recur, and devoted a lot of my time and attention, usually quietly so, to promoting that interpersonal relationship which is epitomized in the word "comrade". Elections are never won by a divided party. I spent many hours as president of the party resolving differing viewpoints and ensuring that conflicts of personality never caused disruption in the party or government.

From the outset, the path to be taken, the policies to be pursued, had to accommodate changing realities without abandoning the principles first enunciated by Norman Manley and pursued under the democratic socialism of Michael Manley. At their core was putting people first.

I often reminded the National Executive Council of the party's obligation to remain the catalyst for progressive change: we have to lead, not simply react. Party groups should be reenergized so that the PNP, as part of its national focus, articulated the interests of the community, of which it forms a part. We needed to provide the leadership the nation needed to restore a sense of decency and national purpose in everything we seek to do.

Much has been written and said about both my personal and leadership style. I do not mind entering a room without causing a stir or drawing attention – what has always seemed more important to me is the impression you have made by the time you leave.

I like to mingle with the crowd. In February 1998, when a test match between England and the West Indies was abandoned because of the poor state of the wicket at Sabina Park, I threw a party on the lawns of Jamaica House to which all visitors to the match were invited. I escaped from my security team and was strolling around when an elderly Jamaican lady said, "I recognize your face. Weren't you the person sitting beside me on the minibus to Ocho Rios?" Her daughter blushed. "Oh no, Mother. That's the prime minister!" When she tried to apologize I simply hugged her and told both of them there was no need for it, or to feel embarrassed.

My style of public speaking changed dramatically when I first took the oath of office as a minister in 1972. I became much more careful and deliberate in my choice of words than in legal practice, because any slip can be maliciously distorted. Once the word is uttered, it cannot be recalled.

In 1988, I had appeared in the Court of Appeal for my plumber, Derryck Latty. When he was arrested and taken to premises he purportedly controlled and shown bags of marijuana, he refused to make any comment after being duly cautioned. The resident magistrate in the Half Way Tree Court found him guilty on the basis that his failure to deny knowledge or ownership of the substance was an admission of guilt. The Court of Appeal upheld my submission that his silence could not be so construed. Hence my often-quoted adage, "Silence cannot be misquoted."

As prime minister, one is never free to advance a personal view on any issue of importance and must avoid commenting on policy which is yet to be decided. Despite the constant pressures, one should also resist the temptation to speak before all the required information has been gathered and assessed.

No one is infallible. If you make a mistake, it is better to be the first to admit it. Ministers are entitled to claim credit for outstanding success in the discharge of their responsibilities, although, invariably, it could not have been done without the full support and often substantial involvement of the prime minister. You cannot seek to capture all the glory. Ministers will also make mistakes, but there are different categories of mistakes. Harsh penalties must be applied where the error is egregious or the motive dishonest.

Whether in cabinet or party executive, my habit was to allow all members to express their views freely, provided this was done with civility. There was no room for rancour or personal abuse, as that would impair collegiality. The goal was to build consensus, within the party and the nation.

In order to encourage sustained growth and spur social renewal, we sought to accelerate our political culture away from confrontation to consultation, from divisiveness to unity, from dependency to self-reliance. Our students were doing better because of our education reforms. Our new telecommunication advances were already showing good prospects for future development. We were passing through the final stages of economic reform and attracting welcome foreign capital for investment, especially in tourism and infrastructure.

No one knew better than I how difficult it would be to set another first: a fourth term for the party and a third term of my own. The political gurus, columnists and pollsters said it was impossible.

The JLP was in desperate need of electoral success. They were buoyant when the Stone polls of November 2000 reflected 44 per cent support for them and 38 per cent for the PNP. The situation worsened for us when, in March 2001, we lost the constituency of North East St Ann to the JLP, which fought the campaign as though the survival of its leader, Edward Seaga, and the party itself depended on it. As was the case when the PNP lost the federal elections in 1958, it did not take us long to identify the only option – the party must get back on the ground, and the government must improve and deliver those programmes which could yield most relief and benefit for the people.

I had to do a clinical analysis and dispassionately examine my own capacity to avert political disaster. After long and earnest soul-searching, I concluded that it was my solemn duty to turn it around, as no one else could in the time remaining. But I made it clear to the National Executive Council in July 2002 that I would not lead the party in further general elections and would retire in time to let my successor set the stage and choose the timing of the general elections to follow.

Maxine Henry-Wilson and Paul Robertson were prepared to leave the cabinet and work full-time as general secretary and campaign director. Their loyalty and their sacrifice made all the difference as we set about recovering lost ground, constituency by constituency. The opposition, the media, the financial moguls predicted that we would be banished. I was certain we could win, and so was my team. We intensified a well-designed programme (Live and Direct) of regular, informed discussions on public policy between the prime minister, his ministers and the public. I made sure that the procedures to ensure a timely response to all letters and telephone calls to the Office of the Prime Minister were followed up.

Our election manifesto, *Advancing the Quality*, captured the essence of our intentions for the fourth consecutive term we were seeking. The visually attractive document promised more of the action that had been changing the face and the quality of Jamaican life over the last five years, in the context of the party's vision:

> Our vision is of a country where individuals are able to fulfil their potential, are in control of their destiny and work – not just for their own personal advancement – but also for the greater good of the nation.
>
> Our vision is of a strong and growing economy producing high-quality jobs, a country in which our people live safely and securely in unity, love, peace and equality. It is a vision that sees a Jamaica that is prosperous and dynamic, with first-class infrastructure, universal education and relevant training of the highest standard.

There was a view that despite our transformational strategies and long list of achievements the party was being overly ambitious even to think of smashing the three-term record. "This will be the end of the PNP monopoly," the naysayers predicted.

Like so many third parties, the National Democratic Movement had failed to win a single seat in the general elections of 1997 or any by-election. Its founding leader, Bruce Golding, had returned to the fold of the JLP, at the insistence of those who made it a condition for financing the campaign. The opponents of the government went all out, but their leadership style was seen as autocratic. The PNP had depth of leadership and no "one don" tendencies.

My team and I remained confident and upbeat. We knew how much work we had done. I had gone all around Jamaica and felt the warmth and positive responses of Jamaicans in every parish. It was therefore with strong faith that I was able to lead my party into the elections with a quiet assurance of victory. We came under severe attack at every step, but we garnered thirty-four seats to the JLP's twenty-six. My decision to lead the PNP in winning a fourth term was vindicated.

There would be no turning back from realizing "our vision of a Jamaica which upholds the fulfilment of human right, dignity for all, and a Jamaica where there is social and economic progress based on shared values and principles of the highest ideals". The victory allowed me to claim the distinction of being the only Jamaican political leader to lead a party to victory in three successive elections.

How did we achieve this feat? We made a sustained effort to keep the party functioning properly at all levels. We ensured inclusiveness by a deliberate strategy to enable the "tendencies" within the party and country to combine for progressive advancement.

Once again, the PNP outclassed and outworked the JLP. The party ran a good campaign, the foundation for which was laid by the high quality of the communications supporting the government's policies and programmes. Our manifesto was meaty, presenting our impressive, solid achievements, past and current, which dwarfed the JLP's record over a comparable period.

So, on the night of 16 October, in my victory speech at the PNP headquarters, I shared with the large and enthusiastic crowd that two days before, my granddaughter Gabrielle Elan had said to me, "Grandpa, P.J. means that you must 'protect Jamaica'."

For the party to win a fourth consecutive term was not only a historic privilege, but also a historic responsibility that had to be discharged by leading the way to unity, harmony, peace and prosperity. I ordered that no motorcades would be allowed, and the tradition of burying the images of defeated opposition candidates in ceremonial coffins would cease. Irrespective of social class, race, gender or political persuasion, I wanted everybody to feel that Jamaica is a land to love, a land to call home.

This could only happen by defusing partisan tensions and reducing political violence. "One Jamaica" could only be achieved through genuine political dialogue. My objective was to secure national agreement on the broad outline of a vision for a new Jamaica; the new governance structure; the role of government; reform of the constitution, the economy, the public sector and the role of civil society.

My fourth swearing-in as prime minister was unique in two respects. For the first time it was not at King's House, the traditional venue, but at Emancipation Park, in open view, so that all citizens could witness and participate in the ceremony. It was also the first time that the prime-ministerial oath of office reflected the reality of Jamaica as a sovereign nation where we pledge to uphold the constitution and laws and recognize the primacy of our people.

Kenny Anthony of St Lucia, Denzil Douglas of St Kitts and Nevis, Perry Christie of the Bahamas, Roger Luncheon as a special emissary from the incumbent chair of CARICOM, President Bharrat Jagdeo, were present to express solidarity and to hear me commit to play my part in all the international forums to which we belong so that the voices of the Caribbean are heard and our interests fully protected.

I promised to choose a team which would serve diligently and with humility and in which there would be no taint of corruption or the abuse of power.

With a reduced but comfortable majority in a chamber of sixty, the choice of two independent members in the Senate was discontinued to permit greater flexibility in appointing the cabinet and ministers of state from a pool of forty-seven.

It took some time for the party to realize how firm was my intention to demit office well before the next election. In the remaining time my goal was to ensure that the foundations of government were entrenched by expanding opportunities through a structure that was inclusive, robust and participatory, alongside increased investment in our human capital through education, training and health.

I also had an overriding obligation to lead in the deepening of regional integration by completing the arrangements for the CSME to expand trade and increase economic cooperation throughout the hemisphere.

In the aftermath of four consecutive defeats, the internal combustion within the JLP made Seaga's continuing leadership intolerable. Bruce Golding emerged victorious and succeeded him as the MP for West Kingston.

I had no hesitation in according the Most Honorable Edward Philip George Seaga all the recognition and courtesies which his contribution to the development of our nation deserved. When the House of Representatives held a special sitting to bid him farewell, I expressed my regret that both of us had been unable to complete the process of full sovereignty by critical constitutional reforms, as embodied in two decisive acts.

The entrenchment in our constitution of a new charter of fundamental rights was still incomplete in a country where our people appreciate the need to hold sacred the indivisible values of human dignity, freedom, equality and the rule of law. We had yet to move away from the monarchical system and become a republic with a president as head of state whose authority is derived directly from the people of Jamaica. Neither happened before my own departure, nor was achieved by the new leaders on both sides of the House before the general elections that followed.

On 26 April 2005, I was privileged to make my fourteenth consecutive presentation as prime minister in the annual budget debate. My thanks to the Almighty for his rich blessings and guidance were followed by my thanks to the people of Jamaica, who had expressed their confidence by placing me at the helm to steer the ship of state.

I spoke of the context in which my service as prime minister had begun. With the dissolution of the supreme Soviet Union, a bipolar world had given way to a single superpower. The social system was weighed down by inequity, divisions and conflicts. The governance structure was still distant and closed. For over a decade, social programmes had been subordinated to reducing the fiscal deficit and the foreign debt. Negative trends in values and social norms were undermining traditional authority systems. Our young people had become alienated. A new era, marked by civility and respect, was necessary to reduce the confrontation and hostility associated with politics.

But I highlighted the journey we had made over thirteen years and expressed satisfaction that in managing the process of change, we were able to underpin Jamaica's democratic system and tradition, while building a stronger and more vibrant economy.

While recognizing the realities both on the domestic and global fronts which we could not ignore, we had also sought to take into account the wishes and aspirations of the people. Our cultural and historical situation had been accorded due importance.

My experience had taught me there was no single blueprint for development that can be applied to all countries regardless of size, history, resource endowment, cultural or political circumstances. There are of course economic principles which cannot be discarded, but a simplistic set of theories or modules for all countries will not of necessity work for Jamaica.

When we decided to stop borrowing from the IMF, we fashioned our own staff-monitored programme based on our own reality and objectives, which was evaluated and approved by the IMF. I knew we had the capacity to devise our own solutions. For us, success really began after we took charge and started to fashion our own solution.

The global imperative dictates that Jamaica becomes internationally competitive. This requires reforming our international trading relationships, as well as having sound internal programmes, policies and projects. To ensure a long-term stable environment, we designed an overall framework involving almost every facet of government.

In my last budget presentation, I reminded the House that independence was intended to make us the masters of our own destiny and architects of our own fortunes.

As soon as it dawned on members of the cabinet, our parliamentarians and the party executive that I was determined to retire from public office, the jostling began. There was no disruption in the pace and scope of government projects, but it proved far more difficult to get the party to concentrate on a work programme to increase policy dialogue within and embrace the wider society in formulating national policy. Simply put, the party's leadership, membership and machinery needed an overhaul to effect economic, political and social transformation in the era of globalization and the emergence of a new national order.

The PNP had every reason to be proud that from its ranks there emerged four candidates of calibre: Karl Blythe, Omar Davies, Peter Phillips and Portia Simpson-Miller. Party chairman Robert Pickersgill and general secretary Burchell Whiteman were there to work with me to ensure that the rules and guidelines were strictly observed. Comrade Desmond Leakey was an early volunteer, who was prepared to refrain from being part of any of the campaign teams, as he knew I would need considerable assistance in putting the party back together once the elections for the party president were over.

In the preceding years, all the pollsters had found, among the other positives associated with the PNP, that we were seen as better able to manage the threat of disunity. Many voters regarded the JLP as fractious and disunited. At the start of our presidential election campaign, early respondents in a poll regarded the four-horse race as an indication of democracy at work. Before the campaign ended, opinion had shifted to the view that the PNP was beginning to drift in the direction of disunity. Despite my best efforts, I was unable to prevent it.

CHAPTER 40

THE CURTAIN FALLS

THE RACE FOR SUCCESSION WAS HOT AND INTENSE. Not surprisingly, party delegates were vigorously courted and there was active jockeying for positions in the new line-up.

Under the watchful eye of the Electoral Advisory Committee staff and the party's electoral commission, led by the general secretary, all arrangements were fine-tuned for voting at Jamaica College. I had enjoyed a good night's sleep, as I refused to watch the West Indies go down to their third defeat in the test series against New Zealand.

I woke up in time to join three longtime friends, Yvon Desulme, Hartley Neita and Jack Wilmot, on my veranda to read the morning papers. In the garden, birds were flitting from flower to flower and pecking at the birdseed scattered about, and an artificial fountain and a stream gurgled. For breakfast that Saturday morning, there was fruit – pegs of naseberry, mango and pawpaw – and saltfish with tomatoes and onions, fried dumplings, orange juice and coffee.

My son, Richard, and his daughter, Gabrielle, came and spent the day.

"It is the first time since I have known you that you are not voting in a party election," he said.

Music pumping from my house system began with a CD blaring mento rhythms. As the morning wore on, the music became ska and rocksteady, with the driving sounds of Prince Buster's "Ten Commandments" and Millie Small's "My Boy Lollipop". There was an interlude of music by Dave Brubeck and Paul Desmond. At noon, red peas soup and dumplings, yam, carrots, came from the kitchen. It was hot and spicy!

No one listened to the radio or television all day. The telephone rang frequently as friends called to wish me a good day, and others with rumours of what was taking place in the voting, which, from many years of experience, I ignored.

At two o'clock a telephone call said counting was about to begin. Jamaican music of the 1960s continued to be played to the shoulder-shaking and head-nodding of the fifteen or so colleagues and friends who had joined us by then.

I decided to go to Vale Royal to receive the results. Dusk was darkening the day when general secretary Burchell Whiteman came to give me the report. We went aside from the group and discussed the day's activities and the results quietly.

Then it was off to the headquarters of the PNP. Old Hope Road, below Mountain View Avenue, to Seaview and all interconnecting roads were choked with vehicles and people. In the dark of the evening, Portia Simpson-Miller's gold-shirted supporters in their skirts or dresses stood out. Hundreds sat on the roadside banks and sidewalks, dejected, as the rumour was that their Mama P. had lost. Then there was silence as I spoke. Sister P.'s "sisters" looked sad. They sat, crowding the roadsides, hands over their heads and moaning and groaning.

They perked up when I said I had the assurance of the cabinet and the parliamentary group that they would support the new president. I then announced the results in alphabetical order – which by pure coincidence reflected the votes each had obtained, in ascending order. Blythe – 204; Davies – 283; Phillips – 1,538; Simpson-Miller – 1,775!

Immediately after the announcement, I left the crowd so that Portia could celebrate her victory with them. An hour later, I received a message: she was on her way to visit me. She came without an entourage, just two police escorts – one a driver – and two of her constituents. I met her on the steps of Vale Royal. We hugged, rocking from side to side, friends since 1969, when, as a young recruit at the National Arena, she had given me a pamphlet for my vice-presidential candidature with my picture on it, and the words, "We say . . . P.J."

"I came to show you my respect," she said.

"Come inside your home-to-be," I invited. We walked into the living room clasping hands, sat side by side on a couch and sipped champagne toasts as we talked about the campaign and its rigours. Then there were two telephone calls, the first from Governor General Sir Kenneth Hall, and the other from his predecessor, Sir Howard Cooke. Her eyes, which had been tired, lit with joy as they congratulated her. She was energized and ready for the challenges ahead and her own campaign to come.

I had run my leg with honesty of purpose and was now ready to pass the baton.

The period before the handover allowed for a smooth transition within both the party and government. At my final meeting of the National Executive Council, I spoke of the need to repair the damage inflicted by the presidential campaign and the danger of descending into infighting which would impede our progress and cause electoral defeat.

I exposed the prime minister–elect to those aspects of the office which are confined to the head of government alone, and to a number of boards over which I presided – the Defence Board, the National Security Council, the Economic Council, National Commission on Science and Technology and the National Road Safety Council, among others.

We held conversations by teleconference with several presidents in the hemisphere and heads of international institutions such as the United Nations and its agencies, the Commonwealth, the Organization of American States and CARICOM.

With the budget for the next financial year already announced, several options had to be verified at the cabinet's final meeting on 27 March, so that the Ministry of Finance could prepare the estimates of expenditure for consideration and approval by the new cabinet.

Before adjourning, we heard from three members – K.D. Knight, Burchell Whiteman and John Junor – who publicly announced their desire to leave politics at the cabinet level. I thanked them sincerely for their service and sacrifice to the country, expressed my gratitude to other members of the government and wished them well in their future endeavours.

On 28 March 2006, the House convened to pay tribute to my service in Parliament. In my reply, I said the 1970s had to be seen as a renaissance in Jamaica's history. Out of that came an epiphany of our arts, music, culture, athleticism and intellectual genius that remains largely unmatched up to the present.

I observed that we were able to reflect during opposition in the 1980s not only on our policies and programmes, but also the approaches needed to balance the plurality of our democratic system without sacrificing the cardinal principles of political morality, justice and equality in the cause of the social and economic advancement of the people.

There were two days between my farewell to Parliament and my retirement as Jamaica's sixth prime minister. During that interval, my mind was brimful with reflections which extended well beyond my fourteen years at the helm. How did I get here? What, I wondered, was the source for my apparent infection by a political virus, seemingly from birth?

On both sides of my family tree, but even more evident and pronounced on the maternal limb, there was acceptance that the sons and daughters of former slaves had an inherent power and right as human beings to create their own destiny. That required the freeing of the mental and creative powers of our own people so that we could find our own place, our own voice and our sense of purpose.

Growing up in the depths of rural Jamaica, I was instilled with the values of mutual respect, especially for the elderly and the infirm, where there flourished spiritual engagement with that life force which is at the heart of Christian/ religious worship. This was buttressed by a passionate love for learning and the knowledge it brings to anyone with the discipline and resolve to acquire it through structured education and training.

I was brought up in an environment – at home, school, church and community – that generated the concept of building a new Jamaica on the foundations of spirituality, mutual trust and respect, regardless of race, colour or creed, as well as hard work, voluntarism and self-reliance. It was these concepts that fuelled a national movement which was particularly sensitive to the special needs of the vast majority of the people.

Universal adult suffrage was a cornerstone, allowing one person, one vote without the obstacles of property rights and income qualification. The leaders so elected were expected to work not just for the people but with the people.

Alongside such electoral empowerment was the joint emphasis on the empowerment of the mind – both sides of it, the intellect and the imagination. This is what afforded many of my generation access to secondary education and eventually to higher/tertiary education. We readily understood that all human acts are acts of intelligence, and without the exercise of the mind, we could not call ourselves a people.

On Wednesday night, I gathered with my personal staff, security officers and Vale Royal staff to say goodbye. It was very touching. A senior member of my security detail broke down and had to be driven home. He claimed that never before had anyone been so kind and considerate to him.

As I woke up on the morning of 30 March 2006, I realized that this would be another landmark day in my life. It was the day fixed for the swearing-in ceremony of my successor, Jamaica's seventh prime minister. It would take place at five o'clock in the afternoon, by which time the brilliant, sweltering sun would have begun its disappearance from the western sky.

There was to be another most telling demonstration of the breadth and depth of my experiences in forty years of public life and the amazing journey I had undertaken as prime minister of my beloved homeland.

Shortly after stirring for the day in my home, in the foothills of St Andrew, which I had so many years before named Uhuru, I received a telephone call from the president of the United States, George W. Bush. He conveyed his appreciation for my contribution to the course of our bilateral and hemispheric relations and his desire to meet personally with my successor as soon as possible. I expressed my gratitude for his kind sentiments, and explained that despite the absence of constitutional term limits, I had decided to depart from the leadership at this time of my own choosing, and by way of a seamless and transparent process. In a warm and friendly conversation, he expressed the hope that I would thoroughly enjoy my years in retirement. I ended our call by wishing him and his family well, in return for his own good wishes.

Another of my final official duties on this, the final day of my fourteen years as head of government, was to receive in my office a special Cuban delegation with a touching personal message from President Fidel Castro Ruz. El Comandante had sent me his best wishes on my retirement and ended with an order. I had missed the celebration of his seventieth birthday owing to my pressing national engagements. His message was that he was serving immediate notice that no excuses would be accepted for his eightieth birthday, and my absence would result in the automatic termination of our friendship of many decades.

Little did I know then that fate would intervene, and that event would have to be postponed because of his illness. When it eventually took place, Fidel could not be present to enjoy it.

The morning of my final day in office was, predictably, a busy one. After a stream of handover exchanges with the cabinet secretary, my permanent secretary, senior advisors and personal support staff, I was ready for my final official call. It was from Patrick Manning, prime minister of Trinidad and Tobago and chairman of CARICOM. He had come directly from the airport and expressed how highly valued was the contribution I had made to CARICOM and the cause of regional integration. Prime Minister Manning reassured me of the firm intention of his government to honour the liquefied natural gas agreements we had signed which would permit the establishment of a jointly owned liquefied natural gas plant in Jamaica. That reassurance was also conveyed to Prime Minister Portia Simpson-Miller after the King's House ceremony and on an official visit to Trinidad and Tobago in the summer. But neither that agreement nor the solemn commitment was ever honoured, as the Government of Trinidad and Tobago reneged, on the excuse of inadequate energy reserves.

The entire staff at Jamaica House gathered outside my office door to bid me farewell. They came from every corner – the main building, the former residence, the cottage, the annex, the Devon Road complex and the grounds. Staff from the Cabinet Office, the Office of the Prime Minister, the auxiliary workers, were all there to shake hands and wave goodbye. Some of the young children – a few from the adjoining basic school and others who had a parent working there – made sure not to miss the occasion.

Quite a few adults and children were seen to shed a tear or two. I myself was deeply touched. As I looked into their faces, I saw staff and security officers who had started with me fourteen years before; some who had risen from junior to senior positions, some who had survived personal tragedies and setbacks – a family of dedicated public servants who had helped, through the ups and downs of the past fourteen years, in their own way, to shape the character of my administration. I also remembered those who had served and gone before.

And so the final morning came to an end.

As my security chauffeur for the past twelve years, Sergeant Selwyn Williams, drove me through the heavy traffic on the short journey from Jamaica House to my home, I realized that I was now in earnest beginning my last few hours as prime minister. That afternoon, as I prepared mentally for the coming ceremony, I thought back to my beginning, how this had come to equip me and others of my generation to grasp the import of the call to take charge of one's affairs in a world that would be shaken by such change.

The need for strategic alliances with sections of the wider world in the post-colonial period was understood by those like me even before independence. With independence, the urgency of this obligation was to become even more evident. It is in this sense that I was well prepared. Thanks to the sophisticated vision of the PNP, the movement to which I gave a lifetime commitment, someone like myself was able to grapple with the challenges of a globalized world.

Flashing quickly across my mental screen were memories of those times in the late 1950s, 1960s and 1970s when even the call for self-reliance, self-government and independence, through investing in the creativity of intellect and imagination of our people, was regarded as pie in the sky and mercilessly criticized. But my upbringing nurtured my own self-confidence, fixity of purpose, positive thinking and a sense of hope in the midst of the harshest of difficulties, strengthened my resolve to carry on and spared me from any paralysis of the will.

As I prepared to carry out my final duties at the end of my amazing personal journey, one on which my country and myself had virtually grown up together, I looked back with some equanimity at what we had achieved. The nation's journey had only just begun, but I had played my part to the best of my ability. It was time to make my exit.

The formalities had yet to be completed. The official car drove out of the gate of Uhuru promptly at 4:30 p.m., after an aide-de-camp temporarily assigned by the Jamaica Defence Force had made sure I was properly sashed and the national insignia suitably pinned to my lapel. The steady pace of the police outriders allowed the prime minister's personal standard on the car to flutter gently in the breeze.

I arrived at the front door of the official residence of the governor general, King's House, precisely on time. After the welcome fanfare by the trumpeters of the Jamaica Military Band, I was escorted to the drawing room upstairs with unusual dispatch. This was due to the understandable anxiety of the governor general to receive in his own hands my letter of resignation. Without this, there would be no vacancy to permit the appointment of my successor as prime minister. I had taken my letter of resignation as prime minister, as well as another to be delivered to the Speaker of the House at the end of the day, to advise him of my resignation as the member of Parliament for Eastern Westmoreland, bringing to an end my career in the legislature.

There was one awkward moment. As I was in the course of handing over my letter to Sir Kenneth Hall, I realized that I had taken the wrong envelope from the car. In a flash, the correct one was retrieved by Seargeant Ralph Webb and the formalities completed. The governor general smiled with relief and at 4:57 p.m. I descended the stairs to take my seat on the platform. The letter to the Speaker, Michael Peart, was delivered at the end of the ceremony.

Norman Washington Manley had run the first leg of the relay to secure our independence. It was now time for me to pass the baton I had received from Michael Norman Manley, who ran the second leg for the PNP. For the first time, running in the lane to which history had assigned us, a woman, Portia Lucretia Simpson-Miller, was to become Jamaica's seventh prime minister, and in so doing shattered the glass ceiling.

In my brief address, I stated how wonderfully privileged I was to have contributed

> to the evolution of our democracy and of the political process which enable us to celebrate in formal Jamaican style a change of leadership by orderly and peaceful means that cannot be surpassed anywhere in the democratic world.
>
> It has been a privilege and a distinct honour to have been able to serve for fourteen years as prime minister of this blessed land. We have had our triumphs and successes, but we have also shared our moments of disappointment. But what is life itself if it is not that?
>
> The journey has been one of peaks and valleys, but never one where any mountain was too high or any valley too dangerous to cause us to falter.

With the undergirding of the blessings of the Almighty and the prayers of the people, I have been fortified and encouraged in all my endeavours and would like on this occasion to say a final word of thanks for the generous support which I have received from all those who wish Jamaica well.

I am confident that the country will be able to rise to new levels of economic growth and witness upward social mobility as we continue to build on the foundations which have been well and truly laid and to profit from the traditions bequeathed to us by earlier generations.

During the course of the reception which followed, I slipped quietly out, got into my private car and departed as just another Jamaican citizen through the gate that leads on to West King's House Road. By then, most of the bustling evening traffic of Kingston had gone. I was home within a few minutes. One of the security officers, who would no longer be in my detail, cried as he made his way slowly down the driveway.

Soon after I reached home, my twelve-year-old granddaughter, Gabrielle, handed me her programme from the just-completed ceremony, on which she had written: "You no longer have to take Five – Take Twenty-five. No More Work, No More Stress – Relax. You're free."

I appreciated more fully what she had written when I went to bed that night – "Dream and fall asleep" – I did not have to wake up next morning to deal with any story in the national news or any item on the national agenda.

Soon after my eyes opened to the dawn, I gave thanks to the Almighty for the good health and strength which had carried me through my leg of the journey. The torch had been passed safely to the next generation for the journey ahead. I prayed for God's richest blessing on the new leaders and the people, and that the hope of our people would not be smothered in doubt and fear.

As the promise of a new day was revealed, and inspired by a song from my childhood, I renewed my personal "vow to my native country, all earthly things above, entire and whole and perfect, the service of our love".

SELECTED BIBLIOGRAPHY

Bertram, Arnold. *A History of Calabar High School*. Kingston: The Calabar Foundation, 2014.

———. *P.J. Patterson: A Mission to Perform*. Kingston: AB Associates, 1995.

Brewster, Havelock, and Clive Thomas. *The Dynamics of West Indian Economic Integration*. Kingston: Institute of Social and Economic Research, University of the West Indies, 1967.

Bryan, Patrick. *Edward Seaga and the Challenges of Modern Jamaica*. Kingston: University of the West Indies Press, 2009.

CARICOM Secretariat. *CARICOM: Our Caribbean Community – An Introduction*. Kingston: Ian Randle, 2005.

Communications Unit, Office of the Prime Minister. *P.J. Patterson: In the Eyes of the World* [collection of tributes on his retirement]. Kingston: Office of the Prime Minister, 2006.

Davis, Carlton E. "A Practitioner's Perspective on Governance". Paper presented at the World Bank Public Sector Day Conference, Washington, DC, 26 April 2004.

Davies, Omar. "An Analysis of the Management of the Jamaican Economy 1972–1985". *Social and Economic Studies* 35, no. 1 (March 1986): 73–109.

De Castro, Steve. *Problems of the Caribbean Air Transport Industry*. Kingston: Institute of Social and Economic Research, University of the West Indies, 1967.

Girvan, Norman, and Richard Bernal. "The IMF and the Foreclosure of Development Options: The Case of Jamaica". Paper presented at the Second Congress of Third World Economists, Havana, Cuba, 26–30 April 1981.

Hughes, Wesley. "A Historical Perspective on Poverty". *The Transforming Landscape of Jamaica*. Kingston: Communications Unit, Office of the Prime Minister, 2006.

Jacques Garvey, Amy, comp. *Philosophy and Opinions of Marcus Garvey, or, Africa for the Africans*. 2nd ed. London: Routledge, 2006.

Manley, Michael. *Jamaica: Struggle in the Periphery*. London: Third World Media, 1982.

Manley, N.W. *Manley and the New Jamaica: Selected Speeches and Writings 1938–1968*. Edited by Rex Nettleford. Kingston: Longman Caribbean, 1971.

McIntyre, Alister, Norman Girvan, George Beckford and Eric Armstrong. *Possibilities for Rationalizing Production and Trade in the West Indies*. Kingston: Institute of Social and Economic Research, University of the West Indies, 1967.

Patterson, P.J. "CARICOM beyond Thirty: Charting New Directions". Presentation at the Twenty-Fourth Meeting of the CARICOM Heads of Government. Montego Bay, Jamaica, 2003.

Planning Institute of Jamaica. *Economic and Social Survey of Jamaica 1975*. Kingston: Planning Institute of Jamaica, 1976.

Ranston, Jackie. *Lawyer Manley*. Vol. 1: *First Time Up*. Kingston: University of the West Indies Press, 1999.

Sherlock, Philip, and Hazel Bennett. *The Story of the Jamaican People*. Kingston: Ian Randle, 1998.

Taylor, Frank Fonda. *To Hell with Paradise: A History of the Jamaican Tourist Industry*. Pittsburgh: University of Pittsburgh Press, 1993.

West Indian Commission. *Time for Action: Report of the West Indian Commission*. Kingston: University of the West Indies Press, 1994.

World Bank. *Governance and Development*. Washington, DC: International Bank for Reconstruction and Development/World Bank, 1992.

INDEX OF NAMES

Blake, Vivian, 44; and party leadership, 60; and Patterson's legal career, 42; and representative politics, 50; and the WIFLP, 33

Blythe, Karl: constituency work, 149; minister of water, 231; and Operation PRIDE issues, 265

Bolívar, Simón: and Jamaica, 310

Boukman, Dutty: rebellion, 31, 298, 299

Bowen, Manley: and the 1986 local government elections, 148; and election boycott, 145

Bowers, Mavis "Pinkie": and SE Westmoreland, 118–119

Boyer, Jean-Pierre: and reparation to France, 299

Bradshaw, Robert: and ACP negotiations, 76; minister of finance of the WIF, 33; and the St Kitts workers' struggle, 7–8;

Brevett, Lloyd: and the Skatalites, 46

Briggs, Wenke: EEC negotiations, 75

Brown, G. Arthur: deputy head of the UN Development Programme, 324; and the WIF, 36

Brown, Headley: and the Iran sugar deal, 81

Brown, Beryl, 11, 12

Brown, Mel: and the 1972 election campaign, 63

Brown, Ralph: and 1992 presidential campaign, 167; and the WIFLP, 33

Brown, Vincent "Bungo", 22

Buchanan, Danny: and SW St Elizabeth, 183

Burke, Paul: and the Appraisal Committee, 137; PNPYO chairman, 144; and Patterson's leadership, 167

Burnham, Forbes: and CARIFTA, 38–39, 101, 235, 283, 284; and the Georgetown Accord, 103

Bush, George W.: and CARICOM, 317; and Patterson's retirement, 397

Bussieres, Jacques: and the financial sector crisis, 203

Bustamante Industrial Trade Union (BITU), 9, 395

Bustamante, William Alexander: and Cacoon Elementary School, 5; and the Commonwealth, 327; foreign policy, 322; and the JLP, 375; and Patterson, 34, 35; and the WIF, 33, 35; and the workers' struggle, 8

Butler, Uriah Buzz: and the Trinidad and Tobago workers' struggle, 8

Byles, Junior, 65

Cameron, David: and enslavement of Africans, 321, 382; open letter to, 381–383

Campbell, Clifford: first Jamaican governor general, 357

Campbell, Colin: and the OPM communications team, 183

Campbell, Monica: and the OPM communications team, 183

Campbell, Lord: chairman of the Booker Group, 74

Capleton, Anthony: and the 1972 election campaign, 63

Carey, Maxwell "Maxie": death of, 53–54, 55, 59; and SE Westmoreland, 120

Cargill, Morris: and the DLP, 33

Carrington, Edwin: and ACP/EEC negotiations, 76

Carrington, Lord: and Zimbabwe, 331

Carter, Eliza Matilda. See Eliza James

Carter, Jimmy: and access to information, 250–251; and Aristide, 300; and the 1997 elections, 192; and Zimbabwe, 331

Carter, Richard (great-grandfather), 5

INDEX OF SUBJECTS